It's Player A versus Player B. Got it?

Actually, since the entire Ryder Cup is at match play, it's about holes won, not total score. A hole is won by the lower score of the two players.

✶✶✶✶✶✶✶✶✶✶✶✶✶✶✶ **SCORING:** ☆☆☆☆☆☆☆☆☆☆☆☆☆☆☆☆

THAT LEADS to the scoring system used throughout the book (as well as on television, in newspapers, and elsewhere) to explain who won and lost Cup matches.

All you really have to remember is that it's depends on who has won the most holes. So if Player A scores a four on the opening hole to Player B's five, Player A is 1-up: He has won one more hole than B to that point. If B wins the second hole, they are back to even. If A then wins the next two holes, after the fourth he is 2-up, and the announcer will say, "Player A is two-up after four." And that's how it proceeds.

What confusion exists comes as the match winds down because players don't have to go all eighteen holes to determine a winner. Say Player A is four holes up (he has won four more holes than Player B) when they reach the fourteenth tee: A is 4-up with five to play (fourteen through eighteen). If A wins the fourteenth hole, he wins the match 5&4—he is five holes up with only four to play, so there is no reason to continue; B can't win the match. If A and B halve the fourteenth hole, A is said to be "dormie": He is four up with four to play and can't lose the match, either winning or halving (and it would be halved only if B wins the last four holes). If B wins the fourteenth hole, A goes to the fifteenth tee three holes up and the match continues until they either finish in a tie or one of them wins.

I'm almost done. Bear with me.

Say A and B are even ("all square" in Cup parlance) as they stand on the eighteenth tee. If they halve the final hole, the match is halved (and in the Cup, each team would win half a point). But if one of them wins the hole, the score would be recorded as a 1-up victory: Literally, it finished with that player 1-up in holes won. This can happen earlier, for example, if they are even after sixteen, then Player A wins the seventeenth. They then would go to the eighteenth hole with A 1-up and one of three things could happen: (1) Player A wins the eighteenth hole and wins the match 2-up; (2) Player B wins the eighteenth hole and the match is halved; or (3) The hole is halved and Player A wins the match 1-up.

I hope you got that. There will be a test next Tuesday.

JFS EXECUTIVE LUNCHEON

With David Feherty

Wednesday, May 16, 2007

DAVID
FEHERTY'S
TOTALLY SUBJECTIVE
HISTORY OF THE RYDER CUP

☆☆☆☆☆☆☆☆☆☆☆☆☆☆☆

ALSO BY
DAVID FEHERTY

SOMEWHERE IN IRELAND, A VILLAGE IS MISSING AN IDIOT

A NASTY BIT OF ROUGH

☆☆☆☆☆☆

ALSO BY
JAMES A. FRANK

10 MINUTES A DAY TO BETTER PUTTING

DAVE PELZ'S SHORT-GAME BIBLE

DAVE PELZ'S PUTTING BIBLE

PRECISION PUTTING

GOLF IN AMERICA

GOLF SECRETS

THE PGA CHAMPIONSHIP: 1916-1984

GOLF MAGAZINE'S COMPLETE BOOK OF GOLF INSTRUCTION

GOLF IN AMERICA: THE FIRST HUNDRED YEARS

GOLF CLUBS OF THE MGA: A CENTENNIAL HISTORY OF GOLF IN THE NEW YORK

METROPOLITAN AREA

GOLF MAGAZINE'S PRIVATE LESSONS

RUGGED LAND | 276 CANAL STREET · FIFTH FLOOR · NEW YORK · NY · 10013 · USA

RuggedLand

Published by Rugged Land, LLC

276 CANAL STREET • FIFTH FLOOR • NEW YORK CITY • NY 10013 • USA

RUGGED LAND and colophon are trademarks of Rugged Land, LLC.

PUBLISHER'S CATALOGING-IN-PUBLICATION
(PROVIDED BY QUALITY BOOKS, INC.)

Feherty, David.
David Feherty's totally subjective history of the
Ryder Cup : a hardly definitive, completely cockeyed,
but absolutely loving tribute to golf's most exciting
event / David Feherty with James A. Frank. -- 1st ed.
p. cm.
ISBN 1-59071-032-0

1. Ryder Cup--History. I. Frank, James A.
II. Title. III. Title: Totally subjective history of the
Ryder Cup.

GV970.3.R93F44 2004   796.352'66
QBI04-200152

Book Design by
HSU + ASSOCIATES

RUGGED LAND WEBSITE ADDRESS:WWW.RUGGEDLAND.COM

AUGUST 2004

1   3   5   7   9   10   8   6   4   2

First Edition

For no apparent reason.

(and Jim McGovern, a fat person.)

Most of the facts in these pages are Jim Frank's, and all of the bullshit is mine. Some of it is even true, honest. Of course, there are many other Ryder Cup accounts, but because it was such a horrendous arse-kicking for so long, I felt compelled to dig deeper for what it was that preserved the Ryder Cup through these early years. So I had to finish this book before I wrote an introduction, largely because I had no idea what it was going to be about.

That's the thing about history, though--if you look at it closely enough it's always *his story*. I wondered how a one-sided, supposedly friendly contest between two nations captured the imagination of the entire golfing world, and why it had such a profound effect on the men who played in it. Professional golfers have always been among the few athletes who are compensated in direct proportion to how well they play, but in this event they weren't paid at all, and perhaps therein lies the reason for the event's success. It was always about a lot more than money.

For their trouble, Ryder Cuppers are paid only enough to cover expenses, (and, in the case of U.S. team members, a donation to a charity of their own choice) and of course they get to keep some of the least fashionable clothing in the history of sport. But they get a chance to be either national heroes, or vilified whipping boys, too.

It all began with that most appealing of traditional feuds, the age-old chestnut—snobs versus yobs. On one side of the ditch the British and Irish were stubbornly proud, and guarded their golfing traditions fiercely, and on the other, America was becoming bigger, getting faster, growing richer, and wanting recognition, perhaps even a little ready-made history of its own. Golf was controlled by Lords and Royals in the British Isles, and by movers and shakers in America. For many, the Ryder Cup was symbolic of the struggle for power in the New World Order. Behind the friendly competition there was a much more serious agenda. Could the pupil become the Master?

It's clear that Samuel Ryder conceived the Ryder Cup, but it was Walter Hagen who performed the delivery. He single-handedly starred, produced, directed, and did the costumes, lighting, and makeup for the first five American teams, and remains, I believe, the most important character in the history of the play. He understood it was a show, and that it would likely spawn plenty of characters, both villains and heroes, on both sides. The Ryder Cup has always inspired antics from its competitors that they would never consider in other events. And again I think it goes back to the absence of money. Few self-respecting professional golfers would descend to the level of gamesmanship often described in the following pages if they were competing against each other for actual *cash*. The fear of being branded a bad sport, or worse, a cheat, is simply too horrifying. That wouldn't be cricket, and it's certainly not golf. However, when a man pulls on a team sweater, some kind of primeval swarm mentality kicks in, and when you make that sweater a flag, well, that's different again. It's not life or death, oh no. It's much more important than that, and some of the rules go out the window. As Bob Dylan wrote:

"Patriotism is the last refuge,
to which a scoundrel clings.
Steal a little and they throw you in jail,
steal a lot, and they make you King."

Making the Ryder Cup team was the greatest achievement of my career, and we lost. But no one can steal those memories from me.

WENTWORTH

1926

THE LOST RYDER CUP

COURSE: WENTWORTH GC
SURREY, ENGLAND
DATE: JUNE 04–05

FINAL SCORE
US: 1-1/2   GB: 12-1/2

ON FRIDAY, SEPTEMBER 17, **2004,** the Thirty-Fifth Ryder Cup Matches will kick off at the Oakland Hills Country Club in Bloomfield, Michigan.

Right?

Well, maybe not. Because what everyone agrees will be the thirty-fifth playing of the Ryder Cup may actually be the thirty-sixth. This discrepancy is only the first of many odd and interesting facts about golf's most exciting event.

The Ryder Cup Matches pit the best golf professionals from the United States against their counterparts from Europe in a biennial—or every two years, if you, like most, can never remember if biennial means twice a year or once every two years—competition.

In the more than seventy-five years that the Matches have been played, their format and the composition of the teams has changed numerous times to reflect changes in the game of golf. But what's important to note here—before you get too bogged down in who played whom, who beat whom, and the difference between foursomes and fourballs—is that the Ryder Cup has become almost a living, breathing thing. It has evolved from a friendly, if somewhat one-sided, competition that was all but ignored by the press and the public into the most exciting, anticipated, and respected event in golf, if not in all of sport. How this happened is a great story, which will be exaggerated dreadfully in the following pages.

Before getting to the Matches, let's set the scene of what golf was like in the old days. Not only will it fill a few more pages (which we are contractually obligated to do), but knowing what went on back then really does give us more of an appreciation of what we have now.

Golf began in Scotland way back when. Oh, sure, there are records of twig-and-berry games being played in China, France, and Holland back then, too. Fine. When those games have their own international competitions, we'll write about them. But golf as we know and love it is a big, hairy, Scottish invention.

The game very likely started when shepherds, looking to kill time between sheep round-ups, swatted at rocks with their crooks. Soon, they were aiming the rocks at rabbit holes. Their sheep, burrowing into the turf to get out of the wind (it's Scotland, remember?), formed the first sand traps, and of course, what self-respecting shepherd could resist the rear end of a sheep sticking out of a hillside?

Despite its fairly lowbrow beginnings among the livestock, golf soon became the sport of the royals. Many of the early Scottish kings played it, but not until

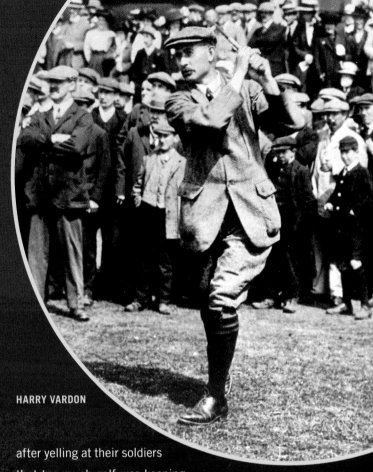

HARRY VARDON

after yelling at their soldiers that too much golf was keeping them from more important things, like archery practice. In 1567, Mary, Queen of Scots, was spotted on the links just a few days after her husband was murdered. She was beheaded soon thereafter, giving new meaning to "losing the front side."

When Scotland and England were united under the same king in 1603, golf began migrating south toward the Sassenachs and from there to points as far as the Royal Navy would carry it. I doubt there's much truth to the rumor that golf came to America as Britain's revenge for losing the Colonies back in 1776. However, there is evidence of the game being played by British soldiers stationed in South Carolina around the time of the War of Independence. Maybe if the Redcoats and the

Minutemen had staged an early Ryder Cup, the whole nasty mess could have been avoided. Instead, it was George Washington 4 & 3 over King George.

But for the most part, golf remained a sport of the aristocracy (i.e., the filthy rich) until the middle of the nineteenth century, when someone found a way to make a ball out of tree sap, meaning it became cheap. Then as now, it was the cost of equipment that made all the difference—that and the price of joining a club, which wasn't so bad then, and only recently has become utterly ridiculous.

Golf settled in America at the end of the nineteenth century, taking root when a few transplanted Scots brought clubs and balls with them from the old country. The USGA was founded in 1894, and the next year the first U.S. Open was held. Not surprisingly, for the first few years that tournament was dominated by British-born club pros, especially sons of Scotland, who'd left towns like St. Andrews and Carnoustie for better paying jobs at the new clubs of the New World.

All those Willies, Jocks, and Sandys made good money teaching golf to the growing upper-class, their pockets full thanks to the Industrial Revolution. Early American golfers included Andrew Carnegie (another son of Scotland, but with an American-made fortune), Cornelius Vanderbilt, and even John J. Rockefeller. So while it had become fairly democratized in the old country, across the Atlantic golf was, once again, a rich man's game.

However, being a club pro, in the Isles or in the States, was still a dual-edged sword. While their rich and powerful students hung on their every burr-rounded bit of instruction ("Aye, sir, ya got tae grrrrrip it in yer fingerrrrrs"), club pros were viewed as barely a step above servants in social class, a stigma that lasted until World War I.

Once the club pros finally formed an organization of their own—the Professional Golf Association (PGA), founded in 1916—their status began to improve. Americans were playing better and entering the pro ranks, but it was still a profession filled with British expatriates, and as might be expected, there were tensions between the home-bred and the foreign-born.

As the ranks of American professionals grew—along with the opportunities for leading players to compete against one another—it was inevitable that someone would suggest that the best golfers on this side of the Atlantic face off against the best from that side. Eventually, the Ryder Cup Matches would be the result. But how does it get there? This is where the story gets muddled.

Start with one of the greatest names golf has ever produced: Sylvanus P. Jermain. According to official PGA history, Jermain, who was the president of the Inverness Club in Toledo, Ohio, deserves at least some of the credit for suggesting a transatlantic match after he invited the great English pros Harry Vardon and Ted Ray to play in the 1920 U.S. Open at Inverness. It probably didn't hurt any that Ray won and Vardon tied for second. (The last time Vardon and Ray had played in the U.S. Open had been 1913, when they were both beaten in a playoff by an unknown twenty-year-old American named Francis Ouimet, whose victory put golf on America's front pages.)

Another version says the idea of a U.S.–Britain match began as a stunt, a way of drumming up circulation for an American golf magazine, which suggested sponsoring such a competition. In late 1920, the PGA voted to give the magazine some funds to help send an American team abroad.

stars, the British trounced the American team, which starred the famous Walter Hagen and featured nine other golfers that few British fans had heard of, 9-3. The Americans didn't win any of the foursome matches (although they halved two of the five), and managed to win only three of the ten singles (halving one—no points were given for halves).

The results notwithstanding, the U.S. team wasn't all that bad. A few weeks later, one of its members, Jock Hutchison (who had been born in St. Andrews), won the Open Championship; Hagen finished sixth. What proved to be most significant, however, were the rules applied

America refers to as an "unofficial international match." Much of the credit for digging up the details of this event goes to another British golf writer, Michael Hobbs. He and Concannon provide the facts from which we're pilfering here.

On April 26, 1926, the *Times* of London reported that, "Mr. S. Ryder, of St Albans, has presented a trophy for annual competition between teams of British and American professionals. The first match for the trophy is to take place at Wentworth on June 4 and 5. The matches will be controlled by the [British] Professional Golfers' Association, but the details are not yet decided."

SAM RYDER AND ABE MITCHELL

The following month, the British magazine *Golf Monthly* reported that a "Walker Cup for professionals" was being arranged, and that Ryder had presented a trophy "for a contest between the two nations to be played alternately in this country and in the US at the time of the Open Championship in the respective countries." It was further reported that Hagen had assembled "a powerful side."

The British team consisted of player-captain Ted Ray plus Abe Mitchell (whose figure would adorn the top of Sam Ryder's cup), George Duncan, Aubrey Boomer, Archie Compston, George Gadd, Fred Robson, Arthur Havers, Ernest Whitcombe, and Herbert Jolly.

By June, the constitution of the U.S. team had shifted a bit, becoming a bit less powerful. Ultimately, the players were Hagen (also captain), Tommy Armour, Bill Mehlhorn, Joe Kirkwood, Al Watrous, Cyril Walker, Jim Barnes, Fred McLeod, Emmett French, and Joe Stein. Two things are worth noting about this crew. First, among the top players not on the team were Gene Sarazen and Johnny Farrell, two native Americans who had chosen not to play in the Open Championship. Second, among those who were playing, Armour and McLeod were Scots by birth, Barnes

and Walker were English, and Kirkwood was Australian, although all lived and worked in the States. The international composition of the American team upset some of the British, who didn't want to play against other "British" players, and, as already noted, didn't sit well with the PGA of America. So before any further international matches would be played, rules for what constituted an American would be necessary.

And, indeed, before the 1927 matches—the first "official" Ryder Cup—it was mutually agreed that a player had to be both born in and resident of the country he represented. However, that was later. The "first" Ryder Cup was still to be held. No word on whether or not a player had to be born a male either.

Despite the questionable citizenship of the U.S. team, they were obliterated, 13 to 1. In the first day's foursome (and in those days, all matches were thirty-six holes, not eighteen as they are today), the Americans went 0 for 5. The tenor of the matches was set in the very first one, when Hagen sent out what was arguably his strongest team—himself and Barnes—and they lost 9&8 to Mitchell and Duncan. The following four foursomes all went to the Brits with identical scores of 3&2. Pissing off Walter Hagen might have been our first mistake.

The singles weren't much better: Mehlhorn managed to beat Compston 1-up, while French halved with Whitcombe, for the only American points. In the other matches, only Armour reached the thirty-sixth hole, where he lost to Boomer 2&1. The other scores included drubbings of 10&9, 8&7, 6&5—a good, old-fashioned whitewashing. But it seemed that everyone had a good time, and Ryder is reported to have said something like "we must do this again." (You have to wonder if he would have been so chipper about it if the boot had been on the

American foot.) Some have taken this to mean that this wasn't the first Ryder Cup, and that Ryder agreed *later* to put up the trophy. In fact, while the trophy might not have been finished in time for the 1926 matches, there is little doubt that it had been commissioned for them.

So was this the first Ryder Cup or not? Officially, no, and feel free to choose whatever reason(s) you like for its having been expunged from the records. Certainly the non-American make-up of the U.S. team was an issue on both sides of the Atlantic. Furthermore, Concannon cites an article from *Golf Illustrated* a few weeks after the matches were finished that said James Ryder, Sam's brother, "decided to withhold the cup" because

of a general strike in early May that forced some of the Americans to change their travel plans, affecting their participation. It might even be felt that the one-sided final score detracted from the event's authenticity. Contrast that with the fact that research into the 1926 competition has been done in Britain. Sour grapes? Probably not. But you never know . . .

So there is our little history lesson, worth remembering as you read what happened over the following three-quarters of a century or so. Make up your own mind as to whether the next match is number thirty-five or thirty-six. Either way, the Ryder Cup is as good as it gets in golf. (And we've won one more than they say, you bastards.)

FINAL SCORE

COURSE:

WENTWORTH GC · SURREY · ENGLAND | 1926

FOURSOMES	SINGLES
Barnes/Hagan lost to Mitchell/Duncan, 9&8	Barnes lost to Mitchell, 8&7
Armour/Kirkwood lost to Boomer/Compston, 3&2	Hagan lost to Duncan, 6&5
Mehlhorn/Waltrous lost to Gadd/Havers, 3&2	Armour lost to Boomer, 2&1
Walker/McLeod lost to Ray/Robson, 3&2	Mehlhorn d. Compston, 1-up
French/Stein lost to Whitcombe/Jolly, 3&2	Kirkwood lost to Gadd, 8&7
	Watrous lost to Ray, 6&5
	Walker lost to Robson, 5&4
	McLeod lost to Havers, 10&9
	French halved with Whitcombe
	Stein lost to Jolly, 3&2
US: 0 GB: 5	**US: 1-1/2 GB: 7-1/2**

TOTAL: US 01-1/2 GB 12-1/2

SAMUEL A. RYDER : (1858–1936)

IF YOU THINK THE RYDER CUP has something to do with yellow moving vans, you are sorely mistaken. Get out of the house more (and away from your television set).

The father of the Ryder Cup was a man who had some problems with his own father. Samuel Ryder—born in Manchester, England, in March 1858—was the son of a local corn merchant. He went to the university in his hometown and then into Dad's business. All the books say that after a few years, young Sam went to his father with a new idea: He wanted to sell "penny packets" of seeds to the English, who are well known for their love of amateur gardening. Dad said no, Sam said goodbye, and in 1898, he moved south to St. Albans (which is about thirty miles north of London), and started the Heath and Heather Seed Company. The business, ahem, blossomed.

In no time at all, and thanks to Ryder's hard work, the company was a great success. But running a company wasn't enough for the tall, energetic Ryder. In 1906, he became the mayor of St. Albans (as well as Justice of the Peace, perhaps looking for another outlet for his flowers), while continuing to run the business with his brother, James. Then, at some point after his fiftieth birthday, in poor health from working too hard, Sam had one of those moments of enlightenment that come to so many hard-charging executive types: His doctor (or maybe it was his minister, for Sam was a religious man) told him that he needed fresh air and exercise. And so he found golf.

Ryder hired a local pro to give him lessons six days a week (never on Sunday), hitting woods and long irons across his vast grounds, chipping over the hedges. When he thought his game was good enough, he joined St. Albans's Verulam Golf Club in 1910. Within a year he was club captain (a post he would hold again in 1926 and 1927), and he continued working on his game with the same fervor that he'd worked at his company. He got his handicap down into single digits for a while, but knew that he'd never get any better starting as late as he did. Then, foreshadowing a trend that would reach its highpoint during the big-money 1970s and 1980s, this corporate titan decided he wanted to hang out with the pros.

In 1923, Heath and Heather sponsored its first tournament, a professionals-only event at Verulam. Promising each contestant a fee of five pounds, and fifty pounds to the winner, the event attracted the likes of former Open Champions Harry Vardon, James Braid, Alexander Herd, and George Duncan, and was won by Arthur Havers, who had won the 1923 Open at Troon just a few weeks earlier (collecting only seventy-five pounds). Also in the field was Abe Mitchell, who still carries the unfortunate label of the best British golfer to never win the Open (although it looks as if Colin Montgomerie may soon displace him). Mitchell was a shy, quiet man, who like most other club pros at the time augmented his small salary by playing in tournaments and exhibitions. Mitchell also was an avid gardener, and perhaps for this reason, he and Ryder became friends. In 1925, Ryder hired Mitchell as his personal instructor, paying him 1,000 pounds a year; besides helping Ryder with his game, this allowed Mitchell to quit his club job and practice his own game in hopes of winning the elusive Claret Jug. Alas, it was never to be.

"I SAY CHAPS, I've just had the most marvellous bloody idea! Let's get a few of the boys from the sheds outside our clubhouses together and start a little argy-bargy with the Americans. We'll give them a damn good thrashing in the morning, then have tea and crumpets, give them a jolly good buggering in the afternoon, and sing "Rule Britannia" out of tune as they sail out of Southampton. What, what?"

☆★☆★☆★☆★☆★☆★☆★☆★☆★☆★☆★☆★☆★☆★☆★☆★☆★☆★

Ryder became a major benefactor of professional golf in Britain, sponsoring numerous tournaments over the years, and attending all the major events. (Not so coincidentally, his seed company had become a leading supplier of grass seed for golf courses on both sides of the Atlantic.) He was involved in sponsoring the 1926 matches pitting the top pros from Britain against those from the United States, who were already coming over to play in the Open Championship at Royal Lytham and St. Anne's. He even donated that event's gold trophy—the one we now call the Ryder Cup—insisting that it be crowned with the figure of a man putting, and that the model for the figure be Ryder's dear friend Abe Mitchell.

About that trophy. For years, it was assumed that Ryder paid for it himself, but more likely he split the 250-pound cost (today, more than $15,000) with the R&A and Britain's Golf Illustrated magazine. It was made by the firm of Mappin and Webb, stands seventeen inches high, weighs four pounds, and is stamped with the date "1927," meaning that it probably wasn't finished in time for the 1926 matches.

For the rest of his life, wherever British pros were playing, it was likely that Sam Ryder was nearby—as long as it was on his side of the ocean. It seems that Mr. Ryder had a great fear of sea voyages. So he passed on accompanying the British team to Worcester, Massachusetts, for the first "official" Ryder Cup in 1927. But he certainly was with them when the matches were played in England in 1929 at Moortown and in 1933 at Southport and Ainsdale. It is probably a good thing that he didn't make the trip to Scioto in Columbus, Ohio, in 1931: The stifling heat that affected the much younger, healthier British golfers likely would have been too much for a man of seventy-three. As it was, he was ill when the British team set sail for the United States in 1935, and he died early the following year. He was buried with his favorite mashie (five-iron).

Joan Ryder, Sam's daughter, said much later that her father was surprised what the event with his name on it had become. "He had the idea that when the Americans came over for a match, he would give a 'small friendly lunch party' for both teams," she said.

Mr. Ryder's party is by no means small, and at times it has been anything but friendly.

☆★☆★☆★☆★☆★☆★☆★☆★☆★☆★☆★☆★☆★☆★☆★☆★☆★☆★

COURSE:

WORCESTER CC | WORCESTER | MASS.

JUNE 03-04

1927

FINAL SCORE:

☆ US 09-1/2   GB 02-1/2

CAPTAINS:

WALTER HAGEN   TED RAY

UNITED STATES

Leo Diegel
Al Espinosa
Johnny Farrell
Johnny Golden
Walter Hagen
Bill Mehlhorn
Gene Sarazen
Joe Turnesa
Al Watrous

GREAT BRITAIN

Aubrey Boomer
Archie Compston
George Duncan
George Gadd
Arthur Havers
Herbert Jolly
Ted Ray
Fred Robson
Charles Whitcombe

"All right..... this could be a long, strange walk."

IN THE EARLY PART OF THE TWENTIETH CENTURY, British expeditions to anywhere were traditionally under-prepared, and seasoned with a splendid dash of heroic idiocy. Take George Mallory for instance, who fancied his chances of nipping up Everest, armed with a coil of rope, a stiff upper lip, and a clean pair of underpants. Naturally, he fell off, and seriously killed himself. How about Shackleton, who froze his balls off on a stroll to the South Pole with a pup tent, walking stick, and a good stout pair of hob-nailed boots? Or maybe he was buggered by a polar bear, who knows? But the difference between these men, and the British Ryder Cup team that boarded the *SS Aquitania* for the six-day crossing of the Atlantic in May 1927, is that the Ryder Cup team came back. The similarity is, none of them knew what they were letting themselves in for.

On paper, the British were favored to capture the first "official" Ryder Cup Match. After all, just a year earlier they had trounced the U.S. team at Wentworth, and the team in 1927 was almost identical in make-up to that of 1926, featuring a trio of Open Championship winners: Ted Ray (who'd won the Open in 1912 and the U.S. Open in 1920), George Duncan (1920), and Arthur Havers (1923). Furthermore, the site of the matches was Worcester Country Club in Massachusetts, which was designed by a hairy Scot, the great Donald Ross. And if that were not enough, the composition of the U.S. team was shaken by new rules, which stated that members of each team had to be born in and a resident of the country for which they were playing. Those same rules had no effect on the visiting team, the rotters!

So why did the British lose? Maybe it was bad luck, of which the British team certainly had more than its fair share, but my best guess is that they were simply gobsmacked by their first experience of America. The problems started with just *getting* them there. Despite their talent for the game, most of the men were still lowly club pros, which meant they had to get permission from largely upper-class memberships to take a few weeks off from their crappy-paying jobs at the beginning of the season. Yet, because they had won the year before, there was no small amount of national pride attached to the matches, and the clubs didn't mind. Most of these members didn't want their professionals in their own *clubhouses*, but it was okay to let them play hooky for a little while, just so long as they gave those Yankees a damned good thrashing. The players also planned to stay for the U.S. Open, which was to be played a few days later at Oakmont, outside Pittsburgh, and many observers thought one of the *British* team might win America's national championship, so reminding the American golfing public that this was still a British pastime. Bloody good show!

The trouble, as it so often is, was money: Britain's *Golf Illustrated* launched a well-intentioned, but somewhat pathetic drive to raise three thousand pounds from the British golfing public to cover the costs of the journey.

TED RAY AND WALTER HAGEN

Solicitations were sent to 1,750 clubs, but only 216 of them contributed a measly average of just over eleven quid each. Sam Ryder kicked in another hundred pounds, but it was left to the magazine to cover the remaining four hundred pounds.

Then there was the team, a tweedy bunch, hand-picked by three former Open Champions Harry Vardon, James Braid, and J.H. Taylor, the "Great Triumvirate" that had dominated British golf at the turn of the century (winning sixteen Opens among them between 1894 and 1914). Unfortunately, despite the presence of the three more recent Open victors, the rest of the team was less than stellar: None of the others had won, or would win, a major championship. Then, at the last moment, the team captain, Abe Mitchell, had to pull out when he was diagnosed with appendicitis. The fifty-year-old Ray was appointed captain, and the team set sail (probably in steerage). But luckily, some mathematical genius realized the team was still short-handed, and Herbert Jolly (Jolly good) was picked at the last minute, hopped on another ocean liner, and joined the team in New York four days late.

And then there was the American team. Thanks to the new rules on citizenship, five players from the 1926 team—Tommy Armour, Jim Barnes, Fred McLeod, Joe Kirkwood, and Cyril Walker—were ineligible, and numerous other strong, but foreign-born, players living in America also were out. But some pretty good replacements were found, including Gene Sarazen, who'd already won the U.S. Open and a few PGA Championships (and would win still more majors) and Leo Diegel (who would win the PGA in 1928 and 1929). And, of course, there was player-captain Walter Hagen, the best golfer of the day, having already won four PGAs (he'd win his fifth later that year) and two Open Championships (with two more to come, in 1928 and 1929).

Just as Hagen took command of the PGA Championship in the twenties, so he ran the Ryder Cup team. Although the official history says that American players were chosen based "entirely on performance during the last three years," it was widely acknowledged that Hagen hand-picked the entire shooting match (he captained the first six teams and played on the first five). And it wasn't only the men he hand-picked. According to his autobiography, *The Walter Hagen Story:*

> "During my years as captain of the Ryder Cup Team I insisted that our fellows be fittingly uniformed. Various manufacturers offered knickers and coats free for our use but I turned them down. Instead I ordered, and paid for, beautifully tailored marine-blue jackets and pale gray trousers from the Alfred Nelson Company in New York. I obtained permission from the army to use an official government eagle ensign embossed with crossed golf sticks and the insigne RYDER CUP TEAM for the pockets. Although I consistently picked my teams for their game and not their beauty, I must admit we stacked up pretty well in the Beau Brummel department, too, when we showed up for the Ryder Team matches."

Brilliant. Not only did Walter want his team to win, he wanted to get them laid too. What a guy.

Arguably better manned but certainly better dressed, the Americans met their opponents when the *Aquitania* docked in New York City, and the British team was let out of the bilges. The landing was eclipsed by another annoying American, Charles Lindbergh, who had dropped in on the Frogs near Paris just a few days before, but that didn't dampen the festivities. The teams were feted with fancy parties and dinners, and they played a few practice rounds just north of New York City to give the Brits a chance to "recover" from the voyage. Recover, my arse. While there is no historical proof, I'd bet the farm that Hagen introduced the boys to ice, and got them all transmembrified. A few years later, Arthur Havers described the team's first few days in an America in the throes of the Roaring Twenties, rich in hope and enthusiasm, and more than two years before the Great Depression: "Everywhere we went we were submerged by hospitality and kindness. Suddenly we were in a world of luxury and plenty so—different from home. It was something we never expected. Even the clubhouses were luxurious with deep-pile carpets, not like the rundown and shabby clubhouses at home."

Beneath Arthur's genteel quote lies this, the first impression of this country that even today slaps every new visitor in the face: "Holy shit, this place is fucking brilliant!" For the men on the British team, it must have been hard, if not impossible, not to feel overawed. Hagen, the evil swine, had one-upped them.

When the teams finally made it to Worcester, the Americans, in typically underhanded fashion, tried to change the already agreed-upon format for the matches. The U.S. team (I mean Hagen, ahem) asked to replace the foursomes with fourballs, a game with which the Americans were more familiar; that any match tied after the regulation thirty-six holes continue until a winner was decided; that each foursomes victory be worth two points instead of one; and that both teams be allowed to substitute a player in the last day's singles (only eight singles' matches were slated, despite each team having nine members) and that the wearing of stupid, or bad-quality trousers should be penalized by the loss of one hole, and the administration of a violent wedgie. The British agreed only to the second to last request.

The Americans shouldn't have worried about foursomes (players alternating shots), as they won three of the four matches on the first day. Johnny Farrell and Joe Turnesa, both new to the U.S. team since 1926, opened the event by hosing George Duncan and Archie Compston, 8&6, and though Ted Ray and Fred Robson were 3-up on Hagen and Johnny Golden at one point in the morning, the Americans scratched back to win 2&1. Gene Sarazen and Al Watrous played like two-dollar ukuleles—going nine-over-par for thirty-four holes—but even that was tuneful enough to beat Arthur Havers and Herbert Jolly 3&2. (The last-minute substitute Jolly admitted afterward that he was in awe of everything he saw in America, and couldn't concentrate on his game.) Finally, despite Leo Diegel relentlessly pissing off Aubrey Boomer and Charles Whitcombe by holing every damned putt he looked at, he and Bill Mehlhorn were down five holes at the halfway point, and were closed out, 7&5 after the thirteenth hole in the afternoon.

Day two's singles were more of the same. It wasn't until the fifth of the eight matches that there was good news for Britain, when Whitcombe halved with Sarazen. It was quite a battle, with the diminutive Sarazen down as many as five holes in the morning, and then back to only two down at the break. They fought hard in the afternoon, with Sarazen getting back to even by the twenty-fifth hole, and Whitcombe taking a one-hole lead on the thirty-fifth, then missing a par putt on the thirty-sixth hole to finish with a halve. Still, he was the only unbeaten player on the British team.

Britain's only win came at the final hole of the final match. Duncan and Turnesa seesawed all day, and it took a long birdie on the thirty-sixth hole to secure the victory. Then the two teams met on the green, shook hands, and walked off together. There was some talk afterward that perhaps there had been too much partying in New York, Hagen purposely running them ragged. No shit, Sherlock. And the absence of Abe Mitchell, the strongest British player, hadn't helped. But even George Philpott, editor of *Golf Illustrated,* admitted, "Several Abe Mitchells would have been needed to alter the result." Captain Ray said the difference was his team's putting, and that the two teams were even until they got on the greens. "I consider we can never hope to beat the Americans unless we learn to putt," he said.

At Oakmont a few days later, Compston was the low member of the British team, finishing seventh. The 1927 U.S. Open was won by Tommy Armour, the transplanted "Silver Scot," who had played for the U.S. Ryder Cup team the year before, but would never be allowed to play again. In typically brainless fashion, no one in the British camp figured out that it might be a good idea to have him play for *them*.

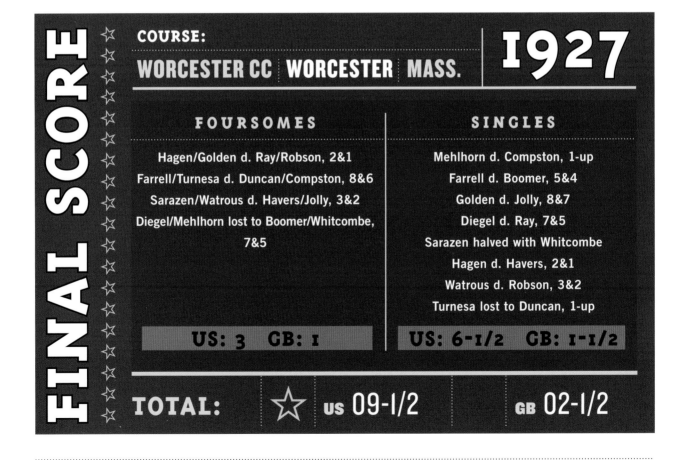

FINAL SCORE

COURSE:

WORCESTER CC : WORCESTER : MASS. | **1927**

FOURSOMES	SINGLES
Hagen/Golden d. Ray/Robson, 2&1	Mehlhorn d. Compston, 1-up
Farrell/Turnesa d. Duncan/Compston, 8&6	Farrell d. Boomer, 5&4
Sarazen/Watrous d. Havers/Jolly, 3&2	Golden d. Jolly, 8&7
Diegel/Mehlhorn lost to Boomer/Whitcombe, 7&5	Diegel d. Ray, 7&5
	Sarazen halved with Whitcombe
	Hagen d. Havers, 2&1
	Watrous d. Robson, 3&2
	Turnesa lost to Duncan, 1-up

US: 3 GB: 1 | US: 6-1/2 GB: 1-1/2

TOTAL: ☆ US 09-1/2 | GB 02-1/2

COURSE:

MOORTOWN GC | LEEDS | ENGLAND

APRIL **26-27**

1929

MOORTOWN

FINAL SCORE:

US 05 ☆ **GB** 07

CAPTAINS:

WALTER HAGEN   GEORGE DUNCAN

UNITED STATES	GREAT BRITAIN
Leo Diegel	Percy Alliss
Ed Dudley	Aubrey Boomer
Al Espinosa	Stewart Burns
Johnny Farrell	Archie Compston
Johnny Golden	Henry Cotton
Walter Hagen	George Duncan
Gene Sarazen	Abe Mitchell
Horton Smith	Fred Robson
Joe Turnesa	Charles Whitcombe
Al Watrous	Ernest Whitcombe

1927   ☆   1931   1933   1935   1937   1947   1949

1929

UNITED STATES

GREAT BRITAIN

FOR SOME ODD REASON, people think that just because a team or an individual did well the last time out, he, she, or it should do well the next time. If the San Francisco 49ers played well last week, they are expected to play well again this week. (That may have been true once upon a time. But today? I don't think so.) And if Rocco Mediate or Darren Clarke wins one Sunday, the pundits and prognosticators say he should have a good chance of winning the next Sunday. But in golf, conventional wisdom is often complete bollocks: The victor is so exhausted from the mental and emotional exertion of the first week (and the inevitable partying that follows) that if he even decides to tee it up the next week, he's unlikely to make the cut. Even more ludicrous is the assumption that a team of golfers that won two years earlier should do well the next time, especially in the 1929 Ryder Cup Matches, as Walter Hagen was once again the American captain.

With a party animal like Wally at the helm, even two years later the lads were probably still hung over. By the end of the 1920s, there was no doubt that America was the world's dominant golf power. Nearly all the best players were now being born there, and then, as now, those that hailed from elsewhere usually moved to the States to face the top competition. Americans dominated in the major championship arena, as well: No non-resident had won the U.S. Open since Englishman Ted Ray in 1920, and none had ever won the PGA Championship, which began in 1916. Across the ocean, the Open Championship was taking on an increasingly American flavor: Particularly galling was the fact that only two British natives won in the 1920s, while six of the ten titles went to either the great showman Walter Hagen or the splendid amateur Bob Jones.

JOHNNY FARRELL WATCHES WALTER HAGEN DRIVE DURING PRACTICE

The preeminence of American golf and the results of the 1927 Ryder Cup made the U.S. team the favorite going into the 1929 Matches. But it was not to be, and fortunately so, for if Great Britain had lost again it is possible the matches would have been discontinued for lack of competition—and interest. Even the English might grow tired of being bent over and given a damned good thrashing by men in strange trousers.

Before the first ball could be struck in anger, the teams had to get together, and again, money was an issue. The Brits needed much less than the three thousand pounds they barely scraped together to cross the Atlantic in 1927, but the public still refused to unzip their pocketbooks. In America, Hagen had gone some way toward helping professional golfers shed their second-class-citizen image, but the British had no such glamorous gadfly. To be allowed into their own clubhouses was still an honor. To finance their trip, the U.S. team played exhibition matches that raised six thousand dollars and took another five thousand from golf-equipment manufacturers and others.

In keeping with Sam Ryder's rules for participation, both teams were full of native sons. But America was a bubbling melting pot and its players could trace their roots the world over. It was widely noted that two of the U.S.

players were of English extraction, and the team was rounded out with players of Irish, Italian, German, Hungarian, Spanish, and Polish descent. It must have been a nightmare to feed them. Bernard Darwin, dean of British golf writers, went so far as to write that Joe Turnesa "had the air of a poor little shivering Italian greyhound"—a line that would get my arse fired today. Captain Hagen protested the restrictions, arguing that foreign-born pros should be able to play for their new country; after all, he said, they'd been able to fight for it in the Great War. My grandfather used to tell me stories about that war, and it never sounded great to me, so I'm with Wally on that one. On the British team, two of the pros were native-born but lived elsewhere: Percy Alliss (father of Peter the Great), taught in Berlin and Aubrey Boomer outside of Paris. In future years, that wouldn't be allowed, and quite right too. The Frogs had folded, and the Sausage-Munchers weren't to be trusted either.

The weather was cool and wet when the Americans landed in northern England, and stayed that way through the practice rounds. So Hagen took his players to the local Turkish baths to help them stay loose. At least that's what the dirty bastard told the press. God knows what they were *actually* up to behind the veil of steam—probably a large portion of rumpy-pumpy with our women. The rain stopped by the time the matches began, and the Americans could shed their extra layers of sweaters and rain gear, which must have been nice for them. The British rain gear was a sweater, rock hard nipples, and more Brylcreem. But while the climate was more welcoming, the British players and spectators were less so.

These Matches may have been the first time a golf crowd really got into the action, the ten thousand locals cheering when their team did well and the Americans hit into trouble. The galleries also watched the Americans hit hundreds of practice balls, something British pros rarely did, preferring instead to hang out in the snug smoking their pipes, getting plastered, and trying to get the Brylcreem off their shiny leather grips. Some of the U.S. team needed extra practice because they had to forsake their normal steel-shafted clubs for clubs with hickory shafts, as the R&A didn't allow steel shafts until November of 1929 (and only then because the Prince of Wales began using them, for both playing golf and his evening spanking). Imagine how spiffing it would be if the USGA could settle our most recent technology argument by sending Prince Charles a non-conforming driver! The player most affected was Horton Smith, who had dominated the U.S. winter tour using steel shafts, but had trouble adjusting; Hagen kept him out of the foursomes, and sent someone to Harrods to buy him a first name.

Even sitting Smith the first day, Hagen set a precedent in 1929 that has remained for the U.S. team: Every player good enough to make the team is good enough to play. Hagen said, "It would be unthinkable to bring them all the way from the States without giving each man a chance to strike a blow for his country," and ever since, no healthy American has sat out the entire event. Again, good on Wally. The man was a God. (In 1927, Al Espinosa was a reserve on the U.S. team and did not play.) The British took a different tack, with captain Duncan playing the best eight of his ten players. He sat Percy Alliss and Stewart Burns out of the Matches, saying they were "short of practice," which was a polite way of saying they weren't playing worth a shite.

The foursomes began almost as they had two years earlier, the Americans winning two matches, the British one, and one halved, despite most of the Americans being so unfamiliar with the format that Hagen had to explain it to

HENRY COTTON AND ARCHIE COMPSTON

LEO DIEGEL

"If you weren't dressed like a big girl, we might have a chance of getting laid."

them. (No kidding. Every American captain since has had to do the same thing). Charles Whitcombe and Archie Compston were 1-up on the tee of the thirty-sixth and final hole, but Whitcombe sliced his drive into a bush, leaving his partner a choice between taking a penalty drop or a gorse enema. You've got to love foursomes—you can hit it sideways all day and never have to play a recovery. The Americans almost refused the gift, though; Joe Turnesa hooked his approach from the left rough—where Johnny Farrell had hooked his drive—so it bounced off the out-of-bounds fence and finished among the trash bags behind a refreshment tent. Farrell lofted a lovely soft shot over a tent full of warm beer and bad cucumber sandwiches to a few feet, Turnesa quivered in the putt to win the hole and halve the match, and then lifted a symbolic leg and pretended to piss on Bernard Darwin's imaginary left foot. (Okay, I made that up, but it would have been cool).

Leo Diegel and Al Espinosa took a big lead early over Aubrey Boomer and George Duncan (who must have been gutted to be drawn to play with someone named Aubrey), and never eased up, winning 7&5. Henry Cotton got his first taste of what would become a long Ryder Cup career, teaming with Ernest Whitcombe against Hagen

HENRY COTTON DRIVING WATCHED BY ABE MITCHELL

and Johnny Golden. As much as 4-down during the afternoon, Cotton staged a single-handed comeback, but the Americans won the last two holes and the match. Despite the format, Hagen was at his punchable best when, before the match, he predicted with a shit-eating grin, "I shall win anyway. I always do." It was left to the two old men, Abe Mitchell and Fred Robson (with a combined age of eighty-six), to score the day's only point for Britain, toppling the experienced Gene Sarazen and the nervous Ed Dudley, who for some reason, just *sounds* nervous.

If the British should have had the edge in the usually Yankee-baffling foursomes, the more talented Americans should have had no problem with the singles. Instead, the British stiffened up some of their famous upper lip, and wiped it all over their opponents.

It began with Charles Whitcombe manhandling Farrell 8&6, a rout that boosted the British spirits. Sarazen was only 1-down after eighteen holes to Compston, then the two threw birdies at each other until Compston pulled away and won 6&4. Facing Boomer, Turnesa lost a morning lead and then the match, 4&3.

Diegel, who would prove to be the only two-match winner for the U.S., became a crowd favorite for his odd

SAM RYDER PRESENTS THE TROPHY TO GEORGE DUNCAN

giraffe-at-the-water-hole putting style, called "Diegeling." Sticking his elbows straight out from his sides and bending over almost horizontal from the waist, he was able to handle pesky short putts; he also Diegeled the living crap out of Abe Mitchell, 9&8 (and launched a nation of "Diegelers"). The only other American win came from the young Smith, who kept the unfamiliar hickory shafts from wrapping around his throat for long enough to win five of the last seven holes and outlast Robson, 4&2.

The biggest grudge match was the biggest rout, captain versus captain. When Hagen learned that he would face Duncan, the American said to his team, "Boys, there's a point for our team right there." But Duncan may have overheard Hagen's men's room remarks and subsequently told a reporter, "This guy has never beat me in a serious match and he never will," a piece of verb-strangling that went unpunished. Hagen showed up for their match dressed entirely in black, but it proved to be his own funeral. He was 5-down at lunch and was quickly devoured in the afternoon when Duncan won the final four holes, ending the match after twenty-eight holes. In a rare moment of total pussyness, Hagen admitted it was "a terrific shellacking."

The only singles match to reach the last two holes was the halve between Ernest Whitcombe and Espinosa, in which neither player ever had a lead greater than two holes and Espinosa had to battle back at the end, winning the last hole for the tie.

The Cup was decided when the young Cotton faced the experienced Watrous. The veteran took an early lead, but Cotton kept cool. When Watrous bogeyed the fifteenth hole, Cotton won the match and allowed a proud Sam Ryder to present his Cup to the British team, who had to be dragged out of the snug.

When the Open Championship was played a few weeks later at Muirfield, Hagen exacted some revenge, running away with the Claret Jug by six strokes. Three U.S. team members took the top three spots, eight Americans were in the top ten, while from the British team only Mitchell and the benched Alliss made the top ten.

A final odd note: The PGA of America's official history reports the 1929 Matches were played May 26–27, while most of the British books say they were April 26–27. Very curious, for while the Americans and British may be separated by a common language, I always thought we used the same calendar. Perhaps Nervous Ed was in charge of the books.

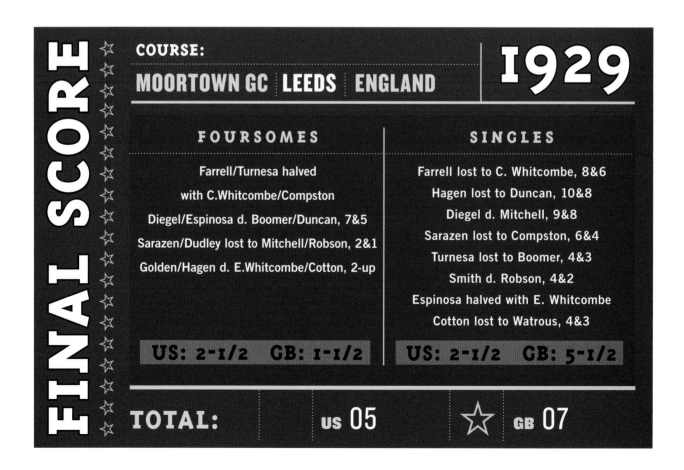

FINAL SCORE

COURSE:

MOORTOWN GC | LEEDS | ENGLAND

1929

FOURSOMES

Farrell/Turnesa halved with C.Whitcombe/Compston

Diegel/Espinosa d. Boomer/Duncan, 7&5

Sarazen/Dudley lost to Mitchell/Robson, 2&1

Golden/Hagen d. E.Whitcombe/Cotton, 2-up

US: 2-1/2   GB: 1-1/2

SINGLES

Farrell lost to C. Whitcombe, 8&6

Hagen lost to Duncan, 10&8

Diegel d. Mitchell, 9&8

Sarazen lost to Compston, 6&4

Turnesa lost to Boomer, 4&3

Smith d. Robson, 4&2

Espinosa halved with E. Whitcombe

Cotton lost to Watrous, 4&3

US: 2-1/2   GB: 5-1/2

TOTAL: US 05   ☆   GB 07

COURSE:

SCIOTO CC | COLUMBUS | OHIO

☆☆☆☆☆☆☆☆☆☆

JUNE **26-27**

1931

SCIOTO

☆☆☆☆☆☆☆☆☆☆☆☆☆☆☆☆

FINAL SCORE:

☆ US **09**   GB **03**

CAPTAINS:

WALTER HAGEN   CHARLES WHITCOMBE

UNITED STATES

☆☆☆☆☆☆☆☆☆☆☆☆☆☆☆

Billy Burke

Wilfred Cox

Leo Diegel

Al Espinosa

Johnny Farrell

Walter Hagen

Gene Sarazen

Denny Shute

Horton Smith

Craig Wood

GREAT BRITAIN

☆☆☆☆☆☆☆☆☆☆☆☆☆☆☆

Archie Compson

William Davies

George Duncan

Syd Easterbrook

Arthur Havers

Bert Hodson

Abe Mitchell

Fred Robson

Charles Whitcombe

Ernest Whitcombe

1927   1929   ☆   1933   1935   1937   1947   1949

1931

UNITED STATES

GREAT BRITAIN

THE CUP MIGHT HAVE BEEN YOUNG, but it was already developing problems that exist to this day. These Matches are usually scarred by internal explosions before a shot is fired, and the causes are familiar—composition of the teams, and naturally, money. In 1931, most of the trouble was in the British camp.

The tour in the States was healthy enough that a few pros could make a living competing and playing exhibitions, but that wasn't the case in Britain. Unless they wanted to starve, top players still had to perform their poxy club job duties, many of which entailed cutting greens, cleaning shoes, repairing clubs, teaching old farts, and generally taking orders from several hundred idiots. (Think of the great old black lockeroom attendant in *Caddyshack*, and you're not far off the mark.) As the game spread, many of these pioneer pros took better-paying club jobs in other countries, which, although it gave them financial security, corroded the Ryder Cup.

In 1931, two players from the previous British team were ruled ineligible: Percy Alliss, who worked at the Wansee Club in Berlin; and Aubrey Boomer, who had swanned off, first to St. Cloud in Paris and then the Royal Golf Club in Belgium. Both men had been attached to these clubs when they made the team in 1929, when Sam Ryder's Deed of Trust for the Matches seems to have been arbitrary. But this year, some bastard was kicking up a stink about it.

The bigger pong however was about money, and involved the young star of the 1929 British team, Henry Cotton, who had won the deciding match two years earlier. Cotton was one of the first British pros to come from privilege, having been educated at public (that's private in America, you fools) schools and sporting more refined tastes. He also wasn't as willing as the older pros to genuflect to the British PGA (largely because he was just as toffee-nosed as they were), and the demand that team members share any money they might make as a result of the Matches just flat-out stuck in his craw. It's sort of ironic that the first British Ryder Cup player who didn't actually *need* money was the first to try to make some.

His plan had been to stay in the States after the Matches to play a few exhibitions and tournaments. The PGA said his earnings would have to be shared by the team, since his transportation was being provided, so Cotton (taking advantage of that splendid education of his) offered to pay his own way and told them that they could stick the trip on the *Aquitania* up their arseholes. But that wasn't cricket at all, and for a few months the two parties sniped at each other, sometimes quite publicly, as when Cotton wrote a long and astonishingly boring article defending himself in Britain's *Golf Illustrated.* If he had read it out loud to them, they probably would have paid him to stop, but still hoping to get him on the team, the PGA offered Cotton the chance to "apologize." Not bloody likely. The bold Henry would have none of it, and even asked Alliss and Boomer to accompany him on a U.S. tour in which they would play exhibitions and attend the Ryder Cup as *journalists!* Henry's writing would have put a double espresso to sleep, but Alliss agreed, and somewhere, in the smoking lounge of some frightfully-awfully posh gentlemen's club, some pompous old duffers swallowed their monocles. It was very public, very unseemly, very un-British, and, if you ask me, totally fucking brilliant. It must have sold a lot of newspapers.

The U.S. team also had a controversy, but it was tiny spuds by comparison. Until he proved that his residence was across the border in the United States, Leo Diegel's place was in jeopardy, because he worked at Aqua Caliente Golf Club in Mexico. (No problema, apparently, when it's done that way around, though I doubt my housekeeper would ever have made the Mexican team.)

The big pre-Match story in the States was how its team was chosen. Five of the players were picked well in advance during the annual meeting/let's-all-get-wrecked-and-fall-down session of the PGA of America. The other three had to earn their spots from a group of fourteen players invited to Scioto Country Club the week before the

SAM RYDER AND THE GREAT BRITAIN TEAM

C.A. WHITCOMBE AND THE GREAT BRITAIN TEAM

Matches to play seventy-two holes of stroke play, with win, place, and show making the squad. It was the only time such a pre-match to make the Ryder Cup Matches was held. I can't imagine they played foursomes.

As a result of all this flaffing around, the teams that finally faced off were markedly different than those that had met at Moortown two years earlier. And, as many journalists (including the strongest British players) noted, the strongest British players were on the sidelines, reporting on—rather than playing in—the Matches. It must have been hysterical.

The British team was not only none too strong, it wasn't exactly sprightly either. Only two players—Syd Easterbrook and Bert Hodson (the last-minute replacement for Cotton)—were under thirty. The Americans were much younger, which became an issue as the temperatures soared. Astonishingly, the British did have something other than their traditional tweeds to wear, but the heat, humidity, and inevitable outbreak of swamp-ass still took its toll on the older gentlemen.

So we can give the Brits a break, not that the American team did. In an event almost as lopsided as the last (and first) time the Matches were in America, the U.S. triumphed easily, 9 to 3.

By this point, even captain Hagen couldn't complain about foursomes being an unfamiliar format for his team. In the very first match, Gene Sarazen and Johnny Farrell (both losers in foursomes in 1929) figured out how to play together and trampled on Archie Compston and William Davies, winning 8&7. What followed wouldn't get much better.

Hagen wanted revenge for the drubbing he suffered at the hands of George Duncan in the singles in 1929. Two years later, the forty-eight-year-old Duncan was originally left off the team (pretty rotten treatment for the winning captain) until the public objected, and he was hastily added back on. As if such treatment wasn't humiliating enough, Hagen salted the wound, combining with Denny Shute to completely sausage Duncan and Arthur Havers, 10&9, still one of the biggest margins of defeat in Cup history. The Americans were 5-up after the first nine holes, 10-up at lunch, and victorious in twenty-seven holes. At least it was mercifully quick in the hundred-degree heat.

Abe Mitchell and Fred Robson, who'd paired together to win the only British point in foursomes in 1929, repeated history, besting Diegel and Al Espinosa with superior putting. The final foursomes saw three rookies and the British captain's brother battle it out; the lead seesawed, but Billy Burke and Wilfred (Wiffy) Cox beat Syd Easterbrook and Ernest Whitcombe (brother of Charles), 3&2. I love it—Billy and Wiffy over Sydney and Ernie sounds like something out of *Sesame Street*.

The singles started like the foursomes, with two American routs. In the first match, Billy Burke—who'd set the Scioto course record while qualifying for the Matches—maintained his standard of play against a tough but eleven-years-older Compston, who was playing in his fourth Ryder Cup (if you include the 1926 Matches). The final score was 7&6, and anyone who watched wouldn't be surprised a week later when Burke won the U.S. Open. (That Open was famous for two reasons: One, Burke faced George Van Elm in a thirty-six-hole playoff; they tied at 149 and had to play another thirty-six, Burke winning by one stroke. Two, it was the first major championship won with steel-shafted clubs.) This one was definitely in black and white.

GEORGE DUNCAN

Sarazen defeated Robson, also 7&6, in a match remembered for a single shot. After taking the first three holes, Sarazen hit his tee shot through the fourth green, his ball finishing in a crack on the cement floor of a refreshment shack. He was about to concede the hole when he noticed an open window overlooking the green. Sarazen and his caddie moved a refrigerator to clear a path for the shot, which he hit through the window and onto the green, finishing ten feet from the hole. In his autobiography, Sarazen recalls making the putt for par; in fact, he missed, and Robson parred to win the hole. (Maybe we should cut the Squire some slack on that one. I think he was 183 years old when he wrote it.) Sarazen had a three-hole lead at lunch and then poured it on, closing out his opponent on the thirtieth hole. (I always think that being beaten by Sarazen must have been a nightmare, like having the crap kicked out of you by Mini-Me.) Lord knows, enough players knew the feeling.

The first of two British points in singles came when Davies beat Farrell 4&3, some retribution for the result of their foursomes match the previous day. In the day's only close matches, Cox topped Abe Mitchell, 3&1, and Espinosa nosed out Ernest Whitcombe, 2&1.

In another epic battle of the captains, Hagen squared off against Charles Whitcombe. Ever the master of gamesmanship, Hagen arrived late to the tee, where he was met by a waiter bearing a martini. Holding the drink in his right hand, Hagen took a few sips while making left-handed practice swings. Then he shifted hands and took a few more sips and a few more swings. When his name was called, Hagen polished off the drink and striped a drive down the middle of the fairway. Whether or not the martini had any alcohol in it is a mystery to this day, but Hagen's golf was wobbly, and he had to summon all his scrambling prowess to reach the turn two holes up. He held on in the afternoon, but not without incident. At the thirty-first hole, Whitcombe hit the wrong ball out of the rough and tried to concede the hole, but Hagen (who might have topped up at lunch) wouldn't let him. He told Whitcombe to find his ball and play the shot again, which Whitcombe did—winning the hole in the process! From gamesmanship to sportsmanship, to "Bollocks! What just happened?" With Hagen's 4&3 victory, the Cup was staying in the United States.

Cotton's stand-in, Hodson, finally got to play in the singles, and probably wished he hadn't. With Cotton stalking the match, notepad in hand, he was horribly hosed, 8&6, by Densmore Shute. Denny, who'd had to qualify for the Matches, made the most of his newly acquired course knowledge, winning both of his matches by huge margins. Havers closed the day by defeating Craig Wood, 4&3, for the other British point.

Someone on the British team had remarked during the week that Britain was having an unusually cold and wet spring and summer. Along the same lines, Bernard Darwin wrote in The *Times* of London, "Cold is the one and only thing that is at all likely to beat the Americans. Similarly, heat is our worst enemy." After Scioto, the British PGA objected to the conditions, and the Matches were never held during an American summer again. (Nobody worried about the British summer, but the Matches were permanently moved to autumn after World War II.)

In the gallery that weekend, along with a couple of famous player/journalists, were two spectators of note. One was Bob Jones, who had won the U.S. Open at Scioto in 1926 and after winning all four majors in 1930, had recently retired from competitive golf with nothing left to prove. The other was an eighteen-year-old Jones fan, who like his idol, parted his hair down the middle and wore knickers; in fact, at one point during the Matches, this young man was mistaken for Jones and admitted into the clubhouse. Years later, that fan would join Scioto Country Club, where he would introduce his son Jack to the game. His name was Charles Nicklaus.

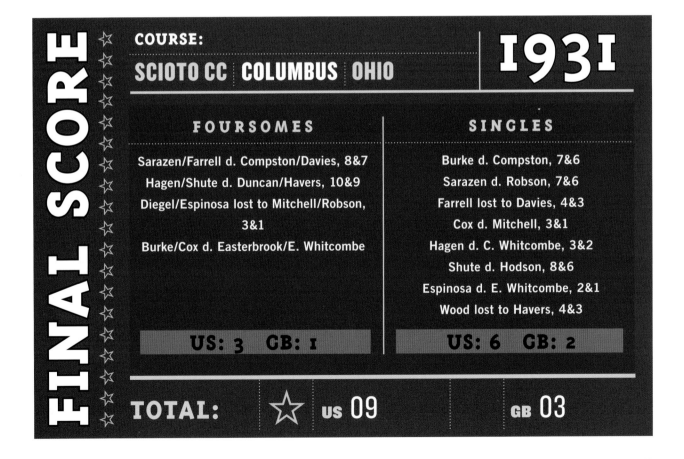

FINAL SCORE

COURSE:

SCIOTO CC · COLUMBUS · OHIO

1931

FOURSOMES

Sarazen/Farrell d. Compston/Davies, 8&7
Hagen/Shute d. Duncan/Havers, 10&9
Diegel/Espinosa lost to Mitchell/Robson, 3&1
Burke/Cox d. Easterbrook/E. Whitcombe

US: 3   GB: 1

SINGLES

Burke d. Compston, 7&6
Sarazen d. Robson, 7&6
Farrell lost to Davies, 4&3
Cox d. Mitchell, 3&1
Hagen d. C. Whitcombe, 3&2
Shute d. Hodson, 8&6
Espinosa d. E. Whitcombe, 2&1
Wood lost to Havers, 4&3

US: 6   GB: 2

TOTAL: US 09   GB 03

COURSE:

SOUTHPORT & AINSDALE GC SOUTHPORT ENGLAND

✩✩✩✩✩✩✩✩✩ JUNE 26-27

1933

✩✩✩✩✩✩✩✩✩✩✩✩✩✩✩

FINAL SCORE:

US 05-1/2 ☆ **GB** 06-1/2

CAPTAINS:

WALTER HAGEN   J.H. TAYLOR

UNITED STATES
✩✩✩✩✩✩✩✩✩✩✩✩✩

Billy Burke

Leo Diegel

Ed Dudley

Olin Dutra

Walter Hagen

Paul Runyan

Gene Sarazen

Denny Shute

Horton Smith

Craig Wood

GREAT BRITAIN
✩✩✩✩✩✩✩✩✩✩✩✩✩

Percy Alliss

Allan Dailey

William Davies

Syd Easterbrook

Arthur Havers

Arthur Lacey

Abe Mitchell

Alf Padgham

Alf Perry

Charles Whitcombe

1927   1929   1931   ☆   1935   1937   1947   1949

1933

THE RYDER CUP OF 1933 FEATURED A FEW FAMOUS FIRSTS AND LASTS.

It was the first time either team had a non-playing captain. And it was the first time decisions made by the captains had a significant impact on the result.

And it would be the last time for twenty-four years that the British, who at this stage were still clinging to the last vestiges of their perceived superiority, would win the Cup. But that's getting ahead of the story.

After the decisive American victory two years earlier, the British PGA wanted a captain who would concentrate on preparing and managing a winning team without the added burden of playing any matches himself, which is a nice way of saying that they wanted someone who, should he open his big fat mouth and put his spikes in it, would at least be easier to throw a sack over and drag out of the way. In the previous three Matches, the American captain, Walter Hagen, had gone 5-1, while the three British captains (Ted Ray, George Duncan, and Charles Whitcombe), were 1-4. Most recently, Hagen had defeated fellow captain Whitcombe 4&3 in the 1931 match that secured the Cup for the U.S. So a non-playing captain was desired, and no one better fit the bill than J.H. Taylor.

Taylor, Harry Vardon, and James Braid were three magnificent tweedheads who comprised the Great Triumvirate that dominated British golf at the turn of the century. Together they won sixteen Open Championships between 1894 and 1914, Taylor winning five and finishing runner-up in six. Besides being a great player, Taylor was a natural leader (he'd helped start the British PGA) and a favorite of the club pro, having worked his way up from caddie to champion. Furthermore, at sixty-two years old, hopefully the old goat wouldn't want to compete.

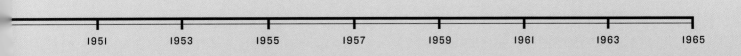

Perhaps thanks to Taylor's captaincy, the months before the Matches were unusually quiet. The committee that picked the British team went with five players from 1931—William Davies, Syd Easterbrook, Arthur Havers, Abe Mitchell, and Charles Whitcombe. Once again, Henry Cotton and Aubrey Boomer were ineligible due to their postings at clubs outside Britain, but this time there was none of the hilarious public bickering that had preceded the previous Matches. And since 1931, Percy Alliss had returned to Britain and was rewarded with a spot on the 1933 team, where he was joined by fellow rookies Arthur Lacey and the two Alfs, Padgham and Perry. All in all, it looked like the chaps had everything in order, and the quest for the Cup might be back on the straight and narrow.

WALTER HAGEN, SAM RYDER AND JH TAYLOR

It was a new-look American team, as well. Hagen was still the captain, of course, joined by returnees Billy Burke, Leo Diegel, Gene Sarazen, Denny Shute, Horton Smith, and Craig Wood; making their first Cup appearances were Ed Dudley, Olin Dutra, and Paul Runyan. Notably absent was that year's U.S. Open winner, Johnny Goodman, who was ineligible because he was an amateur—the last one to win a major championship.

As for those captain's decisions that made a difference? The first one was Taylor's, who brought in a physical-fitness expert from the University of St. Andrews to whip his charges into shape. Every morning at six-thirty, the team would run along Southport beach, their balls hanging out of appalling shorts, scaring the crap out of old ladies, and making dogs run away from their owners. Taylor's Chariots of Fire routine even included forty-one-year-old William Davies, and Abe Mitchell, who at forty-six years old complained bitterly that he couldn't keep his pipe lit. The run was followed by gymnastics and a rubdown (it's not clear who was rubbing whom)—fifty years before fitness trainers became part of the weekly pro tour caravan.

If the atmosphere was smelly before the Matches, it might have been because of Hagen, the devious swine, who didn't show up at the appointed time to exchange the order of play with Taylor. Perhaps a spot of gamesmanship? No doubt, because when a second meeting was set, Hagen was again a no-show. But Taylor had the final word, threatening to jolly well cancel the Matches, and tell Hagen's mummy, if Hagen didn't make their third meeting. Hagen was there, the exchange was friendly enough, and all seemed right in the world.

And then all was turned upside down when the Brits won the foursomes 2-1/2 to 1-1/2. The U.S. hadn't lost the opening day since 1926 (when they were shut out, 5-0). The first match was the most anticipated, Hagen and Sarazen facing Whitcombe and Alliss. It was widely reported that the Americans didn't like each other, which wasn't true but made for good copy in the scummy papers. Hagen, always the master of the dramatic, no doubt wanted to start the Matches with a bang. But he and Sarazen could do no better than tie, and that after fighting back from four down with nine to play.

Mitchell and Havers combined their excellent short games—each leaving the other nothing but short putts—to top Dutra and Shute 3&2. The long-hitting Dutra became the wide-hitting Dutra, and the Brits were up by four holes at the break and coasted in the afternoon. The closest match was Runyan/Wood against Easterbrook/Davies,

THE PRINCE OF WALES COMES TO WATCH THE 1933 RYDER CUP

neither side opening up much of a lead. They were even at lunch before the Brits pulled away. Runyan missed a five-footer on the thirty-fifth hole that would have brought them back within one, and when their opponents disappeared into one of Southport & Ainsdales potty bunkers, the Americans won the thirty-fifth. Both teams played the final hole as if it were dark—a drive into deep rough by Wood, an approach by Davies into another bunker—but both sides scrambled to halve the hole and give the win to the British.

The last match was the only American point in foursomes, and it was hard earned. Perry and Padgham looked to have matters well in hand when they were up by four holes on Billy Burke and Nervous Ed Dudley at

lunch. One of the wins was a fluke: Hitting a blind shot from the rough, Padgham's ball struck Dudley on the leg, and the rules of the day gave the hole to the Brits, who were so far out of position they probably would have lost it. (If that rule had still been in effect in 1991, I would have spent all of the first day aiming at Wadkins.) The pendulum swung back after lunch when the British pair missed a two-footer on the nineteenth hole. This seemed to reinvigorate the Yanks and the match was tied after twenty-four holes. Burke made an anaconda on the thirty-fifth green, the final hole was halved, and the U.S. escaped with its point.

Day two and the singles were nearly overshadowed by the appearance of the Prince of bloody Wales, (a Walter Hagen fan no less!) who decided he wanted to watch a spot of golf. Estimates placed the gallery between fifteen and twenty-five thousand, many who knew nothing about golf but were infected with "Royal Fever." Men with megaphones warned of pickpockets, while stewards holding long lances topped with red-and-white flags tried to control the crowds, with mixed results: The Prince tried to walk along as unfoppishly as he could as his friend Hagen played Arthur Lacey, but he had to repair to the clubhouse to escape the crowds wanting to see him. (Call me old-fashioned, but if he were trying to go unnoticed, he might have wanted to leave the crown on the mantelpiece.) There were no ropes back then, so spectators roamed all over the course, often disrupting play and booing the Americans. Years later, Sarazen said it was more carnival than golf course, but then again, being mistaken for a midget and tossed around for an hour or two would make a man bitter.

Sarazen was the first man out, but only after convincing Hagen that despite his poor play the previous day, he was ready to compete. The captain was willing to concede the point to opponent Alf Padgham, but Sarazen regained his putting touch and ran away after lunch, winning 6&4. In the second match, Olin Dutra took a quick lead over Abe

Mitchell, but then fell apart. Things went so badly for Dutra that in an effort to avoid a stymie—when one player leaves his ball directly in the other's line (in the days before balls were marked and picked up)—Dutra heebied his jeebie, and knocked Mitchell's ball into the hole. Mitchell said, "Ta muchly," and just sneaked by with a 9&8 victory.

Hagen continued his annoying play as captain, relying on fine approaches, good putting, and Arthur Lacey's shock at having the Prince of bloody Wales show up when he least expected it. The Englishman's tee shot on the sixth was so far offline, a spectator (never thinking it could have been from a match in progress), picked the ball up, put it in his pocket, and began walking away. In a brilliantly ironic twist, stewards chased the man down and almost beat the Prince of bloody Wales within an inch of his life. Hagen prevailed, 2&1. Then Wood beat Davies 4&3, coming back from being tied at lunch.

The Americans were a point ahead with four matches still on the course, but suddenly everything broke for the Empire. Alliss bettered Runyan 2&1 when the American short-game wizard did the unimaginable, skinning a sand shot out of bounds on the thirty-fifth hole to lose the match. Leo Diegel and Arthur Havers were even after eighteen holes, but after taking what he described as a "formidable turd," after lunch, Havers pulled away in the afternoon and won 4&3. Whitcombe was 5-down to Smith at the break before finding his form, but it was too late and the American won, 2&1.

So, another perfect Ryder Cup scene was set. They were all tied, with one match left—Easterbrook vs. Shute.

Both were playing in their second Ryder Cup, and both were close to soiling themselves. In 1931, Shute had recorded two incredibly lopsided wins while Easterbrook swallowed a singles loss. This year, Shute had lost his foursomes match while Easterbrook had won. Two good, but at the time hardly great, players (although Shute would go on win the Open and back-to-back PGA Championships), and no one's picks to lock horns in one of the Cup's most exciting matches.

Shute took a quick lead when Easterbrook's putting failed; but then the Brit fought back to cut the American's lead at lunch to one hole. In the afternoon, as they began to sense that their match could prove critical, neither player cracked, but neither could pull away. With four holes left, Shute had a one-hole lead that vanished when Easterbrook holed a long birdie on the thirty-third, then holed an even longer putt for a par to halve the next, and followed up by handling a stymie for another half. Everything—their match and the Cup—was even on the final tee, and dear God, I wish I had this one on VHS!

Both drives found sand. Shute's approach landed in a greenside bunker while Easterbrook played short and safe, in the fairway but far from the green. He pitched onto the green and Shute blasted out of the bunker, both balls finishing about twenty feet from the hole.

It was here that Hagen made his crucial captain's decision, and in retrospect, the wrong one. Chatting with the Prince of bloody Wales, he could have walked across the green and told Shute that a simple two-putt would probably keep the Ryder Cup in America, since matches ending in a tie go to the team holding the Cup. But Hagen stayed put, later saying, "I thought it would be discourteous to walk out on the future king of England."

Like, yeah, I can see Hal Sutton doing that.

Not.

Easterbrook rolled his lag up to about three feet short, and, trying desperately not to let his colon prolapse, watched Shute's putt for the win. Shute overcooked it, rolling his ball six feet past the hole, and with the Cup on the line, putted again—and missed. Syd Easterbrook, Ryder Cup hero, kept it together long enough to hole his three-footer, and win it all. (Shute did find a way to atone for the missed putt: He won the Open Championship a few weeks later.)

Upon receiving the Cup from the Prince of fucking Wales, Taylor resisted the urge to ask what the deal was with him and Waldo, and said, "I am the proudest man in the British Commonwealth of people at this moment." Hagen never lost his cool, admitting in his closing speech that having sailed over with the Ryder Cup, he'd reserved a spot for it on the ship going back.

The "official" Ryder Cup Matches had been held four times and each team had won it twice, always on its own shores. On both sides of the ditch, the public had embraced the matches, the players were keen to be selected, and the level of play was sufficiently high that a wonderfully competitive future seemed imminent. But as stated earlier, it was not to be: This would be the last British win until 1957.

Two more lasts. The 1933 Matches were the last for Samuel Ryder, who died in 1936, and for Abe Mitchell. In three Cup Matches, Mitchell compiled a 4-2-0 record, never losing in the foursomes. He never won the Open Championship he coveted, but his place in golf is secure: He is the wee man with the club, on top of the Ryder Cup trophy.

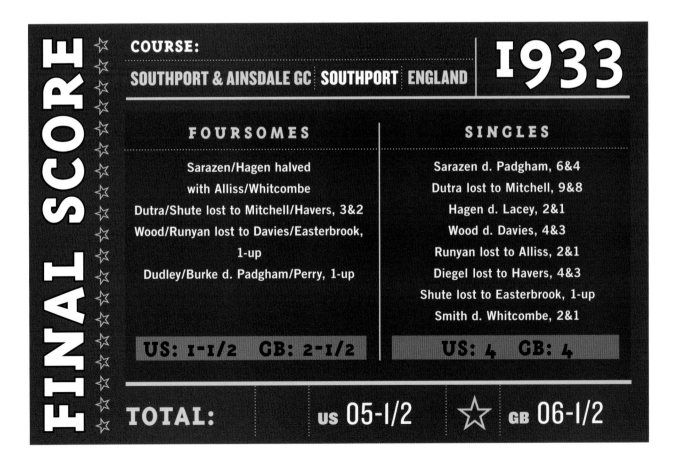

FINAL SCORE

COURSE:

SOUTHPORT & AINSDALE GC · **SOUTHPORT** · **ENGLAND**

1933

FOURSOMES	SINGLES
Sarazen/Hagen halved with Alliss/Whitcombe	Sarazen d. Padgham, 6&4
Dutra/Shute lost to Mitchell/Havers, 3&2	Dutra lost to Mitchell, 9&8
Wood/Runyan lost to Davies/Easterbrook, 1-up	Hagen d. Lacey, 2&1
Dudley/Burke d. Padgham/Perry, 1-up	Wood d. Davies, 4&3
	Runyan lost to Alliss, 2&1
	Diegel lost to Havers, 4&3
	Shute lost to Easterbrook, 1-up
	Smith d. Whitcombe, 2&1
US: 1-1/2 GB: 2-1/2	US: 4 GB: 4

TOTAL: US 05-1/2 ☆ GB 06-1/2

HEROES OF THE RYDER CUP
LEO DIEGEL : (1899–1951)

WALTER HAGEN could play championship golf while remaining calm enough to "stop and smell the flowers along the way." At the other end of the composure spectrum sat (or, more likely, squirmed) Leo Diegel, who was so nervous that he twitched away titles he should have won. At his most jittery he'd race after a shot while it was still in the air, like a jackrabbit on crack, and then begin worrying about the next one even before reaching his ball and assessing the situation. Too bad he was sixty years too early for Prozac.

Mind you, Diegel could hardly be considered a failure. He captured two consecutive PGA Championships, in 1928 and 1929—ending Hagen's run of four straight—as well as thirty-odd other tournaments, including four Canadian Opens in the 1920s, when that competition was considered just a little below a major in importance. But he remains just as well known for chances blown: At the 1925 U.S. Open at Worcester CC in Massachusetts (site of the Ryder Cup two years later), he needed to play the final six holes in even par to win; instead, he went nine over. At the 1933 Open Championship at St. Andrews, holing a short putt on the final green would have lifted him into a tie with Denny Shute and Craig Wood, but he couldn't quite time his stroke with the cheeks of his arse slamming open and shut, and he missed by a mile. His most famous quote was, "They keep trying to give me a championship, but I won't take it."

Diegel competed in four Ryder Cups, from the first in 1927 through 1933, playing in six matches and splitting them 2-1 in singles, 1-2 in foursomes. At Worcester, he paired with Wild Bill Mehlhorn and lost, 7&5, to Aubrey Boomer and Charles Whitcombe, despite sinking two very long putts on holes eleven and twelve in the morning then chipping over an opponent's stymie to squeak out a half on thirteen. He bounced back the next day, beating British playing captain Ted Ray in singles by the same 7&5 score: Diegel's seventy on the first eighteen was the low round of the eight singles matches and easily topped Ray's seventy-eight. His victory also earned the point that won the U.S. its first Cup.

His most notable matches were in a losing cause, in 1929 at Moortown in England. He teamed with Al Espinosa in foursomes to easily dispatch Aubrey Boomer and George Duncan, 7&5, then manhandled Abe Mitchell 9&8 in the singles. "I have certainly never played better golf," Diegel said afterward. "My driver never failed me and my iron shots and putting simply couldn't go wrong." Uh-huh Leo, that'll usually do it.

It was his putting style that made Diegel something of a cult hero. Searching for a yips cure, he adopted an odd posture that became a craze among golfers on both sides of the Atlantic. Bernard Darwin described it thusly: "His chin nearly touched the top of the putter shaft, his elbows were stuck out at the extreme angle physically possible, his wrists were stiff as pokers, and, apparently with his shoulders, he pushed the ball unerringly into the hole." But "diegeling" died a quick death as most amateurs found, as did its namesake, that it didn't banish the nervous twitches for very long.

In his last two Cups, Diegel played only twice—in the foursomes in 1931, singles in 1933—losing both matches. His yipped putt at St. Andrews followed just a few weeks later and was his last spasm in the spotlight.

COURSE:

RIDGEWOOD CC | RIDGEWOOD | NEW JERSEY

☆☆☆☆☆☆☆☆☆ **SEPT. 28-29**

1935

RIDGEWOOD

☆☆☆☆☆☆☆☆☆☆☆☆☆☆

☆ **FINAL SCORE:**

US 09   **GB** 03

CAPTAINS:

WALTER HAGEN   CHARLES WHITCOMBE

UNITED STATES

☆☆☆☆☆☆☆☆☆☆☆☆☆

Olin Dutra

Walter Hagen

Ky Laffoon

Sam Parks

Henry Picard

Johnny Revolta

Paul Runyan

Gene Sarazen

Horton Smith

Craig Wood

GREAT BRITAIN

☆☆☆☆☆☆☆☆☆☆☆☆☆

Percy Alliss

Richard Burton

Jack Busson

Bill Cox

Edward Jarman

Alf Padgham

Alf Perry

Charles Whitcombe

Ernest Whitcombe

Reg Whitcombe

THIS WAS THE FIRST, BUT CERTAINLY NOT THE LAST, nut-crushingly dull Ryder Cup, so I'm not going to spend a whole lot of time on it. When the most interesting story was that three brothers were on the same team, you have to suspect that the matches were far from exciting. Indeed, the final result was an American stampede—and a taste of things to come.

It wasn't as if the British hadn't jumped on the boat with high hopes. Many experts crowed that this was the strongest team they'd ever assembled, but of course one of the things that never changes about the Ryder Cup is that the experts' opinions are often proven to be complete bollocks. The Americans had agreed to change the date from summer to fall to ensure moderate temperatures (and, indeed, the weather was never a factor). Furthermore, the matches were being held on the East Coast—at Ridgewood Country Club, just a few miles from Manhattan— making the journey easier on the visiting team.

And, of course, the British had won the last time, and so on, and so forth, blah, blah, and blah.

So what went wrong? Hey, I'll be buggered if I know. It was nearly seventy years ago and just about everyone who played has been tits up for decades, so really, all we have to go on is the journalism of the day, and God knows we shouldn't take that crap too seriously either. Imagine fifty years from now, someone picking this book up and reading it as if it were factual! Journalists back then just made stuff up (as they do now), *especially* history, largely because it's usually *sooo* damn boring. So, that's where I'm going with this one.

After the matches were done, the British press found no shortage of excuses, including too much clover in the

CHARLES, ERNEST AND REG WHITCOMBE

fairways (which is a beauty), "stage fright" on the part of the players, over-watered greens, underpants-swapping, and not enough time to practice with the larger American ball. (This last excuse had some merit: The Americans played the smaller British ball when they went overseas, and so far neither team had won on foreign soil.) I have no idea what Bernard Darwin of The *Times* of London had to say, but it probably had something to do with the weather not being crap enough again.

Probably the most valid explanation was the lot of the professional on each side of the Atlantic. In America, a growing professional tour allowed players to sharpen their skills while competing against other top players. In Britain, pros still needed to hold those shitty club jobs to survive and had to ask their clubs' permission to play in events such as the Ryder Cup and the Open Championship. Also, American pros were becoming slaves to the driving range, while most Brits believed that practice meant playing another round, preferably after a few bevvies.

But in the end, the reason for the loss was the same as it always has been: One team flat outplayed the other, which was a bummer for the British, but a feeling with which they were going to become accustomed.

The three brothers were the Whitcombes—Charlie, Ernie, and Reggie—stalwarts of British golf in the early twentieth century. Mr. and Mrs. Whitcombe must have been very proud. Charles, a remarkably straight hitter, was the best golfer: Playing captain in 1935, he had been on every Ryder Cup team since 1927 (and would be playing captain again in 1937, then non-playing captain in 1949). He had the longest career of the three (more than twenty years), but would never win the Empire's most coveted prize, the Open Championship. What rotten luck! Ernest, the oldest brother, had played in the 1929 Cup Matches and been playing captain in 1931; he would have won the 1924 Open, having held a three-stroke lead, but ultimately lost the Jug to that irritating bastard Walter wouldn't-you-bloody-know-it Hagen. Reg, the youngest and, for most people's money, the least talented brother, would uphold the family honor, and piss off his two brothers, by winning the Open in 1938, after finishing runner-up the previous year. But this would be Reginald's one and only Ryder Cup.

Besides the Whitcombes, the British selection committee returned Percy Alliss, Alf Padgham, and Alf Perry (winner of the Open Championship a few months earlier), and picked new players Richard Burton (sadly, no relation), Jack Busson, Bill Cox, and Ted Jarman. The Americans had changed their selection procedure yet again, choosing players based on playing records over the previous two years, scoring averages, and of course, drinking buddies of Walter bloody Hagen. Even so, the heart of the team remained intact from 1933—captain Hagen (who by this time should have been a Rear Admiral), plus Olin Dutra, Paul Runyan, Gene Sarazen, Horton Smith, Craig Wood, and joined by first-timers Ky Laffoon; Johnny Revolta; Sam Parks, who had surprised everyone (including himself) by winning the U.S. Open earlier that summer; and a man who could possibly have been the great-great-great-grandfather of the captain of the *Starship Enterprise,* Henry Picard.

For the fourth time in five Matches, the Americans stormed into the lead, winning the first three foursomes. Hagen again paired himself with the midget-from-hell Sarazen, no doubt hoping for something better than the half they managed in 1933. Facing Perry and Busson, the opening holes were a fight but the back nine wasn't, and the Americans were 5-up at the lunchtime snifter. I suspect they might have had a long lunch, because both teams lurched through the second eighteen (the twentieth hole was halved with double bogeys!) until Hagen sobered up his irons and putter and they won going away, 7&6. It was to be Hagen's last Ryder Cup appearance as a player, as he sat himself out of the singles and would be a non-playing captain in 1937: his Cup record was 7-1-1.

American rookies Picard and Revolta had little problem with Padgham and Alliss: Seven holes up at the break, the Americans lost only one hole in the afternoon and won 6&5. A team of British rookies, Cox and Jarman, didn't fare nearly as well, losing 9&8 to Runyan and Smith. The only winning British pair was two Whitcombes, Charles and Ernest, who defeated Dutra and Laffoon. Most of the their action was on the greens, the British missing short putts and the Americans holing long ones, until they finished the first eighteen even. They stayed even or close to it through most of the second round, and were even on the final hole, where the Americans dumped their approach into the sand and lost 1-down.

The singles matches began with hope for the British, who took early leads. Sarazen was as many as four holes down in the morning, but got it back to 1-down at lunch. The little ratbag pulled ahead in the afternoon and ran off a string of birdies over the final holes for a 3&2 win.

If it was annoying to be beaten by the diminutive Sarazen, Paul Runyan must have made his opponents positively suicidal. He would scuttle the ball around like dodgy six-handicapper, but when he got it anywhere near the green he was a genius. He put on a short-game clinic in toppling Richard Burton (who would win the 1939 Open Championship) 5&3. Runyan even won a hole despite Burton laying a stymie (blocking Runyan's ball with his own on the green); when the tables were turned a few holes later, Burton hit Runyan's stymie with his ball. Little wonder that "Little Poison," as the five-foot-seven Runyan was known, was 4-up at lunch and never relinquished his lead.

Brother Reg took an early lead over Revolta and was up by as many as five holes after lunch before his Ryder Cup lobe exploded: Whitcombe bogeyed five of the final nine holes to lose 2&1. The Dutra/Padgham match had a similar feel, Padgham starting with a slight lead, but in the afternoon losing his marbles, and the match with them, 4&2.

The singles were only half over, but the U.S. had won four out of four and was keeping the Cup.

In the matches still on the course, Craig Wood raced out to a quick lead over Percy Alliss and was 3-up at lunch, but unlike the other Americans, he lost ground in the afternoon and fell back to all square after the thirty-third hole. They were still even on the final hole, where Wood hit a fat approach, chipped past the hole, and missed the putt: His bogey lost the hole, and the match to Alliss, 1-up.

Smith also seemed in control, going five up over Cox at the break. But this American also suffered an afternoon attack of shrunken sphincter syndrome, finding everything except a fairway—he was in the sand three separate times on the twenty-fourth hole alone! He chopped and swatted his way to a lovely 45 on the front nine after lunch, giving Cox a one-hole lead. Smith threatened at the finish, but the best he could do was tie Cox for a dispiriting half. But meanwhile, brother Ernie W. was spraying his tee shots so badly he couldn't have hit the sea from the beach, and was lucky to lose to Picard by only 3&2. Not for the last time, there was some seriously shitty golf being played.

The final singles matched the two current national champions, Parks and Perry. Little was known of Parks, a club pro from western Pennsylvania who had had his one and only moment of golf glory earlier that year when he won the U.S. Open. Perry was the more established player and one of the British hopes, but perhaps because the Cup was already lost, he could do no better than tie. The match was close all day, with Perry holding a one-hole lead as they reached the final green, where Parks holed a forty-foot putt to win the hole and a meaningless halve. Hooray, went the crowd, very quietly.

After the dust cleared, some British partisans searched for a silver lining and noted that none of the singles matches was a blowout, most getting to, or near, the final green. "Spiffing boys, we only lost slightly!" Over the next few decades, even that slim glimmer of hope would fade. Looking back on the 1935 Cup, the words of Britain's *Tatler* magazine had a sad and prophetic ring: "Better not go at all than to be beaten like this every year." Fortunately for golf, both teams kept going, and coming, and despite the one-sided nature of the next few contests, because of the diehard spirit of the men who played the first few matches, the Ryder Cup had taken firm root, and was now the most important event in international golf.

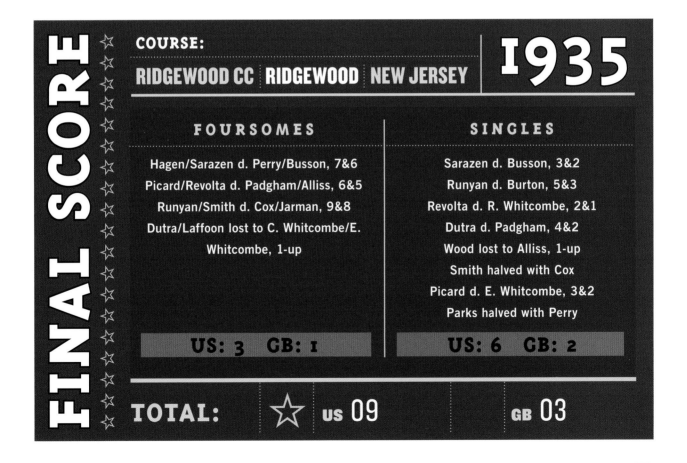

FINAL SCORE

COURSE:

RIDGEWOOD CC | **RIDGEWOOD** | **NEW JERSEY** | **1935**

FOURSOMES	SINGLES
Hagen/Sarazen d. Perry/Busson, 7&6	Sarazen d. Busson, 3&2
Picard/Revolta d. Padgham/Alliss, 6&5	Runyan d. Burton, 5&3
Runyan/Smith d. Cox/Jarman, 9&8	Revolta d. R. Whitcombe, 2&1
Dutra/Laffoon lost to C. Whitcombe/E. Whitcombe, 1-up	Dutra d. Padgham, 4&2
	Wood lost to Alliss, 1-up
	Smith halved with Cox
	Picard d. E. Whitcombe, 3&2
	Parks halved with Perry
US: 3 GB: 1	**US: 6 GB: 2**

TOTAL: ☆ **US 09** | **GB 03**

PAUL RUNYAN (1908–2002)

GOLF IS NOT KNOWN FOR GREAT nicknames: "Golden Bear" and "Merry Mex" are hardly in a class with "Shoeless Joe" or the "Manassas Mauler." One of the best was attached to a five-foot, seven-and-a-half-inch master of the short game named Paul Runyan. His sobriquet was perfect: "Little Poison."

Runyan won fifty tournaments during the 1930s and 1940s, including two PGA Championships, in 1934 and 1938. In the latter, he beat the much-longer-hitting Sam Snead by 8&7, the largest final-round margin of victory while that major was at match play. He was the tour's leading money-winner in 1933 and 1934, and in 1933 won the Radix Award, precursor of the Vardon Trophy, for low scoring average. His low scores were the result of expert pitching, chipping, putting, and his general tendency to piss off a host of players, all of whom looked much better "on paper."

Runyan competed in two Ryder Cups and couldn't have had two more different experiences. As a rookie at Southport and Ainsdale in 1933, he played twice and lost twice. In the foursomes, teamed with Craig Wood against Syd Easterbrook and William Davies, all four played sloppy golf, perhaps nothing uglier than Runyan missing a five-foot putt on the thirty-fourth hole. On the final hole, with the U.S. pair down one, Wood buried the team's drive in long rough, forcing Runyan to summon every bit of his antlike power to wrest the ball out and miraculously get it onto the green. But the Brits scrambled to halve the hole and win the match.

More surprising was Runyan's singles play against Percy Alliss. The two battled for thirty-three holes and were even when Runyan lost the thirty-fourth. On the next, with their balls so close in the bunker they were touching, Alliss got his onto the green then watched as Runyan knocked his sand shot out-of-bounds, giving the Englishman a 2&1 win.

But two years later at Ridgewood, Runyan could not have played better. He and Horton Smith ran roughshod over British rookies Bill Cox and Ted Jarman: Up by six after the morning round, they needed only ten holes in the afternoon to record a 9&8 victory, still one of the biggest margins in Cup history: The U.S. pair had won eleven holes to the Brits two.

In the singles, Runyan faced another rookie, Dick Burton, and proved how a great short game can best a big hitter. On the first hole, Burton laid a stymie on Runyan—and lost the hole when the American holed out anyway. Two holes later, Runyan returned the favor, laying a stymie on Burton, who could do no better than hit his opponent's ball, miss the hole, and go 2-down. Runyan was four holes up at lunch and eventually won 5&3, for the biggest margin of victory on day two.

Runyan became one of the game's foremost teachers (specializing in the short game, of course), but continued playing as well. He won the PGA Seniors in 1961 and 1962, proving again that despite his size, he was big-time.

COURSE:

SOUTHPORT & AINSDALE GC SOUTHPORT ENGLAND

☆☆☆☆☆☆☆☆ JUNE 29-30

1937

☆☆☆☆☆☆☆☆☆☆☆☆☆

☆ **FINAL SCORE:**
US 08   **GB 04**

CAPTAINS:

WALTER HAGEN   CHARLES WHITCOMBE

UNITED STATES
☆☆☆☆☆☆☆☆☆☆☆☆

Ed Dudley

Ralph Guldahl

Tony Manero

Byron Nelson

Henry Picard

Johnny Revolta

Gene Sarazen

Denny Shute

Horton Smith

Sam Snead

GREAT BRITAIN
☆☆☆☆☆☆☆☆☆☆☆☆

Percy Alliss

Richard Burton

Henry Cotton

Bill Cox

Sam King

Arthur Lacey

Alf Padgham

Alf Perry

Dai Rees

Charles Whitcombe

1927   1929   1931   1933   1935   ☆   1947   1949

1937

THERE WERE MANY GOOD STORYLINES HEADING INTO THE 1937 MATCHES.

As usual, high hopes for the British team was one of them because, at least on paper (and especially in the dastardly newspapers, where there was great debate), the home team was looking jolly good.

For one thing, the lads were at home, and no team had lost the Cup playing on its own soil. The make-up of the team was strengthened with the return of Henry Cotton, who had given up his aspirations toward journalism, and his club job on the Continent for one at Ashridge, northwest of London. Cotton was undeniably the country's best golfer and a fan favorite, having put an end to America's ugly stranglehold on the sacred Open Championship.

Before Cotton recaptured the Claret Jug, it had been in American hands almost nonstop since 1921 (except for 1923, when Arthur Havers had outweasled the Yanks at Troon). Not only was it hoisted by Walter Hagen four times and Bobby Jones three, but three of the winners (Jock Hutchison, Jim Barnes, and Tommy Armour) had been born in Britain but then moved to the States, where they improved both their golf and their "prospects." Cotton's victory in 1934 provided hope for those loyal to the Crown, and unleashed a string of successes for the locals: Alf Perry and Alf Padgham won the following two years, providing the only double "Alfie" in the history of the game, and Cotton won again in 1937 (a few weeks after the Ryder Cup), with Reg Whitcombe and Richard Burton closing out the decade. All in all it was a grand old time for John Bull, as they were Englishmen all.

And they were all on the 1937 team, along with returnees Percy Alliss, Bill Cox, Arthur Lacey, and captain Charles Whitcombe, who was hoping that the third time would be the charm. Two rookies also made the squad,

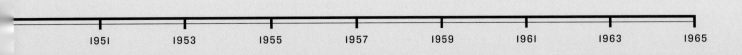

Sam King and the first Welshman to make the team, five-foot-seven Dai Rees, who would pave the way for the even-smaller Woosnam, and Philip Price. (I don't know why, but you don't want to play a Welshman in the Ryder Cup). It was the first of nine Cup appearances for the brilliant Rees, who also would be playing captain from 1955-61. His would prove to be an auspicious debut.

As had been the case since 1933, the British team was picked by committee, so also as usual, the Americans changed their selection policy. As in 1935, part of the team was chosen based on performance over the previous two years on tour, the nod going to Tony Manero (U.S. Open champion in 1936), Denny Shute (PGA, 1936), Horton Smith (Masters, 1936), Henry Picard, Johnny Revolta, and Gene Sarazen. The final four spots would be filled based on six rounds of stroke play—the two-round qualifier for the 1937 PGA Championship (the tournament itself was still a match-play event, and would be until 1958) and the four rounds of the U.S. Open at Oakland Hills outside Detroit. Incredibly, the final two rounds of the Open were on Saturday, June 12, four days before the team was to set sail from New York, which meant the qualifiers would have little time to prepare for several weeks overseas chasing the Cup, the Jug, and no doubt, the poontang. The four were Ralph Guldahl (who won at Oakland Hills), Sam Snead (who finished second), Ed Dudley, and Byron Nelson. Guldahl, Manero, Nelson, and Snead were Ryder Cup rookies, Walter Hagen was their non-playing captain, and the team was described by the British magazine *Golf Monthly* as "the greatest golfing force which has ever come to this country. A splendid spectacle of athletic youth."

(Bloody marvelous—they must have been trying to cheer the British team up.)

Like Rees for the Brits, one of the American rookies was beginning a superb Ryder Cup career. Who? Well hang on there, and I'll tell you, you impatient bastards. Guldahl and Manero would never play again, so we can cross them off immediately, and surprisingly Nelson, despite becoming one of the game's great champions, played for only one more Cup, in 1947. It was Samuel Jackson Snead who would become the workhorse of the U.S. team, playing every year until 1955 and again in 1957, and serving as captain in 1951, 1959, and 1969.

An admitted rube from the mountains of West Virginia, there are hundreds of stories about Snead's lack of sophistication. Shown a picture of himself in the *New York Times,* he asked, "How'd they get that? I've never even been to New York." (I'm sorry, but I still think he had a point.) He was the butt of his teammates' jokes on the voyage over, but he took them well. Personally, having met Mr. Snead on several occasions, I suspect he wasn't as daft as he was happy to make himself look.

"When I felt seasick, the boys said the cure was to eat celery stalks and hard rolls and no other food and then do two hours of dancing every night in the ship's ballroom," the lying old toad wrote in his autobiography, *The Education of a Golfer.* "I tried it," he goes on, "groggy as I was, barely able to roll out of my bunk and pull on my pants, and damned if it didn't work."

Sure, Sammy, and I bet you weren't dancing by yourself either.

The boys also nearly got him into a fight with Tommy Farr, the British heavyweight champion, who was also onboard. Those were lighter days and everything was supposedly in fun. But in over more than fifty years as a pro, Snead usually got the last laugh.

As the matches were beginning, the British got one more bit of good news: The weather forecast was crap. Windy, cold, and threatening nonstop rain, the feeling was the locals would have the advantage. (I can never understand why people think the British and Irish enjoy playing in bad weather. For the record, we think it sucks too). But it was the home team that would be washed away again.

The home audience had seen this movie before, as the Americans took command in the foursomes. For the fifth time in six Cups, the British won only one of the first day's matches.

Captain Whitcombe would be bluntly questioned after putting his two strongest (on paper) players, Cotton and Padgham, out against Nervous Ed Dudley and Byron Nelson. Whitcombe hoped to open with a terrific spanking that would motivate the rest of his team, but despite having won the Open the year before, Padgham's game was weak, and Henry Cotton was probably glad he didn't have to file a story on the way he played. The British pair took an early lead, but fell back and were 1-down at cucumber-crunching time. The wind hurt the locals more than the visitors, as did poor putting: Padgham missed one, "not much longer than my todger," that would have won the twenty-fifth hole. The Americans handled what little was thrown at them, closing out the match on the thirty-fourth hole, 4&2.

The play was better when the most recent U.S. Open champions, Manero and Guldahl, faced the positively naughty-sounding pair of Lacey and Cox. The home boys were a hole up at lunch, then quickly 4-up after twenty-four holes. But the Americans went on a tear, were back to even after thirty, and won three of the final four to take the match, 2&1. "Bollocks!" said Lacey to Cox.

The strongest U.S. pairing appeared to be Sarazen and Shute, and Whitcombe chose to take them on himself, together with Rees. Shute pulled his own ripcord early and was blown away, but Sarazen handled the conditions and his partner's disappearance, and the match was even at lunch. In the afternoon, Rees played like the veteran he wasn't, "carrying his captain on his putter," which must have been dreadfully uncomfortable for Whitcombe. No more than a single hole separated the teams (although Sarazen uncharacteristically missed winning putts on the thirty-fourth and thirty-fifth), and Rees had to sink a tricky six-footer on the last for a half, which he bravely did. A hero was born, and, wouldn't you know it, it was another midget!

The final foursome matched Picard/Revolta against Alliss/Burton. After a slow start, the Brits inched away, holding a three-hole lead at lunch. All three were returned by the twenty-sixth hole, but soon their lead was back to two, which they never relinquished, winning 2&1.

The weather was godawful for the singles, but possibly not as bad as Whitcombe's decision to sit himself and Cox. Furthermore, he kept Padgham in the lineup, and in the leadoff position at that, to face the big-hitting Guldahl. The American was 6-up at the midpoint and ate Alfie's lunch after twenty-nine holes, winning 8&7.

The U.S. team was up by two points, but the tide was about to turn. Shute scrambled on and around the greens to stay close to King, who was 2-up after four holes. They were all square at the break, then Shute took a lead. King was back to even after holing a twelve-foot putt on the thirty-fifth hole, and bravely made a six-foot

DAI REES IS CARRIED TO VICTORY

birdie putt on the last for a half. Meanwhile, Rees had his hands full with Nelson, who took a fast three-hole lead. But heroes rise to the occasion and Rees won four on the trot and was 1-up at lunch despite the wet club flying out of his hands. He then flew away in the afternoon, grabbing a three-hole lead on Lord Byron, which he maintained to the end.

When Cotton had little trouble with Manero, winning 5&3, the overall score was tied, but the U.S. led in three of the four matches still out on the course. The one that looked to be going Britain's way was Alliss vs. Sarazen. The Englishman was 1-up at lunch and 3-up in the afternoon when captain Hagen walked out to remind Sarazen (as if he might have forgotten) of the importance of the match. "Now look here, Shorty, if you win, you can have the bottom bunk tonight."

His player responded, winning three straight holes to draw even. On the par-three fifteenth, Sarazen flew the green, his ball landing in a woman's lap. Sarazen remarked later, "She wasn't too happy about a Yank treating her that way," so she either jumped or picked up the ball and tossed it; either way, it landed on the green a few feet from the hole, and Sarazen holed it for a win. (I'm guessing this women was a Yank.) Sarazen, the dirty dog, dropped a stymie on each of the last two greens, and the bold Percy managed to scoop his way around the first for a half, but the second one got him. The match went to the American, 1-up, effectively stopping the British resurgence.

The last three matches also went to the Americans, Snead handling Burton in a battle of big hitters, 5&4, Nervous Ed out-putting Alfie Perry on the wet greens, 2&1, and Henry Picard clawing and scratching his way past Lacey, 2&1. The U.S. won 8-4, although it could be argued that the match was closer than the score indicated. Which, of course, the British press did. Again, we were only slightly beaten, but at least we were at home, and didn't have to get on that damned boat again. You've got to look for the positive.

With the win, the home-field advantage was finally beaten. The Americans received a congratulatory telegram from President Roosevelt (who had taken five minutes off from watching football), and it was a proud Hagen who strode to the podium for his victory speech. At the last second, either the ever-present wind or a mean-spirited fart from Henry Cotton blew away his notes and he had to ad-lib, mistakenly saying that he was proud to be the captain of the first American team to win on home soil. When some clever bastard in the crowd called him on the mistake, he put up four fingers to indicate his four Open Championships, and said, "You'll forgive me, I'm sure, for feeling so at home here in Britain."

This man should have been the president of these great United States.

He later wrote, "I'm sure that was the fastest recovery shot I ever made."

And I rest my case.

Not only was it Hagen's last Ryder Cup, it was the final appearance for Sarazen, as well. Incredibly, Sarazen, who died in 1999, never captained a Ryder Cup team, but he finished with one of the best records, 7-2-3, and was the only man to play both singles and foursomes in the first six official Cup matches.

In his autobiography, Hagen wrote, "The fact that we'd finally scored a win on British soil was actually more important to us than the win itself." Nobody knew what he meant then, either, and nobody knows now, but it would be twelve years before the Ryder Cup would return to the land of its birth. I hope that makes you all happy, you, filthy Imperialist, nouveau-riche America swine. Don't worry, we'll be back.

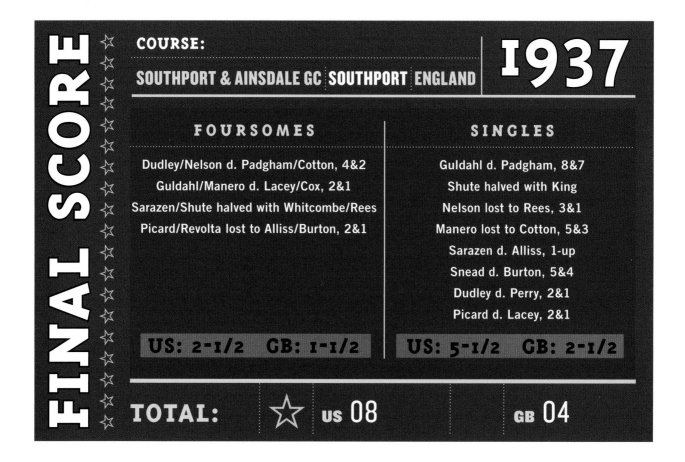

FINAL SCORE

COURSE:

SOUTHPORT & AINSDALE GC **SOUTHPORT** **ENGLAND**

1937

FOURSOMES	SINGLES
Dudley/Nelson d. Padgham/Cotton, 4&2	Guldahl d. Padgham, 8&7
Guldahl/Manero d. Lacey/Cox, 2&1	Shute halved with King
Sarazen/Shute halved with Whitcombe/Rees	Nelson lost to Rees, 3&1
Picard/Revolta lost to Alliss/Burton, 2&1	Manero lost to Cotton, 5&3
	Sarazen d. Alliss, 1-up
	Snead d. Burton, 5&4
	Dudley d. Perry, 2&1
	Picard d. Lacey, 2&1
US: 2-1/2 GB: 1-1/2	US: 5-1/2 GB: 2-1/2

TOTAL: ☆ US 08   GB 04

★ THE WAR

EARLY IN 1939, plans were being made for that year's Ryder Cup. A date and site were chosen—November 18–19, at the Ponte Vendra Country Club, just down the coast from Jacksonville, Florida—and teams were selected.

For the United States, Walter Hagen was to be non-playing captain, leading Vic Ghezzi, Ralph Guldahl, Jimmy Hines, Harold "Jug" McSpaden, Dick Metz, Byron Nelson, Henry Picard, Paul Runyan, Horton Smith, and Sam Snead. Conspicuous by his absence was Gene Sarazen, who supposedly was so mad that he boasted he could pull together ten players of his own and beat Hagen's squad. (Sarazen was a fairly obnoxious little git in his early years.)

Across the Atlantic, it should come as no surprise that the British press and public were optimistic about their boys' chances following the string of successes in the Open Championship. Henry Cotton was chosen as playing captain, with a team of Jimmy Adams, Richard Burton, Sam King, Alf Padgham, Dai Rees, and Charles and Reg Whitcombe. Two players were still to be named, but it never happened.

YEARS

Great Britain declared war on Nazi Germany on September 3. Shortly thereafter, Charles Roe, secretary of the British PGA, cabled his counterparts in the United States: "When we have settled our differences and peace reigns, we will see that our team comes across to remove the Ryder Cup from your safekeeping."

Although the official matches were on hold, the U.S. team kept busy with a series of Ryder Cup–style exhibitions.

Sarazen got his chance to take on the American team in July 1940, when he captained a team of "Challengers" (the members of which were not recorded) against Hagen's squad at Oakland Hills Country Club, outside Detroit. It turns out Sarazen was wrong—his team lost 7-5—but the matches raised $15,000 for the Red Cross.

In 1941, the American PGA again chose a team, although it is unclear if it was done with some hope the war would be over in time or as a way to honor the country's top players. That August, at Detroit Golf Club, 18,000 spectators saw Hagen lead Jimmy Demaret, Ben Hogan, Lloyd Mangrum, Craig Wood, Ghezzi, McSpaden, Nelson, Smith, and Snead against a team of British-born players living in America. Captained by

Bobby Jones and featuring Tommy Armour, that team defeated the Americans 8-1/2 to 6-1/2. In one of the exhibition's highlights, Nelson and McSpaden topped Jones and Sarazen in foursomes, 8&6; then, the next day, Jones came back to top Picard in singles, 2&1.

In 1942 and 1943, Craig Wood was named Ryder Cup captain, but with the war raging and the United States now deep in it, there was no expectation of a transatlantic rematch. The team (including Sarazen both years) was formed for stateside exhibitions, twice facing a squad of "Hagen's Challengers" and winning both times.

Besides raising money for the war effort, the exhibitions had another benefit: They kept America's top golfers in form. The war would be over eventually, the Ryder Cup would resume, and the opportunity to keep in shape would have great benefits for the American side.

Meanwhile, on the other side of the ocean, many of Britain's golf courses were turned into landing strips and civil-defense training grounds. Factories that once made golf equipment were refitted to make arms and supplies, and a generation of young men, including many top athletes, enlisted. In the "Cradle of Golf," the game was all but abandoned for the duration.

COURSE:

PORTLAND GC PORTLAND OR

☆ ☆ ☆ ☆ ☆ ☆ ☆ ☆ ☆ NOV. 01-02

1947

☆ ☆ ☆ ☆ ☆ ☆ ☆ ☆ ☆ ☆ ☆ ☆ ☆ ☆ ☆ ☆

☆ FINAL SCORE:

US 11   GB 01

CAPTAINS:

BEN HOGAN   HENRY COTTON

UNITED STATES	GREAT BRITAIN
☆ ☆ ☆ ☆ ☆ ☆ ☆ ☆ ☆ ☆ ☆	☆ ☆ ☆ ☆ ☆ ☆ ☆ ☆ ☆ ☆ ☆
Herman Barron	Jimmy Adams
Jimmy Demaret	Henry Cotton
Dutch Harrison	Fred Daly
Ben Hogan	Max Faulkner
Herman Keiser	Eric Green
Lloyd Mangrum	Reg Horne
Byron Nelson	Sam King
Ed Oliver	Arthur Lees
Sam Snead	Dai Rees
Lew Worsham	Charles Ward

1927   1929   1931   1933   1935   1937   ☆   1949

1947

GREAT BRITAIN

"IT WOULD BE FAIR TO SAY THAT no one seriously thought we could win the match, but at the same time no one ever dreamt that our fellows would be almost annihilated," wrote Leonard Crawley, one of Britain's leading golf writers. For once, the British were being realistic about their team's chances. But still: 11 to 1?

What happened?

To be fair, it probably was too soon after the war to resume the Matches. Britain's best golfers had lost years of practice and play. Food, clothing, and petrol were still being rationed. And there was no way the British public could afford to give to an appeal for the funds necessary to support a team. So if the Americans wanted to play, they'd have to find a sponsor willing to foot the bill, a modern-day Sam Ryder.

And we have to give them credit: It's a sign of the perceived importance of the event that they found their man.

Robert Hudson was in the fruit-packing business in Oregon, a member of the PGA of America's Advisory Board, and the sponsor of the Portland Open. God knows what would have happened to the Ryder Cup if it hadn't been for him. He agreed to pay for everything for the British team—from transportation to food and uniforms—as long as the Matches were played in Portland. No one liked to have to accept charity, so the atmosphere might have been a little strange on the long voyage on the *Queen Mary*, after which the British had to make a four-day train trek across the U.S. (Englishman Max Faulkner, who would win the Open Championship at Royal Portrush in 1952, was almost as well known for his eccentricities as his golf, and kept the lads amused with tall tales of American history.) Hudson met the team at the dock and, going with Wally's tried-and-tested get-hammered-early method, threw star-studded

HENRY COTTON

parties for them in New York, then accompanied the wide-eyed golfers cross-country, paying for everything along the way, including some of the best meals they'd eaten in nearly ten years. You have to remember, these were men who hadn't seen chocolate or eaten a real egg for the best part of a decade. This trip must have been one long, fantastic dream—with a nightmare ending.

The British were just beginning to play golf again. When the first Open Championship was held after the war, in 1946 at St. Andrews, Sam Snead won by four strokes, and the best British finish was a tie for fourth. The following year, my old boss, Northern Ireland's Fred Daly, won, followed by England's Reg Horne. This was a new generation of players, with little experience at the top levels of the game. The selectors picked three players from the last Cup squad—Henry Cotton (now playing captain), Sam King, and Dai Rees—along with Daly, Horne, and Faulkner, Jimmy Adams, Arthur Lees, Charlie Ward, and Eric Green.

In the States, golf hadn't stopped for the war. The Masters was canceled between 1943 and 1945, the U.S. Open from 1942 to 1945, and the PGA Championship in 1943. But the tour played on and there were plenty of exhibitions to raise money for the Red Cross, USO, and to sell war bonds. Which meant the new American players kept their games sharp, and there were quite a few worthy of consideration for the Ryder Cup. So (and you'll never believe this), a new selection process was employed.

For the first time, points were awarded for tournament finishes during the previous two years: For winning the U.S. Open and PGA Championship a player earned one hundred points, ninety-five went to the Masters winner, eighty for the Western Open, seventy to winners of tour events, followed by a sliding scale of points for top-ten finishes in those same events. Ben Hogan, who began proving himself during the war and had made the 1946 PGA his first major victory, was the playing captain. His team included Herman Barron, Jimmy Demaret, E.J. "Dutch" Harrison, Herman Keiser, Lloyd Mangrum, Byron Nelson, Ed "Porky" Oliver, Sam Snead, and Lew Worsham. It was a formidable lineup that took on the rusty British in 1947.

Snead and Nelson were the only holdovers from the 1937 team. There was no doubt that Snead, who'd qualified for the team on points, was still on top of his game: Perhaps the first man to make the game look like an athletic pastime, he was a superb physical specimen. Only thirty-five, he had finished second to Worsham in the 1947 U.S. Open (after winning at St. Andrews in 1946), and was showing no signs of slowing down.

Byron Nelson was another story. In 1944, a time during which professional golf was dead in the U.K., he'd won thirteen of the twenty-three tournaments he entered, then eighteen of thirty-one in 1945, the year of his amazing streak of eleven victories in a row. He was the most dominant golfer of his time, but he didn't qualify for the Ryder Cup because he'd officially retired from professional golf at the end of the 1946 season due to poor health. So he didn't play a single event in the year of the Cup Matches, yet was invited to join the team. Hogan was convinced that Nelson was still a safe bet.

In Crawley's words, the Americans were "as good a side as any that has ever played against Great Britain, and probably better." He said he would be happy if the visitors won four points. He wouldn't be happy.

With the first Irishman safely ensconced on the team, Murphy's Law applied itself with a vengeance. It seemed that everything that could go wrong did. Back at home, the summer of 1947 had been hot and dry and the courses played firm and fast. In contrast, Oregon had absorbed a record amount of rain that fall, making the Portland Golf Club a barely playable squishfest. An inch of rain fell the night before the matches were to begin, so pools of water were everywhere—in the fairways, on the greens, and filling the bunkers.

Something else happened on the eve of the event: Cotton (the twat) demanded an inspection of the U.S. team's irons, looking for the illegal grooves he thought were imparting too much spin. No non-conforming grooves were found, and the Americans took the challenge in stride. But there was definitely the sense that Cotton was desperate. Also, it occurs to me that if the golf course had indeed been as soft as they say, the extra spin would have been a disadvantage. But Henry was looking for something, or somebody, to blame for what he felt was an impending disaster.

Unable to find relief in the Rules of Golf, Cotton went high, and (hoping he might catch the Almighty in a spare moment between miracles) appealed for divine intervention. Minutes before the first match was to go off, he gathered the British team in his hotel suite, where he lifted a Bible and suggested that they spend a few moments in meditation. But perhaps the Almighty couldn't hear their pleas through the cloud cover, or maybe he was busy creating the Cold War, because he abandoned their cause as soon as the Matches were underway.

The rout began with the opening match, and Cotton was one of its first victims. Paired with Lees against Lew Worsham and Porky Oliver, the captain's putting was ungodly, and he missed, by his own count, eight putts of ten feet or less in twenty-seven holes. The Americans were six up at the break and didn't let up, porking the unfortunate British pair 10&9, which tied the record for the biggest margin of victory in foursomes. Snead and Mangrum also reached lunch 6-up over Fred Daly and Charles Ward. The Brits had a few chances in the afternoon, but the final result was an only slightly less embarrassing 6&5.

The other two foursomes offered the British some hope. Maxie Faulkner and Jimmie Adams were two up on Ben Hogan and Jimmy Demaret at the break, but the Americans proved their mettle by winning four of the first seven holes in the afternoon and retaking the lead. A beautiful pitch by Adams brought the match back to even after fifteen, but on sixteen Hogan hit a six-iron from a fairway bunker to twelve feet and Demaret holed the birdie putt. Winning the final hole gave the U.S. a 2&1 victory.

In the final match, Rees and King had the best opening round for the British and went to lunch up by one over Nelson and Barron. King and Nelson kept the match close as their partners made some poor decisions and poorer shots. The Brits maintained their lead through the twenty-eighth hole, but then Nelson took control, holing putts on the following three holes for wins or halves and sticking his tee shot close enough for a tying birdie on the par-three thirty-fifth hole that secured the match 2&1.

It was the first sweep of the foursomes since the phantom Ryder Cup of 1926. All Cotton could do was hope that the next day would be better. I mean, it couldn't be worse, right?

Wrong. The Americans needed only 2-1/2 points from eight matches to retain the Cup. Hogan was so confident, he kept himself out of the singles (Barron as well), allowing Harrison and Keiser to play. Presumably relying on the same fine form his squad had shown the day before, Cotton sat the same two players he'd held out of the foursomes,

Green and Horne! Neither of these two poor bastards would make another Ryder Cup team, and sadly, it would not be the last time a British captain would hold players out of all the matches.

The scores in the singles look closer than those of the foursomes, but amazingly, only one of the eight matches went to the thirty-fifth hole. It almost isn't fair to go into details, but what the hell, here's a quick account of the carnage.

Harrison was 3-up over Daly at lunch and lost just one hole in the afternoon, winning 5&4. Even closing out the morning round with two birdies, Adams was 1-down to Worsham at the break. The Scot got back to even during the afternoon, but Worsham pulled away over the final nine to win 3&2.

One of the most colorful characters ever to play for Britain, Faulkner had one of its worst records, winning only one match in five Ryder Cups, and it didn't come on this occasion. He was down to Mangrum by six holes at the break, then halved eleven of the next thirteen, and the American won, 6&5. Ward played some of Britain's best golf against Oliver, winning two straight holes after being 4-down at lunch. But it wasn't enough, as Oliver, who reportedly ate more at lunch that the rest of the two teams combined, won two straight of his own to return the lead to four, followed by twelve halves to win 4&3.

The best match saw Arthur Lees (future captain Sam Torrance's first boss at the famous Sunningdale club) fire an even-par round in the morning but still head to lunch 2-down to Nelson, who carded a two under seventy. Both players were one–under par for the first nine in the afternoon before halving all eight holes on the back (actually reaching the thirty-fifth hole), giving Nelson the 2&1 victory.

The fate of the Cup was all but decided when Cotton and Snead faced off. Cotton opened an early lead but gave those holes back and more, and was three down at lunch. The British captain spat out his pacifier and threw all the toys out of the crib a few times that afternoon (much to Snead's glee), and lost more than a few holes by hitting into trees. He managed to cut Snead's lead to one after twenty-seven, but that was when the American raised his game, won four of the final five holes, and picked off Cotton 5&4.

Demaret and Rees traded small leads in the morning, the Welshman 1-up at lunch and maintaining that lead through the twenty-eighth hole. Demaret then took the next three holes and the lead, which he held onto for a 3&2 win. Keiser and King were locked in a similar struggle, going into lunch even. Keiser took an early afternoon lead before King fought back for a two-hole lead after twenty-seven. He added two more on the back nine and halved the last two for a 4&3 win and Britain's only point. Had Herman Keiser's mind been on the task, this might have been the first and only clean sweep in the history of the Matches.

In the book *Hogan*, author Curt Sampson relates a fascinating story. On the eve of the matches, Hogan asked Keiser why he looked so unhappy. Keiser said that he'd recently paid twenty dollars for a "date" with a young lovely who later found out that he was a professional golfer and, presumably, rich. So she raised her fee to a thousand dollars and threatened to accuse him of rape if he didn't pay up. (I hate it when that happens.) Over the last fifty years, many stories of Hogan's character have been told, but this is my favorite. The Hawk just counted out ten hundred-dollar bills and said, "Just pay me when you can, Herm." Damn, but that was a lot of money!

And *that's* a captain.

Once again, what happened? Crawley wrote that the British "looked like a team of good club professionals struggling against the best tournament professionals in the world." The usual excuses were tossed out, in particular the weather and the long journey. But in truth, for almost a decade the British had been kind of busy with one of the most horrific wars in history. People from any generation since can't possibly be expected to understand what it must have been like for that British team. They simply weren't ready, and it would be a long time before they would look ready again.

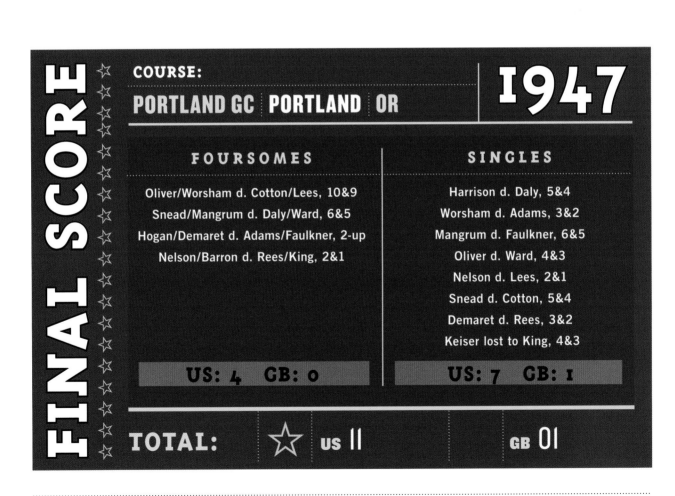

FINAL SCORE

COURSE:

PORTLAND GC | **PORTLAND** | **OR**

1947

FOURSOMES	SINGLES
Oliver/Worsham d. Cotton/Lees, 10&9	Harrison d. Daly, 5&4
Snead/Mangrum d. Daly/Ward, 6&5	Worsham d. Adams, 3&2
Hogan/Demaret d. Adams/Faulkner, 2-up	Mangrum d. Faulkner, 6&5
Nelson/Barron d. Rees/King, 2&1	Oliver d. Ward, 4&3
	Nelson d. Lees, 2&1
	Snead d. Cotton, 5&4
	Demaret d. Rees, 3&2
	Keiser lost to King, 4&3
US: 4 GB: 0	**US: 7 GB: 1**

TOTAL: ☆ US 11 | GB 01

HEROES OF THE RYDER CUP
PERCY ALLISS : (1897–1975)

IF YOU'RE AN AMERICAN, you might wonder if I mean Peter Alliss, whom you probably know as that distinguished-sounding English fellow who occasionally does golf commentary on television. No, I can keep my Allisses straight: This one is Percy, Peter's father and one of the top British golfers in the years before the Second World War.

As a club pro he started in Wales, held a succession of jobs in England, then made a big jump to the Wannsee club in Berlin, Germany, where he was the head man from 1926 to 1932. During that time he won five German Opens as well as two Italian Opens. After returning to England he had his two biggest triumphs, the Professional Matchplay tournaments in 1933 and 1937. Between 1926 and 1938, he had 16 victories in total.

Noticeably absent from his win list was the Open Championship, but it wasn't for lack of chances. He was third in 1931, fourth in 1928, 1929, and 1932, and fifth in 1936. The problems almost always came on the greens: He was blessed with a beautiful swing but what his son called "a none too efficient putting stroke."

Alliss attended five Ryder Cups, but only played in three. He made the 1929 team but was never called upon to play. In 1931, Alliss would have made the team but was ruled ineligible because he was working out of Britain. Henry Cotton, who was at a club in Belgium, was left off for the same reason even though both men had been on the 1929 team: The rules weren't applied uniformly in those days. Alliss and Cotton still went to the '31 matches in Ohio, where they played an exhibition and served as correspondents for British newspapers.

Back in England, Alliss made the Cup squads in 1933, 1935, and 1937, playing in six matches and going 3-2-1. He "debuted" in 1933 teamed with Charles Whitcombe against the dream team of Walter Hagen and Gene Sarazen; the Brits lost a sizable lead and had to live with a half. In the singles, Alliss faced Paul Runyan, he of the magical short game, and was the beneficiary when Runyan surprisingly knocked a bunker shot out of bounds on the 35th hole to lose the match.

Two years later, Alliss split his matches: He and Alf Padgham lost badly to the American rookies Henry Picard and Johnny Revolta, 6&5. In the singles, Alliss was three-down to Craig Wood after the morning but fought back and won the match on the final hole.

He ended his Cup career by winning with Dick Burton over Picard and Revolta, 2&1, then facing Sarazen in The Squire's final Cup appearance. Alliss had a three-hole lead in the afternoon until Hagen, the American captain, gave his player a pep talk that actually worked: Sarazen won the next three holes. At the par-three 15th hole, Sarazen's ball flew long and landed in a lady's lap: It's uncertain whether she stood up or threw the ball back, but whatever, it stopped just a few feet from the hole and Sarazen holed the putt for a win. On the last two holes, Sarazen laid two stymies: On 17, Alliss managed to slide his 35-foot putt past his opponent's ball for a half–"the greatest competitive putt I have ever seen," said Sarazen–but he couldn't repeat at the last and Sarazen won the match, 1-up. It was Alliss' only singles loss in three Cups.

COURSE:

GANTON GC | SCARBOROUGH | ENGLAND

☆☆☆☆☆☆☆☆☆☆☆ SEPT. **16-17**

1949

☆☆☆☆☆☆☆☆☆☆☆☆☆☆☆☆

FINAL SCORE:

☆ US **07** GB **05**

CAPTAINS:

BEN HOGAN | CHARLES WHITCOMBE

UNITED STATES
☆☆☆☆☆☆☆☆☆☆☆☆☆☆

Skip Alexander

Jimmy Demaret

Bob Hamilton

Chick Harbert

Dutch Harrison

Clayton Heafner

Lloyd Mangrum

Johnny Palmer

Sam Snead

GREAT BRITAIN
☆☆☆☆☆☆☆☆☆☆☆☆☆☆

Jimmy Adams

Laurie Ayton

Ken Bousfield

Richard Burton

Fred Daly

Max Faulkner

Sam King

Arthur Lees

Dai Rees

Charles Ward

1927	1929	1931	1933	1935	1937	1947	☆

1949

THE FIRST SEVEN RYDER CUP MATCHES HAD BEEN MARRED by controversies over hot weather, ocean voyages, the nationalities of team members, cold weather, clover in the fairways, train rides, illegal grooves, wet weather, who played and who didn't, even sports jackets, matching slacks, and uncomfortable underpants. But 1949 was the first time there was a burger brouhaha. Yup, meat—of the cow variety, that is.

Food rationing was still in effect in Great Britain, and Robert Hudson, the Oregon fruit-grower who single-handedly saved the 1947 matches by covering the expenses of the British team, didn't think the hosts should have to feed the visiting Americans when they could barely feed themselves. What a nice man Mr. Hudson must have been, and he couldn't possibly have foreseen the righteous indignation his vile vittles would produce. So, disembarking along with the U.S. team at Southampton was more than 1,100 pounds of meat—six hundred steaks, twelve sides of rib-eye, a dozen hams, and twelve boxes of bacon. (What, no fruit? Were they not worried about scurvy, or constipation? Where was the fiber?) Customs officials weren't exactly in the loop (like that never happens) and were unhappy with this special delivery—which, Hudson said, he hoped the British team would share. With a fairly typical degree of sniffyness, His Majesty's finest demanded an import license and the proper fees, and it took some behind-the-scenes bureaucratic bum-sniffing to get the larder out of port and on its long journey north to Ganton, a brilliant heathland course in the north of England.

When the grub finally arrived, rotten or not, it was served to the Americans, and then at a huge banquet attended by the British team, minus their wives, who were offended by what they considered charity, and subsequently gave the whole gig the Heisman. And there, my friends (the first time the wives were involved), went the neighborhood. Their husbands didn't seem to mind though, and ate heartily (although Max Faulkner later remembered the feast being held on the last night, after the matches were over, too late to help give sustenance to the malnourished British team). Having said that, I met old Maxie once, and he thought he was a squirrel. Or maybe it was me.

Anyway, the fattened Americans were led by a very thin Ben Hogan, just seven months after his car had been flattened by a bus on a fog-shrouded highway. Throwing himself across his wife Valerie to protect her, Hogan had suffered appalling injuries and spent two months in the hospital. He was lucky to be alive, let alone hobbling around on crutches and directing his team thousands of miles from home. But even if his captainship was a most-ly sentimental gesture, the flinty Hogan—who would just as soon eat nails as the by-now-notorious nosh—took

LLOYD MANGRUM AND SAM SNEAD

the job seriously. The bastard woke his team up early and made them practice longer and harder than they ever had before. Jimmy Demaret went so far as to ask his captain, "Are we training for golf or the army?" (I don't know what Hogan said, although I did used to watch *Hogan's Heroes,* and I thought he was pretty funny.)

Knowing Hogan, to him it was war and he wasn't above a little covert ops. With the memory of how Henry Cotton had challenged the legality of some of the U.S. team's irons two years earlier, Hogan lodged his own complaint about the grooves in the Brits' clubs. So there! The clubs were rushed to Bernard Darwin, the well-known golf writer and current chairman of the Royal and Ancient's Rules committee: Some reports say Darwin was just beginning dinner, others that he was summoned from his bath, but no matter whether he was supping or soaping, he took the matter in stride, examined the disputed irons, and, even though he wasn't Jewish, agreed that they weren't kosher, saying, "Nothing that a little filing will not put right." Jock Ballantine, the pro at Ganton, was up the rest of the night filing—and cursing. Surprisingly, the British press tended to side with Hogan; not surprisingly, the British players were miffed, and there we went again! People tend to think that Ryder Cup pettiness and gamesmanship started with Ballesteros, but nuh-uh. Old Blue Face was just keeping up appearances.

As if that wasn't enough pre-Match furor for you, wouldn't you frigging know it, the issue of who was on the team resurfaced! On the British side, the player in question was Henry bloody Cotton again, who had won his third Open Championship the year before. Cotton (who as I think I mentioned before was a complete arsehole) had been invited to join the team, opted out, his toffee nose out of joint at not being named captain, and therefore given the chance to avenge the 11-1 hosing in 1947. A reasonably observant follower of the game might have pointed out to old Hank that losing 11-1 the last time out probably didn't help his cause. Much. Instead, the British chose Charles

Whitcombe as captain for the fourth and final time, but since he was a creaky fifty-four, strictly as the non-playing kind. Despite the disastrous results the last time out, the Brits returned seven players who had been porked in Portland—Jimmy Adams, Fred Daly, Max Faulkner, Sam King, Arthur Lees, Dai Rees, and Charlie Ward—plus newcomers Ken Bousfield and Laurence Ayton (who wouldn't play) and prewar veteran Richard Burton.

UNITED STATES RYDER CUP TEAM

"Could we look any gayer?"

As I mentioned earlier, I was an assistant to the great Fred Daly, at Balmoral Golf Club in Belfast, and I can't resist telling one short story about him. Fred was fond of a gin (or three hundred), and one day, after a lengthy liquid lunch, he left the club, hopped into the old orange Hillman Avenger, and headed home, pausing only to swerve through and partially demolish a gas station opposite the entrance to the club. When, some thirty minutes later, a burly Belfast copper banged on his door and asked him what the hell he thought he was doing, leaving the scene of an accident, Fred looked at him, dumbfounded, and said, "Ossifer, that was no accident, I did it on purpose."

Moving right along, using the same points system instituted in 1947, the U.S. team featured five new faces—Skip Alexander, Bob Hamilton, Chick Harbert, Clayton Heafner, and Johnny Palmer—and four returnees—Jimmy Demaret, Dutch Harrison, Lloyd Mangrum, and Sam Snead. (Oddly, the U.S. sent only nine players, which was either ballsy or insulting, I'm not sure which.) It was widely argued that America's best golfers were missing, notably Hogan, who was injured, and Nelson, who had retired and was happy on the ranch.

A third American who should have made the team was Cary Middlecoff, who had won the U.S. Open just three months earlier but had yet to satisfy the American PGA's idiotic five-year membership requirement. (This rule, which would keep many others off the team in years to come, was overturned in 1990.) Gene Sarazen wrote that the waiting period made sense in the early days when an apprenticeship was important to the training of club pros, but in the era of the modern professional golfer, "it is as archaic as the hickory-shafted baffy, the sand tee, and the red golfing jacket." Attaboy Gene. Don't forget the pigskin condom.

Given all this palaver leading up to the matches, the players were understandably anxious. Describing the pressure he felt waiting to hit his first tee shot, Chick Harbert later said, "I have never been so frightened in all my life. You couldn't have driven a pin into my ass with a sledgehammer." I would have liked Chick, I'm fairly sure. Even back then, there was no more stressful event in golf than the Ryder Cup.

Nearly reversing their fortunes of 1947, the British team came out smoking and won the foursomes 3 to 1. In the first match, Johnny Palmer and Dutch Harrison against Jimmy Adams and Max Faulkner, the Americans

71

rushed out to an early lead, but Adams's tee shot at the par-three fifth hole hit the flagstick and finished close enough for an easy birdie. Although the U.S. team fought back, the British pair stayed in command, going to lunch with a three-hole lead then holding on despite some late sketchy play to win 2&1. The second match was similar with Fred Daly and Ken Bousfield taking an early lead, Alexander and Hamilton staging a comeback, and the home team up at the break. The Brits never let the Americans get too close in the afternoon and pulled away at the end to win 4&2.

In the third match, Jimmy Demaret, in purple pants, a bright red sweater, and a horrifying yellow cap, looked like a massive parrot, yet for some reason he didn't clash with his partner, Clayton Heafner, and they ham-and-egged their way past Sam King and Charlie Ward for the only U.S. point on day one. Demaret's drives and approaches set up Heafner's perfect putting, and after taking a one-hole lead in the morning, they closed out the match with four birdies in eight holes—going 3-4-4-3-3-4-3-4—to win 4&3. That's a lot of fours and threes.

The final match was the closest, with Burton and Lees scoring miraculous halves on the last two holes in the morning to finish even with, and dreadfully piss off Snead and Mangrum. Three clutch putts around the turn in the afternoon gave the Brits a two-hole lead, which the U.S. erased and the home team won back. Mangrum's tee shot at the thirty-fifth hole produced a winning birdie, but he missed a putt on the final hole that would have won the hole and halved the match. The 1-up victory gave the British their first lead in the foursomes since 1933, and presumably pissed off Snead and Mangrum even more.

On day two, the weather was perfect, the gallery was excited, and Hogan was close to insanity. Whatever he said to his players—collectively ripping them a new one—worked. The American counterattack started in the first match when Harrison opened 3-3-4-3-3-3 for a four-hole lead over Faulkner and never looked back, coasting to an 8&7 victory. Adams beat Palmer 2&1, Snead handled Ward 6&5, and Rees fired a glorious sixty-five in the morning that set up a 6&4 win over Hamilton. The American managed to keep his sense of humor: Staring at a putt on the twenty-eighth hole, Hamilton looked to the sky and shouted, "You up there, come on down and help. But don't send your son this time; it's a man-sized job." He made that putt, but still lost the match, and with four matches left, the British needed only 1-1/2 points to win back the Cup. But apparently God has a sick sense of humor.

Inspired by (or in fear of) Hogan, the remaining Americans put on a clinic. With six holes to play, Heafner was down a hole to Burton before eagling the thirty-first hole, winning the next three, then dropping a perfect, steaming stymie on the thirty-fifth green to win 3&2. Harbert took his sledgehammer to King, out-driving him by as many as seventy-five yards and taking a five-hole lead into lunch before winning 4&3. Demaret changed palettes for the singles—going only slightly less vomit-ridden with pink pants, blue sweater, and green cap—then colored dear old Arthur Lees black-and-blue, winning 7&6.

The final match is still called one of the best in Cup history. Fred Daly's morning round was a marvelous sixty-six, but not as good as Mangrum's sixty-five, which gave the American a one-hole advantage at the break. That lead was quickly lost in the afternoon, regained, then lost again, so they were even after twenty-seven. Mangrum's finishing kick—3-3-2-4-3—finished off Daly for a 4&3 victory and a marvelous twelve-under-par for thirty-three holes against a brilliant little opponent who was continuing to build a marvelous Ryder resume. I never saw a man shape shots off a wooden club like Fred Daly, three hundred gins or not.

The Americans had won back-to-back in Blighty, and the British didn't seem to have an answer. But they did find a way to chase their ugly American vanquishers from dear old England: The day after the matches ended, the British government devalued the pound sterling, and whatever money the Americans had exchanged was suddenly worth a lot less than that with which they'd started. Demaret spoke for many on his team when he said upon leaving, "All we want of England is out."

All I can say is thank God none of *this* team got into trouble with hookers. It would have cost Hogan a fortune.

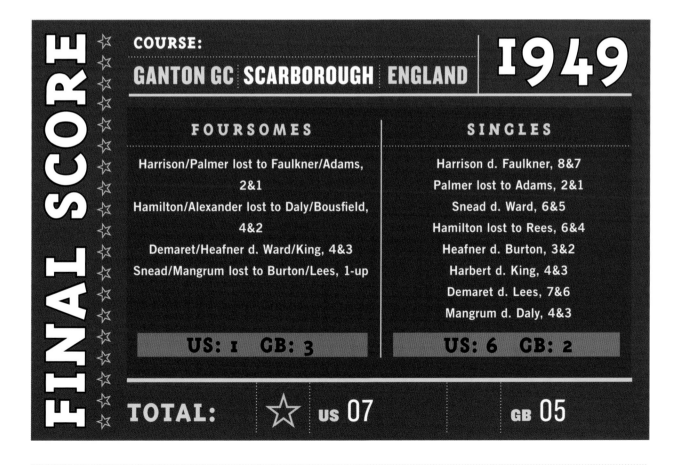

FINAL SCORE

COURSE:

GANTON GC SCARBOROUGH ENGLAND | **1949**

FOURSOMES

Harrison/Palmer lost to Faulkner/Adams, 2&1

Hamilton/Alexander lost to Daly/Bousfield, 4&2

Demaret/Heafner d. Ward/King, 4&3

Snead/Mangrum lost to Burton/Lees, 1-up

US: 1   GB: 3

SINGLES

Harrison d. Faulkner, 8&7

Palmer lost to Adams, 2&1

Snead d. Ward, 6&5

Hamilton lost to Rees, 6&4

Heafner d. Burton, 3&2

Harbert d. King, 4&3

Demaret d. Lees, 7&6

Mangrum d. Daly, 4&3

US: 6   GB: 2

TOTAL: US 07   GB 05

DATE : SEPT 16-17

JIMMY DEMARET (1910–1983)

JIMMY DEMARET isn't the only man to have a perfect record in Ryder Cup play: A dozen Americans went undefeated and untied. But he is the only one to do so in three years (the others just one or two), and he has the most matches—six. Perhaps just as impressive, none of his matches reached the final hole.

He was a flamboyant character with an outgoing personality, quick wit, hideous taste in clothing, and a good singing voice. (Before golfers made enough money, he supported himself as a nightclub singer and continued to entertain the other players in those gentler days when pros traveled and roomed together.) His constant smile and pleasant demeanor were assets after his playing days were through, when he hosted "Shell's Wonderful World of Golf" on television: He was the perfect messenger to spread the good word about golf to the masses.

He was also one hell of a golfer. In roughly twenty years (interrupted by World War II, when he served in the Navy) Demaret won forty-four tournaments and was the first to don the Masters' green jacket three times, in 1940, 1947, and 1950. His best year was 1947, when he won six events, the Vardon Trophy, the money title, and played in his first Ryder Cup.

However, Demaret's unbeaten record almost started with a loss. (Sorry to dwell on the low points, it's the Irish in me.) In his first match, teamed with Ben Hogan (he was one of Hogan's few real friends, and I still can't work out whether or not that was a good thing), the American stars were four down after nine holes to two rookies, Max Faulkner and Jimmy Adams. They battled back, cutting the lead to two by the time the morning ended, then going on a tear after lunch, winning four straight. Then

it was the Brits' turn: They were back to even after the thirty-third hole until Hogan hit a beautiful shot from a fairway bunker and Demaret holed the twenty-foot putt for a birdie and a 2-up American win. He was down again in his singles match to Dai Rees, but overcame a one-hole deficit by winning three straight holes in the afternoon, eventually prevailing 3&2.

In 1949, the Cup was held at Ganton in northeast England, a good but somewhat desolate-looking course Demaret described as "a sort of Pennsylvania Turnpike with tees." Demaret may have found it featureless, but he certainly had an easy trip. With Hogan captaining but not playing as a result of his car crash seven months earlier, Demaret teamed with Clayton Heafner and beat Sam King and Charlie Ward, 4&3: The Americans were only 1-up after the morning round, but came back from lunch hungry, carding four birdies in their last eight holes. Arthur Lees didn't last that long in their singles match, losing 7&6.

Teamed with Hogan again in 1951, they had an easy time against Fred Daly and Ken Bousfield: Up by five after nine, the Americans didn't let their opponents much closer and won 5&4. He was just as overpowering on his own in the singles, putting on a clinic in sand play in defeating Rees again, 2-up, then presenting Rees with his sand wedge.

Rees described the gift as "a typically American generous gesture," but it's unlikely many other pros would have given up a club with which they'd had such success. That was vintage Demaret, although I have to say I did do it once myself, giving my putter to a pro-am partner at St. Pierre in Wales. Of course, I told him to shove it up his arse.

COURSE:

PINEHURST CC (#2) | PINEHURST | NC

☆☆☆☆☆☆☆☆☆ **NOV. 02-04**

1951

FINAL SCORE:

☆ **US 09-1/2**   **GB 02-1/2**

CAPTAINS:

SAM SNEAD   ARTHUR LACEY

UNITED STATES   GREAT BRITAIN

☆☆☆☆☆☆☆☆☆☆☆☆   ☆☆☆☆☆☆☆☆☆☆☆☆

UNITED STATES	GREAT BRITAIN
Skip Alexander	Jimmy Adams
Jack Burke Jr.	Ken Bousfield
Jimmy Demaret	Fred Daly
Dutch Harrison	Max Faulkner
Clayton Heafner	Jack Hargreaves
Ben Hogan	Arthur Lees
Lloyd Mangrum	John Panton
Ed Oliver	Dai Rees
Henry Ransom	Charles Ward
Sam Snead	Harry Weetman

1927   1929   1931   1933   1935   1937   1947   1949

GREAT BRITAIN

"YOU KNEW HE WAS GOING TO BEAT YOU and he knew you knew he was going to beat you." Years later, that line would be applied to Jack Nicklaus. But in 1951, it just as easily could have referred to the U.S. Ryder Cup team.

No one gave the British team much of a chance. Henry Longhurst, the venerable golf writer (and possibly the last television commentator who truly appreciated the value of silence), wrote that his countrymen shouldn't expect to win more than one foursomes and one or two singles. Actually, in fairness, let me back up a little and mention that Henry was often silent because he was too drunk to make a noise—not that that made him a bad person. Anyway Leonard Crawley, describing Pinehurst No. 2—which would play at more than 7,000 yards, the longest Cup course to date—wrote that the British team "would be out-hit to such an extent that they would be unable to cope with their opponents on this fearfully long course."

What made the usually jingoistic British media give up on its team even before they boarded the *Queen Mary?* Let's just say it hadn't been a very good few years for golf in the Old World even without bringing up the two most recent Ryder Cup humiliations.

In 1951 (unlike today), amateur golf was still a big deal, and the two transatlantic matches were proving preposterously one-sided. In the Walker Cup, the American men won 8-4 in 1947 (beating a British team that included Crawley the pencil-squeezer), 10-2 in 1949, and 6-3 in 1951. (Let's rub a little salt in the wound: The Walker Cup began in 1922 and the Brits won only once in the first twenty-two matches—talk about farting into the wind.) The

results of the ladies' Curtis Cup were only slightly more heartening: First played in 1932, it took until the seventh installment, in 1952, for the GB team to win.

In the Open Championship, the homeys were ecstatic with wins by Fred Daly in 1947 and Henry Cotton in 1948. But after them came South African Bobby Locke in 1949 and 1950 (and again in 1952 and 1957), followed by a series of foreign interlopers who would dominate the fifties: Australian Peter Thomson won four times in the decade (and again in 1965), along with one each for Ben Hogan and another South African, Gary Player. A native son wouldn't win again until 1969.

Ah, but there was one brief and shining moment, when England's daft-as-a-brush Max Faulkner won in 1951 at Royal Portrush in Northern Ireland. The sharp-dressed Faulkner was capable of great golf, but also of equally great eccentricity, whether he was using a grab bag of mismatched clubs or farting around with an outlandish swing technique. Heading into the 1951 Open, his practice sessions were spotty at best, but he claimed to have had a premonition that he would win and was signing autographs "Max Faulkner, Open Champion 1951" before hitting his first shot. (Hey, I used to sign "Dick Thrust, Special Agent 1981," but it never did me a damned bit of good). But sure enough, assisted by a "mystery guiding light," Maxie Baby won by two strokes. His Ryder Cup history was less mysterious: Playing in eight matches over five Cups, he recorded only one win (a foursomes match with Jimmy Adams in 1949). His singles career was especially sad, first losing 6&5 to Lloyd Mangrum in 1947, then being steamrolled by Dutch Harrison 8&7 in 1949. He was on the 1951 team, but never a factor. Then again, neither were most of his teammates.

Arthur Lacey was non-playing captain, which was just as well— he'd played on the squad in 1933 and 1937 without winning a point. Along with Faulkner, he had veterans Jimmy Adams, Ken Bousfield, Daly, Arthur Lees, Dai Rees, and Charlie Ward from the 1949 team, plus new boys John Panton, Jack Hargreaves, and Harry Weetman.

There were two new Americans as well: Jack Burke and Henry Ransom. They were joining a much more formidable team—Skip Alexander, Jimmy Demaret, Clayton Heafner, Lloyd Mangrum, and Porky Oliver—plus playing captain Sam Snead, and Ben Hogan. Although Hogan would never fully recover from his car crash, he applied his famous resolve to coming back as a player with amazing results: He won the U.S. Open in 1950 and 1951 (memorably bringing the "monster," Oakland Hills, "to its knees"), as well as the 1951 Masters.

So the American team was the odds-on favorite. In fact, the bastards were already thinking ahead to the next tournament, the North and South, which was to be played at Pinehurst immediately after the Cup was over. The promoters had promised to increase the purse of that event to ten thousand dollars, but once the top players arrived, that promise was taken back, much to the golfers' dismay. I'll be buggered if I can think of a modern-day equivalent to that insult.

The only discomfort for the Americans was the weather. It was so cold and wet during the foursomes that Heafner carried an overcoat to wear between shots. Give me a break. I can understand why Hogan wore pajamas under his golf attire (as a result of his accident, Hogan had circulatory problems in his legs, and often spent the hours after a round in a hot tub), but an overcoat? What a wiener. Conditions were compared to "Carnoustie in the early spring," with some thinking it would offer an advantage to the Brits, who did not "follow the sun" as the American tour pros did, but neither rain, cold, nor gray skies would make a difference. Clayton Heafner could have worn a red silk teddy and fluffy mules—the foursomes went the way they always seemed to, with the Americans in control.

Lacey put out his top pair first, but Faulkner and Rees played well enough to be only 2-down to Heafner and Burke at lunch. However, they then slid away to lose in the afternoon, 5&3. Ward and Lees put together an American-like hot streak in the morning to go to lunch with a three-hole lead over Oliver and Ransom, holding on in the afternoon (just barely) for Britain's only win, 2&1. With Snead driving it long and Mangrum putting true, Jimmy Adams and John Panton could do no better than 5-down at the break and a 5&4 loss. Demaret wasn't at his sharpest, but partnered with Hogan, it didn't matter: The pair was 3-up on Daly and Bousfield at lunch and cruised to a 5&4 victory. As usual, Henry Longhurst's description of that match said it all:

> "Among the gallery in the fourth match, bearing no outward and visible sign connecting him with the proceedings, is a small dark man with grey raincoat, grey cap, grey trousers and inscrutable expression, looking somewhat like a Pinkerton detective on watch for pickpockets. This is the world's greatest golfer, Ben Hogan, participating in a Ryder Cup match. His partner, the normally flamboyant Jimmy Demaret, is concealed in a flowing check ulster with a distinctly Sherlock Holmes air. From time to time they step forward, undress, and give the ball a resounding slam."

I loved old Henry!

The slamming would continue in the singles, but not the next day. For some inexplicable reason—possibly to extend matters long enough to force the golfers to hang around for the North and South—the players were invited to a college football game, the University of North Carolina against Tennessee. The Americans boycotted, preferring to stay in Pinehurst and practice. The away team went to the game, which Faulkner pointed out was markedly different from rugby, in that he'd wager that, "none of those fellows ever got buggered up the arse by a geography teacher." But if the boys thought the result would offer any Faulknerian foreshadowing—visiting Tennessee won, 27-0—they were soon to be sadly mistaken.

On day two (actually three), bathed in sun and under a cloudless sky, the Americans reigned.

Starting the day down 3-1, the Brits needed to come out of the blocks fast, but it didn't happen. In the first match, Burke was six holes up on Adams at lunch, calmly gave up two holes in the afternoon, and coasted to a 4&3 win. That score, and the ease with which the first American won, was about average for the day, though on a more positive note for GB, at least the Prince of fucking Wales didn't show up.

The most interesting match went off second, pitting Demaret, without the luxury of old stone-faced Ben as a partner, against Rees. The Welshman took an early lead and was 1-up at the break. Demaret finally found his form after lunch, making four birdies on five holes around the turn. The difference was Demaret's sand play, with Rees saying later that his opponent got up and down ten times from eleven bunkers. (What I'd like to know is, how badly did Jimmy hit it, to be in eleven frigging bunkers?) On the sixteenth hole, with the match tied, Demaret faced a plugged

BEN HOGAN AND DAI REES (MAY THE BEST MAN WIN)

JOE NOVAK PRESENTS THE RYDER CUP TO SAM SNEAD

lie in greenside sand, and Rees was on the green: The American holed the sand shot for a 1-up lead, halved the seventeenth with another great sand shot, and presumably kissing his camel, won the final hole for a two-hole victory.

In his autobiography, Rees described what happened next: "After I had congratulated Jimmy on his bunker play he made a typically American generous gesture, handed me his sand iron and said: 'Keep it, Dai, as a gift. The one you've got has too sharp an edge and you'll never have any finesse with it...' I took the club to Britain and had it copied for my own set so that, although I lost the match, I came away with a profit." That's the thing about the Ryder Cup: No matter how the conflict is portrayed by media types like us, the players have always felt an affinity with their opponents, a kind of brothers-in-arms thing, if you like. There's a respect there, especially when you've beaten one of the dirty rotten bastards.

A faint glimmer of light for Britain came when the gallant, probably half-baked Fred Daly fought back from three down with three holes to play, won them all, and recorded half a point. However, once Mangrum beat the longer-hitting Weetman 6&5, the Cup was staying in America.

Britain's sole singles victory came when Arthur Lees held off Porky Oliver, making him the only two-time winner for the Brits (he accounted for 2 of their 2-1/2 points) despite the fact that Oliver had threatened to eat him in the middle of the eighth fairway. Hogan had more trouble with Ward than might have been expected: The "world's greatest golfer" was down at one point and held only a two-hole lead at lunch. In the afternoon, both played the front nine in wonderful 33s. On the par-five tenth (their twenty-eighth), Hogan drove into the woods, chipped out, then bombed a three-wood from 300 yards, reaching the front of the green and holing the nearly 100-foot putt for a half. Hogan birdied eleven for another win and prevailed 3&2. God, he must have been a pain in the ass to play.

Alexander's 8&7 win over Panton was remarkable for two reasons: First, after playing his opponent even over the first nine holes, Panton was five holes down at lunch. Second, Alexander had been badly burned in a plane crash just a year earlier and, like Hogan, had to endure a long, arduous recovery. The final match, between Snead and Faulkner, might have been more exciting if the Cup's destination had still been in the balance. Instead, Snead had a four-hole lunchtime lead, and although Faulkner won two holes back early in the afternoon, Snead birdied the thirty-first and thirty-second and closed out the match 4&3.

So Longhurst had been prescient: One foursomes and one or two singles (one and a half, in fact). But the British actually had another singles victory; or, better stated, a doubles. While in Pinehurst, captain Lacey, the dirty old dog, met a wealthy American woman from Pittsburgh whom he later married. Good on you Arthur—I did the same thing, if you leave out the bits about her being wealthy and from Pittsburgh.

Given the way things were going for the British, a love match was better than no match at all.

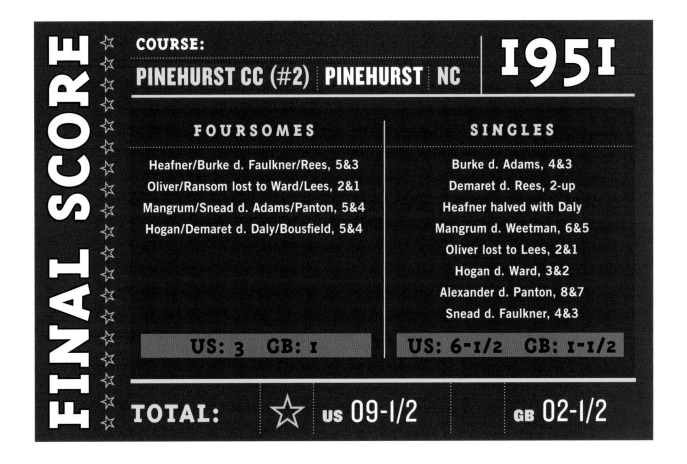

FINAL SCORE

COURSE:

PINEHURST CC (#2) PINEHURST NC | **1951**

FOURSOMES

Heafner/Burke d. Faulkner/Rees, 5&3
Oliver/Ransom lost to Ward/Lees, 2&1
Mangrum/Snead d. Adams/Panton, 5&4
Hogan/Demaret d. Daly/Bousfield, 5&4

US: 3   GB: 1

SINGLES

Burke d. Adams, 4&3
Demaret d. Rees, 2-up
Heafner halved with Daly
Mangrum d. Weetman, 6&5
Oliver lost to Lees, 2&1
Hogan d. Ward, 3&2
Alexander d. Panton, 8&7
Snead d. Faulkner, 4&3

US: 6-1/2   GB: 1-1/2

TOTAL: ☆ **US 09-1/2** **GB 02-1/2**

HEROES OF THE RYDER CUP
ARTHUR LEES (1908-1992)

☆☆☆☆☆☆☆☆☆☆☆☆☆☆☆☆☆☆☆☆☆☆☆☆☆☆☆☆

ARTHUR LEES was typical of so many British pros who vied for the Ryder Cup in the years around World War II. He was a club pro, associated with the gorgeous Sunningdale club near London for almost thirty years—a place where he would later hire a sixteen-year-old assistant named Sam Torrance. He spent most of his time at his job but also managed to compete throughout Europe. He won the 1939 Irish Open and was runner-up in the Czech and German Opens before the war; later, he won three tournaments in Britain: the 1947 Dunlop Masters and the Penfold event in 1951 and 1953, and when he was old enough, the British Seniors in 1959.

This kind of club pro was vital to the Ryder Cup in those years when even the best players had to hold steady jobs that paid the rent but cut into competition. It must have been tough getting permission from one's home club for the two weeks or more necessary to go after the Cup—even then it was a five-day journey across the Atlantic, a few days of practice, two days of play, the journey back, plus days in between.

In four Cups (1947–51 and 1955), Lees played nine matches and amassed a respectable 4-5 record. He went winless in his debut, but then again, so did almost the entire British team, which lost 11-1 in the first post-war resumption. Teamed with Henry Cotton in the opening foursomes, they lost hideously, 10&9, to Lew Worsham and Porky Oliver. In the singles, he had the dubious distinction of losing by the smallest margin, only 2&1 to Byron Nelson. (The only better score was Sam King's 4&3 defeat of Herman Keiser for the sole British point.)

Two years later, Lees paired with Dick Burton in the final foursomes: Their 1-up victory over Sam Snead and Lloyd Mangrum gave the British their first lead in the foursomes since 1933. Facing Jimmy Demaret in the singles, Lees lost 7&6, which was not the worst drubbing of the day.

Lees's heroic year was 1951, for although the U.S. team won big again, 9-1/2 to 2-1/2, he was responsible for eighty percent of his team's points. In the foursomes, he and Charlie Ward took a three-hole lead in the morning over Oliver and Henry Ransom, and managed not to piss it away, winning 2&1. In the singles, Lees met Oliver for the third time in four matches and beat him, 2&1. As a result, Lees became the ultimate trivial statistic—the first Brit to win both his foursomes and singles in the same Cup on U.S. soil. (If you knew that one, you need to stop reading now, start banging your forehead with a metalwood, and only stop when you feel you're ready to get a life.)

In 1955, Lees closed out his Cup career with a split, teaming with Harry Weetman to lose to Jack Burke and Tommy Bolt, 1-up, then topping Ed Furgol in the singles, 3&1. Like so many of the Ryder Cup brethren of his generation, Lees was never on a winning team, yet he lived for the Cup, and never lost faith that someday things would change.

☆☆☆☆☆☆☆☆☆☆☆☆☆☆☆☆☆☆☆☆☆☆☆☆☆☆☆☆

COURSE:

WENTWORTH GC | WENTWORTH | ENGLAND

☆☆☆☆☆☆☆☆☆☆ OCT. **02-03**

1953

☆☆☆☆☆☆☆☆☆☆☆☆☆☆☆☆☆

☆ **FINAL SCORE:**

US 06-1/2   **GB** 05-1/2

CAPTAINS:

LLOYD MANGRUM   HENRY COTTON

UNITED STATES
☆☆☆☆☆☆☆☆☆☆☆☆☆☆☆

Jack Burke Jr.

Walter Burkemo

Dave Douglas

Fred Haas Jr.

Ted Kroll

Lloyd Mangrum

Cary Middlecoff

Ed Oliver

Sam Snead

Jim Turnesa

GREAT BRITAIN
☆☆☆☆☆☆☆☆☆☆☆☆☆☆☆

Jimmy Adams

Peter Alliss

Harry Bradshaw

Eric Brown

Fred Daly

Max Faulkner

Bernard Hunt

John Panton

Dai Rees

Harry Weetman

COULDA, SHOULDA, WOULDA. If ever there was a year that the stars were aligned for a British win, this was it. But like my grandad used to say, "Nearly never bulled a cow," and this one was nearly.

The faithful were encouraged because the Matches were being held at Wentworth, site of the "lost" Ryder Cup of 1926 when the British had spanked the upstart Americans 13-1/2 to 1-1/2. (Hard to believe it was ever that lopsided, isn't it?) No one cared that the earlier Match had been played over the East course while this year's was to be on the West, the famous "Burmah Road." What mattered was that it had been at Wentworth that Sam Ryder said, "We must do this again." The locals hoped that "this again" meant a win, something they hadn't managed since 1933.

Because the U.S. team would be without Hogan, its biggest gun, the composition of the teams also seemed to favor the British. The greatest player of the day, Hogan was having his greatest year. He'd started 1953 by winning his second Masters, then won the U.S. Open for a record-tying fourth time. Having won everything else of importance, he finally captured the Open Championship with an unforgettable performance at Carnoustie that had captured the hearts and minds of golfers the world over. While they didn't like to be beaten, the home crowd knew they had seen something special. But the price of such achievement was expensive for Hogan, who was still suffering from the aftereffects of his horrific 1949 car wreck. The man the Scots had dubbed "the wee ice mon" and whom *Golf Magazine* would eventually call "golf's grim gypsy" refused to play in any event that required thirty-six-hole matches. It must have bent Hogan's mind to do it, but he passed on a shot at the Grand Slam (the PGA Championship, still a match-play event, meant four straight days of thirty-six holes to reach the finals) and skipped the Ryder

LLOYD MANGRUM AND HENRY COTTON

Cup. The British fans were sorry they wouldn't be able to see Hogan play, but they were probably happy enough that as a consequence, their team's chances would be much improved.

Dutch Harrison, veteran of the three previous teams, also opted out, so the American squad under playing captain Lloyd Mangrum featured six new faces: Walter Burkemo, Dave Douglas, Fred Haas Jr., Ted Kroll, Cary Middlecoff (having finally finished his five-year "apprenticeship"), and Jim Turnesa. Joining them were four veterans—Mangrum, Jack Burke Jr., Porky Oliver (I steadfastly refuse to call him Ed), and Sam Snead—but of these, only Snead and Mangrum had played in Britain before. By recent standards, it was a wobbly American team.

The home team was a blend of youth, experience, and the usual dose of institutionalized British optimism, possibly intensified as a result of a new selection process. A few weeks before the Cup was to begin, seventeen players were invited to Wentworth, where they competed in trial matches under the eyes of a Tournament Committee that included non-playing captain Henry Cotton. A number of past Ryder Cup players didn't pass muster (including Arthur Lees and Charlie Ward, the only two Brits to win matches in 1951), but six made it—Jimmy Adams, Fred Daly, Max Faulkner, John Panton, Dai Rees, and Harry Weetman. And there were four new men: Peter Alliss (at twenty-two, the youngest player so far), Harry Bradshaw, Eric Brown, and Bernard Hunt (age twenty-three). For Alliss and Hunt, though both went on to long, successful Ryder Cup careers, it would prove an inauspicious debut.

Despite his checkered Ryder Cup past, Cotton was taking captaincy seriously. At forty-six, it was only on doctor's

SAM SNEAD

LLOYD MANGRUM

orders that he wasn't playing himself (never a model of health, he'd worn himself out with nonstop competition). Like Walter Hagen years earlier, he felt his team should be well fed and well feted: He had them stay in the same hotel as the invaders (standard operating procedure today), procured them the best food (despite the lean times), and even treated the team to a night of theater in London, choosing that most American of musicals, *Guys and Dolls.* Just as important, Cotton made sure they practiced together, and held nightly meetings where he convinced them that the big, bad Americans could be beaten.

And yet despite all that, the Americans dominated the foursomes again. Was it because Cotton left Rees and Faulkner, two of his most experienced players, out of the first day's matches? Again, I'll be Martha Burt if / know. Was it that he threw all his rookies into the fray? Well, it probably didn't help.

In the first match, Douglas and Oliver met Alliss and Weetman. Starting the afternoon with a one-hole lead, the Americans got a break on the twenty-first hole, where they were awarded a free drop where one wasn't deserved. They won the hole with a long putt and never looked back. Well, almost never: On the par-five thirty-fifth, with the Americans dormie 2 (two holes up with only two to play so the worst they could do was halve the match), Oliver drove out of bounds, offering the Brits an opening. But hitting alternate shot, Weetman skied his tee shot, leaving an idiot-mark on his driver, pitched through the green, and twitched a four-footer to win the hole. The hole was halved with bogeys and the U.S. pair won the match, 2&1. Bugger, Bugger, Bugger, and Bollocks!

PETER AND PERCY ALLISS

The two American wins that followed were old-fashioned routs. Mangrum and Snead overpowered Brown and Panton, 8&7. Kroll and Burke kept the steamroller chugging, topping Adams and Hunt 7&5.

The one bright spot (and didn't there always seem to be one?) was the first all-Irish pairing, Fred Daly (from the north) and Harry Bradshaw (south), against Walter Burkemo and Cary Middlecoff. The Americans were down three holes at lunch, fought back to 1-down, and were 3-down again after twenty-seven holes. (Middlecoff had conceded a hole when a ball was buried in a rhododendron.) Burkemo, playing in his only Ryder Cup, caught fire, and the Americans returned to 1-down; it could have been square, but Bradshaw's drive on the thirty-fourth hole was heading OB when it brained, or was headed by a spectator, landed back in play, and led to a scrambling half. At the thirty-fifth, Burkemo's approach hit the flagstick (which back then was an inch thick and weighed about fifteen pounds), but Middlecoff missed the seven-footer that would have tied the match. Still 1-down on the final hole, Burkemo swished a fairway-wood approach to twenty feet while Bradshaw's chip stopped ten feet away. Middlecoff could have halved the match, but his putt slid by. Now it was up to Daly, whose pre-putt routine was quite extraordinary, even under normal circumstances. With a nasty-looking little hickory-shafted blade putter, he would address the ball behind, and then in front, the putterhead jumping back and forth over the top of the ball like a flea bursting for a piss, sometimes as many as fifty times. (He once actually asked me to hit him on the back of his head to get him started.) But the bold wee man finally holed the putt, and secured the victory.

Despite the closing heroics, the old fart who would eventually be Sir Henry Cotton was furious and let his players know it, threatening to "kick their arses" (or, in some reports, "their backsides"). That quote made the next morning's headlines (tabloid journalism had an early start in Britain), and Toots Cotton, Henry's loyal and thoroughly terrifying wife, steamed her way around Wentworth tearing up newspaper placards. I only laid eyes on Toots Cotton once, but she had a face like a sack of hammers. I think she could probably have torn them up just by looking at them.

Maybe Henry threatened to set the missus on the lads, but his words certainly had the desired effect as the Brits played the way they'd long been expected to on day two. After twenty years of being America's doormat, they were up off the floor and ready to fight back.

Down 3-1, Cotton sent out his best players early, willing to gamble on a weak finish for a strong start.

The first match, Rees vs. Burke, had to be delayed ninety minutes due to fog. Visibility was still poor when play began, causing Rees to misdirect approach shots and quickly go 2-down. But once the sun came out, the little Welshman's game shone, and they were even at lunch. Though Rees stumbled again in the afternoon, he holed a long putt at the thirty-fourth to get within one. But on the next hole, two shots left Burke eighty yards from the flag. Using his putter, he hit the "Texas wedge" to nine inches and closed out the match, 2&1. It was not the start Cotton had envisioned.

It was Daly who got things going, firing a sixty-six—"the best golf I have ever played"—to go six holes up on Kroll at the break. When he closed out the match on the twenty-ninth hole, winning 9&7, Daly became only the second British player in history to win both his foursomes and singles in the same year. Back in Belfast, Daly was fast becoming a legend.

Eric Brown (another soup-dragon) met Mangrum in a rematch of the foursomes. Before teeing off, Brown had promised his captain a win and he looked true to his word, taking a two-hole lead into lunch. The American captain embarrassed himself on the multilevel seventh green by four-putting (the ball rolled back to his feet—twice!). Still, most observers expected the rookie to crumble in the afternoon. But a promise was a promise, and after Mangrum evened the match on hole thirty-four, Brown retook the lead on the next with a splendid long iron.

On the final hole, Mangrum made his par five. Brown, putting for eagle, was distracted by Mangrum's bright yellow sweater and asked his opponent to move, which he did. Brown lagged to a foot from the hole and waited for a concession. Instead, Mangrum grumbled, "I guess you can get down in two from there, but let's see you do it anyway." Fuming, Brown took his time, surveyed the putt from all sides, then rolled it in for a 2-up victory.

So much for Sam Ryder's "friendly lunch party." Eric Brown was a friend of my dad's, and they were both total piss artists. The game was on.

The British comeback was expected to end when Snead faced Weetman. And, indeed, Snead held a four-hole lead at lunch and maintained that margin through the thirtieth hole. But over the years Wentworth's final few have jumped up and torn a hole or two in the ballbags of the famous, and suddenly Sam lost control of his driver: Here comes a snapper, there goes a flamer, and he lost five straight holes. Weetman— to whom Snead had referred (in a Ryder Cup-inspired attack of verbal diarrhea) as a "bushy-haired pro with just a fair reputation"—held a one-up lead standing on the final hole, which he parred to preserve one of the most astonishing comeback wins in Cup history (and hand Snead his only singles loss in seven appearances). It was a win that would considerably enhance an allegedly fair reputation.

At this point the matches were tied 4-4.

Of the four matches still on the course, three were still anyone's game. In the fourth, Middlecoff had few problems with Faulkner (yes, poor Max was holding his ankles again), winning much more easily than the 3&1 score would indicate.

Cotton's strategy had almost worked—his experienced players had brought the team close. Now it was up to his rookies, the first of whom was Peter Alliss, who was 1-down to Turnesa at lunch then 1-up with three to play. What ensued was one of the most gut-wrenching finishes in British golf history, but hey, we got Peter the Great out of it, so let's get over it. He certainly did.

Turnesa's drive on the thirty-fourth hole should have sailed out of bounds, but it struck an idiot in the crowd and bounced back into play. (It's an educated lot that goes to a Ryder Cup, and I daresay the poor bastard that headed the Yankee ball back into play got a pretty hard time from those who were paying attention.) From there, Turnesa put his approach into a bunker and got up-and-down for par. Alliss bogeyed when a weak chip was followed by a missed putt, and they were back to even. On the next hole, Alliss's tee shot landed just a few inches out of bounds, but enough to cost him the hole. Turnesa returned the favor on the final hole, driving into the trees along the right side with nothing to do but chip out. Alliss's drive found the middle of the fairway, and a two-iron finished just off the green near the spectator stands. Distracted by the shoes behind him (a yellow sweater had almost gotten Eric

Brown, after all), Alliss fluffed his chip, the ball not even reaching the green. His second chip was better, stopping a yard from the hole. Turnesa missed his par putt, meaning Alliss could win the hole and salvage a precious half. "Then, from that short range, I missed," he wrote later. "Half in six, and for Alliss, a ridiculous, incredible, childish, delinquent six." His one-hole loss was accompanied by a lone voice from the crowd yelling the now immortal, "Hit it, Alliss!"—a remark that most to this day think of as sexist.

There still was Hunt. He had been even with Douglas at the break before the American took a three-hole lead, gave it up, and on the thirty-fifth drove out of bounds (shades of Alliss?) to lose the hole. Hunt then had a one-hole lead on the final hole, where both players reached the green in three, neither close to the flag. Hunt rolled his first putt to a yard away, Douglas two-putted for par, and Hunt, like Alliss before him, wienered out, and missed the three-footer. Losing the hole meant the match was halved and the Cup was staying in the States.

In the final match—which actually finished before the previous two—Bradshaw beat Haas, who had sat out the foursomes. Like his fellow Irishman Daly, Bradshaw won his second point of the matches with a 3&2 victory. But it was too late.

The Ryder Cup had come down to two missed putts on the final hole. So for the first time in twenty years, the matches had become competitive again. How long could they sustain the excitement?

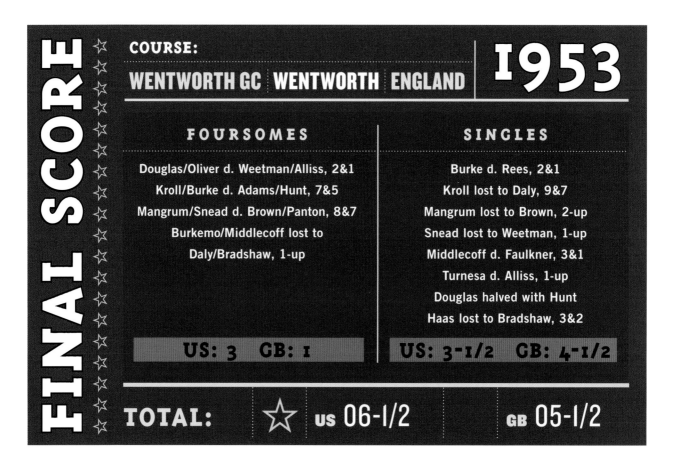

FINAL SCORE

COURSE:

WENTWORTH GC | WENTWORTH | ENGLAND | **1953**

FOURSOMES	SINGLES
Douglas/Oliver d. Weetman/Alliss, 2&1	Burke d. Rees, 2&1
Kroll/Burke d. Adams/Hunt, 7&5	Kroll lost to Daly, 9&7
Mangrum/Snead d. Brown/Panton, 8&7	Mangrum lost to Brown, 2-up
Burkemo/Middlecoff lost to	Snead lost to Weetman, 1-up
Daly/Bradshaw, 1-up	Middlecoff d. Faulkner, 3&1
	Turnesa d. Alliss, 1-up
	Douglas halved with Hunt
	Haas lost to Bradshaw, 3&2
US: 3 GB: 1	US: 3-1/2 GB: 4-1/2

TOTAL: ☆ **US 06-1/2**   **GB 05-1/2**

COURSE:

THUNDERBIRD G&CC | PALM SPRINGS | CA

☆☆☆☆☆☆☆☆☆☆ NOV. **05-06**

1955

☆☆☆☆☆☆☆☆☆☆☆☆☆☆☆☆☆☆☆

☆ **FINAL SCORE:**

us 08   **GB 04**

CAPTAINS:

CHICK HARBERT   DAI REES

UNITED STATES	GREAT BRITAIN
☆☆☆☆☆☆☆☆☆☆☆☆	☆☆☆☆☆☆☆☆☆☆☆☆
Jerry Barber	Ken Bousfield
Tommy Bolt	Harry Bradshaw
Jack Burke Jr.	Eric Brown
Doug Ford	John Fallon
Marty Furgol	John Jacobs
Chick Harbert	Arthur Lees
Chandler Harper	Christy O'Connor Sr.
Ted Kroll	Dai Rees
Cary Middlecoff	Syd Scott
Sam Snead	Harry Weetman

1927   1929   1931   1933   1935   1937   1947   1949

GREAT BRITAIN

AS IF IT WEREN'T BAD ENOUGH that GB couldn't win in America, the way they lost was nothing short of embarrassing. In six tries, they had never scored better than three points, and in the two Matches held in the United States after the war, they had totaled all of three and a half points. The experts offered numerous explanations (or, if you prefer, excuses) for this failure on foreign shores—the players' lack of international experience, unusual course conditions, rigors of travel, and so on. Whatever the reason, the British PGA was determined to change its luck, so in 1955 it changed the method of choosing players, relying on performance rather than on a committee decision. Hardly a stroke of genius, and I know that hindsight is 20/20, but this had taken much too long. An order of merit was established based on the results of select tournaments. The top seven players would automatically make the team, and then a committee would choose the final three. Hey, we couldn't go cold turkey and keep that committee out of it completely. The optimistic view was that this would produce a team of "hot" players; the pessimist said that someone playing well could just as quickly turn "cold." The Americans, for whom the glass always seemed to be overflowing, stuck with their system of giving points for performance over two years, a method that rewarded consistency.

Both teams looked very different from the ones that had battled so furiously at Wentworth. Thanks to the influx of new talent in America, the U.S. team had five fresh faces: the five-foot-five short-game wizard Jerry Barber, Tommy "Thunder" Bolt (nicknamed for his hair-trigger temper), Doug Ford, Marty Furgol, and Chandler Harper. Returning were Jack Burke Jr., Ted Kroll, Cary Middlecoff, and Sam Snead. Lloyd Mangrum had said after Wentworth

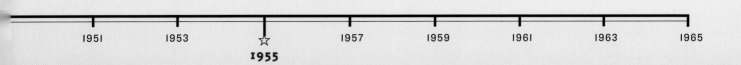

that he would "never, never captain an American team again because of the 9,000 deaths I suffered in the last hour." What a drama queen. He swooned into the arms of Chick Harbert, who was cast as a playing captain no less, despite not having been on a Cup team since 1949, and Mangrum was dubbed ceremonial captain, which certainly seemed a less than fatal position.

Dai Rees, the only holdover from before the war, commanded the visiting squad. Back were Harry Weetman, Harry Bradshaw, and Eric "up yours" Brown, veterans of Wentworth, along with Ken Bousfield (who sat himself both days due to ill health) and Arthur Lees, who'd been around for the loss at Pinehurst. That meant there were four new men: John Fallon, John Jacobs (the only team member under thirty, he would become much more famous in later years as an instructor), Syd Scott, and one of the all-time great consumers of Guinness, Ireland's Christy O'Connor, a man who could start a fight in an empty room.

Notably absent were the goats of Wentworth, Peter Alliss, and Bernard Hunt. Both had played well in the intervening years, but not well enough to qualify automatically. Though we'll never know for sure, it's highly likely that

CHICK HARBERT, ROBERT HUDSON AND DAI REES

when the committee met to pick the last three players for the team, Alliss and Hunt were punished for their final-hole failures two years before. (Their exclusion was a one-match exile, and both would figure in Ryder Cup action for years to come.)

Other changes were in the air. Sam Snead made a suggestion that he thought would be "better for the players and better for the spectators"—replacing foursomes with fourballs (all four golfers play their own balls from tee to green on each hole, with the better score from each team counting). Snead thought the fans would appreciate seeing twice as much golf. And though there was a longstanding notion of British superiority in foursomes—a belief that went back to the Cup's earliest days—the United States had still dominated the foursomes, 26-1/2 to 13-1/2 from the beginning, so any edge that the format might have supposed to give the Brits seems pretty much wholly mythical. Still, the British golf establishment and its press crapped all over Snead's plan. Foursomes was our game, and if you didn't like it, we'd take our bat and ball and go home.

Speaking of balls, for the first time, players could choose between the larger American ball and the smaller

British ball, even switching from hole to hole. Some used the smaller (and, therefore, longer) ball on longer holes and played the larger ball when control, especially around the greens, was important. There's no record of a scientific study (cue the pie charts and spreadsheets) proving whether or not having a choice mattered, but players continued to have the option until 1969, and the USGA and R&A made the larger ball the world's standard a few years later.

The venue also was a first: The first host course to have been built after World War II. Thunderbird Ranch, in Palm Springs, California, was just five years old, one of the swinging new lounge-lizard lairs to spring up in the desert a few hours from Los Angeles. Everything about it was sure to be odd to the Brits: warm weather, palm trees, manmade water hazards, and the wiry Bermuda grass, which required a different style of stabbing around the greens. The home-course advantage would be very much in play (although given the record of matches in America, excuses were hardly to the point).

Speaking of play, Alliss remembers going to a party at Frank Sinatra's house, thick with Hollywood stars even though the Chairman of the Board was out of town. Learning that Alliss was afraid of water and couldn't swim, Johnny Weismuller, a former Olympic swimmer who played Tarzan, decided to teach him—and failed. There supposedly were other hijinks not fit for repeating on a family show, and even fisticuffs between teammates. Who remembers?

After everyone sobered up and found their pants, the matches began under bright sunshine—what else?—and the tone was set early: All four GB tee shots on the first hole missed the first fairway. As for excitement, most observers agreed it came and went with the very first match: Harper and Barber against Fallon and Jacobs, four rookies. Fallon's tee shot landed in a stand of palm trees, and although they managed a gutsy par, Barber holed a five-foot birdie putt. The Brits won a hole back and were even until the sixteenth, where Barber chipped out from the frigging coconuts and into the hole for a birdie. The Americans were 2-up at the break—then 1-down with nine left. But Barber, who was rapidly becoming a Runyanesque pain in the arse, chipped in *again* on the thirty-first hole for a win and nearly repeated three holes later (Harper was decent enough to miss the short putt). The Brits held a one-hole lead on the last when Harper's approach sailed over the green. For the *third* time that day, Barber chipped in, leaving Fallon to make a short, sloping putt for the win. Which he did.

Although the first match off, the battle of the rookies was not the first to finish. Ford and Kroll had already made fast work of Brown and Scott, 5&4, mostly due to Brown's aerosol driving. Burke and Bolt had a much tougher fight with Lees and Weetman, who were one up on the Americans at lunch. The fiery Bolt wouldn't let the lead increase, actually reversing it around the turn so the U.S. pair was up by one on the final hole. Both Bolt and Lees stuck approach shots close—Bolt to four feet, Lees to ten—followed by their partners holing the birdie putts to cement the American victory. The final foursome was a battle of veterans: Snead and Middlecoff against Bradshaw and Rees. It was lost on the greens, the British putting like a pair of steam-driven motorboats and losing 3&2.

Once more for the broken record: United States 3, Great Britain 1. (They should have listened to Snead.)

There was a point during day two that if the matches had suddenly stopped, the British would have won the Cup. But that wasn't a change anyone suggested (Freeze Golf?), and as each contest wore on, the Americans wore down their opponents, leading to the expected conclusion. But it wasn't without its moments.

Those members of the gallery hoping to see Tommy Bolt's head explode weren't disappointed. In the opening match against O'Connor, Bolt was in control early, going 3-up by the break, but then he let it leak away. After lunch, O'Connor won back a few holes, which ignited Bolt's fuse, and he began throwing a wobbly fit the like of which O'Connor had probably never seen. Clubs were flung and the almighty castigated, but Mad Tom managed to calm down, channel his anger into his play and best O'Connor 4&2.

Match number three was the day's best: Middlecoff vs. Jacobs. The Englishman took a fast two-hole lead but gave it back just as quickly and the American took a two-hole lead to lunch. On the strength of his short game, Jacobs ran off a series of birdies and was back to even after twenty-seven holes, then 2-up with three to play. On the thirty-fourth hole, Middlecoff, being a gentleman (I think), conceded a three-footer to Jacobs before canning his own eight-footer for a half. A lesser man than John Jacobs could have been rattled by such a show of confidence. And then on the next hole, Middlecoff drained a twenty-five-foot birdie putt from the back of the green, enough to tighten the sphincter of the most hardened Cup commando. One-up on the final hole, Jacobs faced a slippery five-foot putt that broke at least twelve inches. But bollocks to rookie nerves: He holed it to win, 1-up.

Few of the other matches were as close. Harbert, six holes up on Scott at lunch, didn't mind losing a few holes as he held on for a 3&2 win. Furgol and Lees waged a sloppy battle of crappy bogeys, with Lees prevailing 3&1. As for the chipping magician, Jerry Barber's wedge wand was hexed on day two, and he fell to Brown 3&2.

Snead birdied the first four holes to go 4-up on Rees and held a five-hole lead at lunch, but thanks to four threes in the first six afternoon holes, Rees was back to only 1-down. On the next hole, Snead hooked his drive under a palm tree; he somehow managed to swing a fairway wood in the tight space, miraculously putting the ball onto the green, then holing a long eagle putt. Rees had nothing left and once he three-putted the thirty-first hole, Snead didn't have to work too hard for a 3&1 win.

That left two matches, which, if the British and Irish could win would produce a tie and a huge shot in the arm for golf in the homelands. In a brilliant showing, Harry Bradshaw shot a sixty-five to stay level with Burke through the morning, so there was hope. But the Irishman who'd won both matches two years earlier couldn't find another great round. Burke took a three-hole lead at the turn, and his 3&2 victory meant the Cup could stay and work on its tan. The last match, a battle for personal glory, went to Ford, 3&2.

Despite the loss, the British squad finally had legitimate reasons to be optimistic. Four points was their best showing in America, and hadn't the fate of the Cup come down to the final hole in two matches two years earlier? Things were looking up.

Lord Brabazon, who was president of the British PGA and would later have a famous Ryder Cup course named after him, said at the closing ceremony, "Although we have lost, we are going back to practice in the streets and on the beaches." Did he mean the chaps needed more work from hardpan lies and bunkers, or was he was being allegorical? Or had he simply quaffed too much sherry under the blazing California sun, and thought he was Sir Winston Churchill? Not that it matters. Lords are supposed to say things like that. It's in their job description.

FINAL SCORE

COURSE:

THUNDERBIRD G&CC | PALM SPRINGS | CA

1955

FOURSOMES

Harper/Barber lost to Fallon/Jacobs, 1-up
Ford/Kroll d. Brown/Scott, 5&4
Burke/Bolt d. Lees/Weetman, 1-up
Snead/Middlecoff d. Rees/Bradshaw, 3&2

US: 3   GB: 1

SINGLES

Bolt d. O'Connor, 4&2
Harbert d. Scott, 3&2
Middlecoff lost to Jacobs, 1-up
Snead d. Rees, 3&1
Furgol lost to Lees, 3&1
Barber lost to Brown, 3&2
Burke d. Bradshaw, 3&2
Ford d. Weetman, 3&2

US: 5   GB: 3

TOTAL: ☆   **US 08**   **GB 04**

COURSE:

LINDRICK GC | YORKSHIRE | ENGLAND

☆☆☆☆☆☆☆☆☆☆ **OCT. 04-05**

1957

☆☆☆☆☆☆☆☆☆☆☆☆☆

FINAL SCORE:

US 04-1/2 ☆ **GB 07-1/2**

CAPTAINS:

JACK BURKE JR. | DAI REES

UNITED STATES	GREAT BRITAIN
☆☆☆☆☆☆☆☆☆☆☆☆	☆☆☆☆☆☆☆☆☆☆☆☆
Tommy Bolt	Peter Alliss
Jack Burke Jr.	Ken Bousfield
Dow Finsterwald	Harry Bradshaw
Doug Ford	Eric Brown
Ed Furgol	Max Faulkner
Fred Hawkins	Bernard Hunt
Lionel Hebert	Peter Mills
Ted Kroll	Christy O'Connor Sr.
Dick Mayer	Dai Rees
Art Wall	Harry Weetman

1927   1929   1931   1933   1935   1937   1947   1949

FOR ONCE, the important changes weren't before the matches began but when they were over. Great Britain and Ireland won the Ryder Cup. Bear with me here, I think I'll write that again. Great Britain and Ireland won the Ryder Cup.

Okay, I feel better.

Of course, that's not to say there weren't problems in advance. There certainly were. But they were (almost) forgotten in the jubilant aftermath of the first British victory in twenty-four years.

Controversy surrounded the choice of venue, Lindrick Golf Club, a parkland course in the middle of England that had been picked on the strength of one quality: a rich benefactor. (Hey, whatsisname insisted that the matches be played in Portland a few years earlier, so we're even.) Enter Sir Stuart Goodwin, a wealthy local industrialist, who, like Sam Ryder years earlier, had come to golf late in life. He happened to be at Lindrick, his home course, on the day of an exhibition match featuring the diminutive but legendary twosome of Dai Rees and Fred Daly. Stood up for lunch, good Sir Stuart decided to follow the match despite the pouring rain and was so impressed with the quality of play that he immediately offered to bankroll a tournament in the area. "I like these little fellows, how much are they?" (The Sir Stuart Goodwin Foursomes was played near Sheffield for a few years.) Some time later, with the Ryder Cup drawing near but no site arranged, the British PGA turned to Goodwin, who put up ten thousand smackers with just one condition: Lindrick. So not for the first time and certainly not the last (cases in point: as of this writing, the next two Cups to be held in Britain, 2006 at The K Club in Ireland and 2010 at the Celtic Manor in Wales), money won

18TH FAIRWAY (JUST A FEW YORKSHIRE FOLK OUT TO WATCH THE GOLF)

out. (And I have to complain a little more: The K Club and Celtic Manor are fine courses, but you can find similar ones in virtually every state in the Union. But try finding a Royal Co. Down, Baltray, Portmarnock, or Royal Porthcawl, and be sure to send me a postcard when you do.)

Some thought there were significant problems with Lindrick. It was short, only 6,500 yards, so apparently it would complement the U.S. team's agility with the wedge. (Of course, had it been long, then playing the smaller British ball would have added to the American's length advantage.) It was inland, again playing to the visitors' strengths, as it was similar to the courses they were used to playing in the States (minus the windmill and the clown's mouth). And it was crossed not once but twice by a road, which was not only aesthetically displeasing but could disrupt play. No one needed, say for instance, Jimmy Demaret to be flattened by a cement truck while walking from one green to the next tee. Well all right, maybe the home team could have done with it, but still, it would have been frightfully bad form. Furthermore, Henry Longhurst groused that the clubhouse wasn't fit for an important event, and he was even less impressed with the hotel—"bang on the tramlines of an industrial city"—where the visiting U.S. team was billeted. Henry's paws tended to tremble at the best of times, and the last thing he needed was a train passing nearby. Someone once asked him if he drank a lot, to which the legendary old fart replied, "Heavens no, I spill most of it."

Some weaknesses were addressed. Two new back tees were built, and more important, the greenskeeper prepared the course to aid the home team, going easy on the watering (so fairways and greens would run fast) and growing the rough around the greens. Theoretically, the U.S. players would have to alter their game much as the Brits had had to do in the California desert two years earlier.

And by George, surely not, but the composition of the teams was in question! And cor blimey, this time it was the Americans who were seen to be at a disadvantage!

The British had improved their selection process, awarding points to the top twenty finishers in stroke-play tournaments. So making playing captain Dai Rees's team called for consistency rather than a short spell of good play. Still, the team welcomed only one new member, Peter Mills. Returning from 1955 were Rees, Ken Bousfield, Harry Bradshaw, Eric Brown, Christy O'Connor, and Harry Weetman. Returning from past Cup play was Mad Max Faulkner, and returning from the seventh circle of Ryder Cup hell were Peter Alliss and Bernard Hunt. It was widely regarded as the strongest British team in many a year, and if you were to believe the golfing press, it would face the weakest American squad since hickory underpants and woolen shafts. Jolly hockey sticks, these chaps might just bloody well do it!

Jack Burke Jr. was given his chance to lead as playing captain, but the best Americans were not coming: Sam Snead and Ben Hogan declined Ryder Cup invitations. Cary Middlecoff, a proven Cup performer and 1956 U.S. Open champion, as well as Julius Boros were barred from Cup play for skipping the 1957 PGA Championship in favor of more lucrative exhibitions. Still, the team was hardly a bunch of duffers. Dick Mayer, Tommy Bolt, and Ed Furgol were or would be U.S. Open champions; Burke, Doug Ford, and Art Wall were in the same queue for the Masters; Ford, Burke, Lionel Hebert, and Dow Finsterwald for the PGA. Ted Kroll had played in 1953 and 1957, and now that I come to think of it, I wonder why were these men were regarded as vulnerable? Only Fred Hawkins went without previous or subsequent pedigree.

DAI REES, ERIC BROWN, AND A FAT GUY

The home crowd was cheered by this perceived weakness in the American team. The only clever-clogs out of the bunch was Bernard Darwin, who had been covering the Ryder Cup since its beginning and who offered some sobering thoughts: "The argument that America's best players were left behind does not ring true," he wrote. "No place can be gained in their team without constant proof of great ability. It is true that the team did not contain famous names, but reputation is no guarantee of success."

With the teams and the site supposedly favoring GB, there were sure to be recriminations when, after the first day's foursomes, they found themselves down 3 to 1. That led to the bitterest controversy of them all. But first, some action.

Rees gave his two young pups a chance to get out of the doghouse, teaming Alliss and Hunt in the first match against Ford and Finsterwald. The Americans opened 3-3-3 (birdie-birdie-par) to take a two-hole lead, getting to 3-up and then 4-up before the Brits won three straight and reached lunch just 1-down (Hunt missed a four-footer than would have won eighteen). But then the afternoon looked like the morning, the U.S. pair running out to another three-hole lead and holding on for a 2&1 victory. It was to be the closest match of the day.

Wall and Hawkins also started 3-3-3 against Rees and Bousfield, but the homesters were back to even at the break. Again the Americans went up in the afternoon, but were caught and then passed for a 3&2 loss and the sole British foursomes point.

Kroll and Burke couldn't do much against Faulkner and Weetman in the morning, holding a one-hole lead at lunch. The Americans obviously ate the better meal, for they came out hot and had a four-hole advantage after

KEN BOUSFIELD

twenty-seven holes. Neither Englishman could find the fairway and the match ended at 4&3. The final match was even more one-sided, Mayer and Bolt going 3-up on O'Connor and Brown at the break and coasting to a 7&5 win.

Since he'd played in the foursomes, Rees hadn't had a chance to check his teammates' form, so he called a team meeting and collected their scorecards. He said later that Faulkner and Weetman were the obvious candidates to sit out the singles, but rather than lay down the law, he asked for discussion. Maxie admitted to having played like "rubbish" and volunteered to sit, as he wanted to learn how to play the oboe anyway. Weetman reportedly said much the same (minus the sheet music) and that, all thought, was that.

A short while later, having handed in his the next day's order of play, Rees was approached by a reporter asking for a reaction to Weetman's announcement that he would never again play for a team with Rees in charge. Apparently, Weetman had pitched a complete Miss Piggy, and for many reasons, Rees was shocked: He and Weetman were

DAI REES AND KEN BOUSFIELD

good friends and frequent traveling companions, and he thought the matter had been privately decided to everyone's satisfaction. Rees kept his cool and refused to talk to the reporters who called his hotel room all night long, but in keeping with great British tabloid tradition, the absence of facts didn't spoil their story, and the crap was spread in lumps all over the next day's papers. (After the matches, both men gave their sides of the story to another PGA committee, which overreacted and suspended Weetman from PGA-sponsored tournaments for a year. To his eternal credit, Rees pleaded his fallen friend's case, and the sentence was reduced a few months later.)

When day two began, the British players were fired up. Not only over team politics, but the wind had begun to blow—making the course play longer, possibly disadvantaging the visiting team—and the greens had been cut to make them faster. What a concept! Indeed, six Americans would three-putt the first green. (The maintenance crew had been given incorrect dates, and thinking the matches started a day later, hadn't cut the greens before the foursomes. At least, that was the official line. Personally, I think it's infinitely more likely they were hung over and just wiffed it.)

Either way, despite starting in a hole, Rees was in a good mood, even allowing a change to the American roster. Kroll was ill, and while Rees could have claimed the point, he allowed a substitution: Burke inserted himself into the second spot against the young rookie Mills. But Burke was nowhere near his best, going 5-down to Mills in the morning and eventually losing 5&3, one of the biggest upsets in Cup history.

But that was the second match of the day. It was the first that had everybody talking: the meeting of the mad dogs, Bolt and Brown, both put out first by their captains in hopes that they would either ignite their teams or beat one another to death. (When both were late to the first tee, Jimmy Demaret joked that he had last seen them standing at fifty paces, throwing clubs at each other.) Brown lost the first hole but little else, reaching lunch with a four-hole lead. Bolt cursed his way back to 2-down, but that was all Brown would allow. He increased his lead and won 4&3, only the second time in Cup history the British had won the opening singles match.

Given the nature of the two combatants, it's hardly surprising that the final score wasn't the end of things. They didn't exchange many words during the match, other than Bolt whining about how the Americans had been treated by the fans the previous day, and when the match was over, they may or may not have shaken hands as the following passed between them:

Bolt: "Well, I guess you won, but I didn't enjoy it a bit." (No shit Tommy . . . really?)

Brown: "Nor would I if I'd been licked like you just have . . . Because even you knew when the games were drawn that you never had an earthly hope of beating *me*."

Bolt: "This isn't golf, it's war!" (*Enter Rodney Dangerfield: "Hey everybody, we're all gonna get laid!"*)

In the locker room, Bolt broke a club and continued to complain, mostly about the crowds, saying, "They roared when their guys won, cheered when I missed a putt, and sat on their hands if I played a good shot." Furgol, who listened to the tirade, supposedly said, "Pipe down, you were well and truly licked."

Personally, I find all this talk of men licking each other distasteful, and as for the crowd behavior, bring it on. It's exactly why the Ryder Cup is the greatest event in golf.

With two matches done, the Cup was tied, but not for long: Alliss lost to Hawkins in another surprise, 2&1. But that would be it for the American comeback.

Bousfield took a quick lead on Hebert, leading by five at the break and extending to seven before Hebert won three in a row. But encouraged by reports from Faulkner, who was running around the course playing the oboe badly and giving updates to his teammates (there were no giant scoreboards or walkie-talkies in those days), Bousfield held on for a 4&3 win, and due to the timing of the finishes, it was his point that won the Cup.

Rees, feeling the good vibes from his team, played like a man anxious to watch the other matches: He was 4-up over Furgol after the morning round, 7-up at twenty-seven holes, and won 7&6. Ford holed long putts in the morning but was still 1-down to Hunt at lunch. Hunt took five fast holes in the afternoon and won 6&5.

O'Connor won the first three holes from Finsterwald, but gave them back by lunch. But during the break the Irishman had several pints, then walked into the Lindrick pro shop and bought a new putter (at full retail no doubt), which he used to good effect, winning six of the next eight holes and pocketing a 7&6 win. The Cup's location was already decided well before Mayer and Bradshaw were done, but still they waged the closest match of the day, with Bradshaw holing out a bunker shot in the morning then getting down in two from well off the green on the last hole for a half. It was the only match of the day to reach the final green.

The first British win since 1933 was a colossal achievement. Doormats to the Americans for years in singles, they won all but two of the eight matches, and all by healthy margins. This was no fluke.

Unfortunately, some of the Americans were shitty losers, but to be fair it was probably because they'd had so little practice at it. It wasn't just Bolt, who was clearly feeling shafted. Burke reeled off a string of excuses: the small ball, driving on the wrong side of the road, over-practicing, flagsticks that were too thick and too short, and of course, warm beer and cold women.

But Ed Furgol was right, not just about Bolt but about the entire team: This time, they were well and truly licked. Ugh!

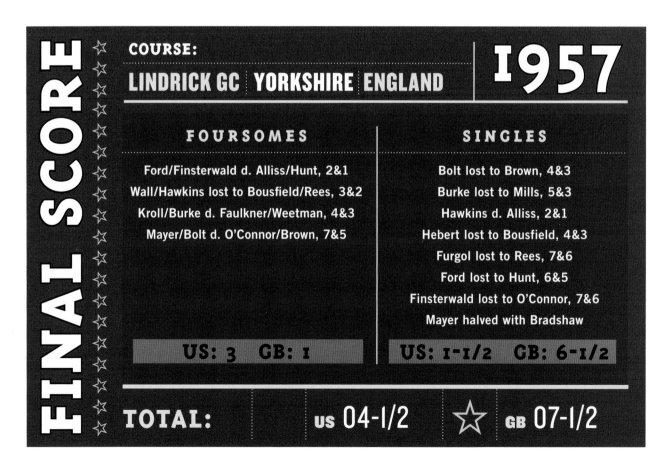

FINAL SCORE

COURSE:

LINDRICK GC | YORKSHIRE | ENGLAND | **1957**

FOURSOMES	SINGLES
Ford/Finsterwald d. Alliss/Hunt, 2&1	Bolt lost to Brown, 4&3
Wall/Hawkins lost to Bousfield/Rees, 3&2	Burke lost to Mills, 5&3
Kroll/Burke d. Faulkner/Weetman, 4&3	Hawkins d. Alliss, 2&1
Mayer/Bolt d. O'Connor/Brown, 7&5	Hebert lost to Bousfield, 4&3
	Furgol lost to Rees, 7&6
	Ford lost to Hunt, 6&5
	Finsterwald lost to O'Connor, 7&6
	Mayer halved with Bradshaw
US: 3 GB: 1	US: 1-1/2 GB: 6-1/2

TOTAL: US 04-1/2 ☆ GB 07-1/2

COURSE:

ELDORADO CC | PALM DESERT | CA

☆☆☆☆☆☆☆☆☆☆ NOV. 06-07

1959

☆☆☆☆☆☆☆☆☆☆☆☆☆☆☆☆☆☆

FINAL SCORE:

US 08-1/2   GB 03-1/2

CAPTAINS:

SAM SNEAD   DAI REES

UNITED STATES	GREAT BRITAIN
Julius Boros	Peter Alliss
Jack Burke Jr.	Ken Bousfield
Dow Finsterwald	Eric Brown
Doug Ford	Norman Drew
Jay Hebert	Bernard Hunt
Cary Middlecoff	Peter Mills
Bob Rosburg	Christy O'Connor Sr.
Sam Snead	Dai Rees
Mike Souchak	Dave Thomas
Art Wall	Harry Weetman

1927   1929   1931   1933   1935   1937   1947   1949

Courtesy of The PGA of America

THE END OF THE EISENHOWER ERA—the white-bread, go-along, placid 1950s—was celebrated with what could have been the dullest Ryder Cup yet. After the upset at Lindrick two years earlier, balance was restored when a strong team had little trouble turning the American golf universe right-side-up again.

But if the action on the course was boring and predictable, what happened off the course was exciting to the point of being dangerous.

The British team—playing captain Dai Rees; holdovers Peter Alliss, Ken Bousfield, Eric Brown, Bernard Hunt, Peter Mills, Christy O'Connor, and Harry Weetman; plus newcomers Norman Drew and Dave Thomas—almost didn't make it to Eldorado Country Club, another brand-spanking-new desert course near Palm Springs. Airplanes were now the preferred mode of transatlantic travel, but in the spirit of team unity, the Brits crossed a stormy ocean on the *Queen Mary,* stomachs in throats (or over the side) most of the way. From New York, they went to Atlanta to meet Bobby Jones, and played in a few exhibition matches, eventually arriving in Los Angeles.

It's 150 miles from LA to Palm Springs, about forty minutes in a small plane. On October 29, the British team, plus a few others including American Doug Ford, were well into the flight when the plane caught up to the backside of a hurricane menacing Mexico. Crossing the San Jacinto Mountains, the plane shuddered and groaned, then dropped from 13,000 feet to 9,000 in a matter of seconds. Hunt, who had given his seat to a flight attendant, was thrown against the roof of the plane. Anything not nailed down flew about. Another attendant was knocked unconscious. Fortunately, anyone who had been drinking heavily was floppy enough to absorb the shock, so once again the Irish saved civilization.

The pilot eventually regained control of the plane, seconds away from disaster. With order restored, Harry Weetman said, "I bloody near messed my pants." Another player responded, "I've got news for you Harry. I did."

About to land in Palm Springs, the plane was turned away because the storm had closed the airport. Back they flew to Los Angeles, where many kissed the ground upon landing. Offered another flight, Rees made one of his most important decisions as captain and chartered a Greyhound bus.

The twenty-nine passengers formed "The Long Drop Club," occasionally meeting to hurl dinner around the room and reminisce. In proper British fashion, the club even had its own tie: a delightful shade of vomit on a background of sky blue, I imagine.

Even before the flight, Peter Mills was bothered by back pain. John Panton, who'd played in 1951 and 1953

SAM SNEAD

(three matches, three losses), was summoned from England as a replacement. By coming late, he avoided the fateful plane ride and the subsequent skid marks, but neither he nor Mills ever got to tee it up, which was a damned shame, and should never happen to any man that qualifies for a Ryder Cup team.

The American team had no such trouble getting to Palm Springs, but they were no less intent on making the British sick. After Lindrick, there would be no complacency, as evidenced by the choice of Sam Snead as playing captain despite his ignominious refusal to play in 1957. With spots secured based on points accrued over two years, a new generation was making its mark: Only three players from the losing team were returning—Ford (winner of the 1957 Masters), Dow Finsterwald (1958 PGA), and Art Wall Jr. (1959 Masters). Julius Boros, who'd made the 1957 team but had to withdraw with a broken leg, was healthy and was joined by first-timers Jay Hebert, Bob Rosburg (1959 PGA), and Mike Souchak. Cary Middlecoff also had his ban lifted and was back.

However, PGA rules continued to weaken the team. Among the players yet to satisfy the five-year waiting period were Billy Casper (who'd won the U.S. Open earlier that year), Ken Venturi, Gene Littler, and most notably, Arnold Palmer (1958 Masters).

The PGA had also, it seemed, forgotten to tell the club that an important event was being held there. Members insisted on being allowed to keep playing until the very last minute, so during their practice rounds, both teams had to wait behind groups of crotchety old hackers who wouldn't let them play through. As if that weren't bad enough, the tees during practice were set all the way back, but once the matches began, the players found themselves hitting from roughly the ladies' tees: It was common practice in the early days of televised golf to make the courses as short and easy as possible; the belief being that the audience wanted to see lots of birdies and low scores. Of course, having practiced from the tips, the players were totally flummoxed by the front tees and the question of what clubs to use on their suddenly much shorter approach shots.

Once the matches began, the excitement was pretty much over. In the first foursomes, Rosburg and Souchak were six holes up on Hunt and Brown at lunch. Hunt was obviously not well, his shoulders wrenched from clinging to the roof of the plane, and suffering bronchitis as well. The U.S. pair took it easy for a 5&4 win.

Finsterwald carried teammate Boros to a sloppy win over Bousfield and Rees. For the first of many times over two days, the water-guarded eighteenth hole was crucial, giving the Americans a one-hole lead in the morning then drowning any hope of a halve when Bousfield, forced to go for it on the thirty-sixth, found the lake to the right of the green, losing 2-up.

Wall and Ford fought a good battle with Alliss and O'Connor, with the Brits getting the best of it. They were 3-up at lunch, extended it to five, but had only a two-hole lead with three to play. Despite leaking oil, the Brits combined to birdie the thirty-fourth hole and close out the match, 3&2, for the team's first point and, more remarkably, Alliss's first win in five Cup matches.

The final foursomes could have gone either way. Snead and Middlecoff were up, down, then up again in the morning, and finished with a one-hole lead. After lunch the swinging continued, and the Brits were 2-up with two to play. Thomas missed a five-footer on the thirty-fifth that would have won the match. Unperturbed, he hit a good drive that Middlecoff couldn't match, hooking into the left rough. Snead had no choice but to go for the green, but his ball dropped into the left-front lake. With the luxury of four shots to win the match, Weetman idiotically passed on laying up and dunked his five-iron in the water to the right. No surprise to anyone, the Americans battled for a bogey five that beat their opponents' six and halved the match. Afterward, Weetman said, "Why did I not play safe? I never do. It's the only way I know how to play, to go for the green. Anyway, I thought it would have been nicer to win 2-up instead of 1-up."

As they say on the telly, let that be a lesson to all of you out there.

In the singles, Drew drew Ford, who was 4-up after nine holes and appeared to be running away from the overmatched Irishman. But the American lead was only one at lunch and stayed that way to the final hole. Knowing the fate of going left or right, Drew hit a wonderful three-wood to the middle of the green and won the hole. Drew drew.

Hopes for a British comeback were short-lived as the Americans won the next four matches: Souchak over Bousfield 3&2; Rosburg topping Weetman, 6&5; Snead (in his final Ryder Cup match) coasting by Thomas, 6&5;

and Finsterwald taking a big lead then holding on, thanks to a near chip-in at the last, to beat Rees, 1-up. The Cup was coming back to the States.

In the battle of the relatives—Jay Hebert was the brother of Lionel, who'd played on the Cup team in 1957; Peter Alliss was the son of Percy, still the Cup's only father-son combo—the Englishman holed numerous long putts but couldn't pull away from the Louisianan with the French-sounding name ("ay-bear"). Alliss was 1-up at lunch then 1-down at the last. This time it was the American who found the water, giving Alliss the hole for a half. (Never having won before, Alliss went undefeated in his third Cup.)

Wall had no problems with O'Connor, winning 7&6. Brown saved a shred of British dignity with a 4&3 victory over Middlecoff. It was to be Brown's last Cup match, and he ended with a perfect record: He was 4-0 in singles, 0-4 in foursomes.

Despite the British win two years earlier, the ease of this victory had observers searching for a way to make the Ryder Cup a fair fight. In the decade just ended, the U.S. teams had gone 4-1, outscoring their opponents 37-23. And the sixties weren't shaping up much better, as the United States had many great players coming along while British prospects were unremarkable.

Among the suggestions was to let the rest of Europe join the British. Or let them recruit other members of the Commonwealth (after all, South Africans Gary Player and Bobby Locke, and Australian Peter Thomson, had won nine of the previous eleven Open Championships). But Sam Ryder's original charter said U.S. vs. Britain, and so it would remain.

Yet when by the time the 1960s dawned, the Ryder Cup would be very different.

FINAL SCORE

COURSE:

ELDORADO CC | PALM DESERT | CA

1959

FOURSOMES

Rosburg/Souchak d. Hunt/Brown, 5&4

Ford/Wall lost to O'Connor/Alliss, 3&2

Boros/Finsterwald d. Rees/Bousfield, 2-up

Snead/Middlecoff halved with Weetman/
Thomas

US: 2-1/2   GB: 1-1/2

SINGLES

Ford halved with Drew

Souchak d. Bousfield, 3&2

Rosburg d. Weetman, 6&5

Snead d. Thomas, 6&5

Finsterwald d. Rees, 1-up

Hebert halved with Alliss

Wall d. O'Connor, 7&6

Middlecoff lost to Brown, 4&3

US: 6   GB: 2

TOTAL: ☆   **US 08-1/2**   **GB 03-1/2**

COURSE:

ROYAL LYTHAM & ST. ANNES | ST. ANNES | ENGLAND

OCT. **13-14**

1961

ROYAL LYTHAM

FINAL SCORE:

US 14-1/2

GB 09-1/2

CAPTAINS:

JERRY BARBER   DAI REES

UNITED STATES	GREAT BRITAIN
Jerry Barber	Peter Alliss
Billy Casper	Ken Bousfield
Bill Collins	Neil Coles
Dow Finsterwald	Tom Haliburton
Doug Ford	Bernard Hunt
Jay Hebert	Ralph Moffitt
Gene Littler	Christy O'Connor Sr.
Arnold Palmer	John Panton
Mike Souchak	Dai Rees
Art Wall	Harry Weetman

1927	1929	1931	1933	1935	1937	1947	1949

THIS WAS THE YEAR EVERYTHING CHANGED EXCEPT THE RESULT.

It was obvious after 1959 that the Ryder Cup was in a spot of bother, both as contest and spectator event. The Americans wanted something more "audience friendly," while the British hoped it (meaning they) could become more competitive without welcoming fuzzy foreign players from outside the Isles. The two alterations to the format—the first changes since 1927—satisfied both sides.

First, all matches were shortened from thirty-six holes to eighteen. This was good for GB, which often led or was close after the morning only to lose to the battle-hardened Americans after lunch. This change—from a marathon to a sprint—also would make the matches more marketable, as the U.S. PGA requested. And splendidly, from your author's point of view, we're now spared from having to do profoundly confusing math when referring to holes played in the afternoon. The nineteenth through the thirty-sixth my arse.

Second, there would be twice as many matches each day, doubling the number of total points—from twelve to twenty-four—the American's desired excitement, and the amount of laundry generated. Theoretically, more matches also would allow captains to use their players more effectively, and reduce the shameful incidence of men qualifying for a team and not playing at all.

Two more changes were suggested: extend the event from two days to three and add fourball matches. (For some unknown reason, the Americans still said they didn't like foursomes, despite their overwhelming mastery in two-man play through the years.) Both modifications would have to wait.

116

DAI REES PUTTING

The changes did have some of the desired effects. At least the matches became closer, even if the final score didn't. Players who didn't play well in the morning could be rested in the afternoon, not only strengthening the team effort, but giving everyone a chance to play.

As a result of the revisions came a perhaps unexpected nuance: a shift in the role of the playing captain. With two slates of matches a day, it was important that captains know how their players were doing in the morning so substitutions could be made for the afternoon. A captain playing his own Ryder Cup match has a hard enough time keeping his gonads out of his throat without having to worry about how well his teammates are doing, and the Americans seemed to grasp this much earlier. U.S. captain Jerry Barber did not play in the morning foursomes, choosing to watch his players instead. The U.S. team also created the job of honorary non-playing captain—in effect, someone else to spectate and report back to the captain on team members' fitness for further battle. Porky Oliver, a salad-swerving veteran of three Cups, was Barber's spare pair of eyes and backup buttocks.

So heading to the fourteenth Ryder Cup matches, the golf world was jazzed. The new format promised excitement. The site was top-drawer: Royal Lytham and St. Annes was the first Open Championship course to host the Cup. And remembering the home team's heroic victory the last time the matches were on home soil, the locals were throbbingly hopeful.

Which of course meant something had to go throbbingly wrong. And it did. To the teams. At the last minute.

The British team was neither particularly strong nor weak. A change in the rules of qualifying meant golfers would have to compete in seven of nine British tournaments to be considered. The talent pool was more of a puddle to begin with, and this shrank it further, although the resulting team was full of recognizable names: Rebounding from Eldorado (and glad not to be flying in) were Peter Alliss, Ken Bousfield, Bernard Hunt, Christy O'Connor, John Panton, and Harry Weetman, along with Dai Rees in his fourth stint as playing captain. The new boys were Neil Coles, Tom Haliburton, and Ralph Moffitt. (You'd either have to be very up on your British golf trivia or a family member not to say "Who?" about two of them, and yes, you're supposed to know Neil Coles.)

On the other hand, the American team was a powerhouse. Returning from past Cups were Barber, Dow Finsterwald, Jay Hebert, Mike Souchak, and Art Wall Jr., who was to take a few days off from making holes-in-one. Four men were making their debut: Along with Bill Collins (again, "Who?") were three superstars in the making—Billy Casper, Gene Littler, and Arnold Palmer, winners of the three previous U.S. Opens. Palmer was the biggest draw: In seven years as a pro, he'd won two Masters, one U.S. Open, and earlier that summer the first of two consecutive Open Championships. American golf was at the height of its glamour, and Palmer was as popular in Britain as he was at home: Arnie's Anglican Army was aching to see him play for the Cup.

They were almost as anxious to see another favorite, Sam Snead, who had declined to compete at Lindrick (a move that many thought contributed greatly to the American loss). But only weeks before the team was to leave for England, Snead was cut. He had inadvertently broken PGA rules, skipping a sanctioned event (the Portland Open, the tournament sponsored by Bob Hudson, who'd saved the Ryder Cup after the war) to play in an unauthorized pro-am in Cincinnati. I'm thinking old Sammy was either getting his pole smoked or his palm greased.

KEN BOUSFIELD

A PLAYER'S BALL COMES TO REST AMONG SPECTATORS

In fairly typical bone-headed style, Snead said of the pro-am, "I figured it wasn't anything more than a glorified exhibition. Five minutes before I'm set to tee off, someone tells me I'd better get permission from the Portland sponsors, so I sent off a wire right away. When I finish eighteen holes, I come into the clubhouse and there's the answer. Permission not granted."

An indication of how much the Ryder Cup meant, Sammy withdrew from the rest of the tournament, hoping it would make amends, but another telegram told Snead that he would be fined five hundred dollars, suspended from the tour for six months, and, worse than all of that, replaced on the Ryder Cup team by Doug holy-crap-you-must-be-joking Ford! (Ford was next in line on the points list. It also helped that he and Snead were the same size, so no alterations were necessary to the uniform.)

To use an expression Sam himself no doubt used, he was "madder than a two-dicked dog." Threatening legal action, his appeal was heard at the PGA's annual meeting—after the Cup matches were over. His suspension was shortened to forty-five days, but sadly, his magnificent Ryder Cup career was over.

Snead's absence was the only cloud over the matches, which began in sunny weather. (Potential botheration had been avoided after Barber realized he'd left the Ryder Cup in the vault of the London hotel in which the team stayed upon arrival in England. The trophy took the train and was on site in time for the opening ceremonies.)

So off we jolly well went with a new format designed to help the homeys, and the first morning's foursomes still went to the evil Americans, three to one. Barber sat out to watch his team, but Rees couldn't resist the mating call of the little cup, and played in this match—and three others. The first foursomes would be his only loss, but even so, he got seriously shafted for not scouting his players. Henry "I'll have one more, and then I'll stay" Longhurst was especially damning, calling for an end to the role of playing captain, self-rule for India, another pink gin, easy on the bitters, and "Oh Christ, that wasn't a fart."

Where was I? Oh yes, with only eighteen holes to decide each point, a fast start was great, but it didn't always guarantee a win. In the first match, Littler and Ford quickly went 2-up but ultimately lost to O'Connor and Alliss, 4&3. (Barber would bench this team in the afternoon.) Wall and Hebert took an early lead and held it, winning 4&3 over Panton and Hunt.

Casper and Palmer (how'd you like to play against those two stiffs?) made their debut against Rees and Bousfield. At the par-five seventh, the Brits were about to win the hole and tie the match when Casper chipped in from rough fifty yards off the green, winning the hole and doubling the American lead. When Casper stuck his tee shot on seventeen to five feet, a distance Palmer rarely missed from, the U.S. pair won, 2&1. The final match, and the only one in the morning to reach the final hole, went to Souchak and Collins, 1-up over Haliburton and Coles.

Seven of the eight teams reappeared in the afternoon, as did the final score, 3-1 in America's favor. O'Connor and Alliss battled mightily with Wall and Hebert, but Alliss's short game (a weak spot throughout his Cup career) proved fatal, and the U.S. pair won on the final hole, 1-up. Panton and Hunt, who'd lost 4&3 in the morning, had a worse time in the afternoon, losing to Casper and Palmer 5&4. Rees and Bousfield used their experience, and some poor American driving, to top Souchak and Collins 4&2. In the final match, Coles and Haliburton again made it to the final hole—after being four down with seven to play—and again they lost by a hole, this time to Barber and Finsterwald.

A 6-2 lead after the first day looked insurmountable, but hope springs eternal in Cupland. After all, twice as many singles matches meant twice as many points.

Harry Weetman opened day two against Ford and took a quick lead that he gave back by the turn. All even at the last, Weetman had a putt to win that he missed, then a three-footer to tie that he also missed, handing his balls and the match on a silver plate to the American. Rookie Moffitt also took the early lead, birdieing the first hole against Souchak, then did nothing else and lost 5&4 to the big-hitting American, who was magnificent. It wasn't only driving that won this day: Souchak single-putted eight of fourteen greens.

Alliss and Palmer dueled all morning, neither pulling more than one hole away, with Arnold trying to get laid eleven times, chipping in twice, and holing out of the sand once to stay close. All square on the last hole, both men were long with their approaches: Alliss's forty-yard chip stopped within three feet of the hole, and Arnie conceded the par, then characteristically ran his twenty-five-footer three feet past. Alliss quickly conceded the comebacker, saying, "That's all right, Arnold, pick it up. We've had a good match; let's leave it that way." The resulting halve was an appropriate finish between two of the game's greatest, enduringly loved characters.

A hot streak on the back nine gave Casper a 5&3 win over Bousfield. Rees never trailed Hebert, winning 2&1, and Coles pressured Littler, firing a string of threes at one point, but having to settle for a halve after the American won the final two holes. Barber struggled against Hunt and lost 5&4. And although both Finsterwald and O'Connor eagled the par-five seventeenth, halving the hole was good enough to give the American the win, 2&1.

Having won five of eight points in the morning singles, the U.S. team led 11-5, meaning one point would keep the Cup. The home team would need a near sweep if they hoped to pull another Lindrick.

With a chance at redemption, Harry Weetman shot a three-under-par thirty-three on the opening nine, but unfortunately for him, Wall went out in two less giving him a two-hole lead at the turn, which he parlayed into a 1-up win. The Cup was staying in the States, a fact made clearer when Souchak beat Hunt 2&1. In between, Alliss finally won his first singles match in five attempts, taking out Collins, 3&2.

The outcome was determined, but Ryder Cup points have always meant everything to Ryder Cup players, and the British didn't stop fighting. Haliburton was the big surprise, grabbing an early two-hole lead over Palmer and taking the match to seventeen, where matching birdies gave Arnold the 2&1 win. The next three matches went to the locals: Rees over Ford, 4&3; Bousfield pipping Barber, 1-up; and Coles besting Finsterwald, 1-up. In the last match, O'Connor and Littler halved.

Winning 4-1/2 to 3-1/2 in the afternoon made the score slightly more respectable for the home team. And if the end result wasn't much of a surprise, there were numerous surprising statistics to emerge from the first "modern" Ryder Cup.

Only one American was over forty years old; five GB players were forty-plus. No Americans were under thirty; two home players were. It was the last time both captains would play; Barber won his foursomes but lost both singles; Rees lost his opening foursomes then won his three following matches (also the best showing on his team). In their Cup debuts, Palmer won three and a half out of four possible points, Casper won three of three, and Littler went winless (one loss, two halves). Playing in his last Cup, Art Wall Jr. was undefeated with three wins, in which he reportedly averaged 1.37 strokes per par three played. Uh-huh.

Also in his last Cup (as a player) was Rees, who finished with a record of 7-9-1. Incredibly, his Ryder career had lasted twenty-four years—from 1937 through 1961—the longest span of any Cup player. His nine appearances isn't a record, since four Cups were cancelled due to World War II. A great player and a great man, he would have fought tooth-and-nail if he'd had the chance.

FINAL SCORE

COURSE:

ROYAL LYTHAM & ST. ANNES **ST. ANNES** **ENGLAND**

1961

FOURSOMES

MORNING

Littler/Ford lost to O'Connor/Alliss, 4&3

Hebert/Wall d. Panton/Hunt, 4&3

Casper/Palmer d. Rees/Bousfield, 2&1

Souchak/Collins d. Haliburton/Coles, 1-up

AFTERNOON

Wall/Hebert d. O'Connor/Alliss, 1-up

Casper/Palmer d. Panton/Hunt, 5&4

Souchak/Collins lost to Rees/Bousfield, 4&2

Barber/Finsterwald d. Haliburton/Coles, 1-up

US: 6   GB: 2

SINGLES

MORNING

Ford d. Weetman, 1-up

Souchak d. Moffitt, 5&4

Palmer halved with Alliss

Casper d. Bousfield, 5&3

Hebert lost to Rees, 2&1

Littler halved with Coles

Barber lost to Hunt, 5&4

Finsterwald d. O'Connor, 2&1

AFTERNOON

Wall d. Weetman, 1-up

Collins lost to Alliss, 3&2

Souchak d. Hunt, 2&1

Palmer d. Haliburton, 2&1

Ford lost to Rees, 4&3

Barber lost to Bousfield, 1-up

Finsterwald lost to Coles, 1-up

Littler halved with O'Connor

US: 8-1/2   GB: 7-1/2

TOTAL: **US 14-1/2** **GB 09-1/2**

HEROES OF THE RYDER CUP
DAI REES (1913–1983)

DAI REES was the first Welshman to play for the Ryder Cup when he debuted in 1937. When his Cup career ended thirty years later, he'd established a number of other firsts as well.

The small (five-foot-seven) Rees was another of those unfortunate British stars to never win the prize he coveted most, the Open Championship. He had numerous chances, including second-place finishes in 1953, 1954, and 1961, and twenty-eight victories around the world, including Britian's PGA Matchplay four times. But where he really shone was in his first love, the Ryder Cup.

Rees played in nine straight Cups (four of those as playing captain; in fact, he was the last playing captain for Britain) and was non-playing captain once, in 1967. He was almost always the team's star, beginning with his first appearance, in 1937.

He opened his Ryder career teaming with his captain, Charles Whitcombe, against Gene Sarazen and Denny Shute, arguably the strongest American team. On a windy day, neither side could make a move, and neither took more than a one-hole lead. Rees carried his team, and needed to hole a slick six-foot putt for a half on the final hole, which he did. He followed that gutsy performance with another in the singles, fighting back from 3-down to Byron Nelson to win, 3&1.

In 1949, Rees faced Bob Hamilton in the singles. The American shot sixty-nine in the morning; good, but not good enough as the Welshman fired a sixty-five—including eight threes—for a four-hole lead at lunch. Rees eventually won 6&4, going twelve-under-par for thirty-two holes with only one five on his card.

In 1951, Rees lost both of his matches, dropping his foursomes with Max Faulkner to Clayton Heafner and Jack Burke, 5&3, then losing his singles to Jimmy Demaret, 2-up, when the American hit outstanding sand shots back to back near the end. After the match, Demaret presented his sand wedge to Rees as a gift.

Rees's greatest year was 1957, when he was both captain and two-time winner on the first British team to beat the Americans in twenty-four years. He actually won his first foursomes in six tries, then defeated Ed Furgol in singles 7&6 on what he called "the most thrilling day of my life."

But he wasn't done, going 3-1 in 1961 as forty-eight-year-old playing captain. It was easily the best performance on his team as he accounted for nearly a third of their 9-1/2 points. He closed his Ryder playing career with a record of 7-9-1, but 5-4 in singles.

In 1967, Rees was brought back as non-playing captain, and although he couldn't recapture the magic of ten years earlier, he did help set British golf on the right course. After the disappointing fifteen-point loss, the visionary Rees called for numerous changes to the administration of golf in Britain; many would be implemented and in time would help make the team competitive again.

As to those records: Rees played in nine Cups; only three men (Nick Faldo, Christy O'Connor Sr., and Bernhard Langer) have played in more, and none of them lost chances to play due to World War II. His five singles wins tie him with four others for second behind Faldo and Peter Oosterhuis with six each. And his five stints as captain is the most for the British/European team. During the years the Ryder Cup was dominated by America, Dai Rees epitomized the spirit of the British and Irish men who paved the way for the event to become the greatest in golf.

COURSE:

EAST LAKE CC | ATLANTA | GA

☆☆☆☆☆☆☆☆☆☆ OCT. **11-13**

1963

FINAL SCORE:

☆ US **23** GB **09**

CAPTAINS:

ARNOLD PALMER JOHN FALLON

UNITED STATES ### GREAT BRITAIN

☆☆☆☆☆☆☆☆☆☆☆ ☆☆☆☆☆☆☆☆☆☆☆

UNITED STATES	GREAT BRITAIN
Julius Boros	Peter Alliss
Billy Casper	Neil Coles
Dow Finsterwald	Tom Haliburton
Bob Goalby	Brian Huggett
Gene Littler	Bernard Hunt
Tony Lema	Geoffrey Hunt
Billy Maxwell	Christy O'Connor Sr.
Arnold Palmer	Dave Thomas
Johnny Pott	Harry Weetman
Dave Ragan	George Will

1927   1929   1931   1933   1935   1937   1947   1949

THROUGHOUT HIS CAREER, Arnold Palmer let his clubs do his talking. But as playing captain of the U.S. Ryder Cup team in 1963 (and the last playing captain, at that), his words were strong:

"I'll only say what I have just told my boys in the locker room," Palmer said in earshot of the British captain, John Fallon. "And that is that I don't think there are ten players in the world who can beat us."

It was hard to argue with Arnold then, and it's flat out stupid now. The Ryder Cup had become an annuity for the Americans, who'd lost only three times in the event's twenty-six years, only once since World War II, and never on home turf. And if anything, the changes recently put into place made Palmer's case stronger.

It was generally acknowledged that the revisions made in 1961—primarily shortening matches from thirty-six holes to eighteen—were done to keep GB competitive, even if it hadn't worked out that way in their debut. So in 1963, when the U.S. PGA asked for a third day of play and two rounds of fourballs, the British PGA could hardly say no, even if those additions played into the Americans' hands. BOLLOCKS!

A third day would have many effects. First, it meant another day of crowds—and their cash. Second, it made the event more attractive for television, a medium that was just beginning to take an interest in professional golf. Third, it probably would favor the Americans, who had more experience with multiday tournaments and the attendant pressure.

Fourball, on the other hand, was an American license to steal. In this game, all four golfers play their own ball from tee to hole, and whoever shoots the lowest score, his team wins the hole (if the two low scores from each team tie, the hole is halved). Giving two better, stronger, battle-hardened Americans a run at each hole was seen as doubling their chances of winning, or as Old Tom Morris didn't used to say, "Not fucking up."

Despite all that, GB still sent a team, which operated under new rules.

Thinking that previous teams had spent too much time farting around in exhibitions and enjoying themselves, travel arrangements were changed. For the first time, the boys came to the United States from the old sod by plane (all except Neil Coles, who was, and remains, deathly-to-the-point-of-soilage afraid of flying), and were accompanied by their wives (bollocks bollocks bollocks!), as well as a delegation from the British PGA. The chance that a bunch of wankers like this would ensure proper conduct was roughly equivalent to that of the Queen Mother getting her tits out at the opening ceremony—but still, at least this trip was to be more serious, and also more luxurious, with the PGA picking up first-class tickets for the entire party. However, the Executive Committee collectively shat in their tweedy drawers when they were presented with the extra costs. In the future, economy class would have to do, and while wives would still be, ahem, *welcome*, they would have to pay for themselves. Like that was ever going to fly—what a bunch of morons.

Did traveling with chaperones and wives affect the outcome of the match? Unlikely. But another new wrinkle certainly did: The captain was through being a player.

In 1961, captain Dai Rees had played in all four matches, and although he went 3-1, the rest of his team was much less successful and lost badly (14-1/2 to 9-1/2). It was thought that playing rather than watching left Rees unaware of his players' conditions, which led to poor choices of pairings and strategy, especially for afternoon matches. That was a mistake not to be made again, and was subsequently lost as a damned good excuse.

The choice of Fallon as captain was a double slap to Rees. Not only was it a repudiation of Rees's performance, but the two men had a history. In 1955, Rees paired Fallon with John Jacobs on the first day and they beat Chandler Harper and Jerry Barber for Britain's only point in foursomes. Despite the victory, Rees sat Fallon during the singles and Fallon never played for the Cup again.

Fallon's team was largely veterans: Peter Alliss, Coles, Tom Haliburton, Bernard Hunt, Christy O'Connor, Dave Thomas, and Harry Weetman. They were joined by Hunt's brother Geoff (only the second time brothers played on the same team), another midget Welshman (what do they feed them?) Brian Huggett, and George Will.

Palmer's troops were formidable. Back were Julius Boros, Billy Casper, Dow Finsterwald, and Gene Littler. The rookies were Tony Lema, Billy Maxwell, Johnny Pott, Bob Goalby, and Dave Ragan. And Arnold would be playing, too, despite a sore shoulder and an enormous penis. Or maybe it was the other way around.

As if Palmer's fighting words weren't enough, British bookmakers pegged the Americans as strong favorites, and in a rare moment of optimism, Henry Longhurst said, "Any British team would do well to win twenty-five percent of the points on U.S. soil . . . . . pass the claret, there's a good fellow, oh bugger it, I've fallen down again!"

Even former Ryder Cup stalwart and ghastly old fart Henry Cotton chimed in, saying the British and Irish "cannot win this match in America": He blamed better practice facilities in America, the big money on the U.S.

128

tour, girls with big honkers, and the smaller British ball (which flew farther but also buried more deeply in sand and rough). "The present top home players," Cotton wrote, "by no means poor performers, are leagues outside the tough American ones."

"And every-one up on their tippy-toes --- and breathe......."

ARNOLD PALMER AND PETER ALLISS

Captain Fallon would have none of it. "That's pre-posterous," he said upon hearing that the outcome had been decided before the matches began. "Except for Palmer, we're as good as their side." Or in other words, fuck Henry, even though he's right.

But on the first morning, Fallon was right. The Brits were tied with the Americans after the first slate of matches, a first in a Stateside Match. In the opening match, Palmer, playing with Pott (who upon hearing he would team with his captain said, "Hell, don't do me any favors. Put me with somebody who'll be just as nervous as I am!"), lost to rookies Huggett and Will, 3&2. In the second, Casper/Ragan vs. Alliss/O'Connor (paired together for the fourth straight time over three Cups), neither team played well, and a par on the final hole won it for the Americans, 1-up. The other two foursomes were halved.

Pleased with their performances, the British players looked forward to more close battles in the afternoon. But during lunch Fallon came up to Hunt and Coles and said, "You boys played so well this morning, I'm going to split you up this afternoon." Obviously the captain hoped their good play would transfer to others, but that wasn't how they saw it. "We couldn't believe our ears," Coles said. "We just sat and gasped."

Coles was paired with Geoff Hunt, Haliburton with Bernard. That any of them came back at all was a moral victory. The U.S. pairs swept all four matches. The most dramatic moment of the matches came when good old Henry Longhurst almost wet his pants, after nearly saying, "Cunt and Holes are one down." Dearie, dearie me.

In order, Maxwell/Goalby (both fresh, having sat out the morning) had no trouble with Thomas and Weetman, 4&3. Palmer wasn't about to lose again, and pairing with Casper he didn't, rolling over Huggett and Will, 5&4. Littler and Finsterwald beat Coles and Geoff Hunt, 2&1. Only the match between Boros/Lema and Haliburton/Bernard Hunt went to the final hole, where America's par beat Britain's bogey.

The next day wasn't much better. True, the Americans were expected to do well in fourball, but this was ridiculous: eight matches, five wins, one loss, two halves. Only Coles and O'Connor, last off in the morning, managed a 1-up win over Goalby and Ragan, and only because O'Connor holed a thirty-foot birdie putt on the last hole. In the afternoon, Fallon kept three of the four teams intact: two of them lost again and the other halved. As for the rested pair, they lost, too.

After the first two days, the U.S. team led 12-4 and needed only four points from the sixteen remaining to keep the Cup. To their credit, the GB lads didn't make it easy, and actually won the morning singles 4-1/2 to 3-1/2.

In the matches worth recounting, Neil Coles (a superb player who never seemed to hit it anywhere but flag high) fought back from 2-down with two to play to halve with Casper. Weetman, who hadn't won a singles since beating Sam Snead in 1953, held off a Boros comeback to win 1-up. Bernard Hunt stayed even with Finsterwald until the American took two sixes, enough for a 2-up British win.

But the match of the morning—and the week—pitted Palmer against Alliss in a rematch of their memorable halve in 1961. Since then, Arnold had won another Masters and another Open Championship (and nearly another U.S. Open, losing to Jack Nicklaus in a playoff). This match was as close as the last, Alliss thrusting, Palmer parrying. The stylish Englishman took a one-hole lead to the seventeenth, where he holed a snaking twelve-footer for a half. With the crowd loudly in Arnold's corner, Alliss faced a sixty-footer on eighteen that he lagged close. When Palmer missed his putt from the back of the green, he conceded Alliss's to give him the win, 1-up. Years later, Alliss said, "When I beat Arnold, I thought they were going to lynch me."

The winning point came in the fourth match of the afternoon, when Littler beat Haliburton, 6&5. But in truth, every one of the Americans won the point because every one of them won his match save Lema, who halved with Alliss. It was a common or garden hosing, 7-1/2 to 1/2. And the final score, 23-9, remains the second biggest margin of victory in Cup history.

To the usual reasons for the British loss—the smaller ball, rigors of travel, less experienced players—Palmer added another. Shock and horror—he said the Americans worked harder. The British players didn't practice enough, spending too much time around the clubhouse rather than beating balls.

Here's a fascinating statistic. In the three morning rounds (one each of foursomes, fourballs, and singles), the teams tied, 8-8. After lunch, the U.S. won 15-1. Sounds like either the Americans were stronger, or the kitchen staff was up to no good.

Among the players making their last Cup appearance were Dow Finsterwald (with a superb 9-3-1 record in four events) and Harry Weetman (2-11-2 in seven). Also leaving the scene was poor Tom Haliburton, who played in six matches over two years and got his plums picked in them all. But Tom was a fighter. All three of his foursome losses went to the final hole; his fourball went to the seventeenth hole; and he took Palmer to the seventeenth in singles in 1961. (The 6&5 singles loss to Littler obviously was an aberration.) In a nice bit of closure, when Haliburton retired from competitive golf shortly after the 1963 Cup, he became the club pro at Wentworth, where it all began.

FINAL SCORE

COURSE:

EAST LAKE CC | ATLANTA | GA

1963

FOURSOMES

MORNING

Palmer/Pott lost to Huggett/Will, 3&2

Casper/Ragan d. Alliss/O'Connor, 1-up

Boros/Lema halved with Coles/B. Hunt

Littler/Finsterwald halved
with Thomas/Weetman

AFTERNOON

Maxwell/Goalby d. Thomas/Weetman, 4&3

Palmer/Casper d. Huggett/Will, 5&4

Littler/Finsterwald d. Coles/G. Hunt, 2&1

Boros/Lema d. Haliburton/B. Hunt, 1-up

US: 6   GB: 2

FOURBALLS

MORNING

Palmer/Finsterwald d. Huggett/Thomas, 5&4

Littler/Boros halved with Alliss/B. Hunt

Casper/Maxwell d. Weetman/Will, 3&2

Goalby/Ragan lost to Coles/O'Connor, 1-up

AFTERNOON

Palmer/Finsterwald d. Coles/O'Connor, 3&2

Lema/Pott d. Alliss/B. Hunt, 1-up

Casper/Maxwell d. Haliburton/G. Hunt, 2&1

Goalby/Ragan halved with Huggett/Thomas

US: 6   GB: 2

SINGLES

MORNING

Lema d. G. Hunt, 5&3

Pott lost to Huggett, 3&1

Palmer lost to Alliss, 1-up

Casper halved with Coles

Goalby d. Thomas, 3&2

Littler d. O'Connor, 1-up

Boros lost to Weetman, 1-up

Finsterwald lost to B. Hunt, 2-up

AFTERNOON

Palmer d. Will, 3&2

Ragan d. Coles, 2&1

Lema halved with Alliss

Littler d. Haliburton, 6&5

Boros d. Weetman, 2&1

Maxwell d. O'Connor, 2&1

Finsterwald d. Thomas, 4&3

Goalby d. B. Hunt, 2&1

US: 11   GB: 5

TOTAL: **US 23**   **GB 09**

COURSE:

ROYAL BIRKDALE GC | SOUTHPORT | ENGLAND

OCT. **07-09**

1965

FINAL SCORE:

US **19-1/2**   GB **12-1/2**

CAPTAINS:

BYRON NELSON   HARRY WEETMAN

UNITED STATES

Julius Boros
Billy Casper
Tommy Jacobs
Don January
Tony Lema
Gene Littler
Dave Marr
Arnold Palmer
Johnny Pott
Ken Venturi

GREAT BRITAIN

Peter Alliss
Peter Butler
Neil Coles
Jimmy Hitchcock
Bernard Hunt
Jimmy Martin
Christy O'Connor Sr.
Lionel Platts
Dave Thomas
George Will

1927   1929   1931   1933   1935   1937   1947   1949

SAMUEL RYDER, ROBERT HUDSON, STUART GOODWIN. Every few years, an individual stepped up, kicked in some money, and saved the Ryder Cup. It happened again in time for the 1965 Matches, and his name was Brian Park. A successful businessman, vice-chairman of the British PGA, and a former captain of Royal Birkdale, site of that year's contest, Park ponied up eleven thousand pounds when no sponsor was on the horizon.

Perhaps more important than Park's financial contribution was his conviction that the Ryder Cup needed to be run more smoothly, and much more for those who came to witness the grand spectacle. He attended the matches in 1963 to see how things were done in America and came back with a cranium full of ideas that were not only applied to the Ryder Cup, but in time to all professional golf in Britain.

Many of Park's improvements benefited the spectators. Whether they were for food, comfort, or safety, few facilities had ever been available to the many thousands who attended golf tournaments in the British Isles. Under Park's command, a tented village was erected, featuring food counters, lavatories, first aid, a mobile post office, and a huge exhibition area where fans could buy everything from golf clubs to sweaters. They could also could buy a 160-page program full of articles and advertisements—a far cry from the traditional one-page-of-toilet-paper pairing sheets.

Park also realized it was important to take care of the press by getting them hammered. The matches at Birkdale welcomed the largest gathering of golf writers ever to Britain. They got their own wooden building near the final green, allowing easy entrance to the nearest bar, which naturally, few of them ever left. Hell hath no fury like a writer sobered. However, it was made easy for them to stumble into players coming off the course, and observation towers around the course that gave reporters and photographers unimpeded views of both the bar and the action were erected. Also, spectators and scribes alike were able to follow the progress of every match as female golfers (including some well-known amateurs) drove Mini Mokes (a kind of British version of the beach buggy) fitted with scoreboards. The records do not show how many innocent bystanders were killed or maimed by these lurching leaderboards, but you know it happened.

With Park in control, the British PGA finally looked like they knew how to organize a Ryder Cup, but they still had to prove that they could win one again, or at least keep it close.

Harry Weetman, who'd been slapped on the wrist by the PGA after falling out with Dai Rees in 1957, had atoned for his sins and was given the captaincy of a team featuring a mix of old and new faces. (Rees was there, too, but as a television commentator.) Back for more were Peter Alliss, Neil Coles, Bernard Hunt, Christy O'Connor, Dave Thomas, and George Will; joining them were Peter Butler (possibly the meanest man ever to play golf), Jimmy Hitchcock, Jimmy Martin, and Lionel Platts, whose clubs looked like a set of four-irons. As always, the British public was quick to forget the results of two years earlier. They were emboldened by the success of GB's amateur team, which had traveled to the States earlier that summer and had, in a shocker, tied the Americans. Weetman had sent the Walker Cup captain, Joe Carr, a telegram that read, "Great golf. Well done. Don't destroy the recipe. Save it for me."

Byron Nelson, whom the players had chosen as captain, led the Americans. (Nelson remembers this practice being followed for just a few years—the PGA picking the players, the players choosing the captain.) He had the usual strong cast of characters: Julius Boros, Billy Casper, Tony Lema, Gene Littler, Arnold Palmer, and Johnny Pott, plus rookies Tommy Jacobs, Don January, Dave Marr, and in his first and only Ryder Cup, Ken Venturi. At the last minute, Pott pulled a muscle in his rib cage and had to withdraw. There was talk of writing home for Mike Souchak, who was next on the points list, but Nelson felt his nine remaining players were up to the task, explaining that they'd earned more than four million dollars in prize money so were "used to holing pressure putts on the big occasion." No word on what Souchak thought of *that* decision.

COURSE | ROYAL BIRKDALE GC, SOUTHPORT, ENGLAND

SENIOR SERVICE SCORE CAR

MATCH NO. |6|

🇬🇧 | | UP

🇺🇸 |1| UP

GENERAL VIEW OF THE COURSE AT ROYAL BIRKDALE (WHAT THE HELL WAS THE FENCE FOR?)

However, it wasn't likely that the Cup would be won or lost on the greens. Heavy rain before the matches had softened the wonderful old links, making it play less linksy and more parkland—slow and tame. Especially over the closing holes—four of the last six were par-fives of more than 500 yards each—the conditions meant no one would be hitting the greens in two, leaving shots in the fifty-- to hundred-yard range. This gave the advantage to the Americans, as Will explained after the fact:

"I noted that the Americans played this shot with their wedges much more stiff-wristed than our team. This produced the low flight, the quick check and then roll. [The Brits tended to hit a higher lob shot that would bounce, sometimes unpredictably.] Perhaps one reason why the Americans excel at this shot is that they invariably play on well-watered greens, whereas we play on a different type of course each week—sometimes fast-running and sometimes soft. Birkdale was in really magnificent condition but the rain prior to the match had made it ideal from the American point of view."

Nice weather for the matches brought out the crowds, 50,000 spectators over the three days. Those in attendance the first day were cheered by the home team's unexpectedly strong showing in the foursomes.

The big upset in the morning was the 6&5 defeat of Palmer and Marr—who didn't win a hole—by Thomas and Will. The locals started birdie-birdie-birdie: Marr, in his first Ryder Cup, later said, "At the start I was nervous, and by the third hole I was downright embarrassed." Marr noticed Arnold's hand shaking as he teed up his ball on the first tee. "That scared me to death," Marr recalled, "and my golf thereafter certainly didn't help Arnold: Some of the places I put him in weren't even on the golf course." O'Connor and Alliss had a similarly big win, 5&4, over Venturi and January. The two American wins were closer, and the morning ended in a 2-2 tie.

While most of the players ate lunch, Palmer and Marr feasted on the driving range and then took a bite out of Thomas and Will, besting them in an afternoon rematch, 6&5. The Americans ran off six straight threes from the second hole to the seventh (a collective five-under-par), mostly on the strength of Palmer's irons and putter. This time, the home team didn't win a hole. Afterward, when asked about the thrashing, all Will could muster was "Blimey!" which, under the circumstances, was very polite. Boros and Lema jumped all over rookies Martin and Hitchcock 5&4, but the brilliant pair of O'Connor and Alliss remained in top form with a 2&1 win over Casper and Littler. Another 2-2 tie and the day ended at 4-4.

Day two's fourballs were almost as close. Seven of the eight matches went to the eighteenth hole, and the U.S. team had a slight lead at the end of the day, winning 5-3. But the score could so easily have been in Britain's favor.

The only decisive win was Palmer and Marr 5&4 over Alliss and O'Connor in the morning. They were the third match off, but the first to finish. The two that followed were crucial to the British team's spirit, and some have argued they were where the Cup was lost. Perhaps, but they certainly proved that the Americans are never to be counted out (and why the U.S. was right to insist on fourballs).

Thomas and Will were four holes up on January and Jacobs with seven to play. Then the wheels fell off. The Americans holed every putt they looked at, and halving the final hole gave the U.S. team an unexpected victory, 1-up. Right behind them, Platts and Butler were 3-up at the turn and got to dormie—four-up with four holes to play—when lightning struck again: Peter Butler three-putted fifteen, and Littler birdied the last three holes to scratch out a half. It might have been the only thing that Butty (who was so mean he would wake himself up in the middle of the night to make sure he hadn't lost any sleep) had ever given away. In the final morning match, Boros and Lema lost 1-up to Hunt and Coles. (And it's here that once again we acknowledge the greatness of Henry "one for the ditch" Longhurst, who wincingly noted that the team of "Hunt and Coles" was the commentator's nightmare.)

A morning that easily could have seen GB taking three points actually finished with the U.S. winning 2-1/2 to 1-1/2. The afternoon ended with the identical score and identical results.

Alliss and O'Connor exacted a measure of revenge on Palmer and Marr, winning 2-up when Alliss hit a magnificent fairway wood onto the can't-be-reached-in-two eighteenth green. Then history repeated itself not once, but twice. January and Jacobs again beat Thomas and Will 1-up. Then Casper/Littler and Platts/Butler again fought to halve, the Brits again losing a four-hole lead, albeit with ten to play. Okay, so Butty gave away two things. In the last match of the day, Venturi finally won a Ryder Cup point (it would be his only one), teaming with Lema for a 1-up victory on Coles and Hunt.

Going 5-3 in fourballs gave the U.S. team a slim 9-7 lead going into singles. It was on the final day that the psychological strain seemed to eat away at the home team, which needed to win early and often, but couldn't.

Captain Nelson sealed victory in the morning, sending out his big guns first—Palmer, Boros, and Lema (who had won the hearts of the British fans when he won the Claret Jug at St. Andrews the year before). They came through as expected with fairly easy wins, as did Marr and Jacobs. In the eight morning singles, Hunt and Alliss won and Will halved for Britain's 2-1/2 points.

When Nelson repeated his strategy in the afternoon—changing the order a bit and leading with Lema, Boros, and Palmer—the Cup was secured. Lema recorded a fast 6&4 win over an ailing O'Connor, then it was just a question of who would notch the winning point. It came from Boros, who parred seventeen to close out his match 2&1 over Hitchcock just seconds before Arnold eagled eighteen to top Butler, 2-up. Behind them, Alliss, Coles, and Platts won their matches for the home team, but the score for the day went down as a lopsided 10-1/2 to 5-1/2.

PETER ALLISS (NOT UNLIKE HIS DEAR OLD DAD)

BRITISH PRIME MINISTER HAROLD WILSON PRESENTS THE RYDER CUP TROPHY TO THE AMERICAN CAPTAIN BYRON NELSON

Ever the gentleman, Nelson said "if the Americans had missed half a dozen putts that they holed and Britain and Ireland had holed half a dozen that they missed. the result might well have been reversed."

What made the difference was playing through pressure, which the U.S. team seemed to do better. Some bright spark calculated that if each game had been stopped after nine holes, the home team would have won, 17-1/2 to 14-1/2, but as far as anyone knows, shortening the matches was never discussed for future meetings.

The star of the week was Tony Lema, who won five out of six matches. "Champagne" Tony hung around a few more weeks, making it to the finals of the Piccadilly Match-Play Tournament where he lost to Gary Player. Tragically, it would be his last appearance in Britain: He died early the next year in a plane crash.

FINAL SCORE

COURSE:

ROYAL BIRKDALE GC | SOUTHPORT | ENGLAND

1965

FOURSOMES

MORNING

Boros/Lema d. Platts/Butler, 1-up

Marr/Palmer lost to Thomas/Will, 6&5

Casper/Littler d. Hunt/Coles, 2&1

Venturi/January lost to O'Connor/Alliss, 5&4

AFTERNOON

Marr/Palmer d. Thomas/Will, 6&5

Boros/Lema d. Martin/Hitchcock, 5&4

Casper/Littler lost to O'Connor/Alliss, 2&1

Venturi/January lost to Hunt/Coles, 3&2

US: 4   GB: 4

FOURBALLS

MORNING

January/Jacobs d. Thomas/Will, 1-up

Casper/Littler halved with Platts/Butler

Marr/Palmer d. Alliss/O'Connor, 5&4

Boros/Lema lost to Coles/Hunt, 1-up

AFTERNOON

Marr/Palmer lost to Alliss/O'Connor, 2-up

January/Jacobs d. Thomas/Will, 1-up

Casper/Littler halved with Platts/Butler

Lema/Venturi d. Coles/Hunt, 1-up

US: 5   GB: 3

SINGLES

MORNING

Palmer d. Hitchcock, 3&2

Boros d. Platts, 4&2

Lema d. Butler, 1-up

Marr d. Coles, 2-up

Littler lost to Hunt, 2-up

Casper lost to Alliss, 1-up

Jacobs d. Thomas, 2&1

January halved with Will

AFTERNOON

Palmer d. Butler, 2-up

Boros d. Hitchcock, 2&1

Lema d. O'Connor, 6&4

Venturi lost to Alliss, 3&2

Marr d. Hunt, 1-up

Casper lost to Coles, 3&2

Littler d. Will, 2&1

Jacobs lost to Platts, 1-up

US: 10-1/2   GB: 5-1/2

TOTAL: US 19-1/2   GB 12-1/2

DATE : OCT. 07-09

COURSE:

CHAMPIONS GC | HOUSTON | TX

OCT. 20-22

1967

FINAL SCORE:

 US 23-1/2 | GB 08-1/2

CAPTAINS:

BEN HOGAN | DAI REES

UNITED STATES | GREAT BRITAIN

UNITED STATES	GREAT BRITAIN
Julius Boros	Peter Alliss
Gay Brewer	Hugh Boyle
Billy Casper	Neil Coles
Gardner Dickinson	Malcolm Gregson
Al Geiberger	Brian Huggett
Gene Littler	Bernard Hunt
Bobby Nichols	Tony Jacklin
Arnold Palmer	Christy O'Connor Sr.
Johnny Pott	Dave Thomas
Doug Sanders	George Will

Courtesy of The PGA of America

BEN HOGAN'S RECORD IN THE RYDER CUP WAS PERFECT. He played three matches
in two years (1947 and 1951) and was undefeated. He captained the team in 1947 and 1949 and was undefeated.
So when the matches came to his native Texas in 1967 and he was named captain, there was no way in hell this
gaping asshole of a man was going to lose.

Hogan's life story is all too well known. He came up from nothing, learned to play golf while caddying (coincidentally, at the same club where the young Byron Nelson—definitely not an asshole—also looped), then struggled as a
young pro before finding his "secret" and breaking through. Once his famous swing became machinelike, he forged
a magnificent career highlighted by two Masters, four U.S. Opens, one Open Championship, and a spectacular car
crash. Then there was the long convalescence, and an amazing return to glory. In life, too, he was undefeated.

He had earned his nickname, the "wee ice mon" for his cold, flinty demeanor. He was a loner, a perfectionist,
and quite possibly a total asshole, but a man for whom the expression "dig it out of the dirt" referred not only to his
work ethic but to his entire life.

The man in the white cap, a smoldering butt dangling from his lips, was possibly the greatest golfer nobody
really ever knew. And he was a man who scared the shit out of just about everyone, including his own team.

And what a team it was—Julius Boros, Gay Brewer, Billy Casper, Gardner Dickinson, Al Geiberger, Gene Littler,
Bobby Nichols, Arnold Palmer, Johnny Pott, and Doug Sanders. No weak links, no nobodies. They were so good that
few observers worried about the absence of the game's best player, Jack Nicklaus. Earlier that year, Nicklaus had

finished the mandatory five-year wait imposed by the PGA, but it left him only nine months to earn enough points to make the team when everyone else had two years. Despite having already won seven majors—including three during the point-amassing period—Jack figured it was missing the cut at the 1967 Masters that kept him off the team. (Incredibly, it was only the second time as a professional he missed the cut in a major. The next time he'd miss at Augusta would be 1994!)

Coming across the ocean to face the American juggernaut was a good British team under captain Dai Rees, who was picked in hopes of resurrecting the glory of Lindrick, now ten years past. Most of the players were experienced Ryder Cuppers: Peter Alliss, Neil Coles, Brian Huggett, Bernard Hunt, Christy O'Connor, Dave Thomas, and George Will had all played in the States four years earlier, and only the gnomelike Huggett hadn't been on the squad at Birkdale. Of the three new men, two of them—Hugh Boyle and Malcolm Gregson—would be making their only Cup appearance. But the third was an exciting young Englishman with great prospects, Tony Jacklin, who just squeaked onto the team, finishing tenth in Cup points.

At the gala dinner before the matches began, each captain introduced his team. Rees "made rather a meal of it," wrote Peter Alliss in his autobiography, "going on about the things each of us had won and done. As we stood up in turn, there were polite ripples of applause."

Then it was Hogan's turn. Each player stood as The Hawk announced his name. When all ten were standing, Hogan said, "Ladies and gentlemen, the United States Ryder Cup team: The finest golfers in the world."

As Alliss put it, "The British ten down before a ball had been hit."

No matter what he said, Hogan didn't treat his players as if they were the world's finest. He ordered them to practice and then, watching them on the range, would walk up and down the line muttering just loudly enough for them to hear, "I've never seen so many god-awful shots in my life." He set a 10:30 curfew, banned them from attending most of the week's social events, and dictatorially decreed that his team would play the smaller British ball.

Hogan was at his imperial assholiest with Palmer. Maybe the fifty-five-year-old was jealous of thirty-eight-year-old Palmer's success: Arnold was about to become the first golfer to earn more than $1 million in a career, and it had taken him only thirteen years to do it; in twenty-two years, Hogan's winnings were barely over $200,000. Hogan was definitely pissed off at Palmer for giving one of the British team members (the identity of the treasonous euro-heathen remains a mystery to this day) a ride in his private plane, but whatever the reasons, the captain made sure "the King" knew who was boss.

In the locker room before the first practice round, Palmer asked his captain, "Say, Ben, is it true that we are going to play the small ball?" Hogan said it was. Arnold pressed on, "Well, what if I don't have any small balls?" Hogan shot back: "Who said you were playing?" And here's a good one—Hogan never, ever called Palmer by his first name! But while he might have been mean enough to threaten to bench the most important person ever to play golf, he wasn't dumb enough to follow through.

Things could not have been more different in the other locker room. Rees ran his team by committee, asking for his players' input on pairings and the order of play. It may have been his way of keeping their spirits up, because nobody gave the Brits a frozen turd's chance in the asshole of hell. The prevailing sentiment was best put by Palmer's agent, Mark McCormack, who wrote, "Americans playing on their home ground are no more likely to lose than Boston is likely to apologize for the tea party." Ha ha farking ha, Mark.

Indeed, like the tea, the British and Irish got dunked.

The first morning's foursomes actually went fairly well for the visitors, with one win—from Thomas and Jacklin—and a half. But the two veteran teams, Alliss/O'Connor and Hunt/Coles, both went down, the latter especially hard. Standing in the middle of the first fairway, Hunt, in his seventh Cup, said to Coles, "I don't think I can hit this." Such is Ryder Cup pressure, but I said something similar to Sam Torrance in 1991, and he hit me.

The matches could—and some would argue should—have ended there. The Brits and Micks were only a point behind, but it was the last time they'd be close.

Much to Henry Longhurst's relief, Hunt and Coles sat in the afternoon, and the rookies Malcolm Gregson and Hugh Boyle were thrown to the lions, Palmer and Dickinson. Arnold could have flown around in his airplane as Dickinson wielded a hot putter to a five-hole lead at the turn and a 5&4 win. Huggett and Will, who'd fought for a valiant tie with Casper and Boros in the morning, staged a rematch in the afternoon and fought just as hard, but a few wayward shots were enough to give the Americans the victory, 1-up. Jacklin and Thomas won again, but Alliss and O'Connor lost, and the American lead had widened to three points.

The fourballs remained America's province. Since being introduced in 1963, sixteen matches had been played and the old sodders had won only three of them. They didn't add any to that column this year, managing only a half from Jacklin and Thomas in the afternoon. In their defense, four of the matches went to the eighteenth hole, where they lost three and halved one. The Americans' near-sweep was accomplished without

ARNOLD PALMER WATCHES GARDNER DICKINSON PUTT

Palmer's participation in the morning: Hogan sat his man down despite two convincing wins the first day. Was it a power trip or smart strategy, resting his top player for later? In public, Palmer told his captain, "Whatever you decide suits me fine." Privately, Arnold admitted that he was a bit tired. And the rest may have done him some good as he and Boros had to battle back from 4-down at the turn to win, 1-up.

Having earned 7-1/2 out of 8 possible points on day two, and needing just three points from sixteen matches to keep the Cup, Hogan probably could have rested his entire team. As it was, the United States won nine matches, lost four, and halved three: Palmer and Geiberger won both of their singles; only Sanders lost both of his. The Cup was safe long before the morning was over.

The fifteen-point margin remains the biggest in Cup history, and many of the individual records are just as impressive. Palmer had gone five for five, as had Dickinson (who Hogan sat during the morning singles). Pott was four for four; Nichols four wins and a half, same as Casper. Only one British player had a "winning" record: Big Dave Thomas was 2-1-2. Of the ten matches to reach the final hole, the Americans lost only one.

That last statistic may have been the most telling, and it led to a long winter of postmortems. Rees, who couldn't be faulted for how his team performed, pressed for significant changes to British golf, including more tournaments to toughen the players, better greens to promote better putting, and adoption of the bigger ball. This last idea became a rallying cry, a vital step toward improving the ball-control skills that were so obviously lacking, especially on and around the greens. (The British PGA ruled that the larger ball would be required for tournament play starting the following year.)

Rees also suggested reducing the teams to eight players each. Others again brought up the idea of expanding the British team to include golfers from throughout the Commonwealth. Such was the depth of despair across the Atlantic that the highly respected golf writer, Henry Longhurst, considered the unthinkable:

> "This is a moment perhaps to ask whether it is really fair to expect the Americans to go on with this match. . . . There is little public interest in it in America and no company regards it as worth televising. . . . The chances of a British team ever beating the USA again are, however much one may bang the patriotic drum, virtually nil."

Beat the USA? Just a close match would do the series a world of good.

FINAL SCORE

COURSE:

CHAMPIONS GC   HOUSTON   TX

1967

FOURSOMES

MORNING

Casper/Boros halved with Huggett/Will

Palmer/Dickinson d. Alliss/O'Connor, 2&1

Sanders/Brewer lost to Jacklin/Thomas, 4&3

Nichols/Pott d. Hunt/Coles, 6&5

AFTERNOON

Boros/Casper d. Huggett/Will, 1-up

Dickinson/Palmer d. Gregson/Boyle, 5&4

Littler/Geiberger lost to Jacklin/Thomas, 3&2

Nichols/Pott d. Alliss/O'Connor, 2&1

US: 5-1/2   GB: 2-1/2

FOURBALLS

MORNING

Casper/Brewer d/ Alliss/O'Connor, 3&2

Nichols/Pott d. Hunt/Coles, 1-up

Littler/Geiberger d. Jacklin/Thomas, 1-up

Dickinson/Sanders d. Huggett/Will, 3&2

AFTERNOON

Casper/Brewer d. Hunt/Coles, 5&3

Dickinson/Sanders d. Alliss/Gregson, 3&2

Palmer/Boros d. Will/Boyle, 1-up

Littler/Geiberger halved with Jacklin/Thomas

US: 7-1/2   GB: 1/2

SINGLES

MORNING

Brewer d. Boyle, 4&3

Casper d. Alliss, 2&1

Palmer d. Jacklin, 3&2

Boros lost to Huggett, 1-up

Sanders lost to Coles, 2&1

Geiberger d. Gregson, 4&2

Littler halved with Thomas

Nichols halved with Hunt

AFTERNOON

Palmer d. Huggett, 5&3

Brewer lost to Alliss, 2&1

Dickinson d. Jacklin, 3&2

Nichols d. O'Connor, 3&2

Pott d. Will, 3&1

Geiberger d. Gregson, 2&1

Boros halved with Hunt

Sanders lost to Coles, 2&1

US: 10-1/2   GB: 5-1/2

TOTAL: US 23-1/2   GB 08-1/2

HARRY WEETMAN : (1920–1972)

HARRY WEETMAN was a mainstay of British Ryder Cup teams throughout the 1950s and early 1960s. A good player who relied on length off the tee plus solid putting, he was a proven champion during those years: Five times in the finals of the British PGA Championship between 1951 and 1960, he won it twice, showing an affinity for match play; he also twice won the Dunlop Masters and four times the Penfold tournament, both top events on the British circuit.

However, in those days a "good" player was rarely good enough against the Americans, whose Cup teams were usually far superior. Weetman's record is proof of that imbalance: He played on seven Cup teams and in fifteen matches, yet accounted for only three points— two wins in singles and two halves in foursomes versus eleven losses.

His moment in the sun—and the sun did shine at Wentworth that year—came in 1953. It was Weetman's second Cup appearance, having lost in the singles two years earlier to Lloyd Mangrum, 6&5, then losing with Percy Alliss to Porky Oliver and Dave Douglas, 2&1, in the previous day's foursomes. Based on the captains' lineups, Weetman found himself matched against the best golfer in the world, Sam Snead, who was 7-1 in Cup matches.

No one was surprised when Snead held a four-hole lead over Weetman after the morning round, although they may have been a little perplexed that the lead hadn't grown with six holes to go. That's when Snead fell apart, going seven-over-par on holes thirteen through sixteen and falling back into a tie. After halving the par-five seventeenth, Weetman birdied and Snead parred the par-five final hole. The Englishman's victory would prove to be Snead's only defeat in seven Ryder Cup singles matches.

Weetman played on every team through 1963, not winning his second match until his final year, when he beat Julius Boros, 1-up, in the morning singles, though Boros exacted his revenge that afternoon, winning 2&1. More shocking than those exercises in futility was his behavior during the 1957 match. Both he and partner Max Faulkner had played poorly in the foursomes and suggested to captain Dai Rees that they sit out the singles. Rees obliged them, then was shocked to hear from a reporter that his friend had said he'd never play for Rees again. The feud cast a pall over Britain's first Cup victory in twenty years and resulted in Weetman's suspension from PGA events for a year. That punishment was later shortened—at Rees's suggestion. And Weetman did, indeed, play for Rees again, in 1959 and 1961.

In 1965, it was Weetman's turn to be non-playing captain. Despite his team's loss to Byron Nelson's squad 19-1/2 to 12-1/2, the captaincy meant that Weetman was back in the good graces of the British golf establishment. Sadly, he died in a car crash in 1972.

COURSE:

ROYAL BIRKDALE GC | SOUTHPORT | ENGLAND

SEPT. **18-20**

1969

FINAL SCORE:

☆ US **16** ★ GB **16**

CAPTAINS:

SAM SNEAD   ## ERIC BROWN

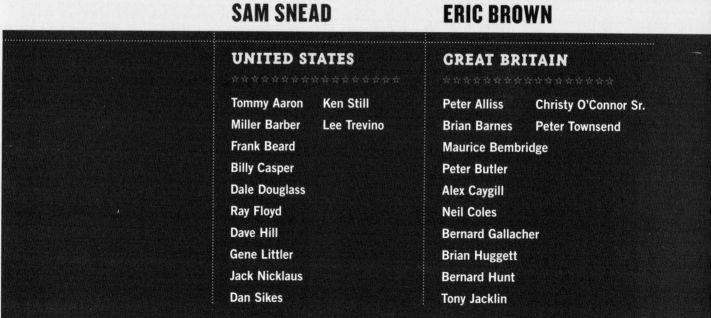

UNITED STATES

Tommy Aaron	Ken Still
Miller Barber	Lee Trevino
Frank Beard	
Billy Casper	
Dale Douglass	
Ray Floyd	
Dave Hill	
Gene Littler	
Jack Nicklaus	
Dan Sikes	

GREAT BRITAIN

Peter Alliss	Christy O'Connor Sr.
Brian Barnes	Peter Townsend
Maurice Bembridge	
Peter Butler	
Alex Caygill	
Neil Coles	
Bernard Gallacher	
Brian Huggett	
Bernard Hunt	
Tony Jacklin	

1967   ☆   1971   1973   1975   1977   1979   1981   1983

1969

HURTLING TOWARD THE SEVENTIES, we're about to get into a more interesting period in the history of the little pot. It's ironic that the Match featuring the debut of Jack Nicklaus and his act of sportsmanship that went down in golf lore was marred by the most acrimonious atmosphere since the dispute over grooves at Ganton two decades earlier. About time too. Frankly, I'm sick of writing about people behaving themselves.

Nicklaus was one of ten rookies on the U.S. team, the size of the squads having been enlarged to twelve, which took a little pressure off the players and gave the captains more options. (And it also might have been a slap at former British captain Dai Rees, who after the embarrassment two years earlier in Houston, had suggested that the size of the teams be reduced. Hey, if it had been up to me, I would have reduced the size of the *American* team only.) Sam Snead, third in a row of elder statesmen to captain the Americans, had only two veterans among his dozen, Billy Casper and Gene Littler. But thanks to the points system they used, all were battle-hardened: Besides Nicklaus, the new blood was Tommy Aaron, Miller Barber, Frank Beard, Dale Douglass, Ray Floyd (who'd won the PGA Championship a month earlier), Dave Hill, Dan Sikes, Ken Still, and the winner of the U.S. Open the year before, Lee Trevino. The team was so strong that the winners of the 1969 Masters and U.S. Open, George Archer and Orville Moody, hadn't qualified.

As for the winner of the Claret Jug that year, Tony Jacklin, he was on the British team and giving the home fans reason for cheer and guarded optimism. Jacklin had proven himself in America, where he'd been playing (and winning) for a few years. He joined a hopeful mix of the wizened and the wet behind the ears: Former Cuppers Peter Alliss (in his last appearance), Peter Butler, Neil Coles, Brian Huggett, Bernard Hunt, and Christy O'Connor

LEE TREVINO

welcomed new boys Brian Barnes, Maurice Bembridge, Alex Caygill, Bernard Gallacher (at twenty, the youngest ever on a British team), and Peter "Tiddler" Townsend—no, not the guitarist for The Who, although that certainly would have been interesting. Leading them was Eric "Fuck you" Brown, famous for his angry confrontations with Lloyd Mangrum and Tommy Bolt in the 1950s.

Another change was the mandatory use of the larger American ball, which might not mean an advantage for either team—the bigger ball was easier to control in the short game, shorter and harder to hit into or across breeze—but would eliminate an excuse from the losing side's post-match ravings.

Speaking of balls, as a player Brown had proven he had them; as captain, he showed he was still willing to get them out and wave them around, damn the consequences. Before the matches began, he instructed his team that they were not to help the Americans look for any errant shots in the thick rough. Some of Brown's players tried to explain that this was meant to keep play moving and avoid accidentally stepping on an opponent's ball, which, they incorrectly believed, would have been a penalty. Yeah, right. The press eagerly took the bone and chewed it, and the Americans took the rival captain's mandate as an act of war. Splendid!

It didn't take long for the hostilities to reach the playing field. In the second match of the morning foursomes, Trevino was paired with Still against Gallacher and Bembridge. On the thirteenth tee, Bembridge asked Still to get

TONY JACKLIN SHAKES HANDS WITH JACK NICKLAUS

out of his field of vision, which was pretty limited anyway, as he's not a whole lot over five feet tall. But the American responded by making an asshole out of himself and a big production of moving everyone—players, caddies, officials—to the other side of the tee box. On the same hole—after Still had hooked his drive into the rough and Trevino could do no better than plug the next shot in a bunker—Still tried to blast out of the sand. The ball appeared to hit Still in the shoulder, which would have been a penalty. Even Trevino thought his partner had been hit, but when he asked, "It hit you, didn't it?" no answer came in reply. To his credit, Trevino told Still to pick up, and conceded the hole. It contributed to a 2&1 win for Gallacher and Bembridge.

The British won three and halved one of those morning matches, giving them a rare opening lead, and a sizeable one at that, 3-1/2 to 1/2. At lunch, while they congratulated one another, Snead was cursing a blue streak at his team. Whatever he said (and we can make a pretty good guess) worked: The afternoon was a near reversal, with the U.S. team winning three and losing one. One of the victories was Nicklaus's Ryder Cup debut, pairing with Sikes to defeat Hunt and Butler, 1-up. The sole British victory came from Jacklin and Townsend, who also had won in the morning. At the end of the first day, the home squad still had the lead, although it had shrunk to a single point.

Local fans were nervous going into day two. Fourballs continued to haunt the GB team, which had been winless in eight matches two years earlier. Breaking up the winning pair of Jacklin and Townsend wasn't a confidence builder, but captain Brown's move worked as Jacklin teamed with Coles to beat Nicklaus and Sikes, while Townsend, who played brilliantly the first two days, played with O'Connor and beat Hill and Douglass. Trevino and Littler, who'd won the previous afternoon, stayed hot and produced America's only point, a 1-up win over Barnes and Alliss. The 2-1/2 to 1-1/2 British win in the morning increased their cushion to two points, and the home crowd started to feel that maybe, just maybe, something special was in the air. Sadly, it was only the stench of Ken Still's shitty attitude.

In the afternoon, Nicklaus sat and Still played. (What the hell was Sam Snead thinking?) That's when the bad blood boiled over in an episode as nasty as any in Cup history.

Again, Still was in the middle of it—actually in the second match, paired with Hill against Huggett and Gallacher (both of whom are capable of getting into a pissing match). On the first green, Huggett asked Hill to stop moving around and told Still to give him room. (His exact words were "I want you behind me from now on.") Pretty good, considering how early it was. On the *second* green, Still's caddie was tending the flag as Gallacher was preparing to putt: Still waited until the Scotsman was about to draw back his blade then yelled at his bagman that a British caddie should be holding the flag. What a gaping asshole—I'd like to have seen him playing Ballesteros.

On the seventh green, with the U.S. pair up two, Hill missed a putt then immediately holed the remaining two-footer. Gallacher snapped at Hill that he'd putted out of turn, and before a referee could step in, Hill picked up Gallacher's marker (which was three feet from the hole), threw it at him, and said, "You can have the hole and the goddamned Cup!" Stomping off the green, Still and Huggett jawed at each other and the crowd hissed the Americans.

On the next green, Still had a short par putt that he wanted to make as a way of giving his partner a read for his birdie try. But Bernard Gallacher, who knew the rules, conceded the putt, picking up Still's ball and handing it to him, which Still said was a penalty (uh, wrong Kenny) and that the hole should go to the U.S. (also wrong, but at least this asshole was consistent). It didn't matter, as Hill made his winning putt, but by that point all four players were fuming, and both captains were on the scene along with Lord Derby, president of the British PGA (who at this stage could have been forgiven for pretending to be as visable as a Nazi war criminal), and the crowd was as hot as the golfers. Eventually calm, or something like it, was restored. But Still never recovered from his anger, leaving Hill to play like a man and ensure a 2&1 victory.

That evening, back in the Prince of bloody Wales Hotel in Southport, Hill and Huggett continued arguing in the hallway outside the hotel restaurant. "But that was the end of it," Huggett reported, "and when immediately after the Ryder Cup we all flew to America for the Alcan tournament, Hill came down the aisle and said to me, 'How about a practice round together?' It was a nice peace offering." (I'd love to know who won that practice round and if the loser paid up.)

The other three matches were quiet, but the Americans continued their fourball dominance, winning two and halving two. Seven of the eight matches had gone to the final hole (the only one that didn't was the nasty business), and the Brits and Bogtrotters had won two, lost two, and tied three, by far their best showing in this format. But the Americans won the day, 4-1/2 to 3-1/2, tying the matches after two days at 8-8.

After the jiggery-pokery of the first two days, the singles matches were peaceful, sportingly fought, and charged with emotion, with the result coming down to the final match.

The Americans took their first lead of the weekend when Alliss lost to Trevino and Townsend fell to Hill. In the fourth match, Casper would beat Barnes, but before that, Neil Coles would fight back from 1-down, birdieing the sixteenth and eagling the seventeenth to defeat Tommy Aaron 1-up. From then on it was all Britain and Ireland: O'Connor over Beard 5&4; Bembridge 1-up on Still (what a damned shame); Butler 1-up on Floyd; and in the battle everyone wanted to see, Jacklin 4&3 over Nicklaus, who couldn't have made a short putt into the hole in a toilet seat.

The British had a two-point lead with the afternoon singles remaining. Three wins and a half from eight matches would bring the Cup home for the first time in twelve years.

The play was neither stellar nor especially close, but the afternoon was exciting as teams traded victories. Dave Hill—who despite everything was undefeated since teaming with Still—won his second singles, defeating Barnes 4&2. Trevino lost to a rested Gallacher 4&3, bringing the Brits one point closer.

Barber had no problem with Bembridge, winning 7&6. Butler took the lead over Douglass, lost it, then played steady and won 3&2. Littler held off O'Connor 2&1, while Coles beat himself and lost to Sikes 4&3. It would come down to the last two matches—Casper vs. Huggett, and the rematch of Jacklin against Nicklaus.

Casper and Huggett seesawed along. They were even at the turn, Casper won the tenth, the next five holes were halved, Huggett won sixteen. The par-five seventeenth was halved when Huggett holed a five-footer. Both hit the green of the par-five eighteenth in two. Casper two-putted, leaving Huggett ten yards from the win, but his first putt rolled five feet past. While sizing up the comebacker, a huge roar erupted on the seventeenth green. Thinking Jacklin had won his match, Huggett realized his putt for a half would give Britain the Cup. He holed it, shook Casper's hand, then fell into the arms of Captain Brown and wept.

TONY JACKLIN AND JACK NICKLAUS

Huggett earned his half, but he had misread (or misheard) what had happened one hole back.

Neither Nicklaus nor Jacklin played his best. They traded the lead, were even at the turn, and stayed that way until Jacklin lost the sixteenth. The roar Huggett heard was the sound of Jacklin holing a long eagle putt on seventeen to tie the match. This was what it was all about—all square, one hole to go, the Ryder Cup on the line.

Both hit good drives on eighteen. Jacklin walked quickly ahead off the tee, but stopped when Nicklaus called his name. "How do you feel?" Jack asked. "Bloody awful," came the reply. "I thought you might," said golf's greatest player. "But if it's any consolation, so do I. A bugger, isn't it?"

Nicklaus put his approach in the middle of the green eight yards from the hole. Jacklin's ball ran to the back of the green, ten yards away, from where he took his time and rolled a beautiful putt that came up about two feet short. Nicklaus overdid his putt for the win, rolling the ball about four feet past.

As usual, Jack took his time lining up his putt, assumed his trademark crouch, and knocked the ball into the middle of the hole. Then he bent down, picked up Jacklin's marker, and offered both it and his hand to the Englishman, saying "I don't think you would have missed that putt, but in these circumstances I would never give you the opportunity."

The match was halved, the Matches were halved, and although the Americans would keep the Cup, everybody came out a winner.

Well, maybe not everybody. Some of Nicklaus's teammates weren't happy with his gesture, and would have preferred to make the young Jacklin sweat it out in front of 10,000 panting countrymen. Publicly, Snead said, "When it happened, all the boys thought it was ridiculous to give him that putt. We went over there to win, not to be good ole boys. I never would have given a putt like that—except maybe to my brother." (In private, Snead let loose with another blue streak, and for the record, no matter what he said he went over there for, he was definitely a good ole boy.)

Given the animosity displayed that week, Nicklaus's act was the perfect way to diffuse the situation and remind everyone that golf is a gentleman's game. And lest we forget, a tie meant the Cup stayed with the Americans. At the closing ceremony, the president of the PGA of America announced that the countries would share the Cup, each team keeping it for a year. With that, he handed it to Lord Derby.

It was as if Jack knew what was in store for the Cup, and understood the importance of the contest, no matter how one-sided it had been for years. If that's what it took for the British to get the Ryder Cup back in their hands, it was okay, no matter how Sam Snead felt. It would be a while before they'd grasp it again.

FINAL SCORE

COURSE:

ROYAL BIRKDALE GC | **SOUTHPORT** | **ENGLAND**

1969

FOURSOMES

MORNING

Barber/Floyd lost to Coles/Huggett, 3&2

Trevino/Still lost to Gallacher/Bembridge, 2&1

Hill/Aaron lost to Jacklin/Townsend, 3&1

Casper/Beard halved with O'Connor/Alliss

AFTERNOON

Hill/Aaron d. Coles/Huggett, 1-up

Trevino/Littler d. Gallacher/Bembridge, 2-up

Casper/Beard lost to Jacklin/Townsend, 1-up

Nicklaus/Sikes d. Hunt/Butler, 1-up

US: 3-1/2   GB: 4-1/2

FOURBALLS

MORNING

Hill/Douglass lost to O'Connor/Townsend, 1-up

Floyd/Barber halved with Huggett/Caygill

Trevino/Littler d. Barnes/Alliss, 1-up

Nicklaus/Sikes lost to Jacklin/Coles, 1-up

AFTERNOON

Casper/Beard d. Townsend/Butler, 2-up

Hill/Still d. Huggett/Gallacher, 2&1

Aaron/Floyd halved with Bembridge/Hunt

Trevino/Barber halved with Jacklin/Coles

US: 4-1/2   GB: 3-1/2

SINGLES

MORNING

Trevino d. Alliss, 2&1

Hill d. Townsend, 5&4

Aaron lost to Coles, 1-up

Casper d. Barnes, 1-up

Beard lost to O'Connor, 5&4

Still lost to Bembridge, 1-up

Floyd lost to Butler, 1-up

Nicklaus lost to Jacklin, 4&3

AFTERNOON

Hill d. Barnes, 4&2

Trevino lost to Gallacher, 4&3

Barber d. Bembridge, 7&6

Douglass lost to Butler, 3&2

Littler d. O'Connor, 2&1

Casper halved with Huggett

Sikes d. Coles, 4&3

Nicklaus halved with Jacklin

US: 8   GB: 8

TOTAL:

 us 16

 gb 16

COURSE:

OLD WARSON CC ST. LOUIS MO

☆☆☆☆☆☆☆☆☆☆ SEPT. **16-18**

1971

☆☆☆☆☆☆☆☆☆☆☆☆☆☆☆☆☆☆

FINAL SCORE:

☆ US **18-1/2** GB **13-1/2**

CAPTAINS:

JAY HEBERT   ## ERIC BROWN

UNITED STATES
☆☆☆☆☆☆☆☆☆☆☆☆☆

Miller Barber	Dave Stockton
Frank Beard	Lee Trevino
Billy Casper	
Charles Coody	
Gardner Dickinson	
Gene Littler	
Jack Nicklaus	
Arnold Palmer	
Mason Rudolph	
J. C. Snead	

GREAT BRITAIN
☆☆☆☆☆☆☆☆☆☆☆☆☆

Harry Bannerman	Peter Oosterhuis
Brian Barnes	Peter Townsend
Maurice Bembridge	
Peter Butler	
Neil Coles	
Bernard Gallacher	
John Garner	
Brian Huggett	
Tony Jacklin	
Christy O'Connor Sr.	

HOW MUCH CONFIDENCE COULD THE GB TEAMS HAVE HAD, having been beaten like an old mule year after year? Didn't it hurt that the American public hardly cared what happened and still their teams won? (These Matches weren't even on television in the States!) But still the Brits showed up, vowing each time that it would be their turn.

In 1971, we had reasons for optimism. Tony Jacklin was continuing to shine on the international stage, proving that his 1969 Open Championship victory was not a fluke by adding the 1970 U.S. Open. The tie at Birkdale two years earlier showed that GB didn't have to be doormats, and that they could hold their own in fourballs. And (gasp of horror!) their team selection process had been changed: The top six players from the money list (Order of Merit) received automatic berths along with six golfers chosen by the troika of returning captain Eric Brown and Cup veterans Dai Rees and Neil Coles. They would look especially for players who hadn't earned enough money on their home tour to qualify but were playing well elsewhere, as Jacklin was doing.

Along with the top six, numbers seven through nine from the Order of Merit made this team: Harry Bannerman, Brian Barnes, Maurice Bembridge, Peter Butler, Coles, Bernard Gallacher, Brian Huggett, Peter Townsend, and in the first of his many Cup appearances, Peter Oosterhuis (all except Bannerman and Oosterhuis had been at Birkdale). The committee also chose Jacklin, of course, as well as Christy O'Connor, who had missed much of the season with injuries and a bout with depression caused by the accidental spillage of a half-pint of Guinness on the third green at Royal Dublin. At Brown's insistence a young up-and-comer named John Garner was also included in

NEIL COLES AND CHRISTY O'CONNOR

PETER OOSTERHUIS AND BERNARD GALLAGHER ENJOY A FREE COKE AND A SUSPICIOUS BOTTLE OF SOMETHING ELSE

the squad. It was a young team, with eight players under thirty.

Nearly 200 members of the British Golf Supporters Association accompanied their boys on a chartered plane to the middle of the American heartland and landed in the middle of a heat wave (100 degrees during the practice rounds). Luckily, the weather would break before the first ball was struck; the American team wasn't likely to be as forgiving.

Four new names made the American squad: Charles Coody (winner of the most recent Masters), Mason Rudolph, J. C. Snead (Sam's nephew, if you believe in West Virginian genetics), and Dave Stockton (1970 PGA Champion)—the U.S. rookies had as many majors as the entire British side. Backing them were eight veterans: Miller Barber, Frank Beard, Billy Casper, Gardner Dickinson, Gene Littler, and the three reigning superstars of golf, Jack Nicklaus, Arnold Palmer, and Lee Trevino, who among them had nineteen majors (including the other three that year). Despite the fact that Trevino had recently had an appendectomy and Casper had broken a toe looking for his hotel room bathroom in the middle of the night, on paper it was a mismatch. As usual.

Looking for an edge, Brown offered a last-minute suggestion: Rather than a day of foursomes and then a day of fourballs, (each followed by an evening of highballs), he proposed changing the order of the games to one round of each the first two days. Brown thought mixing the formats might limit the American threat, especially in fourballs. If he had proposed the change earlier, his wish might have been granted. Instead, it would have to wait.

So the matches were played as planned. What was unexpected was how the action unfolded.

A surprise rainstorm washed out the opening ceremonies and delayed play for more than an hour, but blissfully lowered the temperature by nearly thirty degrees from the practice-round inferno. Once the matches began, they eerily resembled the first morning at Birkdale in 1969 as the Brits won three of four. The best golf was in the one British loss, in which Townsend and Oosterhuis fell to Palmer and Dickinson, 2-up. The tone was set on the first green, where Oosterhuis, who looked like he'd just stepped off the set of *Revenge of the Nerds,* faced his first putt in the Ryder Cup and holed a sixty-foot birdie to go 1-up. The lead went back and forth, never greater than a single hole. On eighteen, with the U.S. pair 1-up, Palmer's approach with a six-iron hit twenty feet past the hole and sucked back for a kick-in birdie and the victory.

In the final match, Hebert paired the long-hitting Nicklaus with the short but dialed-in-with-the-blade Stockton. But Jack's long game was off, negating his partner's touch on the greens, and even he wasn't long enough to position Stockton to reach the par fives. They were 4-down to Jacklin and Huggett after ten holes and lost 3&2. It was the fourth time Nicklaus and Jacklin had met in Cup play, and the Englishman was undefeated with three wins and one half.

Coles and O'Connor, the old men of the British team (thirty-seven and forty-seven, respectively) beat Casper and Barber, 2&1 in the morning, then were replaced in the afternoon by Bannerman and Gallacher, who beat the same American pair by the same scenario. Another British upset in the making? Not quite, as the Americans righted their ship and won two and halved one of the three remaining matches. The halve was almost another American win, Jacklin chipping in from twenty yards off the last green to salvage a tie for partner Huggett against Trevino and Rudolph.

In the final match, Hebert changed strategy and paired Nicklaus with another long hitter, Snead: They had little difficulty with Bembridge and Butler, winning 5&3.

After the home team's comeback, the Brits still led, 4-1/2 to 3-1/2, exactly as they had two years before. Staying close in the fourballs had been crucial to the good British showing at Birkdale, but they were on American soil now, where the Americans were usually close to perfect in better-ball play. Could Brown keep his team focused?

Not exactly. The British captain split up his teams from the first day, sat both Jacklin and Huggett (1-0-1 in foursomes) in the morning, and brought in Garner. Ten GB players teed it up on day two and ten tasted defeat. The Americans swept all four matches in the morning, then won two and halved one in the afternoon. All but one of the eight matches went to the eighteenth hole, but with a sense of déjà vu, the Brits lost five of those seven and halved one.

"I had no idea you were into Irish Dancing."

PETER OOSTERHUIS AND ARNOLD PALMER

The shortest match, a 5&4 win for Palmer and Dickinson over Oosterhuis and Gallacher, featured the only real controversy of the week. On the 208-yard par-three seventh hole, with the U.S. team 1-up, Palmer hit a five-iron to the middle of the green. The shot so impressed Gallacher's American caddy—Jack McLeod, who has been variously described as a "college boy" and a "fifty-five-year-old retired mailman"—that he couldn't help but blurt out, "Great shot. What'd you hit there?" Palmer answered, "A five-iron." Gallacher may or may not have heard the exchange, but he switched from a four-iron to a three and both teams parred the hole.

Before moving to the next tee, the referee announced that the Americans won the hole because McLeod had violated Rule 9a, which prohibits asking advice from the other team. Some reports have Palmer asking the referee if he could ignore the accidental infraction, but Gallacher later said that he thought Palmer was practicing "a bit of gamesmanship . . . and I must say that my high regard for him has never been quite the same again." It wouldn't have mattered what Palmer said or why: Once a referee knows of a violation, he must penalize the guilty party.

To their credit, Gallacher and Oosterhuis put the morning's fracas behind them and won the only British point in the afternoon with a one-hole victory over the medically-challenged team of Trevino and Casper. In the other matches, Jacklin and Huggett returned only to lose to Littler and Snead, 1-up. Palmer and Nicklaus were paired together for the first time and beat Townsend and Bannerman, 2&1 (Townsend played in six matches and lost all six). Coles and O'Connor saved a wee bit of face, bouncing back from four down after five holes to halve with Coody and Beard. But the damage was done and the United States had turned the tables, taking a 10-6 lead into the singles.

The overmatched British and Irish needed a miracle, and for a brief moment looked to be touched by an angel. After Trevino topped Jacklin by one hole, Gallacher halved with Stockton, who hadn't played since losing with Nicklaus the first morning. Then Barnes beat Rudolph, and Oosterhuis continued his fine play, handling Littler 4&3. The lead was down to three.

Any glimmer of light was extinguished by Nicklaus, who was 3-0 since his opening-round loss; he added another notch to his belt with a 3&2 win over the star-crossed Townsend. Dickinson had a surprisingly easy time with O'Connor, winning 5&4 and running his unbeaten Ryder Cup streak to nine straight matches over two years (1967 and 1971). Bannerman was set to register a huge upset, but lost the final hole to let Palmer escape with a half. Beard and Coles also halved. Splitting the morning gave the Americans a five-point lead, just one and half points from keeping the Cup.

Look back at previous matches and you see that GB teams usually fell apart when their backs were to the wall. They often started well but inevitably gagged their way to the final hole. It happened again in St. Louis, where for one moment in the afternoon the visitors were up in six of the eight matches. However, when the final putts had dropped, they'd won only four.

If Trevino was still suffering any ill effects from surgery, it didn't show. He won his fourth of five matches, pummeling Huggett, 7&6. Not only good, but a lucky bastard too, Trevino had played a left-handed wedge shot from under a tree along the fourth fairway, hitting it 120 yards onto the green. He had the decency to smile sheepishly while admitting to Huggett, "I'm as surprised as you are."

The winning point came from rookie Snead with a 1-up win over Jacklin, who hadn't won since the opening match and finished 1-3-1. With the battle for the Cup over, the rest of the matches were for pride, which showed in some cases: Oosterhuis defeated Palmer 3&2, Nicklaus won his fifth straight match, 5&3 over Coles, and Bannerman ended Dickinson's unbeaten streak with a 2&1 win.

For once, the loss had a simple explanation—fourballs. Remove them from the equation and the matches were tied. Even with them, the Brits had their best-ever showing in hostile territory. Flying back across the ocean, the losing team was in surprisingly good spirits, with Brown's wife leading the players and their fans in song, including "My Way." But most critics contended that Brown's way hadn't worked: Why had he selected Garner then played him only once? Why did he drop Coles/O'Connor from the afternoon foursomes and Jacklin/Huggett from the morning fourballs? Why did he sit Bembridge after the first day? Where do babies come from? Eric offered no answers.

He started as many Ryder Cup pissing matches as anyone, went undefeated in four singles matches as a player, and captained the teams responsible for the tie at Birkdale and the best ever showing in America, but Eric Brown's Ryder Cup career was over.

FINAL SCORE

COURSE:

OLD WARSON CC | ST. LOUIS | MO

1971

FOURSOMES

MORNING

Casper/Barber lost to Coles/O'Connor, 2&1
Palmer/Dickinson d. Townsend/Oosterhuis, 2-up
Coody/Beard lost to Bembridge/Butler, 1-up
Nicklaus/Stockton lost to Huggett/Jacklin, 3&2

AFTERNOON

Casper/Barber lost to Bannerman/Gallacher, 2&1
Palmer/Dickinson d. Townsend/Oosterhuis, 1-up
Trevino/Rudolph halved with Huggett/Jacklin
Nicklaus/Snead d. Bembridge/Butler, 5&3

US: 3-1/2   GB: 4-1/2

FOURBALLS

MORNING

Trevino/Rudolph d. O'Connor/Barnes, 2&1
Beard/Snead d. Coles/Garner, 2&1
Palmer/Dickinson d. Oosterhuis/Gallacher, 5&4
Nicklaus/Littler d. Townsend/Bannerman, 2&1

AFTERNOON

Trevino/Casper lost to Gallacher/Oosterhuis, 1-up
Littler/Snead d. Jacklin/Huggett, 2&1
Palmer/Nicklaus d. Townsend/Bannerman, 1-up
Coody/Beard halved with Coles/O'Connor

US: 6-1/2   GB: 1-1/2

SINGLES

MORNING

Trevino d. Jacklin, 1-up
Stockton halved with Gallacher
Rudolph lost to Barnes, 1-up
Littler lost to Oosterhuis, 4&3
Nicklaus d. Townsend, 3&2
Dickinson d. O'Connor, 5&4
Palmer halved with Bannerman
Beard halved with Coles

AFTERNOON

Trevino d. Huggett, 7&6
Snead d. Jacklin, 1-up
Barber lost to Barnes, 2&1
Stockton d. Townsend, 1-up
Coody lost to Gallacher, 2&1
Nicklaus d. Coles, 5&3
Palmer lost to Oosterhuis, 3&2
Dickinson lost to Bannerman, 2&1

US: 8-1/2   GB: 7-1/2

TOTAL: US 18-1/2   GB 13-1/2

COURSE:

MUIRFIELD GULLANE SCOTLAND

SEPT. **20-22**

1973

FINAL SCORE:

US **19**   GB **13**

CAPTAINS:

JACK BURKE JR.   BERNARD HUNT

UNITED STATES

Tommy Aaron	Lee Trevino
Homero Blancas	Tom Weiskopf
Gay Brewer	
Billy Casper	
Lou Graham	
Dave Hill	
Jack Nicklaus	
Arnold Palmer	
Chi Chi Rodriguez	
J.C. Snead	

GREAT BRITAIN

Brian Barnes	Peter Oosterhuis
Maurice Bembridge	Eddie Polland
Peter Butler	
Clive Clark	
Neil Coles	
Bernard Gallacher	
John Garner	
Brian Huggett	
Tony Jacklin	
Christy O'Connor Sr.	

1967	1969	1971	☆	1975	1977	1979	1981	1983
			1973					

THE HONOURABLE COMPANY OF EDINBURGH GOLFERS. Now that's a great name, bulging with history and propriety, and oh so awfully British. Never heard of it? It was the very first golf club, organized in early 1744 on land a few miles from downtown Edinburgh, Scotland, known as the Leith Links.

In March that same year, the HCEG held the game's first recognized competition, which was open to "Noblemen or Gentlemen or other Golfers, from any part of Great Britain or Ireland." A dozen showed up for two rounds over the five-hole course that was played along the Firth of Forth. The winner—to be known henceforth as "The Captain of the Golf"—was a local surgeon named John Rattray, who fired a damned impressive sixty (also, he was probably the first doctor to take Wednesday afternoons off to play golf).

Perhaps more important than the tournament was the fact that it was conducted under the game's first rules, thirteen of them, that dealt with everything from where to tee your ball ("within a club-length of the hole") to what to do if said ball was stopped by a dog ("play it as it lies and stop whyning") or shat on by a horse "Goode luck".

The point of this little history lesson? That Scotland is "the cradle of golf," where the game began its evolution from shepherds violently banging sheep into sandy hillsides and creating the first bunkers, and then swatting seaweed-covered rocks, or however this madness started, to the money-driven circus we know today. And to note, not without irony, that while the Ryder Cup has been contested thirty-five times, sadly only once has the battle been in Scotland. That was in 1973, at Muirfield, which is where those same Honourable Gentlemen moved in 1891 and have been happily laughing at people who aren't members ever since.

THE VICTORIOUS US TEAM DROPS JACK BURKE

Muirfield, one of the world's great golf courses, has hosted fifteen Open Championships, the first in 1892, and the most recent in 2002. For the Americans playing in the 1973 Ryder Cup, two of those tournaments were especially noteworthy: In 1966, it was where Jack Nicklaus won the first of his three Opens, and in 1972 where Lee Trevino captured his second Open (beating both Nicklaus and Tony Jacklin, the great British hope). But they weren't the only members of the U.S. team with their names on the Claret Jug: Arnold Palmer had won in 1961 and 1962, and Tom Weiskopf, a Cup rookie, had won twc months earlier at Royal Troon. So if victories in the host country's national championship were any indication of impending success, the U.S. team was looking good. Like *that* was a shock.

Returning were Tommy Aaron (winner of that year's Masters), Gay Brewer (1967 Masters), Billy Casper (1959 and

PETER OOSTERHUIS

1966 U.S. Opens, 1970 Masters), Dave Hill, and J. C. Snead. The other new faces were Homero Blancas, Chi Chi Rodriguez, and Lou Graham. Collectively, the team owned a lot of majors, and was captained by Jack Burke Jr., who had two majors of his own (1956 Masters and PGA). Many said this was the best American team ever to vie for the Cup.

The home team had majors, too—but only two, both Jacklin's (1969 Open, 1970 U.S. Open). He was joined by eight Cup veterans—Brian Barnes, Maurice Bembridge, Peter Butler, Neil Coles, Bernard Gallacher, Brian Huggett, Christy O'Connor, Peter Oosterhuis, and John Garner—but only one of them had ever been on a winning team (O'Connor in 1957). The rookies were Englishman Clive Clark and Ulsterman Eddie Polland, and the captain was Bernard Hunt, who'd also tasted victory at Lindrick.

TONY JACKLIN

As Hunt saw it, his job was to do everything possible to convince his players that they could upset the American leviathan. Hunt told the world that his team was just as good as the other guys. The new, young players on the U.S. squad, he said, "had barely a decent swing among them," and he noted how many Americans made a Cup team only to vanish. (Of course, that could have been due to a surfeit of talent, something Hunt didn't mention—or have.) He pointed out that British pros had been playing the larger ball since 1968 and were as good as the Americans at controlling it. Furthermore, his boys were playing around the world, gaining valuable experience. "I'd be very surprised if the Americans win this year," Hunt told the press. "Everyone on my side is very keen and very confident."

That was a turd-muncher of a lie, of course, but there were factors in Hunt's favor. The Americans were late flying across the Atlantic, leaving them only two days of practice. Some of the players were unhappy that Nicklaus, who knew Muirfield well, hadn't traveled with the rest of the team, choosing to attend a Miami Dolphins football game instead (he landed in Scotland just a few hours behind his teammates). Trevino joked that he would have liked a few extra hours at home too; seems his wife had just presented him with a daughter.

A bigger advantage for the Brits may have been the adoption of a format change proposed by past-captain Eric Brown two years earlier: one round of foursomes and one of fourballs each of the first two days. Brown hoped shuffling the games would throw off the Americans and end their dominance of team play.

And gag me with a field mouse, but that was exactly what happened. Hunt's team came out on day one eager to prove their captain right and won the morning's first two foursomes and halved the third before Nicklaus and Palmer topped Bembridge and Polland, 6&5.

Having proven that the Americans were mortal, the British didn't let up. The afternoon fourballs were even more one-sided, with the locals winning the first three matches, including the midget partnership of Maurice Bembridge and Brian Huggett taking down Palmer and Nicklaus, 3&1. In the morning, Weiskopf and Casper had played in different pairs and both had lost; paired in the afternoon, they lost again. Trevino had been agitated about something during his morning loss, even grumbling out loud about using Casper's clubs, which would have been a rules violation (it probably was just Lee talking to relieve the tension). He calmed himself in the afternoon and, playing with Blancas, won the only point for the visitors, defeating the British graybeards, O'Connor and Coles, 2&1.

In forty-six years, Britain had never had an opening day like this. Five of eight matches won, one halved. The American gladiators—Palmer, Nicklaus, Trevino, Weiskopf—had all tasted defeat at least once.

If one captain was jubilant, the other was reliving bad memories. Burke had been head man in 1957, the last time the Americans lost the Cup. He said, only half-jokingly, that if his team lost he might not be let back into the country. "We're supposed to win," he'd explained before the matches began, "and if you don't, don't come home."

Sleeping on a three-point lead, the Brits should have been having sweet dreams. But Bernard Gallacher woke up at two in the morning, dizzy and in a cold sweat. (It happens to me all the time, but Bernard hardly drinks.) A few hours later, his wife called a doctor, who diagnosed food poisoning from dinner. By dawn, Hunt learned that one of his stars—with two wins the first day—would be in bed for day two. The team took the news badly. "Some of them looked upon it as a bad omen," said Barnes, who'd partnered Gallacher in both matches the first day. Hunt had to wake Butler, who had yet to play, and tell him to get ready.

Feeling Gallacher's pain, the British managed to split the morning's foursomes. Rising to the occasion, Butler provided the day's highlight, a hole-in-one on the 188-yard sixteenth hole, the first ace in Cup competition. (I guarantee you he didn't even buy himself a drink after that.) But it wasn't enough, as he and Barnes lost to Nicklaus and Weiskopf, 1-up.

In the afternoon, the rest of the home team looked sick: In four matches, all they could muster was a half from Bembridge and Huggett against Trevino and Blancas. Barnes and Butler lost again (how they missed Gallacher!), while Brewer and Casper beat the previously undefeated Jacklin and Oosterhuis, 3&2, the pressure of being Britain's golden boy obviously wearing on Jacklin. "Tony is playing like he's dead beat," said Casper. "The ball is going everywhere."

With their backs to the wall, the Americans had played as if they were all worried about being turned away at U.S. Customs. The big British lead was gone and the teams tied 8-8. As for Bernard Hunt, he admitted to being a bit disappointed, but he remained confident.

But the British captain had to start feeling a touch green around the gills himself as the morning singles progressed. The U.S. won the first three matches, including Weiskopf dispatching a still bilious Gallacher, 3&1. Then Jacklin beat Aaron, 3&1, for GB's only full point of the session. (But it shouldn't have been that close: Aaron, filling in for a tired Palmer, had a bad back and didn't know the course, having played it only once before. It was seen as more proof that Jacklin was chafing under the massive expectations of his countrymen.)

There were three halves: Coles missed a short putt on the last hole and tied Brewer; Bembridge won the last two holes to catch Nicklaus; and Oosterhuis tripped over himself on the last few holes to give Trevino half a point. The Americans were watching the last match particularly closely because Trevino had promised to beat the big Englishman, saying he'd kiss the ass of every man on the U.S. team if he didn't. A half is not a win, and there is reputed to be a famous photo of the Americans with their pants down and their posteriors pointed toward a kneeling, puckering Lee.

To keep the Cup, the U.S. needed only 2-1/2 points in the afternoon, and it didn't take long to get them. In the opening match, Brian Huggett defeated Homero Blancas 4&2 to finish as the only unbeaten player of the week (ironically, Blancas had been unbeaten until then). Then the Americans struck, winning four straight, the Cup-keeping point coming from Snead as it had two years earlier. In that streak, Gallacher didn't have the strength to battle Brewer, Jacklin finally succumbed to the pressure and lost to the much older Casper, and Trevino, having made no promises this time, thumped Coles.

The Cup's home for the next two years assured, the final three matches still had meaning. The forty-nine-year-old O'Connor, with only one win in four matches, battled Weiskopf to the last green, where the legendary Irishman got up and down from the sand to halve the hole and the match. It was a gutsy end to O'Connor's ten-year, thirty-six-match Ryder Cup career. O'Connor's thirty six matches rank him only fifth among British/European players. However, he is tied for first with most total matches lost, twenty one, and alone in first with most singles lost, ten.

Nicklaus, who'd uncharacteristically played safe on the last two holes in the morning and lost both to Bembridge, wasn't about to give the same opponent another chance in the afternoon. The Englishman again kept the match close, but this time Nicklaus finished birdie, birdie, par for a 2-up win, then said to his opponent—whom he'd faced four times—"Hey, you son of a bitch, you can play this game!" He was right on both counts about Maurice.

The last match was also to be Palmer's last. The fact that it was a 4&2 loss to Oosterhuis (who won a record six singles matches) cannot diminish Arnold's record: 22-8-2 in six Cups, one of the best performances in Cup history, from a man who always did more than his fair share to tout the importance of the event.

No matter what the outcome, the captain of the GB team had to be ready for post-match second-guessing, and Hunt was not immune. Should Gallacher have been kept in bed? Where were Polland (who played twice), Clive Clark (who had, in one of the greatest moments of Ryder Cup wussiness, *apologized* to Nicklaus and Weiskopf for "not giving them a better game"), and poor John Garner (who hadn't played at all, which was a crime against humanity)? And how had they done so well the first day only to do so poorly the second? And again, where do babies come from?

Burke had an answer to the penultimate question: "It was the beating on the first day that welded the team together," he said. "We just weren't going to lose."

Hunt agreed: "They were as strong at the finish as they were at the start. I suppose that is because they play so much more than we do. But we're catching up in that department. . . . Getting right down to it, though, I guess they are still a bit better than we are."

A final word about Scotland. Just to prove that the powers that be are not all history-challenged ignorami, the Ryder Cup is returning to the land of golf's birth—in 2014. It's probably already sold out.

FINAL SCORE

COURSE:

MUIRFIELD | GULLANE | SCOTLAND

1973

FOURBALLS & FOURSOMES

FOURSOMES - MORNING

Trevino/Casper lost to Barnes/Gallacher, 1-up

Weiskopf/Snead lost to O'Connor/Coles, 3&2

Rodriguez/Graham halved with Jacklin/Oosterhuis

Nicklaus/Palmer d. Bembridge/Polland, 6&5

FOURBALLS - AFTERNOON

Aaron/Brewer lost to Barnes/Gallacher, 5&4

Palmer/Nicklaus lost to Bembridge/Huggett, 3&1

Weiskopf/Casper lost to Jacklin/Oosterhuis, 3&1

Trevino/Blancas d. O'Connor/Coles, 2&1

US: 2-1/2   GB: 5-1/2

FOURBALLS & FOURSOMES

FOURSOMES - MORNING

Nicklaus/Weiskopf d. Barnes/Butler, 1-up

Palmer/Hill lost to Oosterhuis/Jacklin, 2-up

Rodriguez/Graham lost to Bembridge/Huggett, 5&4

Trevino/Casper d. Coles/O'Connor, 2&1

FOURBALLS - AFTERNOON

Snead/Palmer d. Barnes/Butler, 2-up

Brewer/Casper d. Jacklin/Oosterhuis, 3&2

Nicklaus/Weiskopf d. Clark/Polland, 3&2

Trevino/Blancas halved with Bembridge/Huggett

US: 5-1/2   GB: 2-1/2

SINGLES

MORNING

Casper d. Barnes, 2&1

Weiskopf d. Gallacher, 3&1

Blancas d. Butler, 5&4

Aaron lost to Jacklin, 3&1

Brewer halved with Coles

Snead d. O'Connor, 1-up

Nicklaus halved with Bembridge

Trevino halved with Oosterhuis

AFTERNOON

Blancas lost to Huggett, 4&2

Snead d. Barnes, 3&1

Brewer d. Gallacher, 6&5

Casper d. Jacklin, 2&1

Trevino d. Coles, 6&5

Weiskopf halved with O'Connor

Nicklaus d. Bembridge, 2-up

Palmer lost to Oosterhuis, 4&2

US: 11   GB: 5

TOTAL: US 19   GB 13

COURSE:

LAUREL VALLEY GC | LIGONIER | PA

☆☆☆☆☆☆☆☆☆☆ SEPT. 19-21

1975

☆☆☆☆☆☆☆☆☆☆☆☆☆

FINAL SCORE:

☆ US 21   GB 11

CAPTAINS:

ARNOLD PALMER   BERNARD HUNT

UNITED STATES

☆☆☆☆☆☆☆☆☆☆☆☆

Billy Casper	Lee Trevino
Ray Floyd	Tom Weiskopf
Al Geiberger	
Lou Graham	
Hale Irwin	
Gene Littler	
Johnny Miller	
Bob Murphy	
Jack Nicklaus	
J.C. Snead	

GREAT BRITAIN

☆☆☆☆☆☆☆☆☆☆☆☆

Brian Barnes	Peter Oosterhuis
Maurice Bembridge	Norman Wood
Eamonn Darcy	
Bernard Gallacher	
Tommy Horton	
Brian Huggett	
Guy Hunt	
Tony Jacklin	
Christy O'Connor Jr.	
John O'Leary	

1967   1969   1971   1973   ☆   1977   1979   1981   1983

1975

GREAT BRITAIN

Courtesy of The PGA of America

IT'S HARD TO IMAGINE TODAY, with all the drama and controversy that attends every Ryder Cup, just how testicle-crushingly tedious the event was for many years. God, but it was horrendous at times, but even so, it remained incredibly important to the *players* on both sides. There were some puckering matches of course, and great personal stories and even the occasional nasty rivalry—hey, it was still a chance to play for your country. But for the most part, the long spell of American domination—in the eight matches since the British won in 1957 the best they'd been able to do was a tie, and their average loss was by more than seven points—made for a really boring show.

And in the States, it wasn't even a *show*, because it wasn't on television. All the American public knew of the Ryder Cup was the little article that appeared in their local newspapers carrying a headline that read something like, "U.S. Golfers Win Again—Billy Casper Eats Small Welsh Golfer." If the paper ran the agate type of individual match results, even the most avid golf fan in New Hampshire, North Dakota, or Nevada would see names like "Bembridge" and "Huggett" and ask over their morning mud, "Who are these assholes?"

The lack of fan enthusiasm (at least in the Great Forty-Eight) mixed with the limited capacity of the British to be competitive was taking its toll and raising the inevitable questions: Should players from other countries be considered for the British team? (After all, it wasn't that long ago we owned *this* place, too.) Should there be more players? Fewer? What about the format: Would changing it (again) lead to a closer contest? It was a sign of just how humdrum the Ryder Cup had become that these issues were of greater interest than the matches themselves.

All of which is a way of saying that not only was the Cup as a whole in trouble, but that 1975 was one of the most one-sided, and therefore least exciting, match-ups yet.

But as I said, there was always at least one interesting story every time, and this year there were two. First was Arnold Palmer, who, having made his last appearance as a contestant two years earlier, was serving as American captain, giving him the spotlight for his last act on the Ryder Cup stage. Palmer was forty-six years old and his best years were behind him. But just in case anyone thought he was through, earlier that year he'd won two events in Europe—the Spanish Open and British PGA Championship—and probably close to enough money to earn him a spot on the opposing team. They could have used him.

It was no coincidence that the matches were held at Laurel Valley, a club Palmer had been associated with for years as "playing professional" because it was just minutes from his hometown of Latrobe, Pennsylvania. Arnold's pull was strong enough that nearly 10,000 fans turned out each day of the Cup to slog around the course, made messy by heavy rains just before the matches. The weather was so bad that practice rounds were cancelled and an exhibition featuring Palmer and Bob Hope versus British captain Bernard Hunt and crooner Perry Como was nixed, which was a damned good thing, because the Ryder Cup flame was sputtering. It's a short step from a pre-match exhibition to a pro-am, and that might have snuffed it out completely.

The second story was Jack Nicklaus. At thirty-five and already just about the greatest this idiotic game has ever seen, Jack said that coming into the Ryder Cup he was playing the best golf of his life. He was the Tour's leading money winner in 1975, a year in which he won five events, including the Masters and PGA Championship (his fourteenth and fifteenth professional majors) as well as the World Open, which used to be a hot-shit event that brought together greats from around the globe. He also was one hell of a Ryder Cupper, having played sixteen matches in three years for a record of 10-4-2, with only one loss in singles. He was hot, he was *the* man, and his eagerness to play in what some considered a minor event was of extraordinary importance during the tough years for the Cup.

The rest of the American team were no choppers either—veterans Billy Casper, Ray Floyd, Al Geiberger, Lou Graham, Gene Littler, J. C. Snead, Lee Trevino, and Tom Weiskopf, and first-timers Hale Irwin, Johnny Miller, and Bob Murphy. Of the dozen, only one (Casper) hadn't won a Tour event in 1975, and only two (Snead and Murphy) hadn't already won a major.

The American team was a cannon, and GB sent over a pop-gun. Captain Hunt would have to be a mix of Knute Rockne, Martin Luther King, and Tony Robbins to even get a few points with a squad composed of returnees Brian Barnes, Maurice Bembridge, Bernard Gallacher, Brian Huggett, Tony Jacklin, and Peter Oosterhuis, plus rookies Eamonn Darcy, Tommy Horton, Guy Hunt, Christy O'Connor Jr. (nephew of the great "Himself"), John O'Leary, and Norman Wood.

The fight seemed so unfair that British oddsmakers refused to take money on a U.S. victory. (Bets were being taken on the final score, with the shortest odds on the U.S. outscoring the Brits 2-to-1.) *Golf World* magazine said, "The British are a team that has not proved it could master even the American Walker Cup team." (That wasn't very nice, even by my own low standards.) Nor was the fact that Palmer supposedly was hoping for a clean sweep, a 32-0 win. Givvus a break there, guv!

But it didn't seem at all preposterous after the first morning when the U.S. swept the foursomes. The two teams that had produced fireworks for GB in 1973 weren't worth a flaming fart on opening day: Barnes and Gallacher were dispatched by Nicklaus and Weiskopf, 5&4, and Jacklin and Oosterhuis lost to Geiberger and Miller, 3&1. The rookies didn't fare much better as Horton and O'Leary fell to Trevino and Snead, 2&1, while Wood and Bembridge lost to Littler and Irwin, 4&3. (Littler was one of those great individual stories: He had missed most of the previous season with cancer of the lymph glands, but was very much back and on his game.)

BRIAN BARNES (LARGE MAN IN SMALL SHIRT AND TWO-LEGGED KILT)

Any hopes of a shut-out were over early in the afternoon fourballs when Oosterhuis and Jacklin beat Casper and Floyd, 2&1, followed by Barnes and Gallacher showing some of their old magic and scraping out a half with Nicklaus and Murphy in the only match of the day to reach the final hole. But the other two matches went to the home team, Weiskopf and Graham handling the two Irish rookies, Darcy and O'Connor, 3&2, Trevino and Irwin besting Horton and O'Leary 2&1.

Not only did the Americans have a 6-1/2 to 1-1/2 lead at the end of the first day, but Captain Palmer had shown that no matter how he put his teams together—all of his players had seen action and all the morning pairs were rearranged for the afternoon—they would dominate fairly easily.

Day two wasn't much better for GB—only a half-point better, in fact. The fourballs were played first, and the Brits were winless again, but did manage two halves, one from Oosterhuis and Jacklin against the two Mormons, Casper and Miller, the other Darcy and Hunt versus Geiberger and Floyd. Nicklaus and Snead had little problem with Horton and Wood, winning 4&2, while the problems of Barnes and Gallacher continued with a 5&3 loss to Littler and Graham. (The scores all weekend were somewhat deceiving: While there were some sizable margins of victory, the course was so wet and played so long that even the winners were over par most times.)

One point came to the visitors in the afternoon foursomes, Jacklin and Huggett (in his first appearance at this match) opening up with a 3&2 victory over Trevino and Murphy. But the other three were all resounding American victories—Weiskopf and Miller over O'Connor and O'Leary, 5&3, Irwin and Casper beating Oosterhuis and Bembridge, 3&2, and, by the same score, Geiberger and Graham topping Darcy and Hunt. Again, all twelve Americans had played, but this time Hunt, desperate for any spark of life, had played his dozen as well. The second day score of 6-2 gave the Americans a ridiculous nine-point advantage.

Needing only 3-1/2 points from the sixteen singles matches (yeah, you read that right), the drama was whether or not it would all be over before lunch. (And if it were, would the Brits come back out after stuffing themselves on the free food.) The way the matches played out, the winning point came from Weiskopf, who beat Hunt 5&3 in the seventh singles of the day. But it actually was the fourth match to finish given that two—Trevino vs. Gallacher and Irwin vs. Horton—went to the eighteenth hole, where both were halved. Other than that, Murphy topped Jacklin, 2&1, Oosterhuis (who was almost unbeatable in singles) defeated Miller 2-up (hey, there's a point for GB!), Littler beat Huggett, 4&2, and Casper took out Darcy, 3&2.

The last singles of the morning was by far the most interesting, Nicklaus vs. Barnes. The big Englishman had arrived at the tee wearing ghastly Bermuda shorts and smoking a pipe, and although Jack said he was so focused he didn't notice how his opponent was decked out, something, perhaps the reeking smokestack, or the sight of Brian's legs, definitely got to Mr. Golden Bear. Barnes holed twenty-foot birdie putts on the first two holes to quickly go ahead, Jack three-putted the seventh, and Barnes was 3-up at the turn. It was over at sixteen when Jack bogeyed and lost 4&2.

In the afternoon singles, GB, who'd won three points in the morning, were doing a little better. Although Jacklin lost again (this time to Floyd, 1-up, to finish 2-3-1), Oosterhuis got the better of Snead, 3&2, Horton beat Graham, 2&1, and Wood, who'd only played twice and lost both times, upset Trevino, 2&1. Geiberger halved with Gallacher, Irwin beat O'Leary (who went 0-4) 2&1, and Murphy handled Bembridge (0-3), 2&1.

That left one match, Nicklaus against Barnes again. Jack and Arnie had manipulated the schedule to arrange the rematch. Years later, Barnes recalled, "I remember Jack saying to me on the first tee, 'You beat me once, but there ain't no way you're going to beat me again.' And then he started birdie, birdie and I didn't think I would. But I did." Incredibly, Barnes did win again, fighting back time after time, cutting into Jack's slim leads, drawing back to even, then pulling away with birdies on eleven and twelve and a par on the short fourteenth. One-under-par after seventeen holes, he'd beaten the world's best for the second time in one day, 2&1. "I know how bloody mad he was," said Barnes, "but he never showed it and congratulated me very warmly." Apparently the game's greatest winner was a pretty good loser too.

"I still, all these years on, have difficulty in getting away from it," says Barnesy. "Whenever I attend a corporate outing or dinner I am introduced as the man who twice beat Nicklaus head to head. But you know, I never did consider it as that fantastic. Certainly I enjoyed it at the time, but in my own mind I soon forgot it."

No doubt, people don't forget Brian Barnes's amazing feat (and that is what it was, I don't care what he says!) because there was so damned little else to remember of the 1975 Ryder Cup, particularly if you come from my side of the pond. GB fought back on the last day, and while they still lost the singles 7-1/2 to 8-1/2, at least they got their final score into double digits. What I don't know is if the bookies paid off on the double-the-score bet with the U.S. winning 21-11. My bookie sure as hell wouldn't.

The British, who were used to big headlines whether the Ryder Cup was won or lost, weren't shocked to read the one in the *London Mail* the day after it was all over: DEATH OF THE RYDER CUP. Many people were starting to say out loud that if the matches didn't become more competitive, they wouldn't be around much longer. Bastards, all of them. What a shame it would have been, and what a disgrace to the memory of all the men who'd played against the odds, if we'd just tossed in the towel.

FINAL SCORE

COURSE:

LAUREL VALLEY GC | LIGONIER | PA

1975

FOURBALLS & FOURSOMES

FOURSOMES - MORNING

Nicklaus/Weiskopf d. Barnes/Gallacher, 5&4

Littler/Irwin d. Wood/Bembridge, 4&3

Geiberger/Miller d. Jacklin/Oosterhuis, 3&1

Trevino/Snead d. Horton/O'Leary, 2&1

FOURBALLS - AFTERNOON

Casper/Floyd lost to Oosterhuis/Jacklin, 2&1

Weiskopf/Graham d. Darcy/O'Connor, 3&2

Nicklaus/Murphy halved
with Barnes/Gallacher

Trevino/Irwin d. Horton/O'Leary, 2&1

US: 6-1/2   GB: 1-1/2

FOURBALLS & FOURSOMES

FOURSOMES - MORNING

Casper/Miller halved with Oosterhuis/Jacklin

Nicklaus/Snead d. Horton/Wood, 4&2

Littler/Graham d. Barnes/Gallacher, 5&3

Geiberger/Floyd halved with Darcy/Hunt

FOURBALLS -AFTERNOON

Trevino/Murphy lost to Jacklin/Huggett, 3&2

Weiskopf/Miller d. O'Connor/O'Leary, 5&3

Irwin/Casper d. Oosterhuis/Bembridge, 3&2

Geiberger/Graham d. Darcy/Hunt, 3&2

US: 6   GB: 2

SINGLES

MORNING

Murphy d. Jacklin, 2&1

Miller lost to Oosterhuis, 2-up

Trevino halved with Gallacher

Irwin halved with Horton

Littler d. Huggett, 4&2

Casper d. Darcy, 3&2

Weiskopf d. Hunt, 5&3

Nicklaus lost to Barnes, 4&2

AFTERNOON

Floyd d. Jacklin, 1-up

Snead lost to Oosterhuis, 3&2

Geiberger halved with Gallacher

Graham lost to Horton, 2&1

Irwin d. O'Leary, 2&1

Murphy d. Bembridge, 2&1

Trevino lost to Wood, 2&1

Nicklaus lost to Barnes, 2&1

US: 8-1/2   GB: 7-1/2

TOTAL: US 21   GB 11

COURSE:

ROYAL LYTHAM & ST. ANNES | ST. ANNES | ENGLAND

☆☆☆☆☆☆☆☆☆ **SEPT.** 15-17

1977

FINAL SCORE:

☆ **US** 12-1/2   **GB** 7-1/2

CAPTAINS:

DOW FINSTERWALD   BRIAN HUGGETT

UNITED STATES

Ray Floyd	Lanny Wadkins
Lou Graham	Tom Watson
Hubert Green	
Dave Hill	
Hale Irwin	
Don January	
Jerry McGee	
Jack Nicklaus	
Ed Sneed	
Dave Stockton	

GREAT BRITAIN

Brian Barnes	Mark James
Ken Brown	Peter Oosterhuis
Howard Clark	
Neil Coles	
Eamonn Darcy	
Peter Dawson	
Nick Faldo	
Bernard Gallacher	
Tommy Horton	
Tony Jacklin	

UNITED STATES   GREAT BRITAIN

185

TOTALLY SUBJECTIVE
HISTORY **OF THE** RYDER CUP

THE 1977 RYDER CUP MATCHES, played in England, were just as uneventful as those two years earlier in Pennsylvania. But they had the advantage of being shorter.

After the embarrassing ten-point loss in 1975, any and all ideas for making the Cup more competitive were entertained. The 1977 matches wound up being important, then, for two reasons: First, they proved that a change in format wasn't the answer, and second, they provided a time and place for discussions that would have a very positive effect on the Cup's future.

Someone had the none-too-bright idea that the best way to shrink the size of America's inevitable margin of victory was to reduce the total number of points. (I suppose they were right—if they played only two matches for instance, the most anyone could lose by was, uh, two?) That resulted in a format change that made absolutely no one happy: The first day went from eight matches—one session of four foursomes, another of four fourballs—to one set of five foursomes; day two also went from eight matches to five, all fourballs; and the final day's singles shrunk from sixteen to ten. In defense of this plan, after the last Cup both teams had complained about the pressure and exhaustion of thirty-two matches, which could mean as many as two a day for three days for the top players.

The new format was like swatting a fly with a baseball bat: overkill. There were too few matches and too much time between them—45 minutes!—inserted to suit the television broadcast in Britain. (But there was so little golf played, and it was played so slowly, that the TV coverage was deadly dull, too.) The electric atmosphere of the Ryder Cup—action in many places, roars and groans rolling across the course, fans running from match to match to catch the hot players—was gone. Rather than too much golf, there was too little.

But one other positive to come out of these matches was the introduction of two players who would have magnificent Cup careers: Nick Faldo for GB, and Tom Watson for the United States.

Faldo, in only his second year as a pro (and just a few years removed from being a high-handicapper), was twenty years old and the youngest player to date to make either team. He was joined by other fresh blood—Ken Brown (also twenty, and a nutcase), Howard Clark (twenty-three, and perfectly capable of starting a riot), Mark James (twenty-three, and watching a movie that only he could see), and Peter Dawson (twenty-seven, and the first lefty in Cup competition). Things were looking up, at least in the relief of boredom-off-the-course stakes. The veterans on the team were Brian Barnes, Neil Coles, Eamonn Darcy, Bernard Gallacher, Tommy Horton, Tony Jacklin, and Peter Oosterhuis. The average age of the team was a very young: twenty-eight (quite a change from the "old days" of Abe Mitchell, Henry Cotton, and Harry Weetman). The first-time captain was Brian Huggett, who had just completed a six-match Cup career two years earlier.

The American team, with an average age of thirty-four, also welcomed five newcomers: Hubert Green, who, if he were a dog, would chase your car (yet he still managed to win that year's U.S. Open), Jerry McGee, Ed Sneed, Lanny Wadkins, and, most prominently, Watson, who had won the 1977 Masters and Open Championship, beating Jack Nicklaus in both. Nicklaus led the old-timers on the team, along with Ray Floyd, Lou Graham, Dave Hill, Hale Irwin, Don January, and Dave Stockton. Their captain was Dow Finsterwald, who had lost only three matches in thirteen over four years of Cup play.

Come to think of it, there is an advantage to fewer matches: I have to write less description of what happened. And the less said about this American rout, the better. But since I feel a certain obligation to crap on my predecessors, here goes.

The Americans won the first two days with ease. In day one's foursomes, GB managed one win and one half; in day two's fourballs, one win. What mattered about those two wins is that they came from the same team, rookie Faldo and veteran Oosterhuis. On the first day, they beat Floyd and Graham 2&1; day two, Floyd and Nicklaus, 3&1. No matter what else happened for the British at Royal Lytham, they'd found and anointed a new savior. If I had to pick one player I didn't want to play against, it would have been Raymond, or possibly Wadkins, because they *detested* losing.

The coronation was all the more impressive because Faldo was playing with glandular fever, which had been diagnosed the week before by a doctor who had told his parents (remember, he was twenty) and they'd kept the news from their son. Nice. Lucky it wasn't the clap. It was only on the first morning of Cup play, when he woke up with a rash on his arms, that another doctor told the patient he was sick but that there was no reason he couldn't play if he felt up to it. (Think the good doctor was a golfer? Or had money on the matches?) If it had happened in the States, the entire medical community would have been sued.

Given recent history, it was easy to be dismissive of the British team. But day one easily could have been very different (and if my granny had had balls, she might well have been my granddad). In the first match, the tried-

JACK NICKLAUS

"I'm a little teapot."

TOM WATSON AND NICK FALDO

and-true pairing of Barnes and Gallacher held a one-hole lead over Wadkins and Irwin with five to play, then lost four in a row and fell, 3&1. Just behind them, Coles and Dawson were 2-up with three holes to play over Stockton and McGee, but Stockton, who was (and is) a marvelous putter, dropped a twenty-five-footer on sixteen and a forty-five-footer on seventeen, both for birdies, to draw even. Coles hit a poor drive at the last and the homeys double-bogeyed to lose, 1-up.

Faldo/Oosterhuis came next with their win, followed by Jacklin and Darcy, who also were 2-up with three to play but let Sneed and January back in it for a halve. In the final spot, Watson and Nicklaus had no trouble with James and Horton, winning 5&4.

Day two could have been better, too—if the U.S. team hadn't shown up. Other than the decisive Faldo/Oosterhuis win, only James and Brown had a chance, but they lost, 1-up to Irwin and Graham in a match filled with less-than-stellar play. At least both teams were sloppy: In the other matches, the Americans won 5&4, 5&3, and 5&3.

Okay, who said fewer matches would be more competitive?

With the U.S. ahead 7-1/2 to 2-1/2, the real problem with fewer matches was revealed: There wasn't much

BERNARD GALLACHER AND JACK NICKLAUS

chance for one team to catch up if the other had a big lead. With ten singles to be played, the visitors needed only three points.

They started coming very quickly, Wadkins handling Clark, 4&3, and Graham taking care of Coles, 5&3. For some odd reason, Huggett stuck his best players, Faldo and Oosterhuis, at the bottom of the order, where it seemed unlikely their matches would matter. Then the tide turned when Dawson rudely beat January, twenty years his senior, 5&4, and Barnes squeaked out a 1-up victory over Irwin. But then Hill beat Horton 5&4 for the decisive point.

It was only after the Cup was won that the matches got interesting. Some bastard had stolen Bernard Gallacher's putter just before he was to meet Nicklaus on the first tee. You think that wouldn't be a bummer? But Bernard dashed into the pro shop, bought a Ping Anser (a model he'd never used before), and putting like a demon, was four-up after four holes. However, this was Jack Nicklaus, and as might have been expected he fought back, getting even at sixteen. But rather than crumbling under the pressure, Gallacher holed an eighty-foot (not a typo) birdie putt from one end of the seventeenth green to the other, then rolled in a four-footer to halve the final hole and win the match, 1-up. Great stuff, and one of the great matches in the history of the Cup.

Green and Darcy staged a good fight too (although their two swings made several people in the crowd faint), the American winning 1-up, then Floyd—who was 0-2 having met Faldo and Oosterhuis twice—faced another 0-2 player, James. It was the Englishman who finished 0-3, losing 2&1.

In the next match-up, Faldo, using a graphite-shafted driver (he'd out-driven Nicklaus throughout their fourball, much to Jack's consternation), took a quick lead over Watson, the world number one. They were level at the turn, Faldo pulled ahead, then back to even with one to play. After driving into a fairway bunker, Watson stroked a fifty-foot putt from off the green that hit the flagstick and bounced out rather than in; Faldo's par won the match 1-up. After beating Floyd (twice), Nicklaus, and Watson in successive matches, Faldo said, "I'm really rather enjoying it." They weren't.

In the last match, Oosterhuis also worked his record to 3-0, beating McGee in another seesaw battle, 2-up. Oosterhuis also hit the flagstick on eighteen, but it was with his approach; the easy birdie gave him the hole and the match.

And where, you might ask, was Jacklin? Huggett felt the former star was well off his game and sat him for the singles. That created a big stink, both between the two men and in the British galleries and press, a foofaraw that went on for a few years.

One could argue that the five-point win wasn't that big a deal. But do a little math and you'll see that five points out of twenty was the same as losing by eight out of the thirty-two points played for the last few years. And with the format change having nowhere near the desired effect, the boo-birds were in full squeal again. Something had to be done; this just wasn't cricket (although it might just as well have been).

Something was done, and wisely, behind the scenes. As I said at the beginning, discussions took place that would save the Ryder Cup, and the protagonist was Nicklaus, who in addition to being a great player has always been an astute observer of the game. During the matches, he met with Lord Derby, president of the British PGA, and said, "The matches just aren't competitive enough." According to his autobiography, *My Story,* "We talked about the players' attitudes awhile, then he asked me how I thought we could fix things. I told him the best way I could think of would be to match the USA against a team from the entire European Tour, which by then had brought all the countries of the Continent together with Great Britain and Ireland." The good Lordy D. asked Nicklaus to put his ideas on paper, something to take to both the American and British PGAs: "The crux of my argument," Jack wrote, "could be summed up in the sentence: 'It is vital to widen the selection procedures if the Ryder Cup is to enjoy its past prestige.'"

So something good came out of the matches at Lytham, and it wasn't the dopey format. Nine months later, it was announced that the 1979 Ryder Cup was to be contested by teams from the United States and Europe. A brave new world was about to begin.

FINAL SCORE

FOURSOMES

Wadkins/Irwin d. Gallacher/Barnes, 3&1

Stockton/McGee d. Coles/Dawson, 1-up

Floyd/Graham lost to
Faldo/Oosterhuis, 2&1

Sneed/January halved with Darcy/Jacklin

Nicklaus/Watson d. Horton/James, 5&4

US: 3-1/2   GB: 1-1/2

FOURBALLS

Watson/Green d. Barnes/Horton, 5&4

Sneed/Wadkins d. Coles/Dawson, 5&3

Nicklaus/Floyd lost to Faldo/Oosterhuis, 3&1

Hill/Stockton d. Jacklin/Darcy, 5&3

Irwin/Graham d. James/Brown, 1-up

US: 4   GB: 1

SINGLES

Wadkins d. Clark, 4&3

Graham d. Coles, 5&3

January lost to Dawson, 5&4

Irwin lost to Barnes, 1-up

Hill d. Horton, 5&4

Nicklaus lost to Gallacher, 1-up

Green d. Darcy, 1-up

Floyd d. James, 2&1

Watson lost to Faldo, 1-up

McGee lost to Oosterhuis, 2-up

US: 5   GB: 5

TOTAL: **US 12-1/2**   **GB 07-1/2**

TOM WEISKOP-F
(I call him that because he has so much "f" in him, and I always liked it.)

(b.1942)

TOM WEISKOP-F qualified for the 1977 team but did not play, because he wanted to go to the Yukon and spend some quality time with one of his favorite sheep instead.

The seeds of Tom's problems with the PGA of America had been planted some years earlier. In order to qualify for the US Ryder Cup team, players had to be Class A members of the PGA, and one of the requirements for this status was two-weeks of business school. In 1971, while Lee Trevino was making merry on tour, Weiskop-f was in Baltimore, learning how to fill himself (with beer), and to fill cart batteries (with acid), at least one of which skills was essential for the tour player of the 1970s. Tom actually completed the course, but his paperwork was mishandled by the PGA of America, an uncorrected error that would cost Weiskop-f his place on that year's team. also In addition, Trevino went on to finish a tenth of a shot in front of him in the Vardon trophy (which is the true measure of the player of the year) and the big T felt unrighteously hosepiped. After playing on the winning teams at Muirfield in 1973 and at Laurel Valley in 1975, he wrote a letter to of the PGA of America, requesting that he should not be considered for, or included in, any listing for the 1977 Cup at Royal Lytham. It was a letter

Say, is that man in the sansabelts carrying a gun?

that went unanswered and ignored, even after repeated telephone conversations. In the run-up to selection day, Weiskop-f was second on the money list, but his resolve was unshaken. Plus, (and this is where my heart goes really soft on him) some months earlier he had booked a hunt in the Yukon for the legendary Dall sheep, which would complete for him what sheep-hunters call the "Grand Slam"—a Rocky Mountain Bighorn, a Stone sheep, a Desert sheep and the Dall. (Irish sheep-hunters also perform something like a Grand Slam on their sheep, but it's more of a wrestling hold.)

Weiskop-f was vilified in the press for his decision not to play, but the truth is, he loved the Ryder Cup as much as anyone who played in it. He's a different guy, and one who wanted to see another player get a chance. One of the things I most admire about Tom Weiskop-f is that his life hasn't been just about golf.

And, yes, he got his Grand Slam.

COURSE:

| THE GREENBRIER | WHITE SULPHUR SPRINGS | WV |

☆☆☆☆☆☆☆☆☆☆ **SEPT. 14-16**

1979

☆☆☆☆☆☆☆☆☆☆☆☆☆☆☆☆☆

☆ **FINAL SCORE:**

US 17   **EUROPE 11**

CAPTAINS:

| BILLY CASPER | JOHN JACOBS |

UNITED STATES
☆☆☆☆☆☆☆☆☆☆☆☆☆☆☆

Andy Bean	Lanny Wadkins
Lee Elder	Fuzzy Zoeller
Hubert Green	
Mark Hayes	
Hale Irwin	
Tom Kite	
John Mahaffey	
Gil Morgan	
Larry Nelson	
Lee Trevino	

EUROPE
☆☆☆☆☆☆☆☆☆☆☆☆☆☆☆

Seve Ballesteros	Peter Oosterhuis*
Brian Barnes	Des Smyth*
Ken Brown	
Nick Faldo	
Bernard Gallacher	
Antonio Garrido	
Tony Jacklin	
Mark James	
Michael King	
Sandy Lyle	*captain's picks

| 1967 | 1969 | 1971 | 1973 | 1975 | 1977 | ☆ | 1981 | 1983 |

1979

ADDING CONTINENTAL EUROPE TO what had been the sole province of Great Britain and Ireland didn't suddenly rewrite Ryder Cup history (that's what I'm here for). But it was a start.

After Joan Ryder-Scarfe, Sam Ryder's daughter, approved changing her old man's original Deed of Trust (he'd only agreed to sponsor a match between Britain and the U.S.), it was necessary to figure out who would make the team and how. Although golf had been played on the Continent for years (in fact, some say the old Scots game may have originated in Holland or perhaps evolved from a sport played by the nobles of sixteenth-century France, *perish the thought*), talented European professionals were just coming to the fore. True, a few good golfers had come off the Continent before: Arnaud Massy of France won the Open Championship in 1907, while Belgium's Flory van Donck won twenty-six national titles in the 1930s and 1940s and five times on the early British tour. But it wasn't until 1971 that the British PGA launched the European Tour, and most of the native talent was still in development.

Hey, but at least now there was a *good* reason for changing how the team was selected! The top ten from the Tour's money list would make it, plus two players invited by captain John Jacobs, a former Cup player who was better known as a golf instructor and administrator (he was the first head of the European Tour). Using the new system, his team was a mix of new and old: Brian Barnes, Ken Brown, Nick Faldo, Bernard Gallacher, Tony Jacklin, Mark James, and Peter Oosterhuis were back, joined by Des Smyth, Michael King, Sandy Lyle, and two Spaniards, Severiano Ballesteros and Antonio Garrido, both of whom were among the top ten money winners (Oosterhuis and Smyth were the wild cards).

ANTONIO GARRIDO AND SEVERIANO BALLESTEROS

Ballesteros was the most exciting player on any continent. Young (only twenty-two) and fiery, he possessed a spectacular short game as well as a long game that was long all right, but often wild. He'd exploded onto the scene at nineteen, finishing second in the 1976 Open Championship at Birkdale; he also won his first European Tour event that year, the Dutch Open, and teamed with Manuel Pinero to win the 1976 World Cup for Spain. Suddenly the Spaniards were a force. Teaming with Garrido, he won the World Cup again the next year and began winning on his own around the globe, including in America. In 1979, just two months before the Cup matches, he won the Claret Jug at Lytham by three shots, over, among others, Jack Nicklaus; his final-round, even-par seventy included getting up—and down from a parking lot for a birdie on sixteen. He was the first golfer from the Continent to win the Open since Monsieur Massy. With his glossy blue-black hair, flashing smile, and thunderous Latin temper, Ballesteros was a sight to see, prowling the fairways and hacking from the woods with a mixture of feline grace, elasticity, and unbreakable concentration. He was *exactly* what the Ryder Cup needed.

The American team, under captain Billy Casper, was strong, but nothing like the powerhouses of recent years. There were only four veterans—Hubert Green, Hale Irwin, Lee Trevino, and Lanny Wadkins. Tom Watson had made the team and the trip to the Greenbrier resort in the mountains of West Virginia, but he got a call on the eve of the matches to come home as his wife was giving birth. Mark Hayes was called in at the last minute and joined the other rookies—Andy Bean, Lee Elder (the first black man to play for the Cup), Tom Kite, John Mahaffey, Gil Morgan, Larry Nelson, and Fuzzy Zoeller.

After the disastrous experiment at Lytham, the format was changed as well. The first two days reverted to previous form, four matches each of foursomes and fourballs. The third day remained all singles, but now it was twelve matches, meaning every player on both teams would have the chance to compete.

Unless—and it was a big unless—someone was injured and unable to play. At the end of day two, each captain would put a name in an envelope: If a team member could not compete, the opposing captain would reveal the name in the envelope (presumably that of his weakest link), that man would sit, and the match would be halved. Simple enough.

With so much new to contend with, Jacobs probably expected some problems. But no one was prepared for the behavior of two of his experienced players, Ken Brown and Mark James, who were great pals, still young, and willing to go out of their way to be a pain in the arse to the establishment.

It started at the airport in London, where Jamesy arrived, not wearing his official uniform as required but looking, said Jacobs, "terrible." (I've known Jamesy for twenty-five years, and he's never looked great.) Once at the Greenbrier, the pair skipped a team meeting to go shopping in the resort's arcade then acted like complete arseholes during the opening ceremonies, bored and fidgety (though I don't feel in a particularly strong position to criticize. Take a look at the official team photo for 1991—Torrance and I weren't much better). Once play began, things didn't improve a whole lot.

A nearby hurricane delayed the matches for nearly an hour and flooded parts of the course. But it was nothing compared to the storm that broke after the morning fourballs were over. Jacobs made a statement by leading off

198

with Garrido and Ballesteros, who won the first two holes but ultimately lost a great match to Wadkins and Nelson, 2&1. Ballesteros was starting to get pissed off at Americans in general. Brown and James were next to fall, 3&2, to Trevino and Zoeller. The heroes of 1977, Oosterhuis and Faldo, lost to Elder and Bean, 2&1. Only one European team won, Gallacher and Barnes, 2&1 over Irwin and Mahaffey in the final match of the morning. Despite the changes, America still had its traditional big lead.

Jacobs had to shake up his team in the afternoon, not only for some better luck, but because Jamesy had somehow injured one of his tits. (Officially, it was a chest injury.) Ken Brown (so thin, he was known as "the walking one-iron") hadn't played that much better than his injured mate, but Jacobs kept him in, paring him with the genial Irishman Des Smyth in the first foursomes. That's when the trouble began.

Kenny was bummed not to be playing with his pal Jamesy and for some reason hardly spoke to his partner, rarely a successful strategy in team play. Recording seven bogeys and two pars on the first nine holes, they lost badly to Irwin and Kite, 7&6, the worst loss till then in Ryder Cup foursomes (to be tied in 1991). Afterward, Irwin described what he saw: "Ken hit some just terrible shots. Des hit some good ones, but when he did Ken promptly put him over in jail somewhere. . . . I felt it was obvious there was no rapport between them. There was not even the slightest bit of idle conversation. Smyth didn't play very well and Brown played like he didn't care."

The matches that followed offered hope for Europe. Ballesteros and Garrido defeated Zoeller and Green, 3&2, while Lyle and Jacklin halved with Trevino and Morgan. In the bottom match, Gallacher and Barnes ran into the hottest pairing, Wadkins and Nelson, and lost 4&3. If Paul Runyan was "Little Poison," then Lanny was "Little Bastard." His total of 21-1/2 points won is third all-time on the list of American players, behind only Casper (23-1/2) and Palmer (23). The U.S. lead after day one was three points, 5-1/2 to 2-1/2.

The format flipped on day two, as did the results. Casper broke up his winning teams and rested three of

"Nerd."

"Geek."

HALE IRWIN AND TOM KITE

his four veterans for the morning foursomes and the Euros won the first three matches: Jacklin and Lyle over Elder and Mahaffey, 5&4; Faldo and Oosterhuis back on track with a 6&5 victory over Bean and Kite; and Gallacher and Barnes 2&1 over Zoeller and Hayes. The last match was a repeat of the first-day fourball, Ballesteros and Garrido meeting Wadkins and Nelson, and again the Americans won, 3&2.

Ballesteros and Garrido played Wadkins and Nelson for the third time in the afternoon fourballs, and for the third time the Euros lost, 5&4. Now Seve hated North America, South America, the Americas' Cup, the TransAmerica, American Express, and American Airlines. Irwin and Kite then beat Jacklin and Lyle, 1-up, and it looked as if the visitors were about to suffer another afternoon meltdown. But Gallacher and Barnes won their third match, defeating Trevino and Zoeller 3&2, and Faldo and Oosterhuis squeaked by Elder and Hayes, 1-up. The Europeans had won the day, 5-3, and trailed by one point with twelve singles to go. It was looking like a match, and golf (who'd've thunk it) had united Europe. Even three people in France were interested.

Before those matches could begin, however, there was the affair of the envelope. Jamesy's tit was still killing him, so Casper had to select a player to sit out if he couldn't go the next morning. The captains and officials had discussed the procedure before the matches began, but on the eve of the singles, the Americans asked if Casper could change the name in the envelope: It seems he'd misunderstood the process, and rather than naming his worst player (Morgan, who had a slight injury), he'd selected his best, Trevino. What a Mor(m)on! Casper explained that he thought he was supposed to name the one player he wanted to protect. Jacobs would have been within his rights to refuse, but he told his team that should they come from behind and win, he didn't want any controversy or claims of poor sportsmanship. He allowed Casper to make the switch (which wouldn't happen today without a riot).

Would it have mattered if Lyle had played Morgan instead of Trevino? Probably not, as by time they went out in the last match, the outcome of the Cup had been decided.

For a brief moment, Europe's chances looked good. In the battle of the flaming arseholes, Gallacher, who'd lost only once, met the undefeated

BRIAN BARNES AND BERNARD GALLACHER

Wadkins (who hadn't lost in 1977, either) and Bernard won 3&2, tying the overall score. But the Americans took the next five matches: Nelson ran his record to 5-0 by beating Ballesteros (ay caramba!) 3&2; Kite won 1-up over Jacklin; Hayes went 1-up on Garrido; Bean handled the untested King, 4&3; and Mahaffey outlasted Barnes, 1-up. Faldo beat Elder 3&2, but it did little to erase any of the giant European skidmark. Irwin got to meet Smyth again, and won again, 5&3.

When Hubert Green defeated Peter Oosterhuis, 2-up, it was not only the Englishman's first singles loss in eight matches over five years (how about *that* record), it also provided the Cup-winning point. Brown—who had to play, whether Jacobs wanted him to or not—put a little whipped cream and a cherry on the crap by earning the last European points with a 1-up win over Zoeller. And in the final match, Trevino took Lyle, 2&1. Give each team half a point for the Morgan-James halve, and the final score was 17-11 in America's favor.

Although the Europeans badly lost the singles (8-3, plus the halved match), they found some consolation in the fact that four of those losses had made it to the final hole. And they'd lost the first two days by only one point, much closer than any British team had done on U.S. soil. There was kudos for Faldo (3-1) and Nelson (an incredible 5-0 as a rookie). The Continentals hadn't exactly lit up the sky—both Ballesteros and Garrido won only once in five matches—but a bright future was predicted for Seve, who in eight months would win his first Masters, and begin plotting the downfall of America's Team.

As for James and Brown, upon their return to Britain, they were fined, and got a year's suspension from international team play. (How many events did that keep him out of? One? Two? Big deal.) As for the Ryder Cup, they'd both be back, a lot.

202

FINAL SCORE

COURSE:

THE GREENBRIER | WHITE SULPHUR SPRINGS | WV | 1979

FOURBALLS & FOURSOMES

FOURBALLS - MORNING

Wadkins/Nelson d. Garrido/Ballesteros, 2&1

Trevino/Zoeller d. Brown/James, 3&2

Bean/Elder d. Oosterhuis/Faldo, 2&1

Irwin/Mahaffey lost to Gallacher/Barnes, 2&1

FOURSOMES - AFTERNOON

Irwin/Kite d. Brown/Smyth, 7&6

Zoeller/Green lost to Ballesteros/Garrido, 3&2

Trevino/Morgan halved with Lyle/Jacklin

Wadkins/Nelson d. Gallacher/Barnes, 4&3

US: 5-1/2   EUROPE: 2-1/2

FOURSOMES & FOURBALLS

FOURSOMES - MORNING

Elder/Mahaffey lost to Jacklin/Lyle, 5&4

Bean/Kite lost to Faldo/Oosterhuis, 6&5

Zoeller/Hayes lost to Gallacher/Barnes, 2&1

Wadkins/Nelson d. Ballesteros/Garrido, 3&2

FOURBALLS - AFTERNOON

Wadkins/Nelson d. Ballesteros/Garrido, 5&4

Irwin/Kite d. Jacklin/Lyle, 1-up

Trevino/Zoeller lost to Gallacher/Barnes, 3&2

Elder/Hayes lost to Faldo/Oosterhuis, 1-up

US: 3   EUROPE: 5

SINGLES

Wadkins lost to Gallacher, 3&2

Nelson d. Ballesteros, 3&2

Kite d. Jacklin, 1-up

Hayes d. Garrido, 1-up

Bean d. King, 4&3

Mahaffey d. Barnes, 1-up

Elder lost to Faldo, 3&2

Irwin d. Smyth, 5&3

Green d. Oosterhuis, 2-up

Zoeller lost to Brown, 1-up

Trevino d. Lyle, 2&1

Morgan halved with James (match not played)

US: 8-1/2   EUROPE: 3-1/2

TOTAL: US 17   EUROPE 11

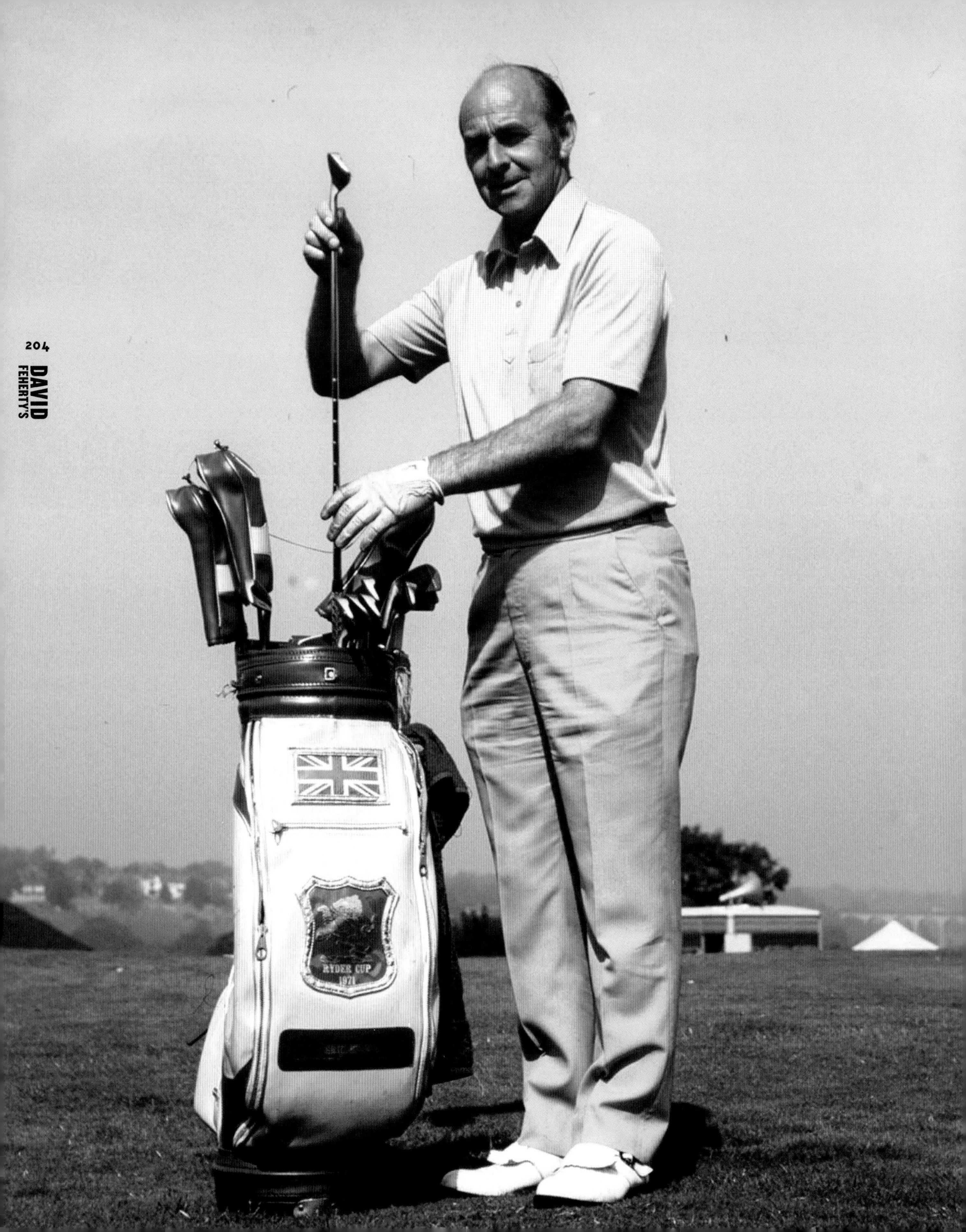
RYDER CUP
1971

ERIC BROWN (b. 1925)

IMMEDIATELY AFTER World War II, Britain had two chances in the Ryder Cup—slim and none. For a long time it was expected that the Americans would prevail and none of the British golfers appeared too angry about losing. Until, that is, Eric Brown came along.

One of Scotland's best in the post-war period, Brown won the Swiss Open and three other national titles between 1951 and 1953, and seven tournaments in Britain in the 1950s. His finest year was 1957, when he won the Vardon Trophy for low scoring average after capturing the Dunlop Masters and finishing tied for third in the Open Championship, just one stroke out of a playoff. It was also a good year for the GB Ryder Cup team, of which Brown was a standout member.

Brown played on four Cup teams, from 1953 to 1959, amassing one of the more unusual records: He played in eight matches and split them—winning all four of his singles and losing all four of his foursomes. Furthermore, his losses were with four different partners and none by a score better than 5&4.

Obviously, Brown played better by himself. He also seemed to play better pissed off. In 1953, against American captain Lloyd Mangrum, Brown had a one-hole lead on the final hole. Putting for an eagle, he asked Mangrum to move, then lagged to a foot away. Listening for the concession, Brown heard instead, "I guess you can get down in two from there, but let's see you do it anyway." Containing his fury, Brown took his time, viewed the putt from every direction, then holed it for a 2-up win.

Brown's American counterpart in anger was Tommy Bolt, known as "Thunder" for his tendency to roar and throw clubs. In 1957, Bolt and Brown faced each other not once but twice. The first time, in foursomes, both were quiet as Bolt teamed with Dick Mayer and roasted Brown and Christy O'Connor Sr., 7&5. But in the singles, the two hotheads put on a display of fireworks.

For the first time in years, the Brits thought they had a chance to win the Cup. Both captains wanted to start the singles with a bang, so they put out their most excitable players. Brown ran out to an early lead and was up four holes at lunch. Bolt got two holes back in the afternoon but then slipped again, eventually losing 4&3. After it was over, Bolt said to Brown, "Well, I guess you won, but I didn't enjoy it a bit," to which Brown reportedly replied, "Nor would I if I'd been licked like you just have." More words passed between them (few, I'm sure, that even I would reprint), and Bolt stormed off saying, "This isn't golf, it's war!" And a war the Americans lost.

In Brown's two other singles, he beat Jerry Barber in 1953, 3&2, and topped Cary Middlecoff in 1959, 4&3, both without incident.

Brown was only slightly less feisty as captain. At Birkdale in 1969, he instructed his team not to help the Americans search for balls lost in the long rough. Despite that, the 1969 Ryder Cup remains famous for one of sport's great acts of sportsmanship: Jack Nicklaus conceding a putt to Tony Jacklin that ended the matches in an overall tie, the best showing for the British since 1957.

In 1971 in St. Louis, Brown's team had their best finish to date on U.S. soil, losing by five points. He was criticized for his handling of the players, but didn't do much to fan the flames other than complaining on the eve of the match about the host's hospitality: "We went to an official dinner and the food was cold," he said. "We came out and had to stand around like tramps because there was no transport to our hotel. These things have made the boys angry. I'm pleased to see that they are just a little bit niggled and they can't wait to get at the Yanks."

Nobody burned like Brown.

COURSE:

WALTON HEATH GC | SURREY | ENGLAND

☆☆☆☆☆☆☆☆☆☆ SEPT. 18-20

1981

☆☆☆☆☆☆☆☆☆☆☆☆☆☆☆☆

FINAL SCORE:

US 18-1/2   **EUROPE 09-1/2**

CAPTAINS:

DAVE MARR   JOHN JACOBS

UNITED STATES

☆☆☆☆☆☆☆☆☆☆☆☆☆☆☆☆

Ben Crenshaw	Lee Trevino
Ray Floyd	Tom Watson
Hale Irwin	
Tom Kite	
Bruce Lietzke	
Johnny Miller	
Larry Nelson	
Jack Nicklaus	
Jerry Pate	
Bill Rogers	

EUROPE

☆☆☆☆☆☆☆☆☆☆☆☆☆☆☆☆

Jose Maria Canizares	Des Smyth
Howard Clark	Sam Torrance
Eamonn Darcy	
Nick Faldo	
Bernard Gallacher	
Mark James*	
Bernhard Langer	
Sandy Lyle	
Peter Oosterhuis*	
Manuel Pinero	*captain's picks

1967   1969   1971   1973   1975   1977   1979   ☆   1983

1981

AS QUICKLY AS SEVE BALLESTEROS BURST OUT of the wings onto the Ryder Cup stage, he fell through a trapdoor and was gone. It had all started out so promising. It didn't matter that he hadn't single-handedly recaptured the Cup or even played all that well in his first appearance, winning only once in five matches is swashbuckling style and precocious talent gave hope to all of Europe—but especially the British, who would let the handsome dago shag the Queen Mother if he could break the American strangehold. And his success since 1979 raised the level of anticipation, too: He won the 1980 Masters and more than half a dozen other tournaments around the globe in the period between Cups, all with a game face that lit up the screen. Like Palmer before, and Norman and Woods after, Ballesteros was made for televised golf. He was brilliant, he was beautiful, and angry, and vulnerable, and innocent enough to show it all. He was pretty interesting, and in a fit of pique reminiscent of Henry Cotton in the 1930s. Long before Brookline, he dropped the European Tour and the Cup establishment into the crapper by raising a stink over that most unseemly of issues: money.

His snit was a direct result of the European team's selection process. As in 1979, the top ten players were to come straight from the tour's Order of Merit, plus two picks made by a three-man committee that included the captain. The two wild cards were expected to be star players who spent so much time competing internationally that they couldn't qualify at home; by that criterion, Ballesteros should have been an easy choice. But he had become so popular that he was demanding, and in many places getting, appearance money—a lot of it. In short, he was Tiger Woods. He knew he was selling a lot of tickets and wanted a piece of the action. When his home circuit

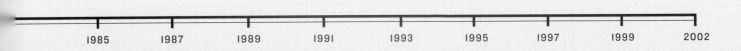

refused (they said they wanted to stop appearance fees entirely but continued to pay some Americans, which took the twig up Seve's ass and turned it sideways) he cut back his play in Europe and even refused to pay the Tour's fifty-pound membership fee. He was taking his bat and ball and going to play with his *new* friends, and everyone could go and boil their heads.

So there!

As the time to pick the team drew near, captain John Jacobs polled those players certain to qualify, and the morons didn't want Ballesteros because he wasn't supporting the tour. He could have been playing on Mars, and I would have picked him, but when the selectors—Jacobs, Neil Coles, and Bernhard Langer (who was leading the Order of Merit)—voted, Seve's only supporter was Jacobs, who as team captain was smart enough to put up with the trouble to get the talent. But Seve was out on his hole.

Almost as controversial was the exclusion of Tony Jacklin, who may not have been in his prime but was twelfth on the money list and had Cup experience. Chosen instead were Mark James, who was eleventh in money but best remembered for his stellar off-course performance two years earlier at the Greenbrier, and Peter Oosterhuis, who was playing in the U.S., and . . . wait a minute. Didn't they say they didn't want players who didn't play in *Europe?* Maybe three didn'ts made a did. Do they?

Sorry.

Anyway, with Oosty and James, the European team returned Howard Clark, Eamonn Darcy, Nick Faldo, Bernard Gallacher, Sandy Lyle, and Des Smyth. New to the squad were Jose-Maria Canizares and Manuel Pinero of Spain, Germany's Langer (who shall hereafter be known as "Herman the German") and in the first of many, the well-known Scottish git, Samuel Robert Torrance. In years to come, many of these players would form the nucleus of winning teams; but this year they were just practicing, overshadowed by an American invasion force.

Captain Dave Marr didn't have the luxury of captain's picks but the ratbag didn't need them. Being forced to take the top eleven players off the two-year points list plus the current PGA Champion gave him one hell of a squad: Back were Ray Floyd, Hale Irwin, Tom Kite, Johnny Miller, Larry Nelson, Jack Nicklaus, Lee Trevino, and Tom Watson; making their debuts were Ben Crenshaw, Bruce Lietzke, Jerry Pate, and Bill Rogers. Together, the U.S. team had won thirty-six majors, including three that year; the European team, without Ballesteros and Jacklin, had none at all. But at least they didn't have Ballesteros.

Oh, shit.

Still, the Americans were careful not to be overconfident. Ben Crenshaw remembers Marr saying to his team, "They want to beat you,' and the emphatic way he said it went right through to the heart of us."
You bastard, Crenshaw. So that's where you heard it!

There was another pre-Cup controversy, one much more easily solved than the personnel issue. When the site for the Matches was announced, it was to be a new course in the middle of England called the Belfry, which also happened to be the new headquarters of the British PGA. Like the team representing Europe, the course would become Ryder Cup–worthy in time. Just a few years old, it was not attractive but challenging (largely due to

LEE TREVINO AND SAM TORRANCE (A RIGHT PAIR OF ARSEHOLES)

DAVE MARR AND LARRY NELSON

the fact that it was frequently top dressed with sewage and small rocks). Even though it had been co-designed by his former Cup teammate Peter Alliss, Brian Barnes (not that he hadn't had a few pints) described the Belfry as little more than a "plowed field." It was an American-style course, with lots of water, which demanded the high, quick-stopping shots that characterized play on the U.S. tour. It didn't seem like a brilliant idea, and before serious damage could be done, the site was changed to Walton Heath, a seriously underranked heathland course south of London, that while far from a traditional links, played fast and featured small greens, two qualities thought to favor the home team.

Why, I do not know.

As the matches approached, all the optoeuromystics searched for good omens. Among those they grasped was the fact that the gap between the last non-American victories was twenty-four years—1933 to 1957—and it was twenty-four years again! We're obviously going to win!

Particularly when the Europeans began better than expected, halving the first morning's foursomes in the rain. As he had done in 1979, Jacobs led with a pair of fuzzy foreigners, Herman the German and Manuel Pinero, who lost to Trevino and Nelson, 1-up. But Lyle and James took care of Rogers and Lietzke, 2&1, followed by Gallacher and Smyth beating Floyd and Irwin, 3&2. It was left to Nicklaus and Watson to fight back from an early deficit to win with relative ease over Oosterhuis and Faldo, 4&3. Even so, a 2-2 tie was encouraging for the Europeans.

Actually, that was boring to write, never mind read. Like the great British public was, I'm hoping this takes a turn for the better soon.

Both captains shuffled their lineups for the afternoon fourballs, which were interrupted by more rain. In the first match, Kite and Miller were lucky to halve with Torrance and Clark, who threw away numerous opportunities to win. James was paired again with Lyle, who was all over the course off the tee but didn't miss a putt; they beat Crenshaw and Pate, 3&2, for their second win of the day. The pairing of Smyth and Canizares was criticized as weak, but a little chemistry developed and they had no trouble with Rogers and Lietzke, winning 6&5. Irwin and Floyd battled with Gallacher and Darcy, Floyd's putting proving the difference in a 2&1 victory. The Euros had controlled the afternoon, winning 2-1/2 to 1-1/2.

211

THE VICTORIOUS U.S. TEAM

Captain Dave Marr had joked before the matches that a submarine was standing by in case the U.S. lost and he had to sneak back into the country. (He also reminded all who would listen that he was a cousin to Jack Burke, the losing American captain in '57.) But while old Dave talked *reeeeal* slow, like a Texan, he was a sharp cookie, and after the poor start he consulted his team, especially the veterans. Trevino and others told their captain that he'd sent out too many rookie pairings and that they needed to put the rookies with pardners who knew not to squat on their spurs. Marr took this advice to heart on day two.

In the morning fourballs, Trevino took Pate under his wing, and they ganged up to *talk* Faldo and Torrance apart, 7&5. Nelson and Kite ended the winning streak of Lyle and James, Nelson holing birdie putts on the last two holes to win 1-up. Herman the German and Pinero didn't let Floyd and Irwin win a hole until sixteen, but by then it was too late as the Europeans won 2&1. The upset winners of day one, Smyth and Canizares, didn't fare so well against Nicklaus and Watson; the Americans, who were well rested, were three-up after nine, posted seven birdies in nine holes, and won more easily than the 3&2 score indicated. The U.S. had grabbed back the lead with a 3-1 morning, and worse was yet to come.

Bollocks! Where the hell is Ballesteros?

Despite downpours and wind, all eight teams played well in the afternoon, with the Americans just better enough to pitch a shut-out. Only one match reached the final hole, Trevino and Pate beating Oosterhuis and Torrance, 2&1. The rest of the matches went to the Americans 3&2—Nicklaus and Watson over Langer and Pinero; Rogers and Floyd over Lyle and James; and Kite and Nelson (now 8-0 in two years) over Smyth and Gallacher.

The U.S. won day two 7-1 (only the 7-1/2 to 1/2 second day in 1967 was more decisive). Jacobs was telling the truth when he said, "It wasn't that our boys played badly. The Americans just excelled."

Well, that and the fact he didn't have Seve.

Down by five points, playing a sodden course that grew longer with every cloudburst, and dispirited from their poor showing, the Europeans came out flat in the singles and stayed that way. Jacobs led off with Torrance, who went to 0-4 in slightly more than two hours, losing to Trevino, 5&3. This would be Trevino's last Cup appearance and he made it memorable: On the first tee, he told his pal Sam, "I'm going to beat the mustache off you." Two golf junkies, they loved to play together. After the loss, (which really pissed him off) Sam showed up for dinner with both teams with an upper lip gleaming white over his tanned mug. It was the first time anyone had seen him without it, and he looked like a damned gerbil.

Trevino, the bastard, was back in the clubhouse drying off before the final match of the day—Nicklaus vs. Darcy—teed off, and joked that he would gladly play again if Jack wanted to stay out of the rain. Never mind the gags, Trevino finished with a fantastic record, 17-7-6 in six Cups and 4-0 at Walton Heath.

It continued to rain on the Europeans' parade as they won only three matches: Pinero defeated Pate, 4&2; Faldo beat Miller (playing in only his second match of the week but also the last of his Cup career), 2&1; and Clark surprised Watson (although it wasn't a shock to the Europeans) 4&3. There were two halves—Rogers vs. Gallacher and Lietzke vs. Langer.

On the American side of the ledger, Crenshaw had no problems with Smyth, 6&4, and Nelson won the deciding point (and his ninth straight match), 2-up over James. I wonder who rattled *his* cage? Irwin topped Canizares 1-up; and Floyd got a rare 1-up win over Oosterhuis.

Two matches deserve more than simply the final score. Kite beat Lyle in one of the most exciting games in Cup history. After eleven holes and a flurry of birdies from both men, they were even, both six-under. At that point, Lyle slowed down but Kite got even hotter: at the sixteenth hole, he was ten-under-par, and he won 3&2. The Ryder Cup as we know it was starting to give birth to itself, inspiring unimaginable bursts of scoring and some of the greatest moments in golf.

Nicklaus declined Trevino's offer, went out in the rain himself, and drowned Darcy, 5&3. This would be Nicklaus's last Cup match, capping a record of 17-8-3 in six years. He finished in style, going 4-0. There was no doubt he would be back as captain—pretty quickly, as it turned out.

This also was Oosty's last Cup, and like Nicklaus, he finished with twenty-eight matches in six years. The big Englishman's record—14-11-3—was especially good for someone who'd endured some of GB's worst years. He would go back to the U.S. and struggle on the PGA Tour, where he had only one victory, the 1981 Canadian Open. In 1977, after going 3-0 at Lytham (including a foursomes win with Faldo over Nicklaus and Watson), the big lad said, "I don't understand it. Here I am beating the top Americans, yet for the rest of the year I'm struggling to stay in the top sixty." There was a simple answer though: Oosty was a Ryder Cup player, one of those who really got it *bad*. To be on that team meant so much to him that he was able to find something deeper within him, the courage to attack and find out how good he really could be. And he was fucking good, believe me, a lot better than some gave him credit for. Most players can't bring themselves to touch the nettle, some grasp it in individual events, but Oosty saved his best for the six Ryder Cup Teams on which he played. The big dork should captain a European team soon, whether or not he lives in America—no one deserves it more.

With a final tally of 18-1/2 to 9-1/2 came the usual noises about changing the selection process, but few questioned including Europe. The three Continentals—Canizares, Pinero, and Langer—had more than held their own. In fact, they were more productive than the GB players, winning 3-1/2 out of a possible 8 points, against 6 out of 24.

Seve had watched the whole thing on the telly, chewing cloves of raw garlic, throwing knives at a picture of Larry Nelson, and shouting "Mierde!' at the top of his voice.

He was perfect. Now, if we could just figure out how to get the asshole back on the team.

FINAL SCORE

COURSE:
WALTON HEATH GC | SURREY | ENGLAND

1981

FOURSOMES & FOURBALLS

FOURSOMES - MORNING
Trevino/Nelson d. Langer/Pinero, 1-up
Rogers/Lietzke lost to Lyle/James, 2&1
Floyd/Irwin lost to Gallacher/Smyth, 3&2
Watson/Nicklaus d. Oosterhuis/Faldo, 4&3

FOURBALLS - AFTERNOON
Kite/Miller halved with Torrance/Clark
Crenshaw/Pate lost to Lyle/James, 3&2
Rogers/Lietzke lost to Smyth/Canizares, 6&5
Irwin/Floyd d. Gallacher/Darcy, 2&1

US: 3-1/2   EUROPE: 4-1/2

FOURBALLS & FOURSOMES

FOURBALLS - MORNING
Trevino/Pate d. Faldo/Torrance, 7&5
Nelson/Kite d. Lyle/James, 1-up
Floyd/Irwin lost to Langer/Pinero, 2&1
Nicklaus/Watson d. Carnizares/Smyth, 3&2

FOURSOMES - AFTERNOON
Trevino/Pate d. Oosterhuis/Torrance, 2&1
Nicklaus/Watson d. Langer/Pinero, 3&2
Rogers/Floyd d. Lyle/James, 3&2
Kite/Nelson d. Smyth/Gallacher, 3&2

US: 7   EUROPE: 1

SINGLES

Trevino d. Torrance, 5&3
Kite d. Lyle, 3&2
Rogers halved with Gallacher
Nelson d. James, 2-up
Crenshaw d. Smyth, 6&4
Lietzke halved with Langer
Pate lost to Pinero, 4&2
Irwin d. Carnizares, 1-up
Miller lost to Faldo, 2&1
Watson lost to Clark, 4&3
Floyd d. Oosterhuis, 1-up
Nicklaus d. Darcy, 5&3

US: 8   EUROPE: 4

TOTAL: US 18-1/2   EUROPE 09-1/2

COURSE:

PGA NATIONAL GC | PALM BEACH GARDENS | FL

☆☆☆☆☆☆☆☆☆☆ OCT. **14-16**

1983

FINAL SCORE:

☆ us **14-1/2**

EUROPE **13-1/2**

CAPTAINS:

JACK NICKLAUS | TONY JACKLIN

UNITED STATES
☆☆☆☆☆☆☆☆☆☆☆☆☆

Ben Crenshaw	Tom Watson
Ray Floyd	Fuzzy Zoeller
Bob Gilder	
Jay Haas	
Tom Kite	
Gil Morgan	
Calvin Peete	
Craig Stadler	
Curtis Strange	
Lanny Wadkins	

EUROPE
☆☆☆☆☆☆☆☆☆☆☆☆☆

Seve Ballesteros	Paul Way
Gordon Brand	Ian Woosnam
Ken Brown	
Jose Maria Canizares	
Nick Faldo	
Bernard Gallacher	
Bernhard Langer	
Sandy Lyle	
Sam Torrance	
Brian Waites	

1967   1969   1971   1973   1975   1977   1979   1981   ☆

1983

Courtesy of The PGA of America

IN 1983, THE EUROPEAN TEAM BLEW THE LID OFF THE RYDER CUP.

Actually, it began in May of 1982, at the first round of the now-defunct Car Care International tournament in England, the very same day my caddie Rodney shit in his pants before getting on a train to work. (Not that that's relevant, it's just one of those things like "Where were you when Kennedy was shot?" A day like that'll linger with you.) Ken Schofield, executive director of the European Tour, asked Tony Jacklin if he would captain the European team sixteen months hence. Jacklin, who was still smarting about having been left off the Cup squad two years earlier, didn't give his answer on the spot; instead, he went off to play his round, shot sixty-five, then came back with a few requests of his own.

Jacklin would take the gig, but he had a few conditions, the most important being that his team would be treated as well as the Americans had been for years. That meant first-class travel and accommodations for his players, their wives or girlfriends, and their caddies, as well as first-class uniforms. (Jacklin remembered all too well wearing plastic golf shoes that fell apart while playing at Laurel Valley in 1975.) "Too many times in the past," the new captain said, "the Ryder Cup has been run, it seemed, more for the officials than for the players. . . . If I were to be captain, it would be run and organized with the players in mind." It was new and strangely frightening concept to the establishment.

The one player Jacklin had in mind was Seve Ballesteros. The best player in Europe, if not the world, Ballesteros was still angry over the tour's stance on appearance money (they were against it, he wanted it) and

SEVERIANO BALLESTEROS (TOO BEAUTIFUL TO BE BAD)

outspoken about his plans to skip the Ryder Cup again, as he had done in 1981. In Jacklin's mind, Seve was the key to Cup success. He was right, too, for no one in the Cup's history had the kind of galvanizing effect on the rest of his team than did Ballesteros.

Tony and Seve met for breakfast during the 1983 Open Championship at Birkdale, where Jacklin laid out his vision of a team that would be treated well and given the tools to win. Perhaps because both men had been left off the team at Walton Heath, the thirty-nine-year-old Englishman was able to get through to the twenty-six-year-old Spaniard. Two weeks after their first meeting Ballesteros agreed to join the team.

The Europeans going to Florida qualified straight off the tour's Order of Merit (although Jacklin demanded some flexibility if necessary): veterans Ballesteros, Ken Brown, Jose Maria Canizares, Nick Faldo, Bernard Gallacher, Bernhard Langer, Sandy Lyle, and Sam Torrance; rookies Gordon J. Brand (not to be confused with Gordon Brand Jr., who would play in later cups), Brian Waites, Paul Way, and Ian Woosnam. At the heart of the team were the "Fab Five"—Ballesteros, Faldo, Langer, Lyle, and Woosnam—all of whom would win majors and, except for Lyle, anchor the Cup team well into the 1990s.

While the European team was ascendant, electrified by the enthusiasm of Ballesteros, the U.S. team was strong but not spectacular. Other than Tom Watson, with seven major championships (among them five Open Championships, the final one just three months before the Cup matches), and to a lesser extent Raymond Floyd with three, the Americans were good players but hardly regarded as world-beaters. In fact, this time there were five rookies on the U.S. team, one more than on the European squad.

Returning with Floyd and Watson were Ben Crenshaw, Tom Kite, Gil Morgan, Lanny Wadkins, and Fuzzy Zoeller. Playing for the first time were Bob Gilder, Jay Haas, Calvin Peete, Craig Stadler, and Curtis Strange. Notably absent was the brilliant Ryder Cupper Larry Nelson, who was undefeated in nine matches over two years and had won the U.S. Open four months earlier. But Nelson hadn't earned enough points to make the team, and the U.S. captain wouldn't get his own picks for another six years.

Also not playing was the most intimidating golfer in history, Jack Nicklaus, although he was the U.S. captain. It is widely believed that Jacklin accepted the captaincy in part because he knew Nicklaus would be his counterpart. But be careful about drawing parallels between their meeting as captains and their singles match in 1969 when Nicklaus famously conceded the eighteenth-hole putt that resulted in a tie. Fourteen years later, neither man was looking for a touchy-feely fuzzy love-fest. There was a feeling that this one might be a balls-out fight.

Jacklin would have sold his granny to win. His demands to the European Tour and the British PGA were intended to foster success, and he spent hours planning, plotting strategy, and sweating the details. He told his players he would only use those who were in form, going so far as to tell poor Gordon Brand that he probably wouldn't make an appearance until the singles, which wouldn't have been so cruel if he hadn't done it on the Concorde flying over. Jacklin was going to ride his thoroughbreds as long as they could run.

Nicklaus took a more democratic approach. He wanted to "ensure that every member of the team gets as near as possible equal golf course time," and planned to pair players who were friends or who he thought would get along.

But he also knew which players could rise to the occasion. He wasn't above a little gamesmanship either, referring to his "inexperienced team" and in the same breath noting that given the strength of the U.S. tour, "it doesn't make a whole lot of difference who plays on our side."

And so the evil chess game began. Jacklin led off the foursomes with a pet pairing, Gallacher and Lyle; Nicklaus sent out his big gun, Watson, with Crenshaw. Both Scots were off their games and they lost, 5&4. Afterward they asked to sit, and Jacklin complied by benching them until the last day.

In the other opening matches, Faldo and Langer beat one of Nicklaus's star pairings, the club-tossing twosome of Wadkins and Stadler, 4&2. Ballesteros wanted to play with countryman Canizares, but Jacklin paired him with the cocky rookie Paul Way, who left a putt on seventeen an inch short, giving a point to Kite and Peete, 2&1. In the final match, Canizares and Torrance smoked Floyd and Gilder off the course by the fifteenth, winning 4&3.

A 2-2 tie was a good start for the Europeans, but Ballesteros wasn't happy and complained that he didn't like "acting like a father to Way and holding his hand." Jacklin responded that was exactly what he wanted from Seve, and that no one was better suited for the job. No word if Seve ever took Way behind the woodshed, but they soon gelled, and started spanking rings around them.

In the afternoon fourballs, Nicklaus rearranged all four teams and sent his remaining four players onto the course; Jacklin kept two pairs intact while playing everyone else except Brand (who really wouldn't play until the final day).

Brian Waites and Ken Brown, penciled in at the last minute for Gallacher and Lyle, scored the upset of the day, defeating Morgan and Zoeller, 2&1. Watson and Haas were in control from the start and beat Faldo and Langer, 2&1. Responding to Jacklin's challenge, Ballesteros went back out with Way and nearly beat Floyd and Strange by himself: He came close to the 578-yard final hole in two and holed a birdie putt to win, 1-up.

In the last match, Torrance partnered Woosnam, who was making his first Cup appearance. "I have never been so nervous," Woosnam recalled fifteen years later. "I was actually shaking on the first tee. Sam whispered to me, 'Don't worry, I'll look after you. It'll be all right.'" [Lucky for Woosie. In my debut, the bastard threatened to strangle *me* on the first green at Kiawah.] "Then *whack!* He shanks his tee shot out of bounds. Then he goes and knocks it out of bounds on the next hole, then he hits in the water. I didn't see him for three holes. But he had seven birdies after that against Ben Crenshaw and Calvin Peete. Good fun, that was." But only after Sam birdied eighteen for a half.

The first day went to the Europeans by a point, 4-1/2 to 3-1/2. It was only the second time the U.S. team had been behind after day one on home ground. That evening, Jacklin's message to his team was direct: "Forget what happened today. You've got to do it all again tomorrow."

Instead, they began to unravel. Waites and Brown had a three-hole lead early and looked primed for another upset, but the troll-and-gnome pair of Stadler and Wadkins fought back, and when Stadler chipped in from twenty-five feet for a birdie on eighteen, the Americans were winners, 1-up. Ballesteros and Way also had a lead but lost it, reaching the final hole 1-down. This time Seve was over the eighteenth green in two, chipped to three feet, then birdied again to salvage a half with Morgan and Haas. If there were any way to eke something out of nothing, Seve would find it.

Unhappy with his play on the first day, Langer asked to sit, but Jacklin wasn't having any of it. He sent the young German out for a third time with Faldo, who holed a number of huge putts, and they beat Peete and Crenshaw 4&2. Going off last, Watson had his third partner in three matches, but it didn't matter as he and Gilder took an early lead and coasted to a 5&4 win over Torrance and Woosnam.

The Europeans had held it together and the second morning ended with the teams tied. In the afternoon foursomes, Jacklin sent two of his teams out for the fourth time and both won: Faldo and Langer took care of Floyd and Kite, 3&2, and finished the first two days with a 3-1 record. The hair on Way's neck was starting to rise and he and Ballesteros took a fast lead over Watson and Gilder, withstood an American rally, and held on for a 2&1 win and a two-day record of 2-1-1. Balancing the books were two American wins: Haas and Strange took Brown and Waites, 3&1, and in the most lopsided victory of the week, Wadkins and Morgan rolled over Torrance and Canizares, 7&5. That night in the European team room, Ballesteros was giving shoulder massages.

Anything to win.

Ten years earlier at Muirfield, the teams were tied 8-8 going into the singles. That time, with sixteen points on the line, the Americans won eleven of them. Jacklin had been on that team. In fact, he had been the only winner for the British side in the morning singles; by the time he played in the afternoon, the Cup was in American hands.

Maybe that inspired his strategy—lead with strength. Jacklin opened with his three best players, Ballesteros, Faldo, and Langer, all of whom—plus Way—had played in every match and won 5-1/2 out of 8 possible points.

With all his other accolades, Nicklaus did not want to go down in history as the first American captain to lose the Ryder Cup at home, and told his players so, ending with, "You guys show me some brass!" (At least that's what he said he said.) Crenshaw felt as if he had gotten a pep talk from Vince Lombardi. Furthermore, for the first time, the matches would be shown on American television. It was only a two-hour telecast on the final afternoon, but no one wanted to lose when the country (even just a small part of it) was watching.

Jacklin's order of play obviously surprised Nicklaus, who'd saved his best—Wadkins, Floyd, and Watson—for last. So instead of a match between Ballesteros and Watson, the two best players in the world, Seve began the afternoon against Zoeller, who was suffering with a bad back (and his usual very average front) and hadn't competed since the first day.

"I told Jack to put me out first because I figured Jacklin would put one of his cripples there, too," said Zoeller. "Imagine my surprise! I started popping painkillers as soon as I learned. Thank goodness they don't give urinalysis to golfers. My eyes were spinning."

But beware the golfer on narcotics. Zoeller took a quick lead that Ballesteros won back and started to build on, hoping a big win would encourage the rest of his team. With seven to play, Seve had a three-hole lead that Fuzzy cut into by winning four in a row, going 1-up with three to play. Ballesteros holed a twenty-foot birdie on sixteen to square the match again. Tied on the last tee, Seve should have had a huge advantage over the aching American, but he hooked his drive into rough so thick that his attempt at hacking out traveled only twenty yards, finishing in a fairway bunker 250 yards from the green.

Zoeller also found the rough with his drive, but his recovery made the fairway. He watched as Ballesteros stepped into the bunker with a three-wood. It was total madness. With the lip of the bunker jutting up only feet in front, only a lunatic would attempt to hit such a shot with such a club. Ballesteros got settled, molded himself to the contours, and with a swish of supernatural strength and grace, picked the ball clean off the top of the sand. It was jaw-dropping to everyone who witnessed it, except to the wizard himself, who was willing his ball on, spitting and hissing at it as it rolled onto the front of the green, twenty feet from the hole. To his credit, Zoeller responded with a clutch shot of his own, a two-iron to ten feet. Ballesteros's birdie try stopped four feet short, Zoeller's rolled close enough for the concession. Seve holed his putt for a half that should have been a win, but still, he had cast a little more of his spell over the Cup.

As expected, Faldo beat Haas, 2&1, and Langer dispatched Morgan, 2-up, giving Europe a two-point edge. But with the strongest Americans at the end, the middle matches became key.

The U.S. dominated, winning 4-1/2 of 6 points: Gilder beat Brand (finally making an appearance), 2-up; Crenshaw took Lyle, 3&1; the forty-year-old Peete outlasted the forty-three-year-old Waites, 1-up; Stadler handled fellow rookie Woosnam, 3&2; and Torrance (With his penchant for drama) at the eighteenth, again birdied the last hole for a half with Kite. In the one European win, Way—who "grew up ten years in three days," according to his captain—beat Curtis Strange, 2&1. With three matches to go, the U.S. team led by one point and for the very first time, viewers in the United States of America were shifting toward the edge of their seats because of the Ryder Cup. These guys were good—even the ones they'd never heard of!

Ken Brown took a big step toward erasing the public's bad memories of him from 1979 by routing Ray Floyd (no easy task), 4&3. It was a shocking fourth loss for Floyd in four matches. More important, the score was tied at thirteen, with two matches left.

After the eleventh hole, Canizares was 3-up on Wadkins, who Nicklaus had positioned near the end because he could "make something happen," which the little ratbag did, by winning two holes and reaching the last 1-down. The teams were now stalking this match, so both men knew its significance. On the long finishing hole, Wadkins laid up to a spot sixty yards from the

US RYDER CUP TEAM

green, then watched as Canizares underhit his third, leaving it in long grass between two bunkers.

Wadkins, the rotten, black-hearted little turd, then hit the shot of the week, a pitch that stopped eighteen inches from the hole. Immediately his team, and a jubilant Nicklaus (Who kissed the divot hole made by Wadkins's club) surrounded him. Said player to captain: "It was only the most important shot of my life, Jack. There's nobody I'd rather have hit it for." Typical bloody Wadkins, ending a sentence with a preposition. "Wait a minute Ethel," said the golf nut to his wife at home in New Jersy. "Jack Nicklaus is kissing a hole in the ground. The next thing you know it'll be my ass." Just how much this little gold cup meant to their heroes began to dawn on viewers. How very cool it was.

Canizares had a chance to win, but his chip from the rough ran through the green, and when he couldn't hole his par putt, he conceded Wadkins's birdie and the vital half point.

So everything rested on the final match, Watson, one of the world's best, versus one of the biggest hearts in British golf, Gallacher, who'd played so poorly in his opening match that he'd asked to be benched. Watson took the early lead, was 3-up after seven, but just 1-up with two to play. At seventeen, a long par-three, both players missed the green not only with their tee shots but with their subsequent chips as well. In an anticlimactic ending, Watson got down in two while Gallacher three-putted. The 2&1 victory gave the Americans the Cup by the slimmest of margins, 14-1/2 to 13-1/2.

In the closest Cup match ever on American soil, neither team led the other by more than a point. The final result was determined by the final hole of the final match. It was a real competition again.

"One thing is certain," said Jacklin afterward, "these matches are going to be as close as this from now on." Nicklaus agreed, saying, "We will not be the favorites when we go to the Belfry in two years. This score was no fluke."

Ballesteros, who needed convincing to play, didn't have to be told how to react. "We were all in the team room feeling down and dejected," Faldo recalled later. "Half of us felt we should have won and the other half were not sure. . . . At that point, in marches Seve. He had his fists clenched and his teeth were bared, just like he is when he's excited, and he kept marching around the room saying to everyone, 'This is a great victory, a great victory.' Then he said, 'We must celebrate,' and he turned the whole mood of the team around. That was the spark, Seve in 1983. By 1985, we knew we could do it."

At the closing dinner, Lanny was presented with a wheelbarrow from the rest of his team, because, as Jack said, "Anyone who could hit a shot like his wedge on eighteen must have a big set of balls."

Later that evening, Crenshaw used it to take Wadkins back to his room.

It was 1983, and suddenly the Ryder Cup was demanding big balls of everyone.

224

FINAL SCORE

COURSE:

PGA NATIONAL GC | **PALM BEACH GARDENS** | **FL**

1983

FOURSOMES & FOURBALLS

FOURSOMES - MORNING

Watson/Crenshaw d. Gallacher/Lyle, 5&4

Wadkins/Stadler lost to Faldo/Langer, 4&2

Kite/Peete d. Ballesteros/Way, 2&1

Floyd/Gilder lost to Canizares/Torrance, 4&3

FOURBALLS - AFTERNOON

Morgan/Zoeller lost to Waites/Brown, 2&1

Watson/Haas d. Faldo/Langer, 2&1

Floyd/Strange lost to Ballesteros/Way, 1-up

Crenshaw/Peete halved with Torrance/Woosnam

US: 3-1/2   EUROPE: 4-1/2

FOURBALLS & FOURSOMES

FOURBALLS - MORNING

Stadler/Wadkins d. Brown/Waites, 1-up

Peete/Crenshaw lost to Faldo/Langer, 4&2

Morgan/Haas halved with Ballesteros/Way

Watson/Gilder d. Torrance/Woosnam, 5&4

FOURSOMES - AFTERNOON

Floyd/Kite lost to Faldo/Langer, 3&2

Haas/Strange d. Brown/Waites, 3&1

Wadkins/Morgan d. Torrance/Canizares, 7&5

Gilder/Watson lost to Ballesteros/Way, 2&1

US: 4-1/2 EUROPE: 3-1/2

SINGLES

Zoeller halved with Ballesteros

Haas lost to Faldo, 2&1

Morgan lost to Langer, 2-up

Gilder d. Brand, 2-up

Crenshaw d. Lyle, 3&1

Peete d. Waites, 1-up

Strange lost to Way, 2&1

Kite halved with Torrance

Stadler d. Woosnam, 3&2

Wadkins halved with Canizares

Floyd lost to Brown, 4&3

Watson d. Gallacher, 2&1

US: 6-1/2 EUROPE: 5-1/2

TOTAL:

US 14-1/2   **EUROPE 13-1/2**

COURSE:

THE BELFRY (BRABAZON COURSE) SUTTON COLDFIELD ENGLAND

★★★★★★★★★☆ SEPT. 13-15

1985

★★★★★★★★★★★★★★★★

FINAL SCORE:

US 11-1/2 ☆ EUROPE 16-1/2

CAPTAINS:

LEE TREVINO   TONY JACKLIN

UNITED STATES		EUROPE	
★★★★★★★★★★★★★		★★★★★★★★★★★★★	
Ray Floyd	Lanny Wadkins	Seve Ballesteros	Paul Way
Hubert Green	Fuzzy Zoeller	Ken Brown*	Ian Woosnam
Peter Jacobsen		Jose Maria Canizares	
Tom Kite		Howard Clark	
Andy North		Nick Faldo*	
Calvin Peete		Bernhard Langer	
Mark O'Meara		Sandy Lyle	
Craig Stadler		Manuel Pinero	
Hal Sutton		Jose Rivero*	
Curtis Strange		Sam Torrance	*captain's picks

1967   1969   1971   1973   1975   1977   1979   1981   1983

UNITED STATES

EUROPE

THE LAST TIME A NON-AMERICAN TEAM WON THE RYDER CUP WAS 1957.

Of the players on the 1985 European squad three hadn't been born yet, and four were born that year.

Okay, so there's a better than average chance that the players who hadn't been born weren't watching the British win, but even those who were around were barely teenagers, and probably more into zit-squeezing and having sex with themselves than the outcome of the matches at Lindrick.

But the European squad's youth did signal one thing: The times they were a-changing, and the momentum was definitely swinging toward the Continent.

The end of GB/Europe's twenty-eight-year streak of frustration began the moment the final putt fell at PGA National in 1983. Even though they'd lost, the Europeans were not hanging their heads in shame or crying over missed putts; they were celebrating. Rather than the usual post-loss accusations and excuses, there was back-slapping, and champagne toasts. A good team had lost to a better one, but not so much better that the losers didn't believe that they had a great chance the next time. Finally, thanks to Jacklin's insistence that they be treated as well as the Americans, even the lesser-known Europeans were starting to feel the way they should—world-class, that is.

Keeping the spirit of 1983 alive was important, so it was no surprise that Tony Jacklin was reappointed European captain. But Jacklin had more requests, and now he wanted to name his own team, all twelve players. "It is not going to be easy to win," he said, "but if I have some control over the weaker end of the team—the top eight or nine should not be a problem—it might just tip the balance." The powers that be were afraid they'd created a monster

THE BELFRY (THE DRIVABLE 10TH AT THE BELFRY MADE FOR THE FOURBALL)

who might pick his mommy or his dog, and wouldn't give Jacklin carte blanche, but they compromised: The top nine on the Order of Merit would qualify; Jacklin would choose the other three.

As a result, his new team looked a lot like his old team. Nine players from the 1983 squad returned—Seve Ballesteros (still the best in the world), Ken Brown, Jose Maria Canizares, Nick Faldo, Bernhard Langer (winner of the 1985 Masters), Sandy Lyle (1985 Open Champion), Sam Torrance, Paul Way, and Ian Woosnam. The other three—Howard Clark and the two Spaniards, Manuel Pinero and Jose Rivero—may not have been at PGA National, but only Rivero was new to Cup play. (Jacklin's three picks were Faldo, Brown, and Rivero.)

The results of 1983 had repercussions for the U.S. team as well. For the first time in years, the Americans were worried, and they responded by changing their selection process. Two years earlier, neither the current U.S. Open or PGA Championship winners—Larry Nelson and Hal Sutton—were on the team: Nelson hadn't won enough points to qualify and Sutton hadn't been a PGA member long enough. The rule was changed so both current champions were automatically in (as long as they were American, and not born female). The other ten players qualified with points won during the previous two years.

Lee Trevino was named captain and given a mix of experienced Ryder Cuppers and greenhorns. Back from 1983 were Raymond Floyd, Tom Kite, Calvin Peete, Craig Stadler, Curtis Strange, Lanny Wadkins, and Fuzzy Zoeller. Hubert Green, who'd hadn't played since 1979, was back as PGA champion. The other four were rookies—Peter Jacobsen, Andy North (U.S. Open), Mark O'Meara, and Hal Sutton. Notably absent was Tom Watson, who'd missed a par putt on the final hole of the PGA a month earlier that would have secured a spot, and you *know* he was bummed. (Watson would have been a rock solid pickarroo, but the U.S. captain was still four years from getting any of those.)

The site was the Belfry, which was to have hosted the Cup in 1981 but had been plucked from the roster when the players objected to the new, undistinguished layout. After significant renovation, including the planting of hundreds of trees, and some top-dressing with actual *soil*, the course was much improved and there now was a world-class hotel on the premises. It was still an "American-style" course, but that no longer scared the home team.

As he had in 1983, Jacklin agonized over every detail, none more so than the pairings. If Trevino was sweating the small stuff, he didn't let it show, although he promised $1,000 to the pair with the best score in the practice rounds, which went to Tom Kite and Calvin Peete, who spent it all in the hotel gift shop on more sunscreen and jewelry.

Just as it had in 1983, Jacklin's strategy failed the first morning. With 25,000 fans crowding the course and cheering the locals, Ballesteros and Pinero won the opening match, 2&1 over Strange and O'Meara. The highlight of the round was Seve's tee shot at the par-four tenth, a short hole with water and trees guarding the green. Trevino had told his players to lay up and wedge on, but Ballesteros hung out his giant cojones and went for the green, his ball just clearing the water and running to the back of the green (where a plaque commemorates the shot). His two-putt birdie gave the Europeans a three-hole lead.

If that was the highlight, the other matches were European lows. Kite and Peete notched an easy 3&2 win over Faldo and Langer, who'd teamed effectively two years earlier but were so shaky this time that the Englishman would sit until the singles (and they wouldn't be paired again for ten years!). Wadkins and Floyd didn't play well, but Lyle

CRAIG STANDLER

PAUL WAY

and Brown played worse and lost 4&3. Stadler and Sutton beat Clark and Torrance 3&2.

Trailing 3-1, Jacklin made a cup of tea, shuffled two teams, sang a quick chorus of "I've got a lovely bunch of coconuts," and brought in three new players. Trevino, although leading, did much the same, keeping two teams intact and bringing in four new men.

Way and Woosnam, called the "Tiny Tots" by their teammates, opened the afternoon fourballs by taking the first three holes then holding off Zoeller and Green to win 1-up. Ballesteros and Pinero could have shared a shirt, and continued their winning ways, beating North and Jacobsen 2&1. Langer and Canizares halved with Stadler and Sutton, and when Floyd and Wadkins handed Howard Clark and Sam Torrance their second loss of the day, 1-up, Sammy headed for the bar. That morning he'd woken up without a trace of a hangover, and he felt his swing had rejected him like a transplanted liver. The Europeans had inched closer though, winning 2-1/2 to 1-1/2, shrinking the American lead to one.

Since 1963, when the matches were extended from two days to three, the British/European team had won the second day only once. Usually they were trounced. This year would be different, thanks to the smallest of mistakes.

Torrance and Clark, 0-2 so far, were the surprise first team off in the fourballs. Howard had been glad to see Sam looking a bit rough at breakfast and they dovetailed beautifully, beating Kite and North, 2&1. The Tots faced Green and Zoeller again and won again, 4&3. O'Meara and Wadkins won the first hole and never looked back, cooling off Ballesteros (who was like a caged animal at lunch) and Pinero, 3&2.

In the last match, Stadler and Strange took a lead but Langer and Lyle clawed back to even at the turn. The Americans took the lead again, increased it to two with two holes left, but Lyle got one back with a twenty-five-foot eagle putt on seventeen. The atmosphere was overpowering on eighteen, when it looked as if the U.S. pair would win the point with a par, especially after Stadler's birdie try stopped eighteen inches away. But the putt was not conceded. "It was for victory on the final green so we had to make him play it," said Lyle. And it was probably the vilest foot and a half in the history of the Cup: Stadler yanked it left, sending the lubed-up home fans into delirium. Instead of a win, the U.S. settled for a half, tying the overall score at six. Momentum shifted, mouths in the crowd foamed, Ronald Reagan shouted "CORNHOLE ME NANCY!" for the first and only time in his life, and the Americans would never lead again.

The boys on the roof at the Belfry Hotel. Take a look at Sam Torrance's face. He's definitely thinking about scaring the shite out of Jacklin.

TONY JACKLIN AND SAM TORRANCE

With Stadler's missed "tiddler" lighting the fuse, the Europeans exploded in the afternoon, winning three of four foursomes. Canizares and Rivero rolled over Kite and Peete, 7&5. Ballesteros and Pinero did much the same to Stadler and Sutton, 5&4. Strange and Jacobsen provided the only point for the visitors with a 4&2 victory over Way and Woosnam, and somebody *finally* beat that little asshole Wadkins. He and Floyd were surprised 3&2 by Langer and Brown. In four matches each, it was Langer's first win, Wadkins's first loss, and I bet there was bad language involved.

With a 3-1 afternoon, the Europeans were going into the final day of singles with a two-point lead as well as the promise of sunshine and a loudly partisan crowd. It was the captains' turn to play: Trevino put his best players in the top three and bottom three matches; Jacklin took a chance and put his best in the middle. Yet again the superstars mostly missed each other, but then without the blind draw we probably wouldn't have the giant-killing stories that have made the Cup so great.

Pinero either jumped for joy when he learned he was leading off against Wadkins, or was horrified beyond all reason. It was hard to tell, but either way he was up for it when the bell rang. All square at the turn, the match

SAM TORRANCE (THE HEART AND SOUL OF THE CUP)

may have been won on ten, where Wadkins was looking at a birdie putt while Pinero was off the green in two. But Pinero, a short game shaman, holed his chip, Lanston (yes, that's his name) missed, and the American eventually lost 3&1. It was a gift the Euros were happy to take.

Both Stadler and Woosnam played some shitty golf, but Stadler's bad was better and he won 2&1. After Floyd's embarrassing forty-one on the front side (hey, it was less than his age), he rallied against Paul Way, who had chances to end the match but uncharacteristically gagged under the pressure of the final holes. Raymond needed to win the final hole for a half, but apparently even he could crack: His tee shot found a bunker and his do-or-die three-wood from the sand died in the water. Way to go, 2-up (and crank up that crowd while you're at it).

The little guys of the European team had taken two of three from America's best, and now was the cream's turn to rise.

Kite had a two-hole lead over Seve at the turn, extending it to three with five to go. But Ballesteros awoke when he got news of Pinero and Way, and put on his dark blue game-face—hitting shots "I never even dream about," said Kite—and holed winning putts on fourteen, fifteen, and seventeen to get back to level. They halved the final hole to halve the match.

Sandy Lyle was the reigning Open Champion and he hadn't won a Ryder Cup match since the first day in 1981. Saving his best for when it mattered, he handled Jacobsen, 3&2. Langer took care of Sutton, 5&4.

At that point, Europe needed one more point, and there were numerous contenders for the honor. It nearly fell to Clark, in a match with O'Meara when the Englishman had a Cup-winning putt on the seventeenth that rimmed the hole and stayed out, but a few seconds later, it was Torrance's chance. Neck-and-neck with North throughout, the crowd-favorite Scot hit a massive drive on the 475-yard eighteenth, leaving only a nine-iron to the green. Andy North made it easier by popping up his tee shot into the water (to the fans' by now *rabid* cheering) and, after taking a drop with a long way to go, he could only watch as Sam hammered a nine iron twenty feet below the hole. Sam's emotions have never been very far from the surface, and he was fighting back tears as he walked across the little wooden bridge to the green. Under a deafening silence with four putts to win, he stroked his little ball up the hill, thrust his arms to the sky when it was halfway there, and birdied the last one more time. For Abe Mitchell, and Alliss & Son, and the Whitcombe brothers, Eric Brown, Tony Jacklin, and every man who had played for the Cup before him, he soaked in the cheers that had been twenty-eight years in coming.

However, he's still a moron as far as I'm concerned.

In the remaining matches, Clark eventually beat O'Meara, 1-up; Green took Faldo, 3&1; Rivero lost to Peete, 1-up; Canizares handled Zoeller, 2-up; and Strange had little problem with Brown, 4&2.

The Europeans had won—big, by five points—and they were rightfully exultant. It was the Americans turn to grouse, mostly about crowds that cheered their bad shots. Trevino dismissed the complainers as crybabies, but Jacklin, upon hearing that one player had been especially critical of the crowds, sniffed, "I bet Hal Sutton can't wait to get back to America and head straight for McDonald's." It wasn't the first time a crowd—or for that matter, a captain—had been nasty and indeed, the Americans were anxious to get back on home soil and recapture the Cup that was rightfully theirs. Because hey, the Europeans couldn't win in America, could they?

FINAL SCORE

COURSE:

THE BELFRY (BRABAZON COURSE) **SUTTON COLDFIELD** ENGLAND

1985

FOURSOMES & FOURBALLS

FOURSOMES - MORNING

Strange/O'Meara lost to Ballesteros/Pinero, 2&1

Peete/Kite d. Langer/Faldo, 3&2

Wadkins/Floyd d. Lyle/Brown, 4&3

Stadler/Sutton d. Clark/Torrance, 3&2

FOURBALLS - AFTERNOON

Zoeller/Green lost to Way/Woosnam, 1-up

North/Jacobsen lost to Ballesteros/Pinero, 2&1

Stadler/Sutton halved with Langer/Canizares

Floyd/Wadkins d. Torrance/Clark, 1-up

US: 4-1/2   EUROPE: 3-1/2

FOURBALLS & FOURSOMES

FOURBALLS - MORNING

Kite/North lost to Torrance/Clark, 2&1

Green/Zoeller lost to Way/Woosnam, 4&3

O'Meara/Wadkins d. Ballesteros/Pinero, 3&2

Stadler/Strange halved with Langer/Lyle

FOURSOMES - AFTERNOON

Kite/Peete lost to Canizares/Rivero, 7&5

Stadler/Sutton lost to Ballesteros/Pinero, 5&4

Strange/Jacobsen d. Way/Woosnan, 4&2

Floyd/Wadkins lost to Langer/Brown, 3&2

US: 2-1/2   EUROPE: 5-1/2

SINGLES

Wadkins lost to Pinero, 3&1

Stadler d. Woosnam, 2&1

Floyd lost to Way, 2-up

Kite halved with Ballesteros

Jacobsen lost to Lyle, 3&2

Sutton lost to Langer, 5&4

North lost to Torrance, 1-up

O'Meara lost to Clark, 1-up

Green d. Faldo, 3&1

Peete d. Rivero, 1-up

Zoeller lost to Canizares, 2-up

Strange d. Brown, 4&2

US: 4-1/2   EUROPE: 7-1/2

TOTAL: US 11-1/2   EUROPE 16-1/2

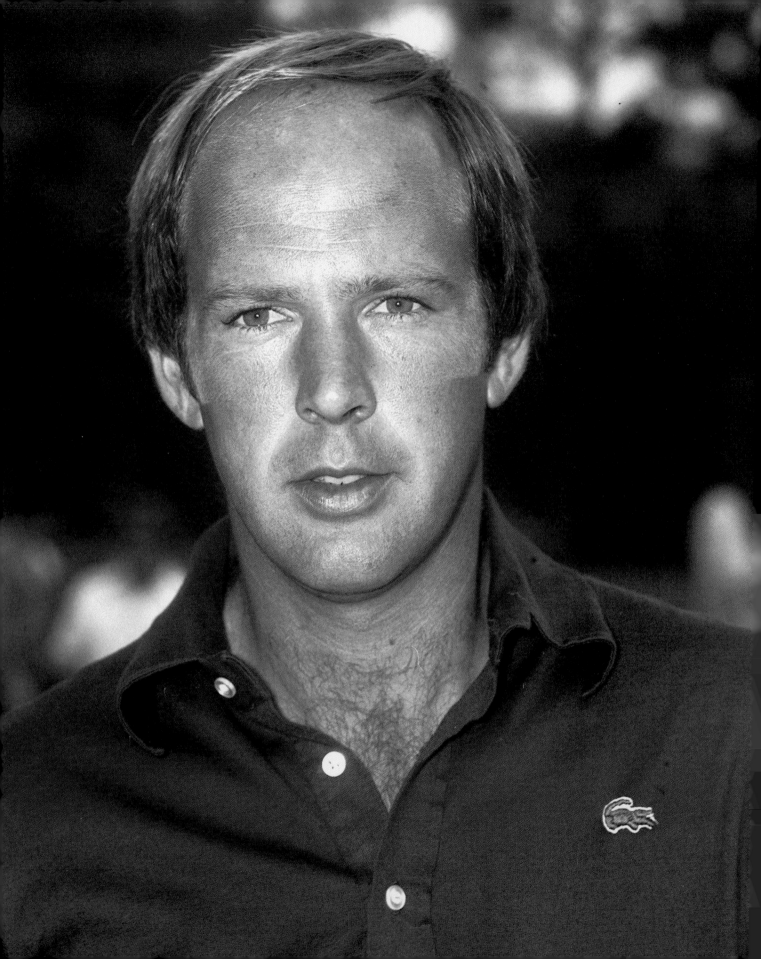

HEROES OF THE RYDER CUP
LARRY NELSON : (b. 1947)

MOST PROFESSIONAL GOLFERS pick up the game at a young age. Not Larry Nelson, who didn't swing a club until he was twenty-one years old and back from military service in Vietnam. With Ben Hogan's *Five Fundamentals of Golf* as his bible, he broke 100 his first time out and 70 within nine months.

Obviously a natural, he turned professional two years later and won his first PGA Tour event in 1979. Over the next ten years he won ten times, including the 1983 U.S. Open and PGA Championships in 1981 and 1987. There also have been a handful of international victories, and since 1997, sixteen wins on the Champions Tour.

Nelson played in his first Ryder Cup in 1979. It was an auspicious debut: He won all five of his matches, four of them over another Cup rookie, Seve Ballesteros. Nelson—who said the opening fourball was only his second time competing at match play—teamed with Lanny Wadkins in all four two-man events. Friday morning, they handled Ballesteros and fellow Spaniard Antonio Garrido (the first Continentals to compete for the Cup), 2&1. Nelson and Wadkins faced the two Spaniards twice on the second day, beating them 3&2 in foursomes and 5&4 in fourballs. Their other victory was 4&3 over Bernard Gallacher and Brian Barnes in the first day's foursomes.

The unbeaten Nelson then faced the 1-3 Ballesteros in singles. The American took a three-hole lead with three opening birdies and cruised to a 3&2 victory. But it was not without excitement: On par-five twelfth, Nelson's drive plugged in the face of a steep bunker and he was lucky to get back into the fairway. From there he hit a fairway wood to six inches for a half. Always self-effacing, Nelson was a little uncomfortable being named most valuable player for the winning (17-11) team. "If there was a hero," he said, "it was Lanny. He spent the first two days teaching me match play and his aggressive nature got me going."

Having learned his lessons well, Nelson remained hot at Walton Heath in 1981. Again in the first match, he teamed with Lee Trevino to defeat two debuting Europeans, Bernhard Langer and Manuel Pinero, 1-up. Playing with Tom Kite he beat Sandy Lyle and Mark James, 1-up, then he and Kite beat Des Smyth and Gallacher, 3&2. Facing James in the singles, Nelson won 2-up, running his unbeaten streak to nine and tying Gardner Dickinson, who won nine straight in 1967 and 1971.

But like Dickinson, nine lives were all Nelson had. On the team again in 1987, he was paired the first morning with rookie Payne Stewart against Ballesteros and another newcomer, Jose Maria Olazabal: In their first of fifteen matches together, the Spaniards prevailed, 1-up. Nelson played three more times in 1987 without a win, losing twice with Wadkins to Langer and Lyle, 2&1 and 1-up, then halving with Langer in a singles match featuring a little controversy: On the final green, Nelson and Langer mutually agreed to concede their short putts for a half. The U.S. was trailing and needed all the points it could get, so some felt Nelson should have taken the chance that Langer would miss and he'd make. But captain Jack Nicklaus (see Nicklaus vs. Jacklin, 1969) agreed with Nelson, saying, "It was a proper gesture on Larry's part."

It was a fitting end to an exemplary Cup career, from one of the most underrated players in history.

COURSE:

MUIRFIELD VILLAGE GC | DUBLIN | OH

SEPT. **25-27**

1987

FINAL SCORE:

US 13 ⭐ EUROPE 15

CAPTAINS:

JACK NICKLAUS | TONY JACKLIN

UNITED STATES		EUROPE	
Andy Bean	Hal Sutton	Seve Ballesteros	Sam Torrance
Mark Calcavecchia	Lanny Wadkins	Gordon Brand Jr.	Ian Woosnam
Ben Crenshaw		Ken Brown*	
Tom Kite		Howard Clark	
Larry Mize		Eamonn Darcy	
Larry Nelson		Nick Faldo	
Dan Pohl		Bernhard Langer	
Scott Simpson		Sandy Lyle*	
Payne Stewart		Jose Maria Olazabal*	
Curtis Strange		Jose Rivero	*captain's picks

UNITED STATES

EUROPE

IT'S HARD TO PINPOINT THE EXACT MOMENT THAT GOLF GOT COOL. Formerly the province of rich, fat white guys, in the mid-1980s it became the obsession of movie stars and CEOs, pop stars and politicians. Baby boomers whose knees hurt from tennis and jogging fell in love with a game that let them spend wads of money on equipment, was perfect for business entertaining, and demanded little or no physical exertion: For many, the real fun was racing around in electric carts with multiple cup-holders.

The golf boom also was a windfall for tour pros, who were getting rich from corporate outings and endorsement deals as well as skyrocketing prize money: In 1960, the total purse on the PGA Tour was $1,335,000; in 1970, $6,750,000; in 1980, $13,370,000. Then, between 1983 and 1987, the money nearly doubled, from $17,600,000 to $32,100,000. (And the run-up continues: In 2002, the purse was up to $200,000,000!)

During this explosion, the Ryder Cup benefited because it was unique—a team event played for national pride. The excitement came to a head at the 1987 matches, which for the first time since 1959 were being held on U.S. soil with the Cup not gathering American dust in an American closet.

The site was Muirfield Village, near Columbus, Ohio, an American-style course created by Jack Nicklaus (who named it after the course on which he won his first Open Championship). Naturally, he was asked to lead the American team. But Nicklaus was saddled with a selection system still based on points won the past two years (plus the current U.S. Open and PGA champions earned automatic berths), and he learned a harsh lesson about golf's new economics: With bigger Tour purses, the best players could compete in fewer tournaments and still get rich,

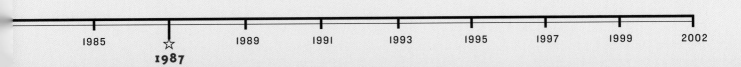

JACK NICKLAUS

which left a lot of Ryder Cup points for those who played especially often, if not especially well.

As a result, the U.S. team was one of the weakest ever. Of the seven returning Cuppers, only four had played in 1985—Tom Kite, Curtis Strange, Hal Sutton, and Lanny Wadkins. Three others were back: Andy Bean (who hadn't played since 1979), Ben Crenshaw (1983), and Larry Nelson (1981, also the 1987 PGA winner). That meant five rookies: Mark Calcavecchia, Larry Mize (1987 Masters), Dan Pohl, Scott Simpson (1987 U.S. Open), and Payne Stewart.

The European team had only two newcomers, Spain's Jose Maria Olazabal (one of three captain's picks) and Scotland's Gordon Brand Jr. (not to be confused with, nor any relation to, Gordon J. Brand, who'd played in 1983 and was English). Nine members had been on the victorious 1985 squad: Seve Ballesteros, Ken Brown (captain's pick), Howard Clark, Nick Faldo, Bernhard Langer, Sandy Lyle (captain's pick), Jose Rivero, Sam Torrance, and Ian Woosnam. Eamonn Darcy, the Irishman with the eccentric swing who'd played in 1975, 1977, and 1981, also was back.

To no one's surprise, Tony Jacklin again was asked to captain. But shortly after accepting the job, he nearly resigned thanks to a Johnny-come-lately to the Cup experience, American television.

With Nicklaus involved at his own course, and the U.S. hell-bent on revenge, executives at ABC predicted strong ratings for the first Cup aired live in the U.S. But that wasn't enough: ABC wanted a fourth day, another round of singles. Colin Snape, the weaselly executive director of the British PGA, took the proposal to Jacklin, who said absolutely not; he thought the U.S. team would be too deep (this was before the teams were set) and that more singles would expose Europe's weaknesses. At the 1986 Open Championship, with both Nicklaus and Jacklin present, the idea was raised again and Jacklin said he would quit if the format were changed. Nicklaus said to forget it, so they did.

Another money-tinged kerfuffle involved one of the sponsors, who also had hopes of Cup-related success. Glenmuir, official clothing supplier to the European team, wanted its logo splashed on all twelve players (that's what they were paying for, wasn't it?), but that would put many of them in violation of their contracts with other manufacturers. If Slazenger was paying Ballesteros zillions, they didn't want him swanning around in Glenmuir, even for one week, and especially not on network telly. The solution was to have them wear the clothing but black out the logos. Another sign of just how golf had become big business.

As the opening ceremonies were ending, Jacklin invited executives from the European Tour for a drink with the team: It was an ambush. For two hours, while the executives (and Torrance) drank, the players ragged on the tour, criticizing everything from course conditioning to the quality of practice balls, both of which were crap. (I mean both practice balls were crap, as for a while it seemed the European Tour had only two.) In retrospect, the administrators realized Jacklin might have set them up as punching bags for the golfers, who were pretty damn freaked-up for the event. "I remember thinking," said Ken Schofield, the tour's executive director, "that if the players were in that sort of mood, God help the Americans!"

As the matches began to unfold the next morning, Jacklin might have worried that he'd let his squad blow off too much steam, but by the end of the day he was a bloody genius again.

Early on, the Americans led in all four foursomes. Strange and Kite, who'd asked to play together, defeated Torrance and Clark, 4&2. Sutton and Pohl faced Brown and Langer, but after losing the opening hole the Americans took control and won, 2&1. However, after that, everything changed.

Wadkins and Mize were 4-up at the turn over Woosnam and Faldo, who were playing together for the first time. This combination, which would rankle the Americans for years, opened its Cup career with a back-nine rally that resulted in a 2-up win. In the final match, Nelson was going for his tenth straight Cup victory and teamed with Stewart against Ballesteros and Olazabal, another new pairing that would prove to have some serious staying power. The U.S. got to 2-up on the front, but the Spaniards eventually won by a hole. The morning ended in a 2-2 tie.

Both captains juggled their lineups in the afternoon, dropping most of the morning losers. Jacklin, who usually relied on a core group of players, changed tactics and sent out three of his remaining four. They played spectacular golf, and Europe swept the fourballs.

Brand and Rivero took care of Crenshaw and Simpson, 3&2. Lyle and Langer went from 2-up on Calcavecchia and Bean to 2-down with five to play, fought back, and notched a 1-up victory with Lyle's par at the last. Faldo and Woosnam continued their success with a 2&1 win over Pohl and Sutton, while Ballesteros and Olazabal, who appeared to be trying to win the pairs division in the world muttering championships, won by the same score over Kite and Strange.

The Americans trailed 6-2 at day's end, and were in shock. This was not meant to happen, and Nicklaus proclaimed that from then on he'd only send out winners. He also appealed to the 20,000 fans for more support, and thousands of tiny American flags appeared on day two. The flags may have helped, but just a little bit as the Europeans padded their lead and gave the raucous 2,000 boosters who'd come across with them more reasons to cheer than the strangely cold beer and massive cocktails.

In the morning foursomes, Kite and Strange, the only team still together after the whitewash, took Brand and Rivero 3&1. Sutton and Mize slowed Faldo and Woosnam, wrestling them to a half. Then Lyle and Langer beat Wadkins and Nelson 2&1, while Ballesteros and Olazabal extended their winning streak to three with a 1-up victory over Crenshaw and Stewart.

Woosnam and Faldo birdied the first five holes in the opening fourballs, enough for a 5&4 win over Strange and Kite. Bean and Stewart finally got a win, beating Darcy and Brand, 3&2. Ballesteros and Olazabal were shown to be human after all, losing to Sutton and Mize, 2&1. But Lyle and Langer, in their third match together, remained invincible, taking Wadkins and Nelson, 1-up.

Europe won the second day, 4-1/2 to 3-1/2. Their lead was five points heading into the singles, so 3-1/2 more would be enough.

Put another way, the U.S. needed nine wins from the twelve matches to win back the Cup. They damn near did it.

The six-foot-four Bean opened against the five-foot-four Woosnam, and height made right as the wee Welshman fell, losing by a hole. Pohl and Clark battled to the last, where Clark's four easily beat Pohl's six for a 1-up European victory. But the Americans reigned supreme in singles (as Jacklin had feared months earlier), controlling the middle matches: After Mize and Torrance halved, Calcavecchia beat Faldo, 1-up; Stewart topped Olazabal, 2-up; Simpson handled Rivero, 2&1; and Kite fought back to defeat Lyle, 3&2. A little more than halfway through, the U.S. team was just one point behind, and it was time for a little old glory-waving from the faithful.

The Darcy-Crenshaw match proved to be the key. After three-putting the sixth to go two down, Gentle Ben beat the everliving shit out of his beloved putter,

"Hit it wherever you want, I'm gasping for a pint."

NICK FALDO AND IAN WOOSNAM

TONY JACKLIN

DATE : SEPT. 25-27

breaking the shaft, making it ineligible for further use and himself into even more of a legend. For such a sweet-natured and calm soul, he could be a raving nutcase on the golf course. Putting with his one-iron, sand wedge, and an unlit Marlboro, he battled back and took the lead at sixteen. But he lost the seventeenth by flying the green, then the eighteenth and the match by driving into the water and, after a drop, dumping his approach in a bunker. The 1-up victory was Eammon Darcy's first win in eleven matches over four years, and it brought Europe to within one point.

Nelson, who'd been undefeated in nine games over two years, had lost his touch and was 0-3 going into the singles, where he faced Herman the German. The American enjoyed a three-hole lead as late as the eleventh hole, but then he lost the next three holes with bogeys. All square at eighteen, both balls were a few feet from the hole when Langer offered "good-good," to halve the match. Nelson thought a second then agreed, conceding the possibility of a make and a miss that would have given the U.S. a much-needed full point. (Of course, it could have gone the other way.)

Langer had mistakenly thought the half would keep the Cup in Europe, when it actually left them a half-point short. But that deficit wouldn't last long because Ballesteros was up on Strange, who at that time was generally acknowledged to be the best player in the world. The thought of being the one to deal the deathblow to the Evil Empire was all the inspiration Ballesteros needed, and despite not having won a singles match in his first three Cups (one loss and two halves), he never gave up the lead he grabbed on the first hole. When Ballesteros won, 2&1, history was made: America had lost at home.

In the final two matches, Wadkins beat Brown 3&2 and Sutton halved with Brand, Jr. The U.S. had won the singles 7-1/2 to 4-1/2, but it wasn't enough.

There were many European heroes in what Faldo called "a real underdog story." Ballesteros won four out of five possible points; Langer, Woosnam, and Faldo each won three and a half out of five; Olazabal took three out of five, Lyle three out of four. The best American performances had come from Sutton and Kite, three out of five each. Strange won only two out of five. Crenshaw lost all three of his matches, and Nelson had half a point from four matches.

Nicklaus became the first American captain to lose on home soil, and there was no whining. As you'd expect, he was the consummate sportsman, saying the Europeans, "played the better golf." But noting that his players didn't win the eighteenth hole in any match, he attacked what he called the "American golf system," saying, "Instead of being aggressive, [American pros] develop a percentage type of style. On the European tour, there is less competition, which puts players in contention more often and makes them better, more aggressive finishers." It was an interesting theory that said in too many words that too much money was creating too much complacency. It would not be the last time the Americans would hear that.

FINAL SCORE

COURSE:

MUIRFIELD VILLAGE GC | DUBLIN | OH

1987

FOURSOMES & FOURBALLS

FOURSOMES - MORNING

Strange/Kite d. Torrance/Clark, 4&2

Sutton/Pohl d. Brown/Langer, 2&1

Wadkins/Mize lost to Faldo/Woosnam, 2-up

Nelson/Stewart lost to Ballesteros/Olazabal, 1-up

FOURBALLS - AFTERNOON

Crenshaw/Simpson lost to Brand/Rivero, 3&2

Bean/Calcavecchia lost to Lyle/Langer, 1-up

Sutton/Pohl lost to Faldo/Woosnam, 2&1

Strange/Kite lost to Ballesteros/Olazabal, 2&1

US: 2   EUROPE: 6

FOURSOMES & FOURBALLS

FOURSOMES - MORNING

Strange/Kite d. Rivero/Brand, 3&1

Sutton/Mize halved with Faldo/Woosnam

Wadkins/Nelson lost to Lyle/Langer, 2&1

Crenshaw/Stewart lost to
Ballesteros/Olazabal, 1-up

FOURBALLS - AFTERNOON

Strange/Kite lost to Faldo/Woosnam, 5&4

Bean/Stewart d. Darcy/Brand, 3&2

Sutton/Mize d. Ballesteros/Olazabal, 2&1

Wadkins/Nelson lost to Lyle/Langer, 1-up

US: 3-1/2   EUROPE: 4-1/2

SINGLES

Bean d. Woosnam, 1-up

Pohl lost to Clark, 1-up

Mize halved with Torrance

Calcavecchia d. Faldo, 1-up

Stewart d. Olazabal, 2-up

Simpson d. Rivero, 2&1

Kite d. Lyle, 3&2

Crenshaw lost to Darcy, 1-up

Nelson halved with Langer

Strange lost to Ballesteros, 2&1

Wadkins d. Brown, 3&2

Sutton halved with Brand

US: 7-1/2   EUROPE: 4-1/2

TOTAL:

US 13

EUROPE 15

COURSE:

THE BELFRY (BRABAZON COURSE) | SUTTON COLDFIELD | ENGLAND

SEPT. 22-24

1989

THE BELFRY

FINAL SCORE:

☆ US 14   ☆ EUROPE 14

CAPTAINS:

RAYMOND FLOYD   TONY JACKLIN

UNITED STATES

Paul Azinger	Lanny Wadkins*
Chip Beck	Tom Watson*
Mark Calcavecchia	
Fred Couples	
Ken Green	
Tom Kite	
Mark McCumber	
Mark O'Meara	
Payne Stewart	
Curtis Strange	

EUROPE

Seve Ballesteros	Sam Torrance
Gordon Brand Jr.	Ian Woosnam
Jose Maria Canizares	
Howard Clark*	
Nick Faldo	
Mark James	
Bernhard Langer*	
Christy O'Connor Jr.*	
Jose Maria Olazabal	
Ronan Rafferty	*captain's picks

1967   1969   1971   1973   1975   1977   1979   1981   1983

UNITED STATES

EUROPE

IN THE EARLY DAYS OF THE RYDER CUP, the English golf writer Bernard Darwin belittled the importance of its captains by asking, "When all is said what can the captain of a golf side do besides putting his men in the best possible order and encouraging them in every possible way?" Tony Jacklin proved that captains could do all that and more, and that they did, in fact, matter.

Though he was fortunate to have been around at the time the Europeans (in particular the Spaniards) were a rising force in world golf, Jacklin was the most effective and influential captain in Cup history. Before he assumed his first command, in 1983, the British and European teams had no wins and one tie in the previous eleven stagings, and none of those ten losses was by fewer than five points (three were by double digits). But when Jacklin came along—and with him a crop of hungry young Continentals—everything changed.

Among his most important accomplishments was convincing his teams that they could, indeed, win: As a former player, he knew what to say and how to say it to fiery, egomaniacal competitors like Seve Ballesteros, who had to be pretty much hummed into playing in 1983. Jacklin also made sure that his players were properly treated. There would be no more flying in coach (it was the Concorde from then on), no more plastic shoes that fell apart on the course (as had happened to him in 1975), and no more traveling solo: Wives and caddies were welcomed.

Jacklin also showed that "putting his men in the best possible order" was a skill. Because each captain prepares his lineups without knowing how the other is arranging his, it takes cunning to divine favorable match-ups. Although Jacklin didn't always guess right, the final results rarely proved him wrong. (It's better to be lucky

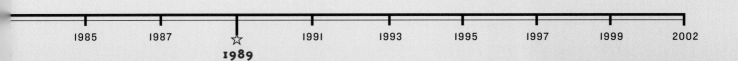

than good, but it's best to be both.) He also concocted some very successful pairings, teaming Ian Woosnam and Nick Faldo, Sandy Lyle with Bernhard Langer, and, most notably, Ballesteros and Jose Maria Olazabal, though that wasn't exactly rocket science.

His record speaks for itself. In 1981, John Jacobs captained the Europeans to a nine-point loss. The next year, under Jacklin and playing in the United States, Europe lost by one point. The year after that, the Americans lost for the first time in twenty-eight years. And in 1987, Jacklin's team accomplished the impossible, winning on American soil for the first time ever. Woosnam spoke for generations of players when he declared after the victory in Ohio that Jacklin deserved a knighthood, or at least a corgi.

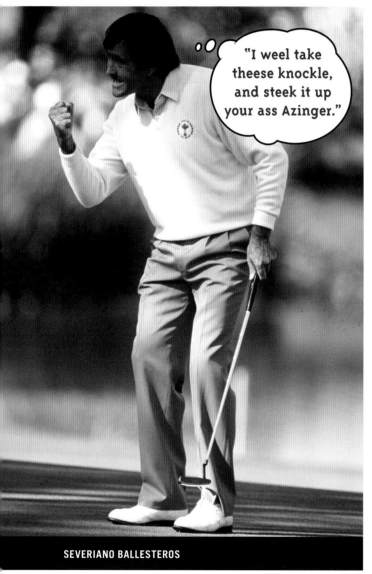

SEVERIANO BALLESTEROS

WIVES OF THE US TEAM PLAYERS

Most observers assumed that the 1989 matches, which were returning to the Belfry (where Europe had won in 1985), would be Jacklin's last stand. His brain and his balls had been through the wringer since the previous matches: His wife, Vivian, had died, and he had been castigated in the fickle British tabloid press for taking up with a much younger woman. (Before the Matches, he married a beautiful Norwegian divorcée, giving the celebrity poonhacks a field day.) But part of being a successful captain had meant dedicating his life to the task, and he was ready to move on. But only after defending the Cup, that is.

Again, the Europeans fielded a stronger team, with eight players back from Muirfield Village: Ballesteros, Faldo, Langer, Olazabal, Woosnam, Gordon Brand Jr., Howard Clark, and Sam Torrance. Three other veterans also returned:

Jose Maria Canizares (from 1985), Mark James (1981), and Christy O'Connor Jr. (who hadn't played since 1975) There was one rookie, the former child prodigy from Ulster, Ronan Rafferty, who, as Europe's top money-winner, had proven he could play. Conspicuous by his absence was Sandy Lyle, who had been on the previous five teams and won the 1988 Masters but was having a disastrous 1989. After failing to qualify on points, Lyle told Jacklin not to waste a captain's pick on him; Jacklin chose Clark, Herman the German, and O'Connor Jr.

Captain's picks were another Jacklin influence, a condition of his accepting the job in 1985. After successive losses, the Americans realized that a little latitude in composing the team might help them too, so in 1989 the U.S. captain was given two picks (or just one if the current PGA Champion hadn't already qualified). Going on points, five veterans made the team: Mark Calcavecchia, Tom Kite, Mark O'Meara, Payne Stewart, and Curtis Strange. Five rookies joined them: Paul Azinger, Chip Beck, Fred Couples, Ken Green, and Mark McCumber.

That left captain Raymond Floyd with two picks (luckily, Stewart had won the 1989 PGA). Floyd, a crusty old veteran, had been chosen to fire up the American team, which he did, in part, by saying things like, "We're going over there to kick butt." (Jacklin's reply: "The cup is going nowhere.") Actually, when you see it in print, they both sounded pathetic—they'd've been better getting into a bitch-slapper with sticks of celery. With his picks, Floyd chose two other crusty old veterans—Lanny Wadkins and Tom Watson—opting for Cup experience over current form.

At the pre-Match dinner, Floyd introduced his team as "the twelve greatest players in the world," echoing Ben Hogan's words of 1967. The boast rang slightly hollow since at the other table sat Faldo, Ballesteros, and Langer, who had won as many majors as the entire U.S. team over the past five years. It probably did nothing for the underwear of his boys either, who after two losses and in hostile territory, were in as tough a spot as any American golfers in history.

"We all told Tony that he should get up and introduce Seve as the thirteenth best player in the world," Faldo recalled later, an indication that even the greatest of the Europeans knew who the alpha male was in this pack. "We knew what Raymond was trying to do, but considering the fact that we had beaten them pretty soundly the previous two matches, it just wasn't appropriate."

The evening ended after the Band of Irish Guards struck up "Land of Hope and Glory" and the Americans beat a hasty retreat.

They were back the next morning. In the opening match, Kite and Strange faced Faldo and Woosnam: The visitors had the honor, but in a nice touch, Kite deferred to the holders of the Cup, and Woosnam hit away. The officials held a quick conference and beginning with the next match, the U.S. teed off first.

That match ended in a half, as did the third, Watson and Beck against Ballesteros and Olazabal (from then on, the Spaniards went off last, winning all three matches). The other two matches went to the U.S. team, Wadkins and Stewart over Clark and James, 1-up, Calcavecchia and Green beating Langer and Rafferty, 2&1.

Exactly as at the Belfry four years earlier, the United States opened with a 3-1 lead. But as also happened in 1985, it was the last time the Americans would have the lead.

Floyd, who was supposed to shake up his team, followed precedent and sent out the four players who'd sat in the morning. Jacklin, whose teams hadn't won a match, stuck with three of them, dropping Langer and Rafferty. They were replaced by Torrance and Brand, who led off the fourballs with a 1-up win over Strange and Azinger. Then Clark and James beat Wadkins and Couples, 3&2. Extending their unbeaten streak to six matches, Faldo and Woosnam beat Calcavecchia and McCumber, 2-up. Batting clean-up, Ballesteros and Olazabal won the first five holes and cruised to a 6&5 victory over Watson and O'Meara. American teams had never even led in any match, and the crowds were juiced up, and in full, knob-waving, gloat mode. It was very loud, and a tough place to be an American.

The second day was kinder to the Americans, who didn't lose any ground but didn't gain any either. In the morning foursomes, Faldo and Woosnam led off by beating Wadkins and Stewart, 3&2, while Ballesteros and Olazabal closed with a 1-up win over Kite and Strange. The middle matches went to the Americans—Azinger and Beck beating Brand and Torrance 4&3, Calcavecchia and Green getting the better of O'Connor and Rafferty, 3&2.

Faldo and Woosnam finally lost, falling in the afternoon's first fourball, 2&1 to Azinger and Beck. Then Kite and McCumber beat Canizares and Langer, 2&1, followed by Ballesteros and Olazabal handling Calcavecchia and Green, 4&2. In the last match on the course, Clark and James were down one hole to Strange and Stewart with four

CHRISTY O'CONNOR

"He's okay!"

O'CONNOR AND HIS WIFE, ANNE, WITH CAPTAIN JACKLIN

to go. An American win would tie things up, but Clark birdied sixteen and the visitors butchered seventeen, turning the lead around. On eighteen, James's drive finished half-in-half-out of a fairway bunker, from where he hit an extraordinary three-iron to within twenty feet of the hole, setting up a two-putt par and a 1-up win. Europe led, 9-7.

Good crowds had enjoyed the first two days despite gray skies. With the sun out on Sunday, the galleries swelled but had to wait until 11:30 for the start of the first match—Azinger vs. Ballesteros, an epic battle between two tough nutcases, darkly decorated by evil gamesmanship from both sides. It was great stuff.

Seve took a quick two holes, and then Azinger won four out of five to lead by two at the turn. At one point, Ballesteros asked Azinger if it would be okay to take a slightly scuffed ball out of play. Azinger was within his rights when he said no, although in any other event he might have agreed. But this was the Ryder Cup, and the asshole took divots out of the rulebook. Seve snarled, "Is this the way you want to play today?" And from then on, they traded swings and needles: When it was Azinger's turn, Ballesteros stood a little too close to his opponent; when Seve wasn't in the fairway, Azinger walked over to make sure Ballesteros didn't improve his lie. There was coughing, jingling of change, at least one beautifully timed caddie-fart, and a fair amount of club rattling.

Holding a one-hole lead on eighteen, Azinger hooked his drive into water. Ballesteros seized the opening, booming his drive over the hazard. After a penalty drop, Azinger smoked a spectacular fairway wood over two spits of water and into a greenside bunker. As an indication of just how great a shot it was, Seve gagged, and hit his second shot into the lake in front. After a penalty drop, he pulled himself together, found the green and holed a slinky twenty-foot downhiller for a bogey that raised a sky-shattering roar from the crowd and earned a clap on the back from his opponent. Well, maybe he just wanted to hit him, but Azinger had already blasted to four feet, and knew he needed his four-footer to halve the hole and win the match. He did just that, earning a slap on the back in return. It was a point to the United States, 1-up, and the most painful defeat in Ballesteros's Ryder Cup career.

In the second match, Beck beat Langer, 3&1, lifting the U.S. team into a 9-9 tie. Then Stewart followed Azinger into the water at eighteen, needed three to get out, and lost to Olazabal, 1-up. By the same score, Rafferty beat Calcavecchia, who not only drowned his tee shot at eighteen but his third shot, as well; it was Rafferty's only point of the week. Kite got one point back with an 8&7 pounding over an out-of-form Howard Clark, but by the time the U.S. team won another, it no longer mattered.

James beat O'Meara, 3&2, and Europe needed only two points to retain the Cup as Couples and O'Connor—both playing only their second match of the week—came to the last tee all square. Both found the fairway, but the American was seventy-five yards longer. Walking with his player, Jacklin said, "Put this on the green and I promise something good will happen." O'Connor hit a two-iron for the ages, from 240 yards to 3-1/2 feet. After the cheers died down, Couples hit a terrible nine-iron, shanking it right of the green. After a chip and missed putt, Couples conceded the hole to O'Connor, who lifted his eyes to the sky and cried. It was his first point in four matches cross two Cups fourteen years apart, and over the next few years the famous Ping two-iron would be auctioned for charity approximately 369 times. "It's the original guv, honest."

The point that retained the Cup came from Canizares, in only his second match. He also came to the eighteenth tied with his opponent, Ken (I'm *not* mental) Green, who had scored five straight threes on holes ten through fourteen but won only two of those holes. Canizares won the fifteenth and they halved sixteen and seventeen. On eighteen, both hit the green in two—Canizares way in the back, Green down front. The Spaniard stroked a beautiful lag from sixty feet that stopped three feet from the hole; Green's fifty-footer was too strong and he missed his six-foot comeback. Canizares holed his par putt for the point that assured a tie.

Too little too late, the Americans won the last four matches. McCumber beat Brand, 1-up, and Watson beat Torrance, 3&1. When Faldo drove into the water on eighteen, he lost to Wadkins, 1-up. Then Woosnam and Strange reenacted the O'Connor-Couples drama: Strange's two-iron finished eight feet from the hole while Woosnam missed the green with an eight-iron, missed his chip, and conceded the hole and the match, 2-up. It was the first point for Strange since he'd halved the first match of the week.

It was only the second tie in Cup history. Jacklin became the first captain from either side to hoist the trophy three times in succession. As expected, he announced his retirement from the captaincy soon thereafter.

Both sides went to great lengths to say that, regardless of the score, golf had been the big winner. However, the Azinger-Ballesteros dick-fencing match signaled the beginning of the end of forty-plus years of more or less gentlemanly behavior. Which is of course, total bullshit. The Ryder Cup had always brought out the best and the worst in its combatants. But starting now, decorum and sportsmanship would seem an even more distant memory.

FINAL SCORE

COURSE:

THE BELFRY (BRABAZON COURSE) SUTTON COLDFIELD ENGLAND | 1989

FOURSOMES & FOURBALLS

FOURSOMES - MORNING

Kite/Strange halved with Faldo/Woosnam

Wadkins/Stewart d. Clark/James, 1-up

Calcavecchia/Green d. Langer/Rafferty, 2&1

Watson/Beck halved with Ballesteros/Olazabal

FOURBALLS - AFTERNOON

Strange/Azinger lost to Torrance/Brand, 1-up

Couples/Wadkins lost to Clark/James, 3&2

Calcavecchia/McCumber lost to Faldo/Woosnam, 2-up

Watson/O'Meara lost to Ballesteros/Olazabal, 6&5

US: 3   EUROPE: 5

FOURSOMES & FOURBALLS

FOURSOMES - MORNING

Wadkins/Stewart lost to Faldo/Woosnam, 3&2

Azinger/Beck d. Brand/Torrance, 4&3

Calcavecchia/Green d. O'Connor/Rafferty, 3&2

Kite/Strange lost to Ballesteros/Olazabal, 1-up

FOURBALLS - AFTERNOON

Azinger/Beck d. Faldo/Woosnam, 2&1

Kite/McCumber d. Canizares/Langer, 2&1

Stewart/Strange lost to Clark/James, 1-up

Calcavecchia/Green lost to Ballesteros/Olazabal, 4&2

US: 4   EUROPE: 4

SINGLES

Azinger d. Ballesteros, 1-up

Beck d. Langer, 3&1

Stewart lost to Olazabal, 1-up

Calcavecchia lost to Rafferty, 1-up

Kite d. Clark, 8&7

O'Meara lost to James, 3&2

Couples lost to O'Connor, 1-up

Green lost to Canizares, 1-up

McCumber d. Brand, 1-up

Watson d. Torrance, 3&1

Wadkins d. Faldo, 1-up

Strange d. Woosnam, 2-up

US: 7   EUROPE: 5

TOTAL: US 14   EUROPE 14

COURSE:

THE OCEAN COURSE | KIAWAH ISLAND | SC

SEPT. **27-29**

1991

FINAL SCORE:

us 14-1/2   EUROPE 13-1/2

CAPTAINS:

DAVE STOCKTON   BERNARD GALLACHER

UNITED STATES

Paul Azinger	Payne Stewart
Chip Beck*	Lanny Wadkins
Mark Calcavecchia	
Fred Couples	
Ray Floyd*	
Hale Irwin	
Wayne Levi	
Mark O'Meara	
Steve Pate	
Corey Pavin	

EUROPE

Seve Ballesteros	Sam Torrance
Paul Broadhurst	Ian Woosnam
Nick Faldo*	
David Feherty	
David Gilford	
Mark James*	
Bernhard Langer	
Colin Montgomerie	
Jose Maria Olazabal*	
Steven Richardson	*captain's picks

1967   1969   1971   1973   1975   1977   1979   1981   1983

UNITED STATES

EUROPE

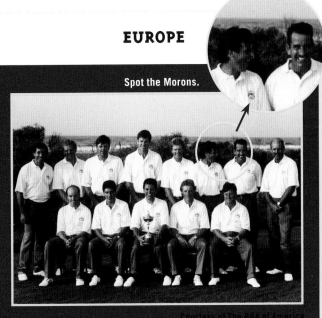

Spot the Morons.

Courtesy of The PGA of America

259

TOTALLY SUBJECTIVE HISTORY OF THE RYDER CUP

YOU HAVE TO SAY THIS ABOUT THE 1991 RYDER CUP MATCHES: They were unforgettable, and not because yours truly played in them (well, that's not the only reason). Today, more than a dozen years later, the Cup everyone remembers is the "War by the Shore." People really are sick bastards.

The U.S. had won the Gulf War just a few months earlier by bombing the crap out a bunch of brown people, and was hungry for another victory. I don't know, but the Americans seemed a little too excited about the chance to beat up on us nice Europeans. It made sense in Kuwait, where they were protecting oil fields and democracy (and oil fields), but really, history tells us that you'll get nothing out of fighting Europe except better chocolate, more expensive wine, and of course, ownership of France. Between flag-waving, camouflage ball caps, falling over a horseshoe crab, and more accusations of cheating (yep, Seve and Zinger went at it again), it was quite a helluva few days. "War by the Shore," indeed.

The hostilities started at the Belfry two years earlier when Ballesteros and Azinger had gone at each other with both their clubs and their mouths. It didn't help that Europe had won the Cup for a third straight time (okay, it was a tie, but we got to keep it and you didn't; that's a win to me!). Then there was Operation Desert Storm, which was like sand in America's shorts, making even mild-mannered fans ornery and loaded for bear. They were spoiling for a good old-fashioned rumble, so we gave it to them.

The choice of golf course was either inspired or expired depending on how you liked your golf. Pete Dye's Ocean Course on Kiawah Island off South Carolina was perfect for match play, but a nightmare for spectators. It was long,

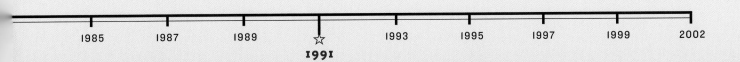

1985   1987   1989   ☆   1993   1995   1997   1999   2002

1991

COLIN MONTGOMERIE

it was exposed to the elements (the wind howled the entire time), and it was harder than Hogan's heart. (Tom Weiskopf, player-turned-architect, called it "an American-style course on links-like land." Yep, that's right, T, and at 7,600 yards, it was pretty much unplayable.)

The captains were hard as well—men's men, if that's not too politically incorrect (not that I give a rat's ass). Dave Stockton, the American leader, wasn't the best-known major-championship winner, like a Nicklaus, a Trevino, or a Hogan. But he'd won two PGAs without much more than a great short game, which meant he was smart. Bernard Gallacher, who'd played in thirty-one Cup matches between 1969 and 1983 (going 13-13-5, pretty damn good in the days of the Brits playing doormat), had been Jacklin's assistant captain in 1989 and also was no dummy. Neither captain was a world-beater, but they were both scrappy and tough.

The teams were about equal, except the Europeans had me. Europe had more rookies (five to three), but our players dominated the World Rankings. It was Europe's stars (and me) against America's depth.

The top three in the world at the time were Ian Woosnam, Jose Maria Olazabal, and Nick Faldo; Ballesteros was fifth. They were all back on the European team, along with veterans Mark James, Bernhard Langer, and Sam Torrance. (Faldo, James, and Olazabal were the captain's picks.) The new boys were Paul Broadhurst, David Gilford, Colin Montgomerie, Steven Richardson, and me. At thirty-three, I was the only rookie not in his twenties: I had managed to make the team by making the top ten in the money list, which many considered to be an act of God, and not one of his best.

All but one of the nine American veterans had been at the Belfry in 1989, and that was Hale Irwin, who hadn't played for the Cup since 1981 but had managed to qualify a decade later. The guys returning were Azinger, Chip Beck, Mark Calcavecchia, Fred Couples, Mark O'Meara, Payne Stewart, the bastard Wadkins, plus Raymond Floydhole, who'd been the captain the last time (Arnold Palmer was the only other guy to do that, captain in 1963 and player in 1965). The rookies were Wayne Levi (who was thirty-eight and had been the PGA Tour's player of the

PAUL AZINGER (GETTING INTO IT)

DATE : SEPT. 27-29

year in 1990, but had been playing like a rat with piles for months); Corey Pavin (leading money winner); and a very hot Steve Pate. Stockton had used his two picks to buy some experience, taking Beck (who'd gone 3-0-1 at the Belfry) and ex-captain Floyd.

One of the players who didn't make the U.S. squad was John Daly, who'd shocked the golf establishment a month earlier by winning the PGA Championship. There was much speculation about Stockton choosing him, but when he didn't, Daly took the high road and sent a fax to the team that said, "Good luck. Now go kick butt!" (Hey, for Johnny that's long-winded, and almost Shakespearean.)

"Kick butt" seemed to be the sentiment of the week.

DAVID FEHERTY AND SAM TORRANCE

Besides a big turnout of American flags, flag pins, and flag clothing, Stockton screened a film called *History of the Ryder Cup* for both teams: When we realized it was a highlight reel of American victories, we were more pissed off than you can imagine. Captain Stockton also introduced his team at the big dinner by saying how much money they'd won, which was kind of tacky too, especially as I didn't have any.

Then there was some moronic local disc jockey that got his listeners to call our hotel rooms in the middle of the night. I don't know what was dumber: The fact that people actually listened to him, or that the prick labeled his stunt, "Wake Up The Enemy." Enemy? Hey, I know it was serious golf, but things obviously were getting out of hand.

The atmosphere went from bad to worse with the very first match. As luck—or shrewd captainization would have it, the Cup began with Azinger against Ballesteros. Beck was playing too, and Olazabal, of course. But to those rooting for a good fracas, it was mano-a-mano.

Showing admirable restraint, Seve waited until the second hole before he demanded a free drop from a bad lie, got it, but still lost the hole. The tension mounted. "By the ninth hole I was livid," Azinger wrote in his autobiography. "When Jose hit his drive off to the right, I was right there to help spot the drop. The referee was intimidated by Seve and Jose, so he simply stood aside and waited to see how we would settle things. Seve and

Jose wanted to drop the ball much farther up the fairway from where I thought the ball had gone into the water. 'You need to drop it right back here,' I said as I pointed to the original position I had indicated. Reluctantly Seve dropped the ball at that spot." (I'd been benched that morning, largely because I was so nervous I couldn't stop weeping, and this incident wasn't helping.)

The Spaniards were three-down at the turn when they accused the Americans of having changed balls back at the seventh hole. (To this day, I'm not sure the hold-off on the call wasn't an effort by Seve to win *every* hole from the seventh!) The Americans didn't deny the mistake, which would have resulted in a penalty if it had been called to the official's attention when it happened, not a few holes later. "Mierde!" and tempers got even hotter. Chip Beck looked angry enough to tear a piece of toast in half, or possibly even crush a grape.

"Looks like a three-wood shot to me."

SEVERIANO BALLESTEROS

There's never been a better angry player than Seve. He and Olazabal won the tenth hole and kept winning, getting back in the lead after sixteen, and when Ballesteros holed a twenty-five-foot, big-breaking birdie putt on the treacherous par-three seventeen, the Europeans won, 2&1.

After the match, the war of words continued. Azinger accused Seve of "always developing a cough at the Ryder Cup," one that erupts when it's his opponent's turn to hit. Ballesteros responded, "The American team has eleven nice guys . . . and Paul Azinger." And all against a background of 25,000 beer-swilling, jingoistic golf junkies with ass-cracks full of dune sand, chanting "USA! USA! USA!" I know, they were getting us back for the Belfry bollock-heads. Fair enough.

There were three other matches that first morning, and they all went to the Americans: Floyd grandfathered Couples around the place 2&1 over Langer and James, Wadkins and Irwin beat Montgomerie and Gilford, 4&2 and Stewart and Calcavecchia squeaked by Faldo and Woosnam, 1-up (this would be a long Cup for Faldo).

The afternoon was less dramatic for everyone but me, because, biting the bullet, Bernard Gallacher played me, thankfully with my best friend in the entire world, the idiot Torrance. We were quickly 1-down to Wadkins

BERNARD LANGER

and O'Meara because I was a nervous wreck. Facing a twenty-footer on the first green, I scuffed the ground behind the ball, and left it four feet wide and six feet short. Wadkins blew a snot bubble. Sam took me aside on the second tee and said, "If you don't pull yourself together, I'm going to join them and you can play all three of us, you useless bastard." We were 3-down at the turn but then I forced my gonads out of my throat and holed a long chip

shot at eleven to win one, then got another with a two at the par-three fourteenth. Sam almost holed his tee shot at seventeen, but so did O'Meara, and all four of us puked our way up eighteen, finding more sand than a cat with diarrhea. It was the last match of the day, and in the gathering gloom, I ended up with a twelve-footer to win the hole and half a point. The Almighty was clearly a total bastard—why me? I read it left edge, and of course, Torrance read it right edge, and I accidentally flinched it off straight, and watched, horrified, as it cruised straight into the back of the hole. I thought I was going to crap myself then, and I almost did right now, just *thinking* about it. I was so happy and relieved I wanted to go home right then, but I remembered we still had two more days of this madness. I had a decent career, with a few wins, and I could clearly play at the highest

"If we played them in the dark, we'd never lose."

SEVERIANO BALLESTEROS AND JOSE MARIA OLAZABAL

level, but nothing had ever felt like the elation I experienced when that ball went into the hole, or the horror at the thought of it missing. I was hooked.

Right behind us, Seve and Ollie had gone off against Zinger and Beck again. Stockton had thought Gallacher might send his best team out first, but he got out-thunk and while there were no fireworks, the result was the same, a 2&1 win for the Spaniards. Pavin and Calcavecchia lost to James and big Steve Richardson, 5&4, then Faldo and Woosnam lost again, 5&3 to Floyd and Couples. Europe won the afternoon 2-1/2 to 1-1/2 and Sam's and my smelly little half point meant the gap was one point at the end of the day. At least / thought that's what it meant, and now I was ready to play a little Ryder Cup, and kick a few famous arseholes.

The next morning Sam and I led off again, this time in foursomes, and my sphincter had managed to tighten up to about 2000 psi again. I struggled on the greens, which had dried out in the constant wind and become as hard as concrete and fast as glass, and we lost 4&2 to the much assholier-than-us pair of Wadkins and Irwin. I was pretty sure I'd have the afternoon off. Calcavecchia and Stewart took James and Richardson, followed by the worst defeat in Faldo's Cup career, a 7&6 drubbing for him and Gilford by Azinger and O'Meara. Faldo had been unhappy with Gallacher's choice as his partner, and he barely spoke to David Gilford (who'd later be a Ryder Cup hero) during the match. Then the unbeatens met: Seve and Ollie against Floyd and Couples, both two-time winners the first day. The Spaniards stayed undefeated, winning 3&2, saving us from being swept.

Gallacher had to do something to change our luck, so he shook up some pairings and sat Faldo down for the first time since 1985. Like Jacklin, the new European captain knew how to put teams together.

The Euros nearly swept the afternoon, winning three and halving one. Woosnam went out first with the tough northerner Paul Broadhurst, making his debut a happy one with a 2&1 win over Irwin and Azinger. In the second,

Steve Pate, who'd been hurt when his limo crashed coming back from the big pre-match dinner, tried to play. (It's at this point that I have a confession to make: It was my limo that caused the crash. We were on our way to Charleston in a cavalcade of limos, and I was sharing a car with Nick Faldo and one of his ex-wives, when my ex-wife asked the driver a stupid question, just as a state trooper was waving us through a red light. The driver looked over his shoulder just as the officer changed his mind, and ended up having to slam on the anchors. We heard the squealing of tires behind, and a few seconds later the crump of a collision as Pater's limo parked itself in the trunk of the one in front, and Pater parked his ribs into a decanter of Jack Daniels. Sorry about that, pal.) Moving right along, he was paired with Pavin—both of them wearing those ugly Desert Storm camouflage hats—and they were lucky to stay as close as they did, only losing to Langer and Montgomerie 2&1. Levi also got his first chance to play, but out of form, he was a load on Wadkins's shoulders and they lost, 3&1, to James and Richardson. That left Ballesteros and Olazabal, who it seemed were tiring from the nonstop action. But these two were unbreakable. From 2-down with six to play against Stewart and Couples, Ollie holed a five-footer on the last hole for a half, and he and Ballesteros virtually danced off the green, re-energizing themselves, the team, and a pretty large European contingent in the crowd, which was making some noise of its own. "Ole, Ole, Ole," went the soccer-style chant. I love the words to that one.

By taking three and a half points in the fourballs, Europe had tied the score at eight. It would all come down to the last day, and the two captains were thinking the same way: Both sent out their old warriors first and saved their stars for near the end. Also, both teams started with a half-point, the result of Pate being unable to play due to my ex-wife, and the name in the European envelope was poor David Gilford, who had to sit out the singles, and was heartbroken.

Faldo and Floyd kicked off the proceedings in a rematch of their Masters playoff the year before. And just like at Augusta, Faldo prevailed, winning 2-up for his only point of this Cup. I was in the second match against a friend of mine, the U.S. Open champ Payne Stewart. I was stinging from having let Sam down the morning before, and was determined to come away with a point. I'd told my caddy. Rodders Wooler, that it didn't matter who I played the next day, I was winning. Payne was off his game and I had an early lead, which began to slip away on the back. But I had two putts to win on seventeen and nearly holed the first one. Payne conceded what was left, giving me my only Ryder Cup win and the first European point of the day.

In the matters that followed, the leads and points swung back and forth. Calcavecchia had a five-hole lead over Montgomerie at the turn, but what should have been an easy win wasn't: Monty holed out from the sand on ten and birdied eleven before losing fourteen to go 4-down with four to play. Then, the world fell out of Calcavecchia's bottom. From left of the green on fifteen he took five to get down. On sixteen, he bogeyed while Monty parred. The par-three seventeenth was the hardest to watch: All Calc had to do was hit the green, but instead he hit something between a shank and a slice (a shlank?) that found the water; both he and Monty had to hit from the drop zone, and the American soon faced a three-footer to win the match. He missed and they were on to the last, where Montgomerie nearly holed a thirty-footer. Calcavecchia had a nine-footer that would have halved the hole and taken the match but it wasn't close and Monty had the half.

Azinger beat Olazabal, 2-up, and Pavin beat Richardson 2&1, thanks to a magnificent bunker shot on seventeen. Ballesteros finished this Cup unbeaten, taking Levi, 3&2. Then the Americans took three of the next four—Beck over Woosnam, 3&1; Couples over Torrance, 3&2; Wadkins over James, 3&2. Only the rookie Broadhurst took a point, from O'Meara, 3&1.

The Americans had a one-point lead with one match left, Langer vs. Irwin. The Europeans needed a win; a halve would give the Cup back to the United States. It was like watching a train wreck: No one could look away.

Irwin took the early lead, Langer fought back. With a win at fourteen, Irwin went 2-up, but it wasn't easy: "I couldn't breathe, I couldn't swallow, I couldn't do anything," he said afterward. Proceeding at his typical snail's pace, Langer won the fifteenth, halved the sixteenth, and won the seventeenth when Irwin three-putted. Langer had scratched back to even, but he had to win the last.

After a missed approach, Irwin hit a poor chip that stopped well short of the hole. The match was in Langer's hands, which were holding his putter thirty feet from the hole. Famous for bad putting (he'd overcome the yips with a series of unconventional grips), he'd actually held his own this week. But on the last he was too bold and rolled his first putt six feet past. Irwin's twenty-footer to win stopped two feet short and was conceded by Langer, who now faced his own putt for the Cup. I'll never forget the look of agony on Bernhard's face as the ball slid by on the right, causing the match to be halved and our Cup to be lost. Hey, the last German under that kind of pressure shot himself in a bunker.

It was arguably the most pressure-packed putt in history and nobody faulted Langer for missing it. "Not even Jack Nicklaus in his prime will make that putt," said Ballesteros. "Not even me!" (To his credit, Langer rebounded well, winning the German Open the next week.) But the Cup was back in American hands. The team celebrated by throwing Stockton into the Atlantic.

The matches could not have been closer: The U.S. held a one-point lead after day one, the teams were tied after day two, and the final score showed only a one-point difference. Despite everything—the histrionics, the over-the-top patriotism, and the blatant displays of bad taste—the golf had been outstanding.

FINAL SCORE

COURSE:

THE OCEAN COURSE KIAWAH ISLAND SC

1991

FOURSOMES & FOURBALLS

FOURSOMES - MORNING

Azinger/Beck lost to Ballesteros/Olazabal, 2&1
Floyd/Couples d. Langer/James, 2&1
Wadkins/Irwin d. Gilford/Montgomerie, 4&2
Stewart/Calcavecchia d. Faldo/Woosnam, 1-up

FOURBALLS - AFTERNOON

Wadkins/O'Meara havled with Torrance/Feherty
Beck/Azinger lost to Ballesteros/Olazabal, 2&1
Pavin/Calcavecchia lost to
James/Richardson, 5&4
Couples/Floyd d. Faldo/Woosnam, 5&3

US: 4-1/2   EUROPE: 3-1/2

FOURSOMES & FOURBALLS

FOURBALLS - MORNING

Wadkins/Irwin d. Feherty/Torrance, 4&2
Calcavecchia/Stewart d. James/Richardson, 1-up
Azinger/O'Meara d. Faldo/Gilford, 7&6
Floyd/Couples lost to Ballesteros/Olazabal, 3&2

FOURSOMES - AFTERNOON

Azinger/Irwin lost to Woosnam/Broadhurst, 2&1
Pate/Pavin lost to Langer/Montgomerie, 2&1
Wadkins/Levi lost to James/Richardson, 3&1
Stewart/Couples halved with
Ballesteros/Olazabal

US: 3-1/2   EUROPE: 4-1/2

SINGLES

Pate halved with Gilford
Floyd lost to Faldo, 2-up
Stewart lost to Feherty, 2&1
Calcavecchia halved with Montgomerie
Azinger d. Olazabal, 2-up
Pavin d. Richardson, 2&1
Levi lost to Ballesteros, 3&2
Beck d. Woosnam, 3&1
O'Meara lost to Broadhurst, 3&1
Couples d. Torrance, 3&2
Wadkins d. James, 3&2
Irwin halved with Langer

US: 6-1/2   EUROPE: 5-1/2

TOTAL:

US 14-1/2   **EUROPE 13-1/2**

HEROES OF THE RYDER CUP

COLIN MONTGOMERIE : (b. 1963)

☆☆☆☆☆☆☆☆☆☆☆☆☆☆☆☆☆☆☆☆☆☆☆☆

THERE SEEM TO BE three Colin Montgomeries: The first is the European Tour superstar who topped the Order of Merit a record seven times and has nearly thirty victories since turning professional in 1987; the second is the major-championship wannabe, with two second-place finishes in the U.S. Open (1997 and tied for second in 1994) and one in the 1995 PGA, yet who has never finished better than tied for eighth in the Open Championship. And the third is a Ryder Cup studmuffin, with one of the best records in British/European team history.

In six Cups from 1991 to the present, Monty has played in twenty-eight matches, compiling a brilliant 16-7-5 record. Along with Tom Kite, he is the only golfer to play at least six singles matches and remain unbeaten (he is 4-0-2, Kite is 5-0-2). His sixteen wins place him fourth all-time for Europe, as do his 18-1/2 total points. So why such an impressive record? According to his official website, the Ryder Cup is "the tournament that inspires him more than any other." Or in other words, it puts a tilt in the big lad's kilt.

Monty had the good luck—or misfortune, depending how you look at it—to debut in 1991 at the "War by the Shore" at Kiawah Island—the same Cup in which yours truly made his sole appearance. He split two team matches, then figured in one of the hardest-to-watch singles of all time, being the unwitting beneficiary of a Mark Calcavecchia swoon: Five down at one point, Monty ended up earning a half point.

In 1993, he was 3-1-1; in 1995, he was 2-3-0; and in 1997 he was 3-1-1 again, with his half in the singles against Scott Hoch lifting Europe from a tie to an outright win. Notice he had only one losing record, that in 1995, when the Europeans won by one point on the strength of a miraculous final-day comeback, and he won his singles match on that day when it mattered most.

But it was in 1999, when he went 3-1-1, that he stepped up and became the team's true leader. He paid a terrible price, being besieged by hecklers so awful that his father had to flee from the course. But the same player who'd let boorish behavior bother him in the past used it as motivation, and he made putts from all over Boston.

The only problem with Montgomerie's performance at Brookline was that his team lost. Not so in 2002 at the Belfry, when he went undefeated (4-0-1) and powered Europe to victory. Paired with Bernhard Langer three times, he had two wins and a half; he and Padraig Harrington handed the American team of Phil Mickelson and David Toms their only defeat. But it was in the singles where his presence was really felt: Wanting to open the final day with a big, inspirational win, he ran over Scott Hoch, 5&4. The rest of the team fed off his success and kept the Americans from starting a comeback like the one three years earlier.

In the States, he's still the dour-looking Scot, the butt of "full Monty" jokes and comparisons to Mrs. Doubtfire. But after all this time he is finally a "man in full." In Britain, despite never winning the Open Championship, he is very much a hero. "It's important that the American team realize how popular I am here in Britain," he said after starring in the "Return of the Cup" in 2002.

Smart Americans do realize it. And they also should realize that they'll be facing him as the European captain one day soon. I've taken my fair share of digs at the big man (as I do at everyone), and sometimes they've missed their mark, wounding him deeply, for Monty is a sensitive soul with issues he'd rather keep to himself. For these, I'm truly sorry. Colin Montgomerie will always be a hero of mine.

☆☆☆☆☆☆☆☆☆☆☆☆☆☆☆☆☆☆☆☆☆☆☆☆

COURSE:

THE BELFRY (BRABAZON COURSE) SUTTON COLDFIELD ENGLAND

SEPT. 24-26

1993

FINAL SCORE:

US 15   EUROPE 13

CAPTAINS:

TOM WATSON   BERNARD GALLACHER

UNITED STATES

Paul Azinger   Payne Stewart

Chip Beck   Lanny Wadkins*

John Cook

Fred Couples

Ray Floyd*

Jim Gallagher Jr.

Lee Janzen

Tom Kite

Davis Love III

Corey Pavin

EUROPE

Peter Baker   Sam Torrance

Seve Ballesteros*   Ian Woosnam

Nick Faldo

Joakim Haeggman*

Mark James

Barry Lane

Bernhard Langer

Colin Montgomerie

Jose Maria Olazabal*

Costantino Rocca   *captain's picks

1967   1969   1971   1973   1975   1977   1979   1981   1983

AFTER THE WAR BY THE SHORE, cooler heads tried to prevail. Summing up the views of the many who were embarrassed by the behavior at Kiawah Island, new American captain Tom Watson said, "This isn't war, this is golf. We're going over there and try like hell to kick their butts. And they're going to try like hell to kick ours. That's as it should be. But when it's over, we should be able to go off together, lift a glass, and toast one another."

Watson almost got his wish.

The selection of the American team was fairly routine. Of the eight U.S. veterans, seven were back from the "war": Paul Azinger, Chip Beck, Fred Couples, Raymond Floyd, Corey Pavin, Payne Stewart, and Lanny Wadkins, along with Tom Kite. Four Americans were on the squad for the first time: John Cook, Jim Gallagher Jr., Lee Janzen, and Davis Love III. John Daly again was the people's choice for a wild-card pick, but Watson wanted experience *and* guts so he went with the forty-four-year-old Wadkins and the fifty-one-year-old Floyd (the oldest man to ever play for either team).

After two narrow losses and the torture of Kiawah, Bernard Gallacher said he was through with the captain's job, but his straight talking and honesty had made him a favorite with his players, all of whom wanted to give him the win he so deserved. He was talked into re-Cupping. Nick Faldo, Mark James, Bernhard Langer, Colin Montgomerie, Sam Torrance, Ian Woosnam, plus captain's picks Seve Ballesteros and Jose Maria Olazabal were returning with him, but there was talk that some of the veterans were past their prime. And the rookies were as succulently green as could be: Peter Baker, Barry Lane, Italy's Costantino Rocca, and the third captain's pick,

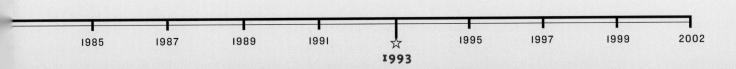

Joakim "Larry" Haeggman from Sweden, the first Scandahoovian on the team.

Watson made his captaincy a 24/7 affair. He spoke to former captains and players from both sides, and questioned coaches from other sports about motivating players and dealing with pressure. When he and his team were practicing at the Belfry, they examined and discussed every hole, especially the last, which had been such a stick up the American butt in 1985 and 1989. His intent was to be prepared for anything.

So it was a surprise when, days before boarding the Concorde for England, the team stepped into a mess the press tagged "Clintongate." President Bill Clinton, president, avid golfer, and well-known poon-hound, invited the team to the White House on their way across the Atlantic. It's a well-known fact that Democrats are shitty golfers (or maybe shitty golfers are Democrats), and most professional golfers are or become staunch conservatives, no doubt the result of having money, hanging around country clubs, and spending their free time hunting, fishing, and laughing at people who don't have pools. Some of the players detested Clinton's tax plans, while others had problems

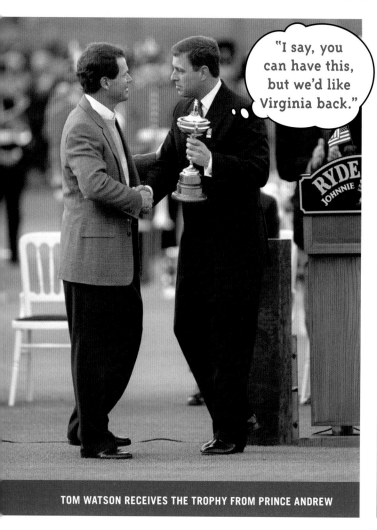

TOM WATSON RECEIVES THE TROPHY FROM PRINCE ANDREW

RAY FLOYD

with his social agenda. Then there was Paul Azinger, who may have abused the language doing it but echoed the feelings of some of his teammates when he said, "I don't want to shake hands with no draft dodger." Leave it to the Zinger to come up with the zinger. That attitude was more than a little insulting if you ask me, and apparently the American captain felt similarly.

Watson showed that he was not only brighter but better than his men when he said, "It doesn't matter who the president is, if you're invited to the White House, you go." So they went, and while there Watson defused the situation with a well-planned speech:

"You know, Mr. President," Watson began, "if you hold the club too far to the right, you're going to get in trouble on the left. If you hold it too far to the left, you're going to have trouble on the right. But if you hold it in the middle . . ." and Clinton chimed in, "You'll get it just right." Everybody laughed and the tension was broken. I'm surprised Zinger didn't point out that the Prez had a fondness of having his club held by someone else.

ROCCA

While Watson was good at getting his team out of trouble, he was less adept when he was the instigator.

Trying to make life as easy as possible for his players, Watson forbade the signing of autographs until the Matches were over. That would even include, he said, the gala dinner two nights before the games began. It was one thing to slight the patrons (who'd coughed up about $300 for the right to mingle), but quite another to defy tradition and not autograph the menus for the other team. But Watson was adamant, and when he politely turned down Sam Torrance's request for a signature, feelings were hurt, noses were out of joint, and it landed all over the next day's newspapers. In fairness, Watson told Torrance he'd be happy to sign the menus later in the week, but for one player to refuse another was a horrible embarrassment, particularly in such a setting. Also, Sammy's near enough to being a Glaswegian that it's very lucky he didn't "pit the heid innim." (You know, the question "Can you sew?" followed by a "Glasgow kiss" and the invitation "Stitch that.") And to top it all off, as usual, the food totally sucked. But Gallacher managed to calm Sam, who can get pissed off (to say nothing of pissed) with the best of them: Sam's only comment to the rabid press corps was that he would let his golf clubs do the talking. Watson spent the final practice day alternately watching his men prepare and apologizing to everyone, including the oak tree to the right of the last green. And the tempest in a ballpoint was over.

Under gray, wet skies and after a two-hour fog delay, the matches began with Pavin and Wadkins against James and Torrance, who had injured his big toe in a sleep-walking/potted plant tackling incident (coincidentally at the Belfry) three weeks earlier. The Americans won, 4&3, as an infection of the big toe came back to bother Torrance. The boys and I christened him "Pus-in-Boots." (It would have far more interesting consequences later.) Azinger and Stewart opened with three straight bogeys against Woosnam and Langer and never got much better, losing 7&5. The job of handling Ballesteros and Olazabal fell initially to Kite and Love: Seve's game was so shaky that he laid up with a nine-iron off the tee of the short par-four tenth; Kite knew an open door when he saw one, grabbed his three-wood, and stuck his shot to five feet for an easy eagle. The Spaniards, who up till then hadn't lost a foursomes match in six tries, would have their revenge. But for now, the first meeting went to the U.S. team, 2&1. The morning ended in a tie when Faldo and Montgomerie beat Floyd and Couples, 4&3. The pairing of Monty and Faldo had raised some eyebrows, and was described by Alister McClean, Monty's caddie, as "Fitness Freak meets Food Freak," but that week they would account for six and a half of the Europeans' thirteen points.

The afternoon fourballs began with a flock of rookies, Janzen and Gallagher against Baker and one grizzled vet, Woosnam. Baker (who said he was so nervous he almost had to change his shorts) was the hero, holing a long, slippery, downhill putt on eighteen to preserve a 1-up win, which was all the more cherished because Baker's baby daughter Georgina had been admitted into hospital the previous evening with suspected meningitis, and he had only played on the insistence of his wife Helen. Pavin and Wadkins continued to mesh well, beating Langer and Lane, 4&2: It was Lanny's twentieth Cup victory, tying him for second among Americans with Billy Casper, two behind Arnold Palmer. It also would be his last win. Going off last, Seve and Ollie won round two against Kite and Love, 4&3.

Match number three remained on the course a long time; in fact, it didn't finish until the next morning. And it was a classic: Azinger and Couples waged a battle royal with Faldo and Montgomerie. The pairs were even after nine, the Americans up one after sixteen, then back to even after seventeen when, with it almost too dark to see, Faldo darted a seven-iron from 160 yards to four feet. Starting again at eight a.m. on a damp Saturday, Monty drove through the eighteenth fairway, Faldo was safe, and Couples found the water. Hitting last, Azinger responded with what he called "the best drive I've ever hit, under the circumstances," sending it twenty yards past Faldo's. From a tough lie, Montgomerie joined Couples in the drink, leaving the match to Faldo and Azinger, who'd done most of the work the previous day as well. Faldo's approach came up fifty feet short while Azinger landed just six yards away. Faldo left his first putt ten feet short on the wet green, then Azinger almost holed his for the win. Faldo calmly drained his putt, looked around at the gallery, and asked, "What's for breakfast?" It had been a great match and finished in a well-deserved half.

277

IAN WOOSNAM

Besides maintaining their one-point lead, Faldo's putt gave the home team momentum. Faldo and Montgomerie barely had time for a cup of coffee and a dump before they were back out, this time against Wadkins and Pavin, who lost 3&2. Then Langer and Woosnam beat Couples and Azinger, 2&1, and Ballesteros and Olazabal took the rubber match with Kite and Love, 2&1, which was nothing short of a miracle, considering some of the places Ballesteros was hitting it. Only Floyd and Stewart slowed the Euro's onslaught, topping Baker and Lane, 3&2.

But how quickly fortunes can turn, and how unlikely the heroes can be! After losing the morning 3-1, Watson sent out the only Americans yet to see action, Cook and Beck, against Faldo and Montgomerie, who had yet to lose. Which they promptly did, 2-up. It was a win that lifted American spirits (Watson later called it "the heart or our victory") and led to two more victories: Pavin and Gallagher over James and Rocca, 5&4, and Floyd and Stewart over Olazabal and Haeggman 2&1. (Haeggman was put in for Seve, which was no surprise to Billy Foster, Ballesteros's caddie, who said that his man "couldn't hit a cow on the arse with a banjo.") In the one European win, Baker once again provided the heroics, carding six of the team's eight birdies in only thirteen holes, as he and Woosnam thrashed Couples and Azinger, 6&5.

It had been a long day—starting with the finish of a match from the previous afternoon, featuring non-stop action, and even a minor Seve blow-up (he tossed his toys out of the crib over a drop area). When it was over, each team had won four matches, and the Europeans still had their one-point lead.

The night before the singles, Watson was told that Torrance's toenail had to be removed and he couldn't walk, let alone play. Sammy was heartbroken to miss a Ryder Cup match, but he'd have to sit out, drinking heavily. But just as importantly, Watson had to pick an American to sit as well. Wadkins offered to stand down, saying that as a captain's pick he shouldn't play in place of someone who had qualified. Watson called it "one of the greatest gestures I've ever seen anyone make," then used it to fire up his men, telling each one on the first tee to "play this one for Lanny." What a little shit! He even knew how *not* to play and still win.

The other medical issue was potentially more dangerous. The Bakers had again spent the night in each other's arms at the hospital with eleven-month-old Georgina, still showing symptoms of spinal meningitis. But by morning, it had been fortunately diagnosed as a bad ear infection and Baker was back and ready to go, sleep be damned. In his locker was a get-well card, signed by the entire American team. At least *he* got an autograph.

The first match pitted Couples (with only a half point in four matches) against Woosnam (4-0), and to no one's surprise, Woosie took the lead. But they came to the last all even, and on the very hole where he'd collapsed in 1989, Couples hit an eight-iron to eight feet then watched Woosie get inside him by a foot. Freddie just missed, Woosie conceded the tap-in, and then ran his putt three and a half feet past, giving the crowd a group nervous breakdown. He knocked it in, but afterward, the wee Welsh warrior admitted it was the toughest short putt of his life.

After being three down with seven to play, Beck beat Lane, 1-up. Then Europe ran off three straight wins: Montgomerie over Janzen, 1-up; Baker, incredibly given his previous few hours, 2-up over Pavin; and Haeggman a surprising 1-up on Cook. Then it was America's turn—Stewart over James, 3&2, and Gallagher (in what had been Wadkins's spot) over a positively suicidal Ballesteros, 3&2; and Kite easily over Langer, 5&3. This would be Kite's last Ryder Cup: His seven-year record was 15-9-4, including a perfect run in singles (five wins, two halves).

The teams were tied, 12-1/2 points a side, and Europe was ahead in two of the three remaining matches.

Robin Love, Davis's seven-months-pregnant wife, had as usual walked every step of the way with her man, and had exhausted herself on Friday, with doctors worrying she might have induced a premature delivery. But her condition improved, and she sent Davis out, obviously relieved and ready to go. In a collapse that would have fit in perfectly at Kiawah, Rocca held a one-hole lead over Love, but he three-putted seventeen, missing a short one that wasn't conceded. On eighteen, all even, Love split the fairway with his drive while the Italian flew well right. Rocca's approach was well short, off the green fifty yards from the hole. The door was open, but Love finished short as well, on the green, but forty feet away. Rocca chipped long and two-putted for bogey. Love, after leaving his first putt four feet short, settled over the ball, backed off, settled in again, and holed out for the turnaround win. Davis could see that Costantino was distraught, and put his arm around his shoulder, as did Ballesteros, who was also in tears, more from frustration with himself. The press the following day was, to say the least, less than kind to Rocca.

Needing just a half point to tie, Floyd made his last Cup match memorable, never letting Olazabal take the lead and beating him 2-up for the winning point. In the final match, reigning PGA champion Azinger halved with Faldo, after the Englishman had made a hole-in-one on sixteen, only the second ace in Cup history.

America's 15-13 victory never looked easy. Neither Azinger nor Couples had a win, both going 0-3-2, while old man Floyd was 3-1, Wadkins was 2-1-1, and rookie Beck was 2-0. For Europe, Woosnam won 4-1/2 out of 5 possible points, easily the best performance of the week. But his half came in the singles, when the rest of the old guard—Ballesteros, Olazabal, Langer, and Faldo—had just one half among them.

The papers suggested that maybe they were too old, or needed more fiber in their diet, or something, but whatever the reason for the loss, it just wasn't acceptable. After all, now we were supposed to be winning this damn thing!

FINAL SCORE

COURSE:

THE BELFRY (BRABAZON COURSE) | **SUTTON COLDFIELD** | **ENGLAND**

1993

FOURSOMES & FOURBALLS

FOURSOMES - MORNING

Pavin/Wadkins d. Torrance/James, 4&3

Azinger/Stewart lost to Woosnam/Langer, 7&5

Kite/Love d. Ballesteros/Olazabal, 2&1

Floyd/Couples lost to Faldo/Montgomerie, 4&3

FOURBALLS - AFTERNOON

Janzen/Gallagher lost to Baker/Woosnam, 1-up

Pavin/Wadkins d. Langer/Lane, 4&2

Azinger/Couples halved with
Faldo/Montgomerie

Kite/Love lost to Ballesteros/Olazabal, 4&3

US: 3-1/2   EUROPE: 4-1/2

FOURSOMES & FOURBALLS

FOURSOMES - MORNING

Wadkins/Pavin lost to Faldo/Montgomerie, 3&2

Couples/Azinger lost to Langer/Woosnam, 2&1

Floyd/Stewart d. Baker/Lane, 3&2

Kite/Love lost to Ballesteros/Olazabal, 2&1

FOURBALLS - AFTERNOON

Cook/Beck d. Faldo/Montgomerie, 2-up

Pavin/Gallagher d. James/Rocca, 5&4

Couples/Azinger lost to Baker/Woosnam, 6&5

Floyd/Stewart d. Olazabal/Haeggman, 2&1

US: 4   EUROPE: 4

SINGLES

Wadkins halved with Torrance

Couples halved with Woosnam

Beck d. Lane, 1-up

Janzen lost to Montgomerie, 1-up

Pavin lost to Baker, 2-up

Cook lost to Haeggman, 1-up

Stewart d. James, 3&2

Love d. Rocca, 1-up

Gallagher d. Ballesteros, 3&2

Floyd d. Olazabal, 2-up

Kite d. Langer, 5&3

Azinger halved with Faldo

US: 7-1/2   EUROPE: 4-1/2

TOTAL: US 15   EUROPE 13

COURSE:

OAK HILL CC | ROCHESTER | NY

☆☆☆☆☆☆☆☆☆☆ **SEPT.** 22-24

1995

FINAL SCORE:

US 13-1/2 ☆ EUROPE 14-1/2

CAPTAINS:

LANNY WADKINS   BERNARD GALLACHER

UNITED STATES

Fred Couples*   Loren Roberts

Ben Crenshaw   Curtis Strange*

Brad Faxon

Jay Haas

Peter Jacobsen

Tom Lehman

Davis Love III

Jeff Maggert

Phil Mickelson

Corey Pavin

EUROPE

Seve Ballesteros   Philip Walton

Howard Clark   Ian Woosnam*

Nick Faldo*

David Gilford

Mark James

Per-Ulrik Johansson

Bernhard Langer

Colin Montgomerie

Costantino Rocca

Sam Torrance   *captain's picks

THE STATISTICS ARE WORTH REPEATING.

In the first twenty-two Ryder Cups—when it was the best of Britain against America's finest—the U.S. was the easy and consistent conqueror: Three wins for Britain versus nineteen for the U.S., and no GB wins in their last ten attempts at going it alone. But beginning in 1979, when the Continentals signed on, a one-sided rout turned into a fair and fascinating fight: five wins for the U.S. and two for Europe, plus a tie that kept the Cup on the right side of the Atlantic. They were nearly all close battles, and included the first-ever foreign win on American soil.

In less than a decade, the Cup went from big snooze to big news. Fans turned out by the thousands whether the matches were here or there (or, if you prefer, there or here); corporations poured millions into sponsorship; American television (years behind the BBC) devoted hours of live coverage and was rewarded with good ratings. The Ryder Cup had become the greatest event in golf. People still loved to watch the Masters and the other majors, but they didn't do so from the edge of their seats.

So it isn't only hindsight that allows me to label those Cassandras who started worrying about the Cup's future absolute idiots. Okay, the U.S. had won two in a row in 1991 and 1993, Europe's heroes were aging, and the only major championship in which a European seemed capable of contending was the Masters (where they'd won six of the last eight). But the European Tour was the second-best circuit in the world by a large margin, with more and better players coming on all the time, the aging Euro superstars were still winning, and, more importantly, had a wealth of international experience. And it wasn't as if the Americans had a lock on the majors, as players from other

parts of the world—especially Southern Africa and Australia—were making their presence known (which would result in the creation of that Ryder Cup-wannabe, the Presidents Cup).

NICK FALDO

LANNY WADKINS (IN LOVE WITH THE CUP)

So it was a little early to be writing elegies for the Ryder Cup. For some of its "old" players, maybe. But the Cup itself was doing just fine, thank you very much.

In 1995, team composition was the big story for both sides. In Europe, there was some controversy over the loss of one captain's pick (down to two), which could have presented a problem when it came time for choosing among the many players dividing their time between Europe and the U.S. Bernard Gallacher, back for the third (and lucky?) time as captain, eventually chose Nick Faldo and Ian Woosnam. They joined a team already bulbous with Cup experience: Seve Ballesteros, Howard Clark, David Gilford, Mark James, Bernhard Langer, Colin Montgomerie, Costantino Rocca, and Sam Torrance. Two newcomers made the squad: Per-Ulrik Johansson of Sweden and Philip Walton of Ireland.

Notably absent from the team was Jose Maria Olazabal, winner of the 1994 Masters, who was suffering from a persistent tootsie problem, a serious condition that threatened to end his career, and about which he would never complain. (It's also important to note that during the two years in which he suffered, Olazabal never even considered asking for a cart.) It would take another year or so before a maverick German physician diagnosed a problem in Olazabal's back, which would allow him to return for future Cup play. But until then, it meant Gallacher had to find a new partner for Seve.

In America, Lanny Wadkins, a captain's pick in 1993, was the pick as captain in 1995. He also added Cup experience with his selections, balancing five rookies by choosing Fred Couples and Curtis Strange. Curtis was a surprising selection to some because his Ryder record was under fifty percent, and he hadn't won on the PGA Tour since 1989. But that last win was the U.S. Open and it was at the same Oak Hill. (Lanston also remembered Strange winning the U.S. Open in 1988, over Faldo in a playoff, so the choice was more than justified.) The other American veterans were Ben Crenshaw, Jay Haas, Peter Jacobsen, Davis Love III, and Corey Pavin; the rookies were Brad Faxon, Tom Lehman, Jeff Maggert, Phil Mickelson, and Loren Roberts.

The average age of the Europeans was thirty-six, same as the Americans. The Europeans had seven players over thirty-seven, the Americans had five over forty, and each side had only one player under thirty—Johansson and Mickelson. The real statistical advantage was in experience: thirteen majors for the European side, six for the U.S.; and fifty-one Cups for Europe versus fifteen for America. If anything—going by that statistics crap—the edge had to be with Europe.

Which explains, of course, why the Americans jumped into the lead right away.

In the opening foursomes, Gallacher tried to recapture some Belfry magic by re-teaming Faldo and Monty. Playing in rain that turned to hail, they faced Lehman and Pavin, whom Wadkins described as a "bulldog and a Jack Russell." The Americans took an early lead, but not without incident: On the second hole, Faldo chipped through the green then conceded a short putt to Lehman, who didn't hear and putted out. Faldo (who has a tendency to mumble) snapped, "When I say it's good, it's good!" The bulldog later said, "I told him to speak clearly. Then he claims he said a couple of times that my putt was good. I wasn't going to put up with any crap . . ."

And there we went again.

The U.S. pair, four up after five, lost the lead, and the teams were even after fifteen. The match stayed square to the last, which both sides played like idiots until Lehman holed a four-footer for par and a 1-up win.

The wins alternated. Torrance and Rocca toppled Haas and Couples, 3&2. Love and Maggert had little trouble with Clark and James, winning 4&3. Langer and Johansson took an early lead but needed all eighteen to beat Strange and Crenshaw, 1-up. And the morning was halved.

Three of the four European teams from the morning returned for the fourballs, but Wadkins dismembered like a mad surgeon, and turned out none of the same pairings. And the U.S. won three of the four matches. Ballesteros opened the afternoon with his first new partner since 1985, David Gilford. They beat Jacobsen and Faxon, 4&3, and Gilford was the star. But we have to give the Americans an assist: Thinking Faxon had made par on seven, in one of the most magnificently boneheaded gestures in Ryder Cup history, Jake picked up his ball. In fact, Brad had taken a penalty drop behind a tree, meaning he recorded a bogey. Gilford's par gave the Europeans their first lead, which they never relinquished. As for Seve, he hit a few good shots, but spent most of his time up his partner's shirt, advising him how to handle the tricky, wet greens. Gilford, a mild mannered part-time cattle breeder who had been devastated by the result of the stupid question incident at Kiawah, felt he had a point to prove, and while he appreciated his partner's enthusiasm, said, "I still have to play my own game." When Gilly holed the winning putt on the fifteenth green, Seve hugged him so tightly, his hat fell off.

But the rest of the afternoon was all-American. Maggert and Roberts, two straight hitters, could do nothing wrong in rolling over two fat smokers, Rocca and Torrance, 6&5. Couples and Love were 4-up after six on Faldo and Monty and finished with a 3&2 victory. Gallacher had written Langer and Johansson into the final slot during the morning round when they had held a comfortable lead; but they fell apart late and nearly lost the match. As a result, they were two tired Europuppies when they met Pavin and Mickelson, who won easily, 6&4, giving the U.S. a 5-3 lead at day's end.

Saturday morning went to the Europeans, 3-1. Faldo and Montgomerie—taking abuse from the press and the galleries for Nick's alleged behavior the previous morning (the papers called them "Snooty and the Blowfish")—

handled best buddies Strange and Haas, 4&2. Torrance and Rocca never trailed Love and Maggert, winning 6&5 in a match that included the third hole-in-one in Cup history, Rocca's five-iron at the sixth. It's a stupid game. The day before, the same European pairing had lost 6&5 to a team that included Maggert. Roberts and Jacobsen scored the only U.S. point of the morning, winning 1-up on Woosnam and Walton. Langer paired with Gilford to end the morning with a 4&3 win over Lehman and Pavin.

As quickly as the momentum was with the Europeans, it was gone—as was the afternoon, which the U.S. won, 3-1. Faxon and Couples defeated Torrance and Montgomerie 4&2; Haas and Mickelson beat Ballesteros and Gilford 3&2; and Pavin and Roberts faced Faldo and Langer in a fantastic battle that went to eighteen, where Pavin chipped in (is it me, or did that little ratbag do that more than anyone in history?) for a birdie and the 1-up win. The only European win was by Woosnam and Rocca (who was rapidly soothing his old Belfry scar with his third win in four matches) over Love and Crenshaw, 3&2.

So the day ended in a 4-4 tie, which gave the U.S. a two-point lead going into the singles. Remarkably, it was the first American lead heading into the final day since 1981, giving Captain Wadkins confidence but also leading him to note that, "a two-point lead is not big enough."

On Sunday, Seve persuaded captain Gallacher to let the team play in his lucky navy blue, instead of the

COLIN MONTGOMERIE

286

scheduled green. (He wasn't superstitious but he felt this, combined with making everyone sit backwards on the toilet and hum the Peruvian national anthem, would ensure victory.) In the opening singles, he faced Lehman. Both players were 1-1, and it wasn't pretty. Gallacher told Seve he was putting the erratic superstar first because "you can't lose us the Ryder Cup in that position." Hardly inspiring, but prophetic, as Ballesteros (who couldn't have hit the bathroom floor with a bladder full of beer) had to get it up and down from several different area

"Come here you feelthy English peeg."

SEVERIANO BALLESTEROS AND DAVID GILFORD

codes to stay close on the front nine, then use every bit of gamesmanship he could muster, and ultimately lost 4&3 to the solid American. In the second match, Jacobsen kept taking, and then losing leads to Clark. When the Englishman aced the eleventh, he took his first lead of the match, which he turned into a 1-up win, after a nightmare downhill four-footer for par on eighteen. (There had only been two aces in the Cup in the first 68 years, then two in the same year. Like I said, stupid game.)

James beat Maggert, 4&3. Woosnam and Couples, who'd met in 1993 and halved, met again and halved again, the only shared point of the week. Love and Rocca, who'd also been matched in a memorable singles tussle two years earlier, met again, Love having less trouble this time, winning 3&2.

Gallacher stacked his best players in the middle of the pack and they lived up to their captain's trust. Gilford nearly threw away a one-hole lead with one to play, but Faxon missed a six-footer on eighteen that would have salvaged a half point. Monty the magnificent, who'd lost the PGA Championship in a playoff to Australian Steve Elkington just a month before, gained a small measure of confidence with a 3&1 win over Crenshaw, finishing the match with three threes. Sam Torrance eased past Loren Roberts to win 2&1. Then Pavin defeated Langer, 3&2, and with three matches left, the teams were tied at 12-1/2.

Strange faced Faldo in the Englishman's record-setting forty-first Cup match. It was a reprise of the U.S.

Open strokeplay playoff of 1988 (which Curtis won, 71-75). Strange had a one-hole lead after fifteen, and held it after both bogeyed sixteen. Both of them nearly butchered seventeen, but Faldo got a read off Strange's missed par putt and rolled in a huge seven-footer to square the battle with one hole to play.

Then he hooked his tee shot into the left rough on the last. Curtis followed a good drive with a poor approach that found the rough short of the green, and Faldo wedged out to about ninety-five yards. Neither man could have been in their happy place, but Faldo struck a beautiful wedge to five feet. Strange, standing in the deep grass of the steep upslope short of the green, did all he could to chip to seven feet. Curtis, 0-2 and hoping to vindicate Wadkins for his captain's pick, struck a putt that hit the right side of the hole and cruelly stayed out. Faldo (who at 1-3 was also a captain's choice) had his eyes glued closed throughout, and when he opened them, he was left with one of the biggest, and nastiest, putts of his incredible career.

"Everything was shaking," he said later, "everything except the putter." The putt was fast and broke to the right, but found the hole for "the greatest scrambling par of my life." He'd won the match, 1-up, and given the Europeans the lead for the first time all week. Said Woosnam, "I knew then we had won the Ryder Cup."

But not so fast, shorty. There were two matches left, both featuring Europe's rookies, Walton and Johansson. Walton dueled with Haas, who'd played in 1983, when he went 2-1-1. A dozen years later, he was 1-2 going into the singles, and he found himself three holes down with four to play to the Dubliner with the squeaky voice. Thanks to a little luck and magic, he battled back, but came up empty on the last, losing the hole, and the match by a hole. The Cup was heading back to Europe on the Concorde.

Per-Ulrik Johansson lost 2&1 to Phil Mickelson, but it didn't matter. It was time for horrendously out-of-tune refrains of "When Irish Eyes are Smiling" and enough crap champagne to drown the population of Dublin. It was one hell of a party, thanks to Europe putting on the kind of singles exhibition—winning them 7-1/2 to 4-1/2—that used to be an American specialty. But in the end (actually on the eighteenth hole), the Europeans prevailed by winning four of the five singles that reached the last green and halving the other.

It had taken Bernard Gallacher ten Ryder Cups—seven as a player, three as the captain—to finally be on the winning team. At the closing ceremony, Wadkins congratulated his fellow captain but offered some friendly advice: "Enjoy your two years with this pretty little thing," Lanny said, "because we're going to be back fighting like hell in 1997 in Spain."

The Cup was finally going to the Continent.

FINAL SCORE

COURSE:

OAK HILL CC | ROCHESTER | NY

1995

FOURSOMES & FOURBALLS

FOURSOMES - MORNING

Pavin/Lehman d. Faldo/Montgomerie, 1-up

Haas/Couples lost to Torrance/Rocca, 3&2

Love/Maggert d. Clark/James, 4&3

Crenshaw/Strange lost to Langer/Johansson, 1-up

FOURBALLS - AFTERNOON

Jacobsen/Faxon lost to Ballesteros/Gilford, 4&3

Maggert/Roberts d. Torrance/Rocca, 6&5

Couples/Love d. Faldo/Montgomerie, 3&2

Pavin/Mickelson d. Langer/Johansson, 6&4

US: 5   EUROPE: 3

FOURSOMES & FOURBALLS

FOURSOMES - MORNING

Strange/Haas lost to Faldo/Montgomerie, 4&2

Love/Maggert lost to Torrance/Rocca, 6&5

Roberts/Jacobsen d. Woosnam/Walton, 1-up

Pavin/Lehman lost to Langer/Gilford, 4&3

FOURBALLS - AFTERNOON

Faxon/Couples d. Torrance/Montgomerie, 4&2

Love/Crenshaw lost to Woosnam/Rocca, 3&2

Haas/Mickelson d. Ballesteros/Gilford, 3&2

Pavin/Roberts d. Faldo/Langer, 1-up

US: 4   EUROPE: 4

SINGLES

Lehman d. Ballesteros, 4&3

Jacobsen lost to Clark, 1-up

Maggert lost to James, 4&3

Couples halved with Woosnam

Love d. Rocca, 3&2

Faxon lost to Gilford, 1-up

Crenshaw lost to Montgomerie, 3&1

Strange lost to Faldo, 1-up

Roberts lost to Torrance, 2&1

Pavin d. Langer, 3&2

Haas lost to Walton, 1-up

Mickelson d. Johansson, 2&1

US: 4-1/2 EUROPE: 7-1/2

TOTAL: US 13-1/2   EUROPE 14-1/2

HAL SUTTON (b. 1958)

EVERY FEW YEARS, a player comes onto the PGA Tour carrying a heavy load: the burden of being the next "sure thing," or even worse, "the next Nicklaus." In the early 1980s, Hal Sutton wore both tags, and for a while lived up to them. In 1982, his first full year as a pro, he won a tournament, had eight top-ten finishes, and ranked eleventh in money. The next year he hit paydirt, winning the PGA Championship in style and the Tournament Players Championship and finishing atop the money list. The next few years weren't bad—a few wins and more than enough money for a kid whose daddy was in the oil bidness—but they were hardly Nicklausian. And then he was in freefall, a "Whatever happened to?"

In the late nineties, reaching his forties and finally in a happy marriage (his fourth), Hal seemed to grow up and into his potential. He won six times from 1998 to 2001. Just as important, he became a force, a rock, a mensch. And nowhere was his presence felt more powerfully than in the Ryder Cup.

Sutton played on two losing Cup teams during his early career. At the Belfry in 1985, he opened with a win, teaming with Craig Stadler to top Howard Clark and Sam Torrance, 3&2. But in the three matches that followed, he had one loss and one half in team play then lost to Bernhard Langer in singles, 5&4. The partisan crowds cheered loudly as the home team won for the first time in twenty-eight years, and Hal made the mistake of criticizing them. British captain Tony Jacklin tarred him as an ugly American when he said, "I bet Hal Sutton can't wait to get back to America and head straight for McDonald's."

He fared better at Muirfield Village in 1987 when the Europeans won in the States for the first time. Going 2-1-2 and turning in one of the best American performances,

he and Larry Mize were the only team to beat the partnership of Seve Ballesteros and Jose Maria Olazabal in its maiden year. But Hal's downward spiral had begun.

Which made his return to form and the Ryder Cup all that much sweeter. He qualified for the 1999 team at Brookline and made the most of it, leading the American team with 3-1/2 points from five matches. He was the heart and soul of the squad, mixing maturity and emotion. Captain Ben Crenshaw called him "the backbone of the team," and he never showed more spine than when he opened the Sunday singles with a 4&2 win over Darren Clarke, a victory that energized a team that entered the day trailing by four points and emerged a historic winner.

Most of his other matches had significance as well. Sutton and Maggert beat Lee Westwood and Darren Clarke for America's only point on the first morning. His win with Maggert over Colin Montgomerie and Paul Lawrie first out on Saturday gave hope to a team trailing by four. Even that afternoon's half with Justin Leonard against Miguel Angel Jimenez and Olazabal was noteworthy because it featured a Sutton-fueled comeback. He proved that desire is more important than youth.

Three years later, Sutton played only twice at the Belfry. He and Scott Verplank beat Clarke and Thomas Bjorn, 2&1, on the first afternoon. Then he sat until the singles, where he faced Langer and lost to him again, 4&3, as Europe won the Cup.

Hal Sutton really "gets" the Ryder Cup. He has had plenty of elation and disappointment in his life and his career, and will have all that experience and more to draw on as the American captain in 2004. He's a friend of mine, and a true gentleman whom I've always admired for his chin-up attitude, obvious sense of fairness, and his abnormal interest in fine shotguns.

COURSE:

VALDERRAMA GC | SOTOGRANDE | SPAIN

☆☆☆☆☆☆☆☆☆ SEPT. **26-28**

1997

☆☆☆☆☆☆☆☆☆☆☆☆☆☆☆☆

FINAL SCORE:

US **13-1/2** ☆ EUROPE **14-1/2**

CAPTAINS:

TOM KITE   SEVE BALLESTEROS

UNITED STATES   EUROPE
☆☆☆☆☆☆☆☆☆☆☆☆   ☆☆☆☆☆☆☆☆☆☆☆☆

Fred Couples*	Mark O'Meara	Thomas Bjorn	Lee Westwood
Brad Faxon	Tiger Woods	Darren Clarke	Ian Woosnam
Jim Furyk		Nick Faldo	
Scott Hoch		Ignacio Garrido	
Lee Janzen*		Per-Ulrik Johansson	
Tom Lehman		Bernhard Langer	
Justin Leonard		Colin Montgomerie	
Davis Love III		Jose Maria Olazabal*	
Jeff Maggert		Jesper Parnevik*	
Phil Mickelson		Costantino Rocca	*captain's picks

THE NOISE BEFORE THE PREVIOUS FEW CUPS had been relatively quiet: little controversy, few squabbles. The fighting was confined to the field of play. But for nearly two years before the 1997 matches, the uproar was deafening, it smelled vaguely like a garlic fart, and it bore a very strong Spanish accent.

For the first time, the matches would be held on the Continent, on the southern coast of Spain. The locale was chosen as a way of thanking Seve Ballesteros (and, indirectly, all of Continental Europe) for making the event exciting again. I'll make no bones about it: Jacklin might have dressed it up and done the hair and makeup, but Seve made the Ryder Cup into the sexy beast it is today. And if the Cup was to be in his home country, it certainly made sense that the insane son-off-my-beech should be the European captain.

However, not everybody was happy with either choice. "The Spanish couldn't run a raffle," said Tony Jacklin (who *lived* near the Vallderrama club), speaking for the many who worried that the country's infrastructure and the relaxed attitude of its citizenry would create problems. The pessimists weren't entirely wrong: There were logistical headaches, everything from hours-long traffic jams to bug-infested, crumbling hotel rooms. But except for heavy rainstorms that delayed matches and soaked the course, the golf went off almost without incident.

Predictably, the same could not be said for Seve's captaincy. Beginning the moment he was named, he was spectacularly frantic and obnoxious, alienating anyone and everyone who dared to challenge his authority. He accused Cup executives of taking bribes from the millionaire owner of Valderrama to stage the match there. (What he didn't say was that he wanted it played on a nearby course *he'd* designed.) Seeking any advantage for his team, he insisted

17TH GREEN (LOVELY FOR A HOME SITE, BUT NOT FOR GOLF)

"Jim Nantz told me he was going to be captain."

U.S. PRESIDENT GEORGE BUSH AND U.S. PLAYER'S WIVES

that the order of play be changed, and it was: For the first time since fourballs were added in 1963, they would precede foursomes. And, most selfishly, he was unhappy with the process for selecting his team.

Like Bernard Gallacher two years earlier, Ballesteros had to make due with two, rather than three, captain's picks. That meant he would be forced to choose among the many Europeans shuttling between their home circuit and the U.S. PGA Tour. He knew early on he wanted Nick Faldo and Sweden's Jesper Parnevik. But he also wanted his old pairs-mate, Jose Maria Olazabal, who was on the mend after two years of agony with a bad toe (actually a pinched nerve in his back). How to get three players with two picks? Leave it to Seve.

When the number-ten player on the Order of Merit, Spain's Miguel Angel Martin, injured his wrist in July, Ballesteros saw his opening. Despite assurances from Martin that he'd be fine, Seve insisted on a physical exam. When Martin refused, Seve tossed him from the team and picked the number-eleven player, who just happened to be Olazabal. Most players and administrators backed Martin, but that didn't deter Seve, who ranted, raved, and generally pouted until he got his way. In the end, Martin was allowed to attend team functions, wear the team uniforms, and appear in team photos, but not play. He came to Valderrama for one day, leaving before the Matches began. At least one Spaniard knew how to behave.

Ballesteros hoped Olazabal would strengthen a team that was old and weak. The core of the team was well-worn: Faldo (making his eleventh Cup appearance), Olazabal (fifth), Bernhard Langer (ninth), Colin Montgomerie

"If you let me win, I weel never try to play again."

SEVERIANO BALLESTEROS

(fourth), and Ian Woosnam (eighth); two other "veterans," Per-Ulrik Johansson and Costantino Rocca, were making their second and third appearances, respectively. Plus, there were five rookies: Parnevik, Thomas Bjorn (the first Dane), Darren Clarke, Ignacio Garrido, and Lee Westwood.

By comparison, Tom Kite's American squad was hailed as one of the greatest ever. Returning were Fred Couples and Lee Janzen (both captain's picks), Brad Faxon, Tom Lehman, Davis Love III, Jeff Maggert, Phil Mickelson, and Mark O'Meara (but only Couples, Love, and O'Meara had more than one previous Cup experience). The American rookies were the real reason for the excitement: Jim Furyk, Scott Hoch, Justin Leonard, and especially Tiger Woods.

Upon final announcement of the American team, Lehman said, "This team looks like the future of golf." Said Love (on only his third Cup team but third in Cup experience), "You put Woods and Mickelson on a team and I'd feel like I'm two down when I walk to the first tee." Captain Kite was cautiously optimistic, saying, "It does look awesome, but you know how it will be."

How it would be was messy. As if there wasn't enough belching, O'Meara raised the issue of paying Ryder Cuppers, saying, "This isn't about greed. It's just the right thing to do." Most players were quick to defend the current system—even though they received an extremely small stipend to cover expenses, while organizations on both sides of the Atlantic made millions—but the issue wasn't dead; it would return.

Then there was the issue of Seve, architect of evil. It had become customary for the captain of the home team to request changes to the host course, usually to benefit his squad, but most felt that Ballesteros (who was paid a handsome fee by the very man he accused of attempted bribery) had overdone it, especially on the par-five seventeenth hole, where he redesigned the green so it was narrow, severely contoured, and protected by a steep slope that funneled into a pond. He also had the grounds crew grow rough across the fairway, negating the American's long-hitting advantage. ("I never much cared for a par-five where you hit driver, sand wedge, sand wedge," said Lehman.) The hole, like most of the rest of the golf course, was pretty average before the changes, and much worse afterward, but it would make an impact throughout the matches. As would Seve. It was a bad joke, but the Europeans knew the punchline. We knew the Valderrama layout intimately, having played our year-end tour championship there for almost a decade.

MARTIN, GARRIDO, BALLESTEROS, OLAZABEL AND JIMENEZ

It was a relief when the matches finally began, nearly two hours late thanks to the frog-strangling downpour that rumbled through in the wee hours of Friday morning. Love and Mickelson faced Olazabal and Rocca in fourballs, and the lead swung back and forth. When both Americans missed birdie putts on the last, the Europeans drew first blood, 1-up. At one point, members of the gallery had used cellphones to disturb Mickelson during his swing, and though he won the hole, it wouldn't be the last time the crowds got overly involved. Their was a fair amount of American representation in the crowd, but Seve's demeanor had the homeys stroppy from the word go.

In the matches that followed, the victors alternated: Couples and Faxon defeated Faldo and Westwood, 1-up; Parnevik and Johansson topped Lehman and Furyk, 1-up; and in the only match that didn't reach the final hole, Woods and O'Meara took the birdieless Montgomerie and Langer, 4&2. The morning was halved, but it was seen as a European victory and provided exactly the psychological advantage Seve had hoped for, starting with fourballs.

Ballesteros left three of his four teams intact while Kite kept only one (Woods and O'Meara) and sent the rest of his men into battle. In another seesaw fight that went to the final hole, Hoch and Janzen beat Rocca and Olazabal 1-up, taking the afternoon's only full point for the United States. The last match out finished quickly, with Monty and Herman the German taking their revenge on Woods and O'Meara, 5&3.

Thanks to the late start, the middle matches had to be suspended due to darkness. The next morning, the course was wetter, longer, and slower still due to more rain that again delayed the start. It was a superhuman effort from the grounds crew that made the place even close to playable. When the remaining games finally resumed, Faldo and Westwood beat Maggert and Leonard, 3&2; it was Faldo's twenty-fourth Ryder Cup point, moving him ahead of Billy Casper on the all-time list. What a player. I don't care how many majors anybody has won (Faldo has six); this is one of the greatest records in golf. Then Parnevik and Garrido halved with Lehman and Mickelson. It had taken two days, but the first day ended with the Euros ahead, 4-1/2 to 3-1/2.

On the second day, seven of the eight matches made it to the now-infamous seventeenth hole and three ended there. At Seve's direction, the hole had been cut two yards from the front of the green (on tour, a hole is rarely placed less than four yards from any edge). It would prove a butt-puckering position, to say the least.

With fourballs again opening play, Love and Couples faced Montgomerie and Clarke. The Americans took a lead, lost it, got it back, then gave it up for good when Monty holed a slippery birdie putt on seventeen for a one-hole advantage the Europeans held to the end. The trickle of Monty's putt opened a floodgate of European victories as Bjorn and Woosnam beat Faxon and Leonard 2&1, then Woods and O'Meara lost to Faldo and Westwood, also 2&1. Both matches finished on seventeen, where Woods's putt from off the back of the green raced across the surface, past the hole, down the shaved bank, and into the water to horrible jeers from gloating fans.

That left Lehman and Mickelson to salvage something from the morning, which they did with a half against Garrido and Olazabal. This match also featured the seventeenth hole, where Mickelson hit a two-iron out of the rough from 240 yards; the ball just cleared the water, hit near the flag, ran forward, then stopped and rolled back to five feet. Lehman called it "the single greatest shot I've ever seen." Garrido's three-wood had flown the green and into a bunker, from where he faced a treacherous explosion to a hole that must have looked as if it were in the water: Mustering up all his courage, under the laser beam stare of his childhood hero, the rookie Spaniard played the perfect splash, which took forever to roll down the green and stop six feet away. Lehman called it "maybe the second greatest shot I've ever seen." It proved crucial as Mickelson missed his eagle putt, Garrido holed his birdie, and they remained tied. On eighteen, Olazabal holed a twelve-foot par putt to ensure the half. The Europeans had won the morning, 3-1/2 to 1/2: The U.S. had not won a match!

As all this was going on, Seve was popping up everywhere like a demented prairie dog. He raced around, about, and underneath the course through a series of maintenance tunnels in his bright blue, souped-up cart, talking to his players, gesticulating wildly, barking into his walkie-talkie, waving, leopard crawling, and earning the nickname "Captain Frantic." Kite was more low-key, quietly watching the matches and chatting with Michael Jordan (who rode in the captain's much slower cart) and former president George the First, a friend from back in Texas. He was much less visible, as (and you're not going to believe this) no one had told him about the existence of the tunnels, which made getting around the crowds a great deal easier. The difference in the teams was reflected in the captains: Kite would let his squad win; Ballesteros would will his to victory, or resort to poison and/or snipers in the cork oaks.

The afternoon was only slightly better for the visitors. In the one match that finished on the day it began, Monty and Herman took an early lead and held on for a 1-up win over Janzen and Furyk. The other matches had to wait till the next morning to finish, when Hoch and Maggert finally won a point for the U.S. team, fighting back from 3-down after five to top Faldo and Westwood, 2&1. The much-vaunted Woods continued to struggle, teaming with Leonard for a half with Parnevik and Garrido. And in a rare blowout, Couples and Love, 1-up when darkness fell, started the morning with five bogeys and eventually fell to Rocca and Olazabal, 6&4.

The Europeans had embarrassed the Americans, winning the second day (okay, two days) 6-2. That gave them a five-point advantage with the singles to come. On Saturday night, Kite had asked President Bush to talk to the U.S. team. "I wouldn't call it a speech," Bush said. "Just remarks of encouragement, nothing that will live in history to rival the Gettysburg Address." Whatever he said, it seemed to spark the Americans in singles, when they finally performed the way everyone, including themselves, expected.

Needing points in a hurry, Kite put his best players out first. Ballesteros saved his power for the end in case they had to stop an American rally. As it happened, they were both wrong.

For the third straight Cup, Couples and Woosnam met in the singles: The previous two had both been halves, but this time, Couples won convincingly, 8&7. But anyone taking the trouncing as a good omen for the U.S. would have been disappointed. From then on, the stars fell: Love lost to Johansson, 3&2, and Woods was cut down 4&2 by Rocca. Leonard could only halve with Bjorn, who had been 4-down after four. America's big guns, winners of three majors in 1997, had been muzzled and the Europeans needed only one point to keep the Cup.

But it wouldn't come easy. Mickelson beat Clarke, 2&1, costing the Irishman a Ferrari that had been promised him by his equipment sponsor if he finished the Cup with a perfect record. Janzen topped Olazabal 1-up. At one point during the next match, Seve came running up to Parnevik and was met with "Get the fuck away from me." While he didn't want to see him at that moment, Parnevik later admitted, "I don't know what he did, but whatever it was, it worked." Apparently not well enough, though, as O'Meara beat him 5&4. It worked for good in the next match, when Langer beat Faxon 2&1 for the fourteenth point, ensuring a tie that would keep the Cup in Europe. Maggert then beat Westwood, 3&2, and the winning point was actually a half, picked up by Monty, who, urged by Captain Prairie Dog B., conceded a long putt on the last green in his match with Hoch. (The gig was over now, so it was time for Seve to be sporting—the man would make a chameleon blush.) The U.S. won the final two matches— Furyk over Faldo, 3&2, Lehman beating Garrido, 7&6—and the final one-point victory was proof of just how close the Americans came, winning seven of the twelve matches and halving two others. If just one of the top players had won! That sort of speculation had been a Ryder Cup staple for seventy years.

Afterward, the U.S. press engaged in the kind of postmortem pissing and farting contest that had been perfected by the British over so many years of losing: Kite had been out-captained; the best Americans had played worst (which they had—Woods, Love, and Leonard winning only one match among them); the U.S. team was too lazy, too spoiled, too concerned with money and perfect teeth, should have visited the course before the matches. Plus, of course, Seve did this, Seve did that . . . And they (just like I) didn't know the half of it.

Before the 1997 Cup had begun, Kite talked about what, for the Americans, had been the good old days: "Thirty years ago, you invited the British over, beat up on them, had a couple of cocktail parties, and sent them home. That's not true anymore." How right he was.

FINAL SCORE ☆☆☆☆☆☆☆☆☆☆☆☆☆☆☆☆☆

COURSE:

VALDERRAMA GC | SOTOGRANDE | SPAIN | 1997

FOURBALLS & FOURSOMES

FOURBALLS - MORNING

Love/Mickelson lost to Olazabal/Rocca, 1-up

Couples/Faxon d. Faldo/Westwood, 1-up

Lehman/Furyk lost to Parnevik/Johansson, 1-up

Woods/O'Meara d. Montgomerie/Langer, 4&2

FOURSOMES - AFTERNOON

Hoch/Janzen d. Rocca/Olazabal, 1-up

Maggert/Leonard lost to Westwood/Faldo, 3&2

Lehman/Mickelson halved with Parnevik/Garrido

O'Meara/Woods lost to

Langer/Montgomerie, 5&3

US: 3-1/2   EUROPE: 4-1/2

FOURBALLS & FOURSOMES

FOURBALLS - MORNING

Love/Couples lost to Montgomerie/Clarke, 1-up

Faxon/Leonard lost to Bjorn/Woosnam, 2&1

O'Meara/Woods lost to Faldo/Woosnam, 2&1

Lehman/Mickelson halved with Garrido/Olazabal

FOURSOMES - AFTERNOON

Janzen/Furyk lost to Montgomerie/Langer, 1-up

Hoch/Maggert d. Faldo/Westwood, 2&1

Leonard/Woods halved with Parnevik/Garrido

Couples/Love lost to Olazabal/Rocca, 6&4

US: 2   EUROPE: 6

SINGLES

Couples d. Woosnam, 8&7

Love lost to Johansson, 3&2

Woods lost to Rocca, 4&2

Leonard halved with Bjorn

Mickelson d. Clarke, 2&1

O'Meara d. Parnevik, 5&4

Janzen d. Olazabal, 1-up

Faxon lost to Langer, 2&1

Maggert d. Westwood, 3&2

Hoch halved with Montgomerie

Furyk d. Faldo, 3&2

Lehman d. Garrido, 7&6

US: 8   EUROPE: 4

TOTAL: US 13-1/2   EUROPE 14-1/2

COURSE:

THE COUNTRY CLUB | BROOKLINE | MA

☆☆☆☆☆☆☆☆☆☆ **SEPT.** **24-26**

1999

☆☆☆☆☆☆☆☆☆☆☆☆☆☆☆☆

FINAL SCORE:

☆ **US** 14-1/2   **EUROPE** 13-1/2

CAPTAINS:

BEN CRENSHAW   MARK JAMES

UNITED STATES		EUROPE	
David Duval	Hal Sutton	Darren Clarke	Jean Van de Velde
Jim Furyk	Tiger Woods	Andrew Coltart*	Lee Westwood
Tom Lehman*		Sergio Garcia	
Justin Leonard		Padraig Harrington	
Davis Love III		Miguel Angel Jimenez	
Mark O'Meara		Paul Lawrie	
Jeff Maggert		Colin Montgomerie	
Phil Mickelson		Jose Maria Olazabal	
Steve Pate*		Jesper Parnevik*	
Payne Stewart		Jarmo Sandelin	*captain's picks

1967   1969   1971   1973   1975   1977   1979   1981   1983

IF THE OVER-THE-TOP PARTISAN ANTICS AT THE "War by the Shore" in 1991 would

have upset Samuel Ryder, the "Battle of Brookline" probably had him revolving in his grave. While the matches were exciting and the result a surprise—thanks to the greatest final-day comeback in Cup history—the magnificence of the golf was tainted by knee-jerk reaction.

We probably should have been prepared for trouble since the big pre-Cup controversy was the issue of paying players. Should they be paid for representing their countries? Were the organizing bodies making too much at the players' expense? What would constitute fair compensation?

These questions and others threatened to overshadow the PGA Championship at Medinah, outside Chicago. But PGA of America executives did something unusually wise, holding a meeting for American Cup hopefuls (those already on the team and those with a chance) where they promised that a financial plan would be announced soon after the Cup. They were true to their word, promising to donate $200,000 in the name of each player (and captain), split between his choice of charity and university. I'm sure the PGA still made a pretty penny, but $2.6 million to good causes is better than nothing. A lot better.

Also going on at Medinah was the last-minute scrambling for points and U.S. captain Ben Crenshaw's last chance to watch those players hoping to be plucked for one of his picks. The day after Tiger Woods won the PGA by a stroke over Sergio Garcia, Crenshaw's team was set. It featured only one newcomer—David Duval—and an impressive list of veterans: Woods, Jim Furyk, Justin Leonard, Davis Love III, Mark O'Meara, Jeff Maggert, Phil

"Screw the majors!"

BEN CRENSHAW AND PHIL MICKELSON

Mickelson, Payne Stewart (1999 U.S. Open winner), Hal Sutton, and captain's picks Tom Lehman and Steve Pate.

For Europe, captain Mark James' team was greener than a kindergarten Kleenex, with seven players making their first Cup appearances: Garcia, already a force, and displaying all the usual Spanish passion; Scot Andrew Coltart (a captain's pick); Padraig Harrington; Miguel Angel Jimenez; Paul Lawrie (1999 Open Champion); the insane Swede Jarmo Sandelin; and Jean Van de Velde, the handsome waterboy of Carnoustie (who by the way, is *perfect* for TV). Returning were Darren Clarke, Monty, Jose Maria Olazabal, Jesper Parnevik (captain's pick), and Lee Westwood; only Monty and Ollie had more than one year of previous Cup chops. But as James said, "In my experience, experience is overrated." Mark James is probably the funniest man ever to play golf, and has an incredible ability to look the most miserable doing it, too. He's not deadpan. Think extinct-for-millions-of-years-pan, and for this reason, he was not particularly well liked or understood by Americans. Now that he's playing the Champions Tour, all that will change.

Right about now it's worth recalling that the U.S. had lost the previous two meetings by a total of two points and that many (especially those professional vipers, the golf media) were questioning how much the rich, pampered Americans really *wanted* to win. It was unlikely anyone would have said about the U.S. team what Seve Ballesteros had said about his squad after Valderrama: "My players played with their hearts, and that is why we won." Dead fucking right.

If the U.S. was going to prove it had the heart to go with its game, Gentle Ben was the perfect choice to apply CPR and elicit the necessary devotion from his boys. Few American golfers have been so loved. He did everything possible to get his players prepared and pumped. (For more insights into Ben's approach to being captain than I can rip off here, read his autobiography, *A Feel for the Game*. It's vintage Crenshaw, sappy and steely, warm, wise, and comfortably crumpled at the edges.) Ben knew he had to forge a team from a dozen individuals, part of which he accomplished by turning one of the lounges in Boston's Four Seasons Hotel into a game room, complete with ping-pong table (that was Payne Stewart's idea), big-screen television, and videogames.

The European team made camp one floor down. There's no record of the teams playing practical jokes on each other or fighting over elevators and luggage carts. They saved their energy for the course. (For the European view of the Cup experience, plus a lot more, read James's candid and beautifully written memoir, *Into the Beat Pit.*)

Turned out Jamesy was right (the arsehole usually is), and the wet-behind-the-ears Europeans shocked the Americans out of the gate.

Knowing he needed a fast start, Crenshaw led off the foursomes with his two strongest teams. However, Duval and Mickelson were all over the course in losing to Montgomerie and Lawrie, 3&2, and Woods and Lehman fell 2&1 to Parnevik and Garcia, who developed an instant chemistry. They turned out to be an inspired bit of pairing by James, a buzzsaw that ran undefeated through four different American teams; their first win also was a nice bit of tit-for-tat as Sergio got Tiger back for pipping him at the PGA. In the bottom matches, Jimenez and Harrington, two rookies, were quickly down to Love and Stewart, but came back to weasel out a precious half. The U.S. finally won one, Maggert and Sutton over Westwood and Clarke, 3&2. The matches were close: Half of the four-man battles over the two days went to the eighteeth, another four ended at seventeen. And most went to the Europeans: In the afternoon fourballs, when three of four went to the final hole, the U.S. couldn't muster anything more than a half point.

Mickelson and Furyk shot a better ball score of sixty-two and still lost to Parnevik and Garcia, 1-up; it didn't help that Mickelson missed short birdie tries on sixteen and eighteen. Teamed with Leonard, Love holed a long eagle putt on fourteen and another for birdie on eighteen but still they could only manage a half with Montgomerie and Lawrie, who also were rolling their rocks (I've always wanted to say that). Jimenez and Olazabal took care of Sutton and Maggert, 2&1, then Woods and Duval were beaten 1-up by Westwood and Clarke, the latter making six birdies on his own.

There was action outside the ropes, as well, where 30,000 fans a day (way more than the Country Club could contain) had too much to drink and not enough room. Whether they were juiced, squeezed, or just fresh, the fans got on the players, and not only the Europeans. Brookline was a tough room to work, and I have a personal theory as to why. Anyone that's traveled the States knows that Boston is a different city anyway, a great sports town with crazy fans that call a spade a "fuckin' shovel," and a giant gaping asshole in the middle of it known as "The Big Dig." It looks like every Irishman that ever came here is trying to tunnel his way home, and in 1999 it could take an hour and a half to drive to the other side of the street. By the time the Beantowners got to Brookline, a lot of them were ready for several dozen beers and some *serious* heckling. At Fenway, they were used to being ignored by batters and pitchers alike, but against the deafeningly silent background of a Ryder Cup match, they had targets that *had* to hear them.

The worst of the abuse was directed at Monty, who, bless his soft heart and thin skin, attracts morons the way Arnold attracted pretty girls. Monty and I have a little history, dating back to when we played together in Europe. All my life I've poked fun at people whom I really like, as a perverted way of offering them the chance to prove their character. And it's not just me either, it's kind of a rite of passage on the European Tour, trial by insult, if you like. If a man could take it and give it back, we always thought more of him, but Monty was always different, easily wounded,

and retrospect I wish I hadn't been so tough on him. I didn't give him the *Mrs. Doubtfire* nickname (that was another pro, Englishman John Hawksworth), but it was attributed to me in the British press, and it followed the big lad across the Atlantic to Brookline. If he had dressed in a tweed skirt, horn-rimmed glasses, and a good stout pair of walking shoes and had a publicity shot taken with a vacuum cleaner, people here would have fallen in love with him, but it just wasn't in his nature to do such a thing, and so it went the other way. It was brutal, with idiots shouting, "Nice tits, Mrs. Doubtfire," and worse. The verbal abuse was so bad that Monty's father had to leave the course. The American fans got on their own, too, particularly Duval and Mickelson, who along with O'Meara were very vocal about wanting to be paid, but Monty got the vast majority of the punishment.

The Americans were like punch-drunk fighters after the first day, dazed and confused upon finding themselves down 6-2. Hal Sutton, who, while compiling the best American record became something of a spiritual leader, tried to rally his team by relating something he'd learned in 1985 when playing on the first American squad to lose in twenty-eight years. "We can't play to keep something bad from happening," Sutton told his

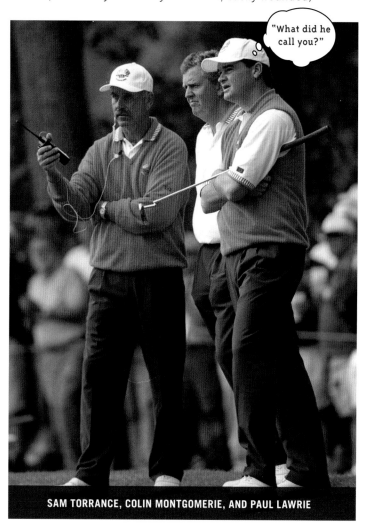

SAM TORRANCE, COLIN MONTGOMERIE, AND PAUL LAWRIE

mates. "We have to play to make something good happen."

Saturday's foursomes did start with something good for the Americans as Sutton and Maggert, the only U.S. pair with a first-day win, led off by beating Montgomerie and Lawrie 1-up, despite the round taking five hours plus a lightning delay. Then Furyk and O'Meara couldn't make a birdie and lost to Clarke and Westwood, 3&2. Woods was paired with Pate, his third partner in as many matches, and eagled the fourteenth to beat Jimenez and Harrington, 1-up. But any momentum was snuffed when Parnevik and Garcia notched their third win, taking Stewart and Leonard—who had five bogeys to the Euros' five birdies in the first eleven holes—by 3&2. The teams had split, 2-2.

The afternoon fourballs ended with another tied score, but a few small incidents would prove to pay big dividends for the Americans on the final day. Mickelson switched putters and teamed with Lehman to hand Westwood and Clarke their first defeat, 2&1. After resting in the morning, Love and Duval nearly beat Parnevik and Garcia, but Sergio, at nineteen the youngest Cupper ever, holed a seven-foot birdie on the final green to halve the match: This was one of the best matches of the week, Love nearly holing out for a double eagle and Parnevik pitching in from fifty feet.

Off the tree, skip on the pond, nothing but green!

JESPER PARNEVIK AND SERGIO GARCIA

Leonard, who hadn't looked comfortable and putted dreadfully in two winless matches, asked to be put back into action on Saturday afternoon with Sutton. Crenshaw obliged, saying, "I have a hunch that Justin's putter will get hot." Johnny Miller, doing color commentary for NBC, said he had a hunch about Leonard, too, that he "should go home and watch on television." Leonard's putting didn't improve, the team blew a few chances, and they had to settle for a half with Jimenez and Olazabal. But Miller's comment about Leonard became a rallying point for the Americans: "It was one more thing to motivate us," Crenshaw said. "Like we didn't have enough already."

The final match of the day was the only American loss, Woods and Pate falling to Montgomerie and Lawrie, 2&1. Tiger continued to struggle, especially on the greens. He wasn't alone—poor putting nagged the Americans both days—as reflected in the two-day score, ten to six. The pundits were quick to report that no team had ever come back from more than two points down to win. And the Europeans needed only four points to retain the Cup.

There are two moments of the 1999 Ryder Cup that I'll never forget. Everyone knows the first, which is coming up. The other was Crenshaw's press conference Saturday night. Ben is an emotional guy who spent two years getting himself, his team, and every imaginable detail ready for the three days of play. There is no way in his wildest dreams he thought he'd be four points down going into Sunday. I don't know how they'd describe it in Texas, but when he sat down to face the bloodthirsty scribes, he looked like he'd been hit on the head with a bag of dicks. He was exhausted.

After fielding the obvious questions and defending every decision he'd ever made, he snapped, or as he wrote in his book, "something jolted me back into reality." Most of the people listening probably thought he'd fallen through the rabbit hole into Wonderland when he said, "I'm going to leave you all with one thought, and I'm going to leave. I'm a big believer in fate. I have a good feeling about this. That's all I am going to tell you." And then he left.

There were no secrets about what went on at the hotel that night. The Europeans had a leisurely dinner, James and his assistant Torrance prepared the lineup for the singles, and it was an early night.

In the American lounge, Crenshaw waved the flag, raised the roof, and called in the artillery. Tony Robbins could have taken some lessons from Ben that evening. He showed a video of great shots and dramatic moments in Cup history that also included George C. Scott as Patton and John Belushi from *Animal House* ("nothing's over until we say it's over!"). Then George W. Bush, still governor of Texas, came in and read the famous letter from Colonel William Travis, who was defending the Alamo (which is the single most disappointing national monument in the U.S. Do yourself a favor; if you need to see a half-finished building swarmed by Mexicans, visit any building site south of Tulsa instead). The last words of the letter are "Victory or death," and I have no doubt which one the Americans were banking on. Finally, they went around the room and everyone spoke, even Davis Love's wife Robin, who went last, and quoted the late instructor Harvey Penick, who'd been like a second father to Crenshaw: "Take dead aim," she reminded them.

I've been in a few locker rooms and player meetings, but I can't believe there's ever been a revival meeting that packed more hellfire and damnation than this one. And holy shit, but it worked. I was there, and as hard as it was to watch, I couldn't help but feel that something truly special was in the air. It was the most remarkable afternoon of drama and tension I've ever experienced.

Crenshaw sent Lehman and Sutton—two older, experienced, and highly respected players—out first to "set the tone," which they did, beating, respectively, Westwood, 3&2, and Clarke, 4&2. From that point on, it was off to the races: Mickelson over Sandelin (in his first Cup appearance), 4&3; Love over Van de Velde (also making his debut), 6&5; Woods over Coltart (the third rookie who sat until the singles), 3&2. Then Duval got his game back and took it to Parnevik, 5&4, and Pate beat Jimenez, 2&1. In the first eight matches, only Harrington scored a point for the Europeans, beating O'Meara 1-up. Meanwhile, in matches eleven and twelve, Furyk beat Garcia 4&3, and Lawrie beat Maggert, also 4&3, for only the second European point.

With two matches still on the course, the U.S. led fourteen to twelve and needed a half to win. Europe needed two wins to keep the Cup.

Cue the second moment, in the match no one will ever forget, Leonard against Olazabal. Having been dissed on national television and playing nowhere near his standards, Leonard must have thought he was stuck in his own personal *Groundhog Day*; 3-down after nine holes, 4-down after eleven. (Two years earlier, he'd had a four-hole lead on Thomas Bjorn and blown it, settling for a half.)

Then, miraculously, he rewrote the script: As Crenshaw predicted, Leonard's putter started smokin' and he went par-par-birdie-birdie to tie the match at fifteen. They were still tied at seventeen, where both approaches hit the green but finished on the lower tier, Ollie twenty-five feet away, Leonard forty-five. And then Leonard's putt, up the hill, perfectly paced, just a little break, and in.

There was pandemonium, a human explosion of excitement, relief, and "Up yours, Johnny!" Suddenly there was dancing on the green, and a riot of silicone jugs and tousled blond hugs. There was jumping and yelling before someone remembered that Olazabal (who was standing dumbfounded, and the only one *really* in need of a hug) still had a chance to halve the hole.

It was a defining moment in so many ways—of the American comeback, of the incredible emotional pressure— but why did we see such a crack in the arse of good sportsmanship? Kneeling at the greenside with Torrance, I was in several strange positions. A European Ryder Cup player who wanted desperately for the brotherhood to prevail, yet elated to be living in America, I had good friends on both teams. I'd spent the previous months reading about and listening to how these Americans supposedly didn't care about each other, had little regard for the Ryder Cup, were interested only in money, and had no concept of how to be a "team." (For the record, none of the Americans had ever asked for money for any other reason than they wanted to direct a very small percentage of the massive profit generated by the event toward charities of their own choosing.) As I watched the events unfold, the world around me seemed to drift into slow-motion and the deafening roar of the crowd quickly muted. Shit, I thought, these guys look like they care about each other to me, and about the Ryder Cup, and it didn't look like it was about the money. If this wasn't a "team," then Johnny Miller's brain was a blowfish. The premature celebration on the seventeenth green was a giant "up yours" to everybody that had doubted these men and their commitment to Cup and country. From 1927, every man that played on either team realized how special it was to touch that little gold cup, to carry the hopes of their country, their captain, and their teammates. Apart from the worst shirts in the history of sport, the men from 2001 were no different.

Olazabal nearly holed his birdie putt, but nearly wasn't enough. And with that, Justin could do no worse than halve the match, giving America the winning half point. (And, indeed, Olazabal won the eighteenth to halve the match.) Behind them, Montgomerie and Stewart were locked in a tight match that was suddenly meaningless: After watching in disbelief from the seventeen fairway, dear Payne Stewart, who had battled with hecklers all day on his opponent's behalf, conceded a putt on eighteen to give Monty the win. It was a characteristically sweet gesture, and a month later he was gone.

A few ugly minutes overshadowed three days of spirited but gentlemanly competition. There were some exemplary efforts, notably those of Montgomerie, Parnevik, Garcia, and the rookie Lawrie, all of whom finished 3-1-1. Only

JUSTIN LEONARD

Sutton matched that score for the States. The rest of the Americans scrambled: Love had one win and three halves, Leonard one loss and three halves, O'Meara and Stewart no wins. Woods won only two points, Duval one and a half. But when it mattered on Sunday, facing a four-point deficit, they won 8-1/2 of 12 points.

That night, I walked from the Copley Plaza over to the Four Seasons for a few bevvies with the boys, hoping that they weren't too devastated by the loss. When I got there, they were in full swing, all of them somewhere between Anheuser and Busch, with occasional tears, but mostly drunken cheers, and predictions of how it would be the next time at the Belfry. I got hugs from every brother but Monty, and big Darren Clarke deliberately poured a beer all over my crotch. Lovely, but where *was* Monty? I had stayed away from the team room all week, not wanting to upset him during the matches, as I knew he was having a hard enough time of it. At a pre-match cocktail party, his wife, Eimar, had told me that she would never forgive me for what I had done to him. I really needed to see him, but he was in his room, apparently shattered by the effort he had put in and crestfallen over the result. Jamesy and his wife Jane were their usual philosophical selves (well, Jamesy was, and Jane was threatening to kill anyone that wasn't European with a furled-up umbrella), and Sam and Suzanne Torrance were just lovers as usual, playing tonsil-hockey on the sofa, when in walked Monty, in a purple mood. He went to the buffet, shoveled some Caesar salad on to a plate, got in front of me, and said, "What are you doing here? You have no right to be here."

I waved around the room and said, "Monty, I'm a Ryder Cup player, just like you. There are plenty of us in here."

Then he took his plate and hurled it at me, but there must have been dressing on his hand or something, because it slipped and shot sideways, almost decapitating a waiter who had just walked in, carrying a tray of crudités. It had taken all week, but finally he made a bad swing. It was chaos, followed by stony silence, as the big lad stamped off with his head down, past everybody, and back to his room. I looked at captain Jamesy, who was staring at the carpet. It was no use—I had to go. Monty deserved to be in that room with his teammates, and I knew that while I remained, he wouldn't come back. So I apologized to the boys, kissed the wives, and stumbled back onto the streets of Boston utterly heartbroken. I found an empty Bud can and with my hands in my pockets, kicked it all the way back, into the lobby, up the elevator, and into my room at the Copley Plaza, with tears streaming down my face. (I still have the can—how weird is that?) Monty had been such a rock all week, and had played so bravely, and I knew that no matter how badly I was feeling, it was worse for him. And it was, at least in part, because of me.

Ben Crenshaw called it "The miracle that will live forever in our hearts."

Sam Torrance, one of James's assistants, said it was "One of the most disgusting things I have seen in my life." And that fat bastard used to share rooms with *me!* The chance for revenge would be sweet when the matches returned to the Belfry in two years, when Sammy would be the European captain.

But then the whole world changed.

FINAL SCORE

COURSE:

THE COUNTRY CLUB : BROOKLINE : MA

1999

FOURSOMES & FOURBALLS

FOURSOMES - MORNING

Duval/Mickelson lost to
Montgomerie/Lawrie, 3&2
Lehman/Woods lost to Garcia/Parnevik, 2&1
Love/Stewart halved with Jimenez/Harrington
Maggert/Sutton d. Westwood/Clarke, 3&2

FOURBALLS - AFTERNOON

Mickelson/Furyk lost to Parnevik/Garcia, 1-up
Love/Leonard halved with Montgomerie/Lawrie
Sutton/Maggert lost to Jimenez/Olazabal, 2&1
Woods/Duval lost to Westwood/Clarke, 1-up

US: 2   EUROPE: 6

FOURSOMES & FOURBALLS

FOURSOMES - MORNING

Sutton/Maggert d. Montgomerie/Lawrie, 1-up
Furyk/O'Meara lost to Clarke/Westwood, 3&2
Woods/Pate d. Jimenez/Harrington, 1-up
Stewart/Leonard lost to Parnevik/Garcia, 3&2

FOURBALLS - AFTERNOON

Mickelson/Lehman d. Westwood/Clarke, 2&1
Love/Duval halved with Parnevik/Garcia
Leonard/Sutton halved with Jimenez/Olazabal
Woods/Pate lost to Montgomerie/Lawrie, 2&1

US: 4   EUROPE: 4

SINGLES

Lehman d. Westwood, 3&2
Sutton d. Clarke, 4&2
Mickelson d. Sandelin, 4&3
Love d. Van de Velde, 6&5
Woods d. Coltart, 3&2
Duval d. Parnevik, 5&4
O'Meara lost to Harrington, 1-up
Pate d. Jimenez, 2&1
Leonard halved with Olazabal
Stewart lost to Montgomerie,1-up
Furyk d. Garcia, 4&3
Maggert lost to Lawrie, 4&3

US: 8-1/2   EUROPE: 3-1/2

TOTAL:

 US 14-1/2   EUROPE 13-1/2

COURSE:

THE BELFRY (BRABAZON COURSE) **SUTTON COLDFIELD** ENGLAND

☆☆☆☆☆☆☆☆☆☆ **SEPT.** 27-29

2002

☆☆☆☆☆☆☆☆☆☆☆☆☆☆

FINAL SCORE:

US 12-1/2 ☆ **EUROPE** 15-1/2

CAPTAINS:

CURTIS STRANGE   SAM TORRANCE

UNITED STATES
☆☆☆☆☆☆☆☆☆☆☆☆

Paul Azinger*	Scott Verplank*
Mark Calcavecchia	Tiger Woods
Stewart Cink	
David Duval	
Jim Furyk	
Scott Hoch	
Davis Love III	
Phil Mickelson	
Hal Sutton	
David Toms	

EUROPE
☆☆☆☆☆☆☆☆☆☆☆☆

Thomas Bjorn	Phillip Price
Darren Clarke	Lee Westwood
Niclas Fasth	
Pierre Fulke	
Sergio Garcia*	
Padraig Harrington	
Bernhard Langer	
Paul McGinley	
Colin Montgomerie	
Jesper Parnevik*	*captain's picks

CAPTAIN TORRANCE'S FAVORITE COLOR. MONKEY-SHIT BROWN.

EUROPEANS MIGHT NOT HAVE BEEN AWARE OF the American media coverage before the last Cup and how it had affected the U.S. team, but it would have been pretty hard not to notice this time. It's all too easy for those of us who are lucky and good enough to make a living from professional golf to forget that we live in the real world. Lots of money, perks like courtesy cars, free meals, and equipment, plus the adoration of fans create a cocoon of privilege and a sense of invincibility. But soon after the 1999 Ryder Cup was over, our perfect existence was shattered, not once but twice.

One month after Brookline, Payne Stewart died in a private jet crash. It hollowed out all of us in the world of golf. It could have been any one of us in that little Lear, but Payne Stewart was more than a little different. He was so familiar, so touchable, and so loved that millions, inside and outside of golf, were drawn to the TV screen, watching the fateful jet inch across the screen again and again like a ghastly CNN video game. It *couldn't* happen, but it did, and it left a smoking crater on the landscape of golf that can never be filled. And there was no event in which Payne Stewart's character shone through better than the Ryder Cup. More than anything in his career, he loved to play for his country.

The second awful reality check was the horror of September 11, 2001. Growing up with troops on the streets of Ulster, with the carnage of frequent bombings and sectarian murders in the news all the time, it shouldn't have affected me as badly as it did the average American, but for me, it might have been worse. This wasn't supposed to happen here, not in the land of the fresh start. This place was exempt from the kind of religiously-driven insanity that boils up and suppurates out from centuries of evil, cruelty, and intolerance-in-the-name-of-God, over in the old countries. But suddenly, the stench was upon us, and the whole world reeled, for despite what anyone might have heard or read about anti-American sentiment, America, and the American dream, is much loved throughout this little planet. But people don't write letters of commendation, only complaint. Countless millions, perhaps billions, still dream of living in this amazing place, and to see it violated in such a way was utterly horrifying. It still hurts to think about what happened and why, and to see how our world has changed—living in fear, many of our freedoms challenged, and knowing that the world we're leaving our children is not as safe as the one in which we grew up.

Nothing was immune from the aftermath, including the Ryder Cup, which was to have been played a little more than two weeks later in England. With the teams picked and ready to go, the decision was made to postpone the matches for a year but otherwise change as little as possible: The teams and the venue would remain.

If there was some good to come out of the tragedy, it was the washing away of the bad blood from Brookline. After the eleventh of September 2001, fighting would be reserved for something more important than a golf match between rich men in bad shirts. There was no room for hostility among friends. Sport thrives on competition, one side will always lose and the other win. But more than ever, we needed to remember that what were doing was not life and death, and that when the games were through, we could sit together, have a drink, and laugh.

But it was a shitty way to be reminded.

There was ample evidence at the Belfry that the world was a different place. There was a heavy cloak of security, men carrying machine guns, watching the thousands of spectators, conducting searches, and taking no chances. No one objected.

The pre-Match ceremonies were emotionally charged. Jets overhead, the many speeches and prayers, even the fluttering of the flags took on extra meaning. If you weren't affected, you weren't human.

And there couldn't have been two better captains to handle the circumstances than Curtis Strange and Sam Torrance. Curtis gets a bum rap sometimes for his bluntness, but he is a very thoughtful and sincere man who deserves an enormous amount of credit for his accomplishments both on and off the course. A modern Ryder Cup captain has to go through twenty-four months of bullshit before the bell rings, all kinds of press conferences, PGA committee meetings, the wardrobe debacle, opening ceremony arrangements, menus and seating, team selection, etc. It never ends. Curtis was someone the players could respect and would listen to throughout the extra year of waiting (although no one was more anxious to get going).

Sam Torrance had waited his whole life for this moment. In Europe, a player's career is measured in two dimensions. First, by the amount of wins, and second by his Ryder Cup record. For so many years, European players realistically had only one major championship in which to play, as it was almost impossible to qualify for the Masters, PGA, and U.S. Open from the European money list, and so the Ryder Cup had gradually become more and more huge until this moment, at which point it had consumed Sam completely, and he was ready. I was there to work the first day TV coverage for USA Network, and Sam had booked me a room over the center of the putting green at the Belfry. It was so small I had to have most of the furniture taken out, but it didn't matter. I could simultaneously get on my bed, order room service, cut my toenails, throw open the window, and show both teams my arsehole as they practiced. It was the perfect location.

The teams were evenly matched in many ways, notably the mix of veterans and rookies: The U.S. had three rookies, Europe four. As usual, the Americans placed higher in the world ranking, but that's not always a fair measure, as events on the U.S. Tour are worth more in points than events anywhere else. Remember, this European team was playing for Sam Torrance, which was worth about fifty points on the ranking list in itself.

Returning for the U.S. were Mark Calcavecchia, David Duval, Jim Furyk, Scott Hoch, Davis Love III, Phil

CURTIS STRANGE

SERGIO GARCIA AND LEE WESTWOOD

PAUL AZINGER HOLES HIS BUNKER SHOT ON THE 18TH

Mickelson, Hal Sutton, and the world's undisputed number one, Tiger Woods. There were three rookies—Stewart Cink, David Toms, and Scott Verplank, the last a captain's pick, as was veteran Paul Azinger. Six of the world's top twelve were on the team, while only one player (Sutton, the hero of 1999) wasn't in the world's top fifty.

Europe was bringing two golfers from the top twelve, four who were out of the top fifty, and a slew of questions about players whose games and rankings had slipped in the extra year. There was discussion about changing the teams, perhaps adding another player to each side, but ultimately, thanks to Sam and Curtis, it was decided to stay with the original twenty-four. (Anyone who qualified for a Ryder Cup team would be a Ryder Cup player.) The veterans were Thomas Bjorn, Darren Clarke, Padraig Harrington, Bernhard Langer, Colin Montgomerie, Lee Westwood, and the two captain's picks, Sergio Garcia and Jesper Parnevik. The rookies were Niclas Fasth, Pierre Fulke, Paul McGinley, and Phillip Price, with the last two in particular having suffered dramatic reversals of fortune in the intervening twelve months.

This was Langer's tenth Cup and Montgomerie's sixth, but no one else on the European team had more than two prior appearances. The U.S. team wasn't much more experienced with Cup play, but they had fourteen major championships (Woods accounting for eight of those; the rest were divided among six others), while Europe had only two, both from the alte mensch, Langer.

Said Torrance of the teams, "They have one Tiger, but I have twelve lions." (Not bad, from a big pussy like him.)

Sam also had the home-course advantage: The Europeans were 2-1-1 in Ryder Cups at the Belfry. He added to that advantage by exercising his right as home-team captain to mess around with the course. This proved to be significant, especially slowing the greens well below PGA Tour–level speed. He also had the fairways narrowed at 280 yards, which took the driver (or the fairway) out of the hands of long hitters like Woods and Mickelson.

At the short, par-four tenth hole, which had been drivable in previous Cups, Torrance had the tee moved back. The hole would play 310 yards, calling for a 265-yard pop to carry the water. This change affected both teams, but hurt the U.S. more: The first two days, Duval was the only

American to go for the green, during the Saturday afternoon fourballs. He made birdie, sparking a team win, but that was it. The Europeans enjoyed a slight statistical advantage on the hole.

Opening with fourballs—which once, many years before, was thought to favor the Americans—Europe jumped out to a quick lead. In the first match, Strange put two tigers together, Woods and Azinger, but they lost to Clarke and Bjorn 1-up when the big Dane holed a twenty-five-foot birdie putt on the last hole: Woods had seven birdies on his own ball, and he and Zinger combined for a best-ball sixty-three; Clarke and Bjorn carded a best-ball sixty-two. The magic had started early.

Torrance found more when he paired the exciting and excitable Garcia with a struggling Westwood. They had little difficulty with Duval and Love, winning 4&3, the first of three straight victories, and with nine birdies between them, Montgomerie and Langer topped Hoch and Furyk by the same 4&3 score. (Montgomerie had more than shown his Ryder Cup mettle before, but this week he would be Godlike.) The only U.S. point came from Mickelson and Toms, who had a three-hole lead with six holes to play and nearly lost it, holding on to a 1-up win over Harrington and Fasth.

The 3-1 European lead was their biggest opening margin since the format change in 1979 that created two sets of matches each of the first two days. It proved to be a huge psychological boost, even though the Americans wouldn't lose another four-match series. Didn't matter: The image of American invulnerability had cracked.

SAM TORRANCE (A CREATURE IN HIS NATURAL HABITAT)

The U.S. bounced back in the afternoon foursomes, losing only one match, but it was a big one: Woods and Calcavecchia fell to Garcia and Westwood (who was supposed to be struggling) 2&1, when Tiger missed two short putts on the back nine. Sutton and Verplank saw their first action, against Clarke and Bjorn, and won the last two holes to take the match 2&1. In the third match, Mickelson and Toms were down three holes, went birdie-eagle-birdie on fifteen, sixteen, and seventeen to catch Montgomerie and Langer, and held on for the half when Langer missed an eight-foot birdie on eighteen. Cink and Furyk scored a relatively easy 3&2 win over Harrington and McGinley. By taking the afternoon 2-1/2 to 1-1/2, the U.S. had closed the European lead to a single point.

In 1999, European captain Mark James had kept three rookies on the bench until the singles, when all three lost. Sammy wasn't going to make that mistake, so Saturday morning he sent out his remaining first-timers,

Fulke and Price, who lost to Mickelson and Toms, 2&1. With that victory, the U.S. drew even for the first time since Friday morning. (One European still had yet to make an appearance: Parnevik, who was a captain's pick after winning three times on the PGA Tour in 2000–1, but had injuries and a poor 2002.) Playing in the last match, Love and Woods recorded their first victories of this Cup, beating Clarke and Bjorn, 4&3. By finishing well ahead of the second and third matches, the win gave the U.S. its first lead of the match. But it wouldn't last long.

Westwood and Garcia remained undefeated, beating Cink and Furyk 2&1, but Garcia's antics—he was thoroughly enjoying playing to the crowd and the television cameras—annoyed the Americans, and not for the last time. In the last match to finish, Montgomerie and Langer, who'd first played as a team in 1991, won their fifth match together (against one loss and one halve), defeating Verplank and Hoch, 1-up. The morning had been split 2-2, and the Europeans maintained their one-point advantage.

The afternoon fourballs were the closest session of the week, with three games going to eighteen, the fourth to seventeen. In the first match, Parnevik finally appeared and, paired with fellow Swede Fasth, lost to Calcavecchia and Duval 1-up. Mickelson and Toms had their unbeaten streak snapped by Montgomerie and Harrington, 2&1 (but Monty's streak remained alive, 3-0-1).

Garcia, who was being compared to Seve Ballesteros for both his good play and nonstop cheerleading, finally went overboard. He and Westwood were paired again and had yet to lose, and they met Woods and Love in a great match. When Westwood drove the tenth green, Sergio jumped on his partner's back in celebration, stirring up the crowd and totally pissing off the Americans, who had forgotten he was only *twenty-two.* But the tables turned over the last holes: Sergio three-putted seventeen to fall back into a tie, then both he and Westwood missed par putts of less than six feet on eighteen, handing the U.S. pair the win.

In the final match, Hoch and Furyk had a two-hole lead after fourteen, but McGinley birdied fifteen and sixteen to lift Clarke and himself into a tie. Hoch won the seventeenth, but both Americans bogeyed eighteen to lose the hole and finish in a tie. That also tied the overall score, 8-8, for the first time since the "War by the Shore" in 1991.

If there was any controversy at the 2002 Ryder Cup, it swirled around Strange's lineup for the singles. He would get (and accept) all the blame for saving his strongest players until the end, ultimately giving up too many points early to Torrance's strategy of leading with strength. "I thought he [Torrance] took one hell of a gamble by frontloading his team like he did," Curtis said afterward, "but they got on the board early and the crowd got into it. I think that's exactly what he wanted." The truth of the matter was that it didn't matter. Curtis and Sam could have loaded their teams into a shotgun and aimed it at the pairing sheet for all the difference it would have made. With all the history and emotion that Sam had in him, his team simply wanted to win more, and was going to, no matter what. This one was for the "Hairy One." I stood on the putting green with Sam and the players as the matchups made their way off to the first tee every fifteen minutes. Sam would go down with each of them, and then come back to the putting green, looking more and more green around the gills. I had just been into the bar to get a pint of Guinness to straighten me up, when he spotted me talking to Phillip Price. He nodded at the covered porch, and I took it inside. Seconds later, he ducked in, closed the double doors behind him, snatched my glass, and drained it in one massive swallow. Then he wiped the cream off his mustache with my sleeve, burped enormously, and without a word, headed back out the door into the fray. To his credit, he only needed two more pints that morning.

Again, Monty was the key, opening the day with a big 5&4 win over Hoch (who finished 0-3-1). It was all but over on the first hole, where the big Scot holed a thirty-foot birdie putt to take the lead. "The noise that was generated from that putt was quite unbelievable," Monty said after the match. "I've never heard that noise before. I was shocked and shattered by it. And the noise reverberated around the whole course. It was momentum." Momentum for his team, which followed his lead, and momentum for a crowd that never stopped cheering and yelling.

The next matches to finish were also big European wins, Langer 4&3 over Sutton, Harrington 5&4 over Calcavecchia, Bjorn 2&1 over Cink. Just as important as winning was that fact that these matches ended quickly, so the scoreboards were turning blue well before Toms topped Garcia 1-up (Sergio drove into the water on eighteen) and Duval halved with Clarke. Then Verplank, who had been a controversial captain's pick, beat Westwood, 2&1.

With five matches to go, the score was 12-1/2 to 10-1/2. Two points would bring the Cup back to Europe.

The first came from one of the greatest upsets in Ryder Cup history: Price, number 119 in the world, defeated Mickelson, number two, 3&2. Early in the week, Price had been asked in a press conference if he thought he should withdraw from the Cup, such was the state of his faltering game. But buoyed by support from Torrance, his teammates, sports psychologist Alan Fine, and the galleries (who unfurled many Welsh flags on Sunday), he played the round of his life, making five birdies, including a twenty-five-footer on the sixteenth hole to end the match and bring Europe within one point.

Immediately after Price was right, Azinger and Fasth reached the eighteenth green: The Swede had a one-hole lead and was sitting twenty-five feet from the hole while Zinger was in the left greenside bunker, his ball on a downslope. "I understood the situation, the gravity of the circumstances," Azinger said afterward, knowing that he had to halve the hole to keep the match alive. One of the most remarkable competitors in history, Azinger holed out his bunker shot, momentarily quieting the fans and giving the U.S. a glimmer of hope when Fasth missed his birdie putt and they each took half a point. But the Americans would have to win all three remaining matches to tie the Cup, and keep it.

Which was where they stood when Furyk and McGinley reached the eighteenth hole all even. Earlier that morning, I'd tackled Paul on the putting green and thrust into his hand a solid-gold, four-leaved clover ball marker inscribed ALWAYS END YOUR DAY WITH A 69, given to me by my wife on our wedding day. (The ball marker, that is.) He was an Irish rookie on the team, unknown to most Americans (as I had been at Kiawah), and I told him that I thought it might work one more time. Paul was left of the green in two, and Furyk in the bunker Azinger had visited only moments earlier, in almost the exact same spot. McGinley got his ball onto the green, about eight feet away. Furyk, needing to hole his explosion to win the match, almost pulled an Azinger, the ball rolling over the right edge but not dropping in. He had his par, meaning McGinley had to sink his for the half and the Cup.

"All the rookies had breakfast together this morning because we all teed off late," Fulke said after it was all over. "We all agreed that one of us was going to be the hero today."

Minutes earlier, it had been Price. Then it was McGinley, who made his par and in the tradition of captain Torrance—who'd canned the winning putt on the same green in 1985 to end a twenty-eight-year victory drought—threw his arms in the air and basked in the crowd's deafening approval. Minutes later, the bastard tossed himself into the lake in front of the green, with my wedding present from the wife in his pocket. It was a tense few hours all right, but I got it back.

The two remaining matches went in the book as halves. Fulke parred sixteen to draw even with Love, they both parred seventeen, and knowing the Cup was changing continents, both players agree to concede the final hole and share the point. Finally, in a match without meaning, Woods, the world's best player, had to work for his halve with Parnevik, who had been struggling with his nerve and his game for months. But this was the Ryder Cup, and all bets were off.

With a 7-1/2 to 4-1/2 final-day charge, the Europeans put an emphatic stamp on the first Ryder Cup of the twenty-first century. Led by the most beloved player in the history of European golf, the Europeans were collectively twenty-four-under par on Sunday versus seven-under for the Americans. The U.S. won only two matches. A man having his worst year halved with the number one player in the world, while the number two lost to a golfer whose name he likely didn't know.

It was thrilling theater, astonishing golf, and just as exciting as the Battle at Brookline but with almost none of the spite, and no bad behavior. The crowds were polite, there was little or no heckling, and the players hoisted a few hundred together after it was over. Best of all for me, Sam led the incredible war-horse Montgomerie over by the hand, and put him in front of me. Monty smiled the biggest, warmest smile I've ever seen, threw his arms around me, lifted me off the ground, and I got to thank him and tell him that no matter what he'd read or heard, he'd always been a hero to me. Finally, after the debacle at Brookline, I got a hug from the one brother I needed most. He'll never know how much it meant to me, or to Sam.

Taking a leaf out of the Torrance-Feherty manual, later that same evening David Duval joined the lads in the team room, and got all slobbered up like the rest of us. He wasn't the only one, but at one stage, he, Jesper Parnevik, and I used a sleeping Darren Clarke as a sofa in the middle of the dance floor. It's one of my favorite photos.

Captains Strange and Torrance had spent the previous year doing all they could to ensure this Ryder Cup was built on sportsmanship and love for the game, and with the memory of 9/11 still fresh, they *both* succeeded brilliantly. The following day I had to do a corporate outing at Pebble Beach, and when I got there, crumpled and hung-over, I realized I'd left some things at the Belfry: about a billion brain cells, and my golf clubs.

But I had the memories of another great Ryder Cup to play with forever.

FINAL SCORE

COURSE:

THE BELFRY (BRABAZON COURSE) **SUTTON COLDFIELD** ENGLAND

2002

FOURBALLS & FOURSOMES

FOURBALLS - MORNING

Woods/Azinger lost to Clarke/Bjorn, 1-up

Duval/Love lost to Garcia/Westwood, 4&3

Hoch/Furyk lost to Montgomerie/Langer, 4&3

Mickelson/Toms d. Harrington/Fasth, 1-up

FOURSOMES - AFTERNOON

Sutton/Verplank d. Clarke/Bjorn, 2&1

Woods/Calcavecchia lost to Garcia/Westwood, 2&1

Mickelson/Toms halved with Montgomerie/Langer

Cink/Furyk d. Harrington/McGinley, 3&2

US: 3-1/2   EUROPE: 4-1/2

FOURSOMES & FOURBALLS

FOURSOMES - MORNING

Mickelson/Toms d. Fulke/Price, 2&1

Cink/Furyk lost to Westwood/Garcia, 2&1

Verplank/Hoch lost to Montgomerie/Langer, 1-up

Woods/Love d. Clarke/Bjorn, 4&3

FOURBALLS - AFTERNOON

Calcavecchia/Duval d. Fasth/Parnevik, 1-up

Mickelson/Toms lost to
Montgomerie/Harrington, 2&1

Woods/Love d. Garcia/Westwood, 1-up

Hoch/Furyk halved with Clarke/McGinley

US: 4-1/2   EUROPE: 3-1/2

SINGLES

Hoch lost to Montgomerie, 5&4

Toms d. Garcia, 1-up

Duval halved with Clarke

Sutton lost to Langer, 4&3

Calcavecchia lost to Harrington, 5&4

Cink lost to Bjorn, 2&1

Verplank d. Westwood, 2&1

Azinger halved with Fasth

Furyk halved with McGinley

Love halved with Fulke

Mickelson lost to Price, 3&2

Woods halved with Parnevik

US: 4-1/2   EUROPE: 7-1/2

TOTAL:

US 12-1/2   **EUROPE** 15-1/2

DATE : SEPT. 27-29

Player - USA	Years Played	Years	No. of Matches	R.C. Records W-L-H	Singles Record W-L-H	Foursomes Record W-L-H	Four-Balls Record W-L-H	Total Points Won	Point Pct*
Tommy Aaron	1969-73	2	6	1-4-1	0-2-0	1-1-0	0-1-1	1.5	.25
Skip Alexander	1949-51	2	2	1-1-0	1-0-0	0-1-0	0-0-0	1.0	.50
Paul Azinger	1989-91-93-2002	4	15	5-7-3	2-0-2	2-2-0	1-5-1	6.5	.43
Jerry Barber	1955-61	2	5	1-4-0	0-3-0	1-1-0	0-0-0	1.0	.20
Miller Barber	1969-71	2	7	1-4-2	1-1-0	0-3-0	0-0-2	2.0	.29
Herman Barron	1947	1	1	1-0-0	0-0-0	1-0-0	0-0-0	1.0	100
Andy Bean	1979-87	2	6	4-2-0	2-0-0	0-1-0	2-1-0	4.0	.67
Frank Beard	1969-71	2	8	2-3-3	0-1-1	0-2-1	2-0-1	3.5	.44
Chip Beck	1989-91-93	3	9	6-2-1	3-0-0	1-1-1	2-1-0	6.5	.72
Homero Blancas	1973	1	4	2-1-1	1-1-0	0-0-0	1-0-1	2.5	.63
Tommy Bolt	1955-57	2	4	3-1-0	1-1-0	2-0-0	0-0-0	3.0	.75
Julius Boros	1950-59-63-65-67	5	16	9-3-4	3-2-1	5-0-2	1-1-1	11.0	.69
Gay Brewer	1967-73	2	9	5-3-1	2-1-1	0-1-0	3-1-0	5.5	.61
Billy Burke	1931-33	2	3	3-0-0	1-0-0	2-0-0	0-0-0	3.0	100
Jack Burke Jr.	1951-53-55-57-59	5	8	7-1-0	3-1-0	4-0-0	0-0-0	7.0	.88
Walter Burkemo	1953	1	1	0-1-0	0-0-0	0-1-0	0-0-0	0.0	.00
Mark Calcavecchia	1987-89-91-2002	4	14	6-7-1	1-2-1	4-1-0	1-4-0	6.5	.46
Billy Casper	1961-63-65-67-69-71-73-75	8	37	20-10-7	6-2-2	8-5-2	6-3-3	23.5	.64
Stewart Cink	2002	1	3	1-2-0	0-1-0	1-1-0	0-0-0	1.0	.33
Bill Collins	1961	1	3	1-2-0	0-1-0	1-1-0	0-0-0	1.0	.33
Charles Coody	1971	1	3	0-2-1	0-1-0	0-1-0	0-0-1	0.5	.17
John Cook	1993	1	2	1-1-0	0-1-0	0-0-0	1-0-0	1.0	.50
Fred Couples	1989-91-93-95-96	5	21	7-10-4	2-1-2	1-6-0	4-3-2	9.0	.43
Wilfred Cox	1931	1	2	2-0-0	1-0-0	1-0-0	0-0-0	2.0	100
Ben Crenshaw	1981-83-87	4	12	3-8-1	2-2-0	1-2-0	0-4-1	3.5	.29
Jimmy Demaret	1947-49-51	3	6	6-0-0	3-0-0	3-0-0	0-0-0	6.0	100
Gardner Dickinson	1967-71	2	10	9-1-0	2-1-0	4-0-0	3-0-0	9.0	.90
Leo Diegel	1927-29-31-33	4	6	3-3-0	2-1-0	1-2-0	0-0-0	3.0	.50
Dave Douglas	1953	1	2	1-0-1	0-0-1	1-0-0	0-0-0	1.5	.75
Dale Douglass	1969	1	2	0-2-0	0-1-0	0-0-0	0-1-0	0.0	.00
Ed Dudley	1929-33-37	3	4	3-1-0	1-0-0	2-1-0	0-0-0	3.0	.75

Olin Dutra	1933-35	2	4	1-3-0	1-1-0	0-2-0	0-0-0	1.0	.25
David Duval	1999-2002	2	6	1-3-2	1-0-1	0-1-0	0-1-0	2.0	.33
Lee Elder	1979	1	4	1-3-0	0-1-0	0-1-0	1-1-0	1.0	.25
Al Espinosa	1927-29-31	3	4	2-1-1	1-0-1	1-1-0	0-0-0	2.5	.63
Johnny Farrell	1927-29-31	3	6	3-2-1	1-2-0	2-0-1	0-0-0	3.5	.58
Brad Faxon	1995-97	2	6	2-4-0	0-2-0	0-0-0	2-2-0	2.0	.33
Dow Finsterwald	1957-59-61-63	4	13	9-3-1	3-3-0	4-0-1	2-0-0	9.5	.73
Raymond Floyd	1969-75-77-81-83-85-91-93	8	31	12-16-3	4-4-0	4-8-0	4-4-3	13.5	.44
Doug Ford	1955-57-59-61	4	9	4-4-1	2-2-1	2-2-0	0-0-0	4.5	.50
Ed Furgol	1957	1	1	0-1-0	0-1-0	0-0-0	0-0-0	0.0	.00
Marty Furgol	1955	1	1	0-1-0	0-1-0	0-0-0	0-0-0	0.0	.00
Jim Furyk	1997-99-2002	3	11	3-6-2	2-0-1	1-3-0	0-2-1	4.0	.36
Jim Gallagher Jr.	1993	1	3	2-1-0	1-0-0	0-0-0	1-1-0	2.0	.67
Al Geiberger	1967-75	2	9	5-1-3	2-0-1	2-1-0	1-0-2	6.5	.72
Bob Gilder	1983	1	4	2-2-0	1-0-0	0-2-0	1-0-0	2.0	.50
Bob Goalby	1963	1	5	3-1-1	2-0-0	1-0-0	0-1-1	3.5	.70
Johnny Golden	1927-29	2	3	3-0-0	1-0-0	2-0-0	0-0-0	3.0	100
Lou Graham	1973-75-77	3	9	5-3-1	1-1-0	1-2-1	3-0-0	5.5	.61
Hubert Green	1977-79-85	3	7	4-3-0	3-0-0	0-1-0	1-2-0	4.0	.57
Ken Green	1989	1	4	2-2-0	0-1-0	2-0-0	0-1-0	2.0	.50
Ralph Guldahl	1937	1	2	2-0-0	1-0-0	1-0-0	0-0-0	2.0	100
Jay Haas	1983-95	2	8	3-4-1	0-2-0	1-2-0	2-0-1	3.5	.44
Fred Haas Jr.	1953	1	1	0-1-0	0-1-0	0-0-0	0-0-0	0.0	.00
Walter Hagen	1927-29-31-33-35	5	9	7-1-1	3-1-0	4-0-1	0-0-0	7.5	.83
Bob Hamilton	1949	1	2	0-2-0	0-1-0	0-1-0	0-0-0	0.0	.00
Chick Harbert	1949-55	2	2	2-0-0	2-0-0	0-0-0	0-0-0	2.0	100
Chandler Harper	1955	1	1	0-1-0	0-0-0	0-1-0	0-0-0	0.0	.00
Dutch Harrison	1947-49-51	3	3	2-1-0	2-0-0	0-1-0	0-0-0	2.0	.67
Fred Hawkins	1957	1	2	1-1-0	1-0-0	0-1-0	0-0-0	1.0	.50
Mark Hayes	1979	1	3	1-2-0	1-0-0	0-1-0	0-1-0	1.0	.33
Clayton Heafner	1949-51	2	4	3-0-1	1-0-1	2-0-0	0-0-0	3.5	.88
Jay Hebert	1959-61	2	4	2-1-1	0-1-1	2-0-0	0-0-0	2.5	.63
Lionel Hebert	1957	1	1	0-1-0	0-1-0	0-0-0	0-0-0	0.0	.00
Dave Hill	1969-73-77	3	9	6-3-0	3-0-0	1-2-0	2-1-0	6.0	.67
Scott Hoch	1997-2002	2	7	2-3-2	0-1-1	2-1-0	0-1-1	3.0	.41
Ben Hogan	1947-51	2	3	3-0-0	1-0-0	2-0-0	0-0-0	3.0	100

Hale Irwin	1975-77-79-81-91	5	20	13-5-2	3-1-2	6-1-0	4-3-0	14.0	.70
Tommy Jacobs	1965	1	4	3-1-0	1-1-0	0-0-0	2-0-0	3.0	.75
Peter Jacobsen	1985-95	2	6	2-4-0	0-2-0	2-0-0	0-2-0	2.0	.33
Don January	1965-77	2	7	2-3-2	0-1-1	0-2-1	2-0-0	3.0	.43
Lee Janzen	1993-97	2	5	2-3-0	1-1-0	1-1-0	0-1-0	2.0	.40
Herman Keiser	1947	1	1	0-1-0	0-1-0	0-0-0	0-0-0	0.0	.00
Tom Kite	1979-81-83-85-87-89-93	7	28	15-9-4	5-0-2	7-5-1	3-4-1	17.0	.61
Ted Kroll	1953-55-57	3	4	3-1-0	0-1-0	3-0-0	0-0-0	3.0	.75
Ky Lafton	1935	1	1	0-1-0	0-0-0	0-1-0	0-0-0	0.0	.00
Tom Lehman	1995-97-99	2	10	5-3-2	3-0-0	1-2-1	1-1-1	6.0	.60
Tony Lema	1963-65	2	11	8-1-2	3-0-1	3-0-1	2-1-0	9.0	.82
Justin Leonard	1997-99	2	8	0-3-5	0-0-2	0-2-1	0-1-2	2.5	.31
Wayne Levi	1991	1	2	0-2-0	0-1-0	0-0-0	0-1-0	0.0	.00
Bruce Lietzke	1981	1	3	0-2-1	0-0-1	0-1-0	0-1-0	0.5	.17
Gene Littler	1961-63-65-67-69-71-75	7	27	14-5-8	5-2-3	4-3-1	5-0-4	18.5	.67
Davis Love III	1993-95-97-99-2002	5	21	8-9-4	3-1-1	3-3-1	2-5-0	10.0	.46
Jeff Maggert	1995-97-99	3	11	4-5-0	1-2-0	4-2-0	1-1-0	6.0	.55
John Mahaffey	1979	1	3	1-2-0	1-0-0	0-1-0	0-1-0	1.0	.33
Tony Manero	1937	1	2	1-1-0	0-1-0	1-0-0	0-0-0	1.0	.50
Lloyd Mangrum	1947-49-51-53	4	8	6-2-0	3-1-0	3-1-0	0-0-0	6.0	.75
Dave Marr	1965	1	6	4-2-0	2-0-0	1-1-0	1-1-0	4.0	.67
Billy Maxwell	1963	1	4	4-0-0	1-0-0	1-0-0	2-0-0	4.0	100
Dick Mayer	1957	1	2	1-0-1	0-0-1	1-0-0	0-0-0	1.5	.75
Mark McCumber	1989	1	3	2-1-0	1-0-0	0-0-0	1-1-0	2.0	.67
Jerry McGee	1977	1	2	1-1-0	0-1-0	1-0-0	0-0-0	1.0	.50
Bill Melhorn	1927	1	2	1-1-0	1-0-0	0-1-0	0-0-0	1.0	.50
Phil Mickelson	1995-97-99-2002	4	16	8-5-3	3-1-0	1-1-2	3-2-1	9.5	.59
Cary Middlecoff	1953-55-59	3	6	2-3-1	1-2-0	1-1-1	0-0-0	2.5	.42
Johnny Miller	1975-81	2	6	2-2-2	0-2-0	2-0-0	0-0-2	3.0	.50
Larry Mize	1987	1	4	1-1-2	0-0-1	0-1-1	1-0-0	2.0	.50
Gil Morgan	1979-83	2	6	1-2-3	0-1-1	1-0-1	0-1-1	2.5	.42
Bob Murphy	1975	1	4	2-1-1	2-0-0	0-1-0	0-0-1	2.5	.63
Byron Nelson	1937-47	2	4	3-1-0	1-1-0	2-0-0	0-0-0	3.0	.75
Larry Nelson	1979-81-87	3	13	9-3-1	2-0-1	4-2-0	3-1-0	9.5	.73
Bobby Nichols	1967	1	5	4-0-1	1-0-1	2-0-0	1-0-0	4.5	.90
Jack Nicklaus	1969-71-73-75-77-81	6	28	17-8-3	4-4-2	8-1-0	5-3-1	18.5	.66

Andy North	1985	1	3	0-3-0	0-1-0	0-0-0	0-2-0	0.0	.00
Mark O'Meara	1985-89-91-97-99	5	14	4-9-1	1-4-0	1-3-0	2-2-1	4.5	.32
Ed Oliver	1947-51-53	3	5	3-2-0	1-1-0	2-1-0	0-0-0	3.0	.60
Arnold Palmer	1961-63-65-67-71-73	6	32	22-8-2	6-3-2	9-3-0	7-2-0	23.0	.72
Johnny Palmer	1949	1	2	0-2-0	0-1-0	0-1-0	0-0-0	0.0	.00
Sam Parks	1935	1	1	0-0-1	0-0-1	0-0-0	0-0-0	0.5	.50
Jerry Pate	1981	1	4	2-2-0	0-1-0	1-0-0	1-1-0	2.0	.50
Steve Pate	1991-99	2	5	2-2-1	1-0-1	1-0-0	0-2-0	2.5	.50
Corey Pavin	1991-93-95	3	13	8-5-0	2-1-0	2-2-0	4-2-0	8.0	.62
Calvin Peete	1983-85	2	7	4-2-1	2-0-0	2-1-0	0-1-1	4.5	.64
Henry Picard	1935-37	2	4	3-1-0	2-0-0	1-1-0	0-0-0	3.0	.75
Dan Pohl	1987	1	3	1-2-0	0-1-0	1-0-0	0-1-0	1.0	.33
Johnny Pott	1963-65-67	3	7	5-2-0	1-1-0	2-1-0	2-0-0	5.0	.71
Dave Ragan	1963	1	4	2-1-1	1-0-0	1-0-0	0-1-1	2.5	.63
Henry Ransom	1951	1	1	0-1-0	0-0-0	0-1-0	0-0-0	0.0	.00
Johnny Revolta	1935-37	2	3	2-1-0	1-0-0	1-1-0	0-0-0	2.0	.67
Chi Chi Rodriguez	1973	1	2	0-1-1	0-0-0	0-1-1	0-0-0	0.5	.25
Loren Roberts	1995	1	4	3-1-0	0-1-0	1-0-0	2-0-0	3.0	.75
Bill Rogers	1981	1	4	1-2-1	0-0-1	1-1-0	0-1-0	1.5	.38
Bob Rosburg	1959	1	2	2-0-0	1-0-0	1-0-0	0-0-0	2.0	100
Mason Rudolph	1971	1	3	1-1-1	0-1-0	0-0-1	1-0-0	1.5	.50
Paul Runyan	1933-35	2	4	2-2-0	1-1-0	1-1-0	0-0-0	2.0	.50
Doug Sanders	1967	1	5	2-3-0	0-2-0	0-1-0	2-0-0	2.0	.40
Gene Sarazen	1927-29-31-33-35-37	6	12	7-2-3	4-1-1	3-1-2	0-0-0	8.5	.71
Denny Shute	1931-33-37	3	6	2-2-2	1-1-1	1-1-1	0-0-0	3.0	.50
Dan Sikes	1969	1	3	2-1-0	1-0-0	1-0-0	0-1-0	2.0	.67
Scott Simpson	1987	1	2	1-1-0	1-0-0	0-0-0	0-1-0	1.0	.50
Horton Smith	1929-31-33-35-37	5	4	3-0-1	2-0-1	1-0-0	0-0-0	3.5	.88
J.C. Snead	1971-73-75	3	11	9-2-0	3-1-0	2-1-0	4-0-0	9.0	.82
Sam Snead	1937-47-49-51-53-55-59	7	13	10-2-1	6-1-0	4-1-1	0-0-0	10.5	.81
Ed Snead	1977	1	2	1-0-1	0-0-0	0-0-1	1-0-0	1.5	.75
Mike Souchak	1959-61	2	6	5-1-0	3-0-0	2-1-0	0-0-0	5.0	.83
Craig Stadler	1983-85	2	8	4-2-2	2-0-0	1-2-0	1-0-2	5.0	.63
Payne Stewart	1987-89-91-93-99	5	19	8-9-2	2-3-0	4-5-1	2-1-1	9.0	.47
Ken Still	1969	1	3	1-2-0	0-1-0	0-1-0	1-0-0	1.0	.33
Dave Stockton	1971-77	2	5	3-1-1	1-0-1	1-1-0	1-0-0	3.5	.70

				R.C. Records W-L-H	Singles Record W-L-H	Foursomes Record W-L-H	Four-Balls Record W-L-H	Total Points Won	Point Pct*
Curtis Strange	1983-85-87-89-95	5	20	6-12-2	2-3-0	4-4-1	0-5-1	7.0	.35
Hal Sutton	1985-87-99-2002	4	16	7-5-4	1-2-1	4-1-1	2-1-1	9.0	.56
David Toms	2002	1	6	4-1-1	1-0-0	1-0-1	2-1-0	4.5	.75
Lee Trevino	1969-71-73-75-79-81	6	30	17-7-6	6-2-2	5-3-2	6-2-2	20.0	.67
Jim Turnesa	1953	1	1	1-0-0	1-0-0	0-0-0	0-0-0	1.0	100
Joe Turnesa	1927-29	2	4	1-2-1	0-2-0	1-0-1	0-0-0	1.5	.38
Ken Venturi	1965	1	4	1-3-0	0-1-0	0-2-0	1-0-0	1.0	.25
Scott Verplank	2002	1	3	2-1-0	1-0-0	1-1-0	0-0-0	2.0	.65
Lanny Wadkins	1977-79-83-85-87-89-91-93	8	34	20-11-3	4-2-2	9-6-0	7-3-1	21.5	.63
Art Wall	1957-59-61	3	6	4-2-0	2-0-0	2-2-0	0-0-0	4.0	.67
Al Watrous	1927-29	2	3	2-1-0	1-1-0	1-0-0	0-0-0	2.0	.67
Tom Watson	1977-81-83-89	4	15	10-4-1	2-2-0	4-1-1	4-1-0	10.5	.70
Tom Weiskopf	1973-75	2	10	7-2-1	2-0-1	3-1-0	2-1-0	7.5	.75
Craig Wood	1931-33-35	3	4	1-3-0	1-2-0	0-1-0	0-0-0	1.0	.25
Tiger Woods	1997-99-2002	3	15	5-8-2	1-1-1	2-3-1	2-2-0	6.0	.40
Lew Worsham	1947	1	2	2-0-0	1-0-0	1-0-0	0-0-0	2.0	100
Fuzzy Zoeller	1979-83-85	3	10	1-8-1	0-2-1	0-2-0	1-4-0	1.5	.15

Player –EUROPE	Years Played	Years	No. of Matches	R.C. Records W-L-H	Singles Record W-L-H	Foursomes Record W-L-H	Four-Balls Record W-L-H	Total Points Won	Point Pct*
Jimmy Adams	1947-49-51-53	4	7	2-5-0	1-2-0	1-3-0	0-0-0	2.0	.29
Percy Alliss	1929-31-33-35-37	5	6	3-2-1	2-1-0	1-1-1	0-0-0	3.5	.58
Peter Alliss	1953-57-59-61-63-65-67-69	8	30	10-15-5	5-4-3	4-6-1	1-5-1	12.5	.42
Peter Baker	1993	1	4	3-1-0	1-0-0	0-1-0	2-0-0	3.0	.75
Seve Ballesteros	1979-83-85-87-89-91-93-95	8	37	20-12-5	2-4-2	10-3-1	8-5-2	22.5	.61
Harry Bannerman	1971	1	5	2-2-1	1-0-1	1-0-0	0-2-0	2.5	.50
Brian Barnes	1969-71-73-75-77-79	6	25	10-14-1	5-5-0	2-4-0	3-5-1	10.5	.42
Maurice Bembridge	1969-71-73-75	4	17	6-8-3	1-3-1	3-5-0	2-0-2	7.5	.44
Thomas Bjorn	1997-2002	2	6	3-2-1	1-0-1	0-2-0	2-0-0	3.5	.58
Aubrey Boomer	1927-29	2	4	2-2-0	1-1-0	1-1-0	0-0-0	2.0	.50
Ken Bousfield	1949-51-55-57-59-61	6	10	5-5-0	2-2-0	3-3-0	0-0-0	5.0	.50
Hugh Boyle	1967	1	3	0-3-0	0-1-0	0-1-0	0-1-0	0.0	.00
Harry Bradshaw	1953-55-57	3	5	2-2-1	1-1-1	1-1-0	0-0-0	2.5	.50
Gordon Brand Jr.	1987-89	2	7	2-4-1	0-1-1	0-2-0	2-1-0	2.5	.36
Gordan Brand Sr.	1983	1	1	0-1-0	0-1-0	0-0-0	0-0-0	0.0	.00

Paul Broadhurst	1991	1	2	2-0-0	1-0-0	0-0-0	1-0-0	2.0	100	
Eric Brown	1953-55-57-59	4	8	4-4-0	4-0-0	0-4-0	0-0-0	4.0	.50	
Ken Brown	1977-79-83-85-87	5	13	4-9-0	2-2-0	1-4-0	1-3-0	4.0	.31	
Richard Burton	1935-37-49	3	5	2-3-0	0-3-0	2-0-0	0-0-0	2.0	.40	
Jack Busson	1935	1	2	0-2-0	0-1-0	0-1-0	0-0-0	0.0	.00	
Peter Butler	1965-69-71-73	4	14	3-9-2	2-3-0	1-4-0	0-2-2	4.0	.29	
J.M. Canizares	1981-83-85-89	4	11	5-4-2	2-1-1	2-1-0	1-2-1	6.0	.55	
Alex Caygill	1969	1	1	0-0-1	0-0-0	0-0-0	0-0-1	0.5	.50	
Clive Clark	1973	1	1	0-1-0	0-0-0	0-0-0	0-1-0	0.0	.00	331
Howard Clark	1977-81-85-87-89-95	6	15	7-7-1	4-2-0	0-4-0	3-1-1	7.5	.50	
Darren Clarke	1997-99-2002	3	12	4-6-2	0-2-1	1-2-0	3-2-1	5.0	.40	
Neil Coles	1961-63-65-67-69-71-73-77	8	40	12-21-7	5-6-4	4-8-1	3-7-2	15.5	.39	
Andrew Coltart	1999	1	1	0-1-0	0-1-0	0-0-0	0-0-0	0.0	.00	
Archie Compston	1927-29-31	3	6	1-4-1	1-2-0	0-2-1	0-0-0	1.5	.25	
Henry Cotton	1929-37-47	3	6	2-4-0	2-1-0	0-3-0	0-0-0	2.0	.33	
Bill Cox	1935-37	2	3	0-2-1	0-0-1	0-2-0	0-0-0	0.5	.17	
Fred Daly	1947-49-51-53	4	8	3-4-1	1-2-1	2-2-0	0-0-0	3.5	.44	
Eamonn Darcy	1975-77-81-87	4	11	1-8-2	1-3-0	0-1-1	0-4-1	2.0	.18	
William Davis	1931-33	2	4	2-2-0	1-1-0	1-1-0	0-0-0	2.0	.50	
Peter Dawson	1977	1	3	1-2-0	1-0-0	0-1-0	0-1-0	1.0	.33	
Norman Drew	1959	1	1	0-0-1	0-0-1	0-0-0	0-0-0	0.5	.50	
George Duncan	1927-29-31	3	5	2-3-0	2-0-0	0-3-0	0-0-0	2.0	.40	
Syd Easterbrook	1931-33	2	3	2-1-0	1-0-0	1-1-0	0-0-0	2.0	.67	
Nick Faldo	1977-79-81-83-85-87-89-91-93-95-97	11	46	23-19-4	6-4-1	10-6-2	7-9-1	25.0	.54	
John Fallon	1955	1	1	1-0-0	0-0-0	1-0-0	0-0-0	1.0	100	
Niclas Fasth	2002	1	3	0-2-1	0-0-1	0-0-0	0-2-0	0.5	.15	
Max Faulkner	1947-49-51-53-57	5	8	1-7-0	0-4-0	1-3-0	0-0-0	1.0	.13	
David Feherty	1991	1	3	1-1-1	1-0-0	0-1-0	0-0-1	1.5	.50	
Pierre Fulke	2002	1	2	0-1-1	0-0-1	0-1-0	0-0-0	0.5	.25	
Bernard Gallacher	1969-71-73-75-77-79-81-83	8	31	13-13-5	4-3-4	5-6-0	4-4-1	15.5	.50	
Sergio Garcia	1999-2002	2	10	6-3-1	0-2-0	4-0-0	2-1-1	6.5	.65	
John Garner	1971-73	2	1	0-1-0	0-0-0	0-0-0	0-1-0	0.0	.00	
Antonio Garrido	1979	1	5	1-4-0	0-1-0	1-1-0	0-2-0	1.0	.20	
Ignacio Garrido	1997	1	4	0-1-3	0-1-0	0-0-2	0-0-1	1.5	.38	
David Gilford	1991-95	2	7	3-3-1	1-0-1	1-2-0	1-1-0	3.5	.50	
Malcolm Gregson	1967	1	4	0-4-0	0-2-0	0-1-0	0-1-0	0.0	.00	

Joakim Haeggman	1993	1	2	1-1-0	1-0-0	0-0-0	0-1-0	1.0	.50
Tom Haliburton	1961-63	2	6	0-6-0	0-2-0	0-3-0	0-1-0	0.0	.00
Padraig Harrington	1999-2002	2	7	3-3-1	2-0-0	0-2-1	1-1-0	3.5	.50
Arthur Havers	1927-31-33	3	6	3-3-0	2-1-0	1-2-0	0-0-0	3.0	.50
Jimmy Hitchcock	1965	1	3	0-3-0	0-2-0	0-1-0	0-0-0	0.0	.00
Bert Hodson	1931	1	1	0-1-0	0-1-0	0-0-0	0-0-0	0.0	.00
Tommy Horton	1975-77	2	8	1-6-1	1-1-1	0-2-0	0-3-0	1.5	.19
Brian Hugget	1963-67-69-71-73-75	6	24	8-10-6	3-3-1	5-3-2	0-4-3	11.0	.46
Bernard Hunt	1953-57-59-61-63-65-67-69	8	28	6-16-6	4-3-3	1-9-1	1-4-2	9.0	.32
Geoffrey Hunt	1963	1	3	0-3-0	0-1-0	0-1-0	0-1-0	0.0	.00
Guy Hunt	1975	1	3	0-2-1	0-1-0	0-1-0	0-0-1	0.5	.17
Tony Jacklin	1967-69-71-73-75-77-79	7	35	13-14-8	2-8-1	8-1-4	3-5-3	17.0	.49
John Jacobs	1955	1	2	2-0-0	1-0-0	1-0-0	0-0-0	2.0	100
Mark James	1977-79-81-89-91-93-95	7	24	8-15-1	2-4-1	1-7-0	5-4-0	8.5	.35
Edward Jarman	1935	1	1	0-1-0	0-0-0	0-1-0	0-0-0	0.0	.00
Miguel Angel Jimenez	1999	1	5	1-2-2	0-1-0	0-1-1	1-0-1	2.0	.40
Per-Ulrik Johansson	1995-97	2	5	3-2-0	1-1-0	1-0-0	1-1-0	3.0	.60
Herbert Jolly	1927	1	2	0-2-0	0-1-0	0-1-0	0-0-0	0.0	.00
Michael King	1979	1	1	0-1-0	0-1-0	0-0-0	0-0-0	0.0	.00
Sam King	1937-47-49	3	5	1-3-1	1-1-1	0-2-0	0-0-0	1.5	.30
Arthur Lacey	1933-37	2	3	0-3-0	0-2-0	0-1-0	0-0-0	0.0	.00
Barry Lane	1993	1	3	0-3-0	0-1-0	0-1-0	0-1-0	0.0	.00
Bernard Langer	1981-83-85-87-89-91-93-95-97-2002	10	42	21-15-6	4-3-3	11-6-1	6-6-2	24.0	.57
Paul Lawrie	1999	1	5	3-1-1	1-0-0	1-1-0	1-0-1	3.5	.70
Arthur Lees	1947-49-51-55	4	9	4-5-0	2-3-0	2-2-0	0-0-0	4.0	.44
Sandy Lyle	1979-81-83-85-87	5	18	7-9-2	1-4-0	3-3-1	3-2-1	8.0	.44
Jimmy Martin	1965	1	1	0-1-0	0-0-0	0-1-0	0-0-0	0.0	.00
Paul McGinley	2002	1	3	0-1-2	0-0-1	0-1-0	0-0-1	1.0	.33
Peter Mills	1957	1	1	1-0-0	1-0-0	0-0-0	0-0-0	1.0	100
Abe Mitchell	1929-31-33	3	6	4-2-0	1-2-0	3-0-0	0-0-0	4.0	.67
Ralph Moffitt	1961	1	1	0-1-0	0-1-0	0-0-0	0-0-0	0.0	.00
Colin Montgomerie	1991-93-95-97-99-2002	6	28	16-7-5	4-0-2	7-3-1	5-4-2	18.5	.66
Christy O'Connor Jr.	1975-89	2	4	1-3-0	1-0-0	0-2-0	0-1-0	1.0	.25
Christy O'Connor Sr.	1955-57-59-61-63-65-67-69-71-73	10	36	11-21-4	2-10-2	6-6-1	3-5-1	13.0	.36
John O'Leary	1975	1	4	0-4-0	0-1-0	0-2-0	0-1-0	0.0	.00
JosJ Maria Olaz<bal	1987-89-91-93-97-99	6	28	15-8-5	1-5-0	7-2-1	7-2-3	17.5	.63

Peter Oosterhuis	1971-73-75-77-79-81	6	28	14-11-3	6-2-1	3-6-1	5-3-1	15.5	.55
Alf Padgham	1933-35-37	3	7	0-7-0	0-4-0	0-3-0	0-0-0	0.0	.00
John Panton	1951-53-61	3	5	0-5-0	0-1-0	0-4-0	0-0-0	0.0	.00
Jesper Parnevik	1997-99-2002	3	11	4-3-4	0-2-1	2-0-2	2-1-1	6.0	.53
Alf Perry	1933-35-37	3	3	0-2-1	0-0-1	0-2-0	0-0-0	0.5	.17
Manuel Pinero	1981-85	2	9	6-3-0	2-0-0	2-2-0	2-1-0	6.0	.67
Lionel Platts	1965	1	5	1-2-2	1-1-0	0-1-0	0-0-2	2.0	.40
Eddie Polland	1973	1	2	0-2-0	0-0-0	0-1-0	0-1-0	0.0	.00
Phillip Price	2002	1	2	1-1-0	1-0-0	0-1-0	0-0-0	1.0	.50
Ronan Rafferty	1989	1	3	1-2-0	1-0-0	0-2-0	0-0-0	1.0	.33
Ted Ray	1927	1	2	0-2-0	0-1-0	0-1-0	0-0-0	0.0	.00
Dai Rees	1937-47-49-51-53-55-57-59-61	9	17	7-9-1	5-4-0	2-5-1	0-0-0	7.5	.44
Steven Richardson	1991	1	4	2-2-0	0-1-0	0-1-0	2-0-0	2.0	.50
Jose Rivero	1985-87	2	5	2-3-0	0-2-0	1-1-0	1-0-0	2.0	.40
Fred Robson	1927-29-31	3	6	2-4-0	0-3-0	2-1-0	0-0-0	2.0	.33
Constantino Rocca	1993-95-97	3	11	6-5-0	1-2-0	3-1-0	2-2-0	6.0	.55
Jarmo Sandelin	1999	1	1	0-1-0	0-1-0	0-0-0	0-0-0	0.0	.00
Syd Scott	1955	1	2	0-2-0	0-1-0	0-1-0	0-0-0	0.0	.00
Des Smyth	1979-81	2	7	2-5-0	0-2-0	1-2-0	1-1-0	2.0	.29
Dave Thomas	1959-63-65-67	4	18	3-10-5	0-4-1	3-2-2	0-4-2	5.5	.31
Sam Torrance	1981-83-85-87-89-91-93-95	8	28	7-15-6	2-3-3	3-7-0	2-5-3	10.0	.36
Peter Townsend	1969-71	2	11	3-8-0	0-3-0	2-2-0	1-3-0	3.0	.27
Jean Van de Velde	1999	1	1	0-1-0	0-0-0	0-0-0	0-1-0	0.0	.00
Brian Waites	1983	1	4	1-3-0	0-1-0	0-1-0	1-1-0	1.0	.25
Philip Walton	1995	1	2	1-1-0	1-0-0	0-1-0	0-0-0	1.0	.50
Charles Ward	1947-49-51	3	6	1-5-0	0-3-0	1-2-0	0-0-0	1.0	.17
Paul Way	1983-85	2	9	6-2-1	2-0-0	1-2-0	3-0-1	6.5	.72
Harry Weetman	1951-53-55-57-59-61-63	7	15	2-11-2	2-6-0	0-4-2	0-1-0	3.0	.20
Lee Westwood	1997-99-2002	3	15	7-8-0	0-3-0	4-2-0	3-3-0	7.0	.45
Charles Whitcombe	1927-29-31-33-35-37	6	9	3-2-4	1-2-1	2-0-3	0-0-0	5.0	.56
Ernest Whitcombe	1929-31-35	3	6	1-4-1	0-2-1	1-2-0	0-0-0	1.5	.25
Reg Whitcombe	1935	1	1	0-1-0	0-1-0	0-0-0	0-0-0	0.0	.00
George Will	1963-65-67	3	15	2-11-2	0-3-1	2-3-1	0-5-0	3.0	.20
Norman Wood	1975	1	3	1-2-0	1-0-0	0-1-0	0-1-0	1.0	.33
Ian Woosnam	1983-85-87-89-91-93-95-97	8	31	14-12-5	0-6-2	4-3-2	10-3-1	16.5	.53

*Note: To better evaluate a player's performance in the Ryder Cup, the percentage category reflects the number of total points earned versus the number of matches (possible points) played.

UNITED STATES	EUROPE
HIGHEST MARGIN OF VICTORY	
1967 in Houston, Texas 23 ½ to 8 ½	1985 in The Belfry, England 16 ½ to 11
1947 in Portland, Oregon 11 to 1	1957 in Yorkshire, England 7 ½ to 4 ½

UNITED STATES	EUROPE
TOTAL POINTS OVER 34 MATCHES	
Team points 440.5	319.5
Foursome points 126.5	90.5
Four-Ball points 85	72
Singles points 229	157

UNITED STATES	EUROPE
MOST TIMES ON RYDER CUP TEAM	
Lanny Wadkins 8 (1977-79-83-85-87-89-91-93)	Nick Faldo 11 (1977-79-81-83-85-87- 89-91-93-95-97)
Raymond Floyd 8 (1969-75-77-81-83-85-91-93)	Christy O'Connor Sr. 10 (1955-57-59-61-63-65-67-69-71-73)
Billy Casper 8 (1961-63-65-67-69-71-73-75)	Bernhard Langer 10 (1981-83-85-87-89-91-93-95-97-02)
	Dai Rees 9 (1937-47-49-51-53-55-57-59-61)

UNITED STATES	EUROPE
YOUNGEST PLAYER	
Horton Smith in 1929 – age 21 years and 4 days	Sergio Garcia in 1999 – age 19 years, 8 months, 15 days
Tiger Woods in 1997 – age 21 years, 8 months, 27 days	Nick Faldo in 1977 – age 20 years, 1 month, 28 days
Horton Smith in 1931 – age 23 years, 1 month, 5 days	Paul Way in 1983 – age 20 years, 7 months, 3 days
Tiger Woods in 1999 – age 23 years, 8 months, 25 days	Bernard Gallacher in 1969 – age 20 years, 7 months, 9 days

UNITED STATES	EUROPE
OLDEST PLAYER	
Raymond Floyd in 1993 – age 51 years, 20 days	Ted Ray in 1927 -age 50 years, 2 months, 5 days
Don January in 1977 – age 47 years, 9 months, 26 days	Christy O' Connor Sr. in 1973 -age 48 years, 8 months, 30 days
Julius Boros in 1967 – age 47 years, 7 months, 17 days	

UNITED STATES	EUROPE
MOST MATCHES PLAYED	
Billy Casper 37	Nick Faldo 46
Lanny Wadkins 34	Bernard Langer 42
Arnold Palmer 32	Neil Coles 40
Raymond Floyd 31	Seve Ballesteros 37
Lee Trevino 30	Christy O'Connor Sr. 36
Tom Kite, Jack Nicklaus 28	Tony Jacklin 35

MOST POINTS WON

Billy Casper	23 ½	Nick Faldo	25
Arnold Palmer	23	Bernard Langer	24
Lanny Wadkins	21 ½	Seve Ballesteros	22 ½
Lee Trevino	20	Colin Montgomerie	18 ½
Jack Nicklaus	18 ½	JosJ Maria Olaz<bal	17 ½
Gene Littler	18	Tony Jacklin	17
Tom Kite	17	Ian Woosnam	16 ½
Hale Irwin	14	Bernard Gallacher	15 ½
Raymond Floyd	13 ½	Peter Oosterhuis	15 ½
Julius Boros	11	Neil Coles	15 ½

BEST POINT PERCENTAGE (MINIMUM OF 3 RYDER CUP MATCHES)

Jimmy Demaret (6-0-0)	100%	Colin Montgomerie (16-7-5)	66%
Jack Burke (7-1-0), Horton Smith (3-0-1)	86%	Abe Mitchell (4-2-0)	65%
Walter Hagen (7-1-1)	83%	JosJ Maria Olaz<bal (15-8-3)	61%
J.C. Snead (9-2-0)	80%	Seve Ballesteros (20-12-5)	59%
Sam Snead (10-2-1)	79%	Percy Alliss (3-2-1)	58%

MOST SINGLES MATCHES

Arnold Palmer	11	Neil Coles	15
Jack Nicklaus	10	Christy O'Connor Sr.	14
Lee Trevino	10	Peter Alliss	12
Gene Littler	10	Nick Faldo	11
Billy Casper	10	Tony Jacklin	11
Lanny Wadkins	8	Bernard Gallacher	11
Raymond Floyd	8	Bernard Langer	10
Tom Kite	7	Brian Barnes	10
Sam Snead	7	Bernard Hunt	10

Most Foursome Matches

Lanny Wadkins	15	Nick Faldo	18
Billy Casper	15	Bernard Langer	18
Tom Kite	13	Seve Ballesteros	14
Arnold Palmer	12	Christy O'Connor Sr.	13
Raymond Floyd	12	Tony Jacklin	13
Lee Trevino	10	Neil Coles	13
Payne Stewart	10		

MOST FOUR-BALL MATCHES

Billy Casper	12		Nick Faldo	17
Lanny Wadkins	11		Seve Ballesteros	15
Raymond Floyd	11		Bernhard Langer	14
Lee Trevino	10		Ian Woosnam	14
Fred Couples	9		JosJ Maria Olaz<bal	12
Arnold Palmer	9		Neil Coles	12
Jack Nicklaus	9		Tony Jacklin	11
Gene Littler	9		Colin Montgomerie	11
Davis Love III	9		Sam Torrance	10

MOST MATCHES WON

Arnold Palmer	22		Nick Faldo	23
Lanny Wadkins	20		Bernhard Langer	21
Billy Casper	20		Seve Ballesteros	20
Lee Trevino	17		Colin Montgomerie	16
Jack Nicklaus	17		JosJ Maria Olaz<bal	15
Tom Kite	15		Ian Woosnam	14
Gene Littler	14		Peter Oosterhuis	14
Hale Irwin	13		Tony Jacklin	13
Raymond Floyd	12		Bernard Gallacher	13

MOST SINGLES MATCHES WON

Arnold Palmer	6		Nick Faldo	6
Billy Casper	6		Peter Oosterhuis	6
Sam Snead	6		Peter Alliss	5
Lee Trevino	6		Brian Barnes	5
Tom Kite	5		Neil Coles	5
Gene Littler	5		Dai Rees	5

MOST FOURSOME MATCHES WON

Lanny Wadkins	9		Bernhard Langer	11
Arnold Palmer	9		Nick Faldo	10
Billy Casper	8		Seve Ballesteros	10
Jack Nicklaus	8		Tony Jacklin	8
Tom Kite	7		JosJ Maria Olaz<bal	7
Hale Irwin	6		Colin Montgomerie	7

MOST FOUR-BALL MATCHES WON				
Lanny Wadkins	7		Ian Woosnam	10
Arnold Palmer	7		Seve Ballesteros	8
Billy Casper	6		Nick Faldo	7
Lee Trevino	6		JosJ Maria Olaz<bal	7
Jack Nicklaus	5		Bernhard Langer	6
Gene Littler	5		Colin Montgomerie	5
Fred Couples, Corey Pavin	4		Peter Oosterhuis	5
Hale Irwin, J.C. Snead	4		Mark James	5
Raymond Floyd, Tom Watson	4		Bernard Gallacher	4

MOST MATCHES LOST				
Raymond Floyd	16		Christy O'Connor Sr.	21
Curtis Strange	12		Neil Coles	21
Lanny Wadkins	11		Nick Faldo	19
Billy Casper	10		Bernard Hunt	16
Fred Couples	10		Bernhard Langer	15
Tom Kite	9		Sam Torrance	15
Davis Love III	9		Mark James	15
Payne Stewart	9		Peter Alliss	15
Mark O'Meara	9		Tony Jacklin	14
Tiger Woods	8		Brian Barnes	14
Ben Crenshaw	8		Bernard Gallacher	13
Arnold Palmer	8		Ian Woosnam	12
Jack Nicklaus	8		Seve Ballesteros	12
Fuzzy Zoeller	8			

MOST SINGLES MATCHES LOST				
Raymond Floyd	4		Christy O'Connor Sr.	10
Jack Nicklaus	4		Tony Jacklin	8
Mark O'Meara	4		Neil Coles	6
Ian Woosnam	6		Harry Weetman	6

MOST FOURSOME MATCHES LOST				
Raymond Floyd	8		Bernard Hunt	9
Lanny Wadkins	6		Neil Coles	8
Fred Couples	6		Sam Torrance	7

Tom Kite	5	Mark James	7
Billy Casper	5	C. O'Connor Sr., P. Alliss, B. Langer	6
Payne Stewart	5	N. Faldo, B.Gallacher, P. Oosterhuis	

MOST FOUR-BALL MATCHES LOST

Curtis Strange	5	Nick Faldo	9
Davis Love III	5	Neil Coles	7
Paul Azinger	5	Bernhard Langer	6
Mark Calcavecchia	4	Seve Ballesteros	5
Raymond Floyd	4	Sam Torrance	5
Tom Kite	4	Christy O'Connor Sr.	5
Fuzzy Zoeller	4	Peter Alliss	5
Ben Crenshaw	4	Brian Barnes	5
Lanny Wadkins, Jack Nicklaus	3	George Will	5
Billy Casper, Hale Irwin, Fred Couples	3	Tony Jacklin	5

MOST MATCHES HALVED

Gene Littler	8	Tony Jacklin	8
Billy Casper	7	Neil Coles	7
Lee Trevino	6	Bernhard Langer	6
Davis Love III	4	Sam Torrance	6
Fred Couples, Julius Boros	4	Brian Hugget	6
Tom Kite, Hal Sutton	4	Bernard Hunt	6

MOST SINGLE MATCHES HALVED

Gene Littler	3	Bernard Gallacher	4
Tom Kite	2	Neil Coles	4
Fred Couples	2	Bernhard Langer	3
Arnold Palmer	2	Sam Torrance	3
Jack Nicklaus	2	Peter Alliss	3
Lanny Wadkins	2	Bernard Hunt	3
Hale Irwin	2	Seve Ballesteros	2
Lee Trevino	2	Ian Woosnam	2
Billy Casper	2	Christy O'Connor Sr.	2
Justin Leonard, Paul Azinger	2	Colin Montgomerie	2

MOST FOURSOME MATCHES HALVED			
Phil Mickelson	2	Tony Jacklin	4
Billy Casper	2	Charles Whitcombe	3
Gene Sarazen	2	Nick Faldo	2
Lee Trevino	2	Ian Woosnam, Dave Thomas	2
Julius Boros	2	Brian Hugget, Harry Weetman	2
		Ignacio Garrido, Jesper Parnevik	2

MOST FOUR-BALL MATCHES HALVED			
Gene Littler	4	JosJ Maria Olaz<bal	3
Raymond Floyd	3	Sam Torrance	3
Billy Casper	3	Tony Jacklin	3
Fred Couples	2	Brian Hugget	3
Lee Trevino	2	Colin Montgomerie	2
Al Geiberger	2	Seve Ballesteros	2
Miller Barber	2	Bernard Langer	2
Johnny Miller	2	Maurice Bembridge	2
Craig Stadler	2	Peter Butler	2
		Lionel Platts	2
		Bernard Hunt	2
		Dave Thomas	2
		Neil Coles	2

TEAMS WINNING ALL POINTS IN A SERIES

FOURSOMES

United States won all foursomes 4-0 in 1947

United States won second series foursomes in 4-0 in 1963

United States won first series foursomes 4-0 in 1975

United States won second series foursomes in 4-0 in 1981

FOUR-BALL

United States won first series four-ball 4-0 in 1967

United States won first series four-ball 4-0 in 1971

Europe won first series four-ball 4-0 in 1987

Europe won first series four-ball 4-0 in 1989

SINGLES

No side has ever had a clean sweep in the singles

RELATIVES IN RYDER CUP MATCHES

FATHER AND SON

Percy Alliss (1929-33-35-37) and Peter Alliss (1953-57-59-61-63-65-67-69),

Antonio Garrido (1979) and Ignacio Garrido (1997)

BROTHERS

Charles Whitcombe (1927-29-31-33-35-37), Reg Whitcombe (1935) and Ernest Whitcombe (1929-31-35)

Bernard Hunt (1953-57-59-61-63-65-67-69) and Geoffrey Hunt (1963)

Joe Turnesa (1927-29) and Jim Turnesa (1953)

Jay Hebert (1959-61) and Lionel Hebert (1957)

UNCLES AND NEPHEWS

Christy O'Connor Sr. (1955-57-59-61-63-65-67-69) and Christy O'Conner Jr. (1975-89)

Sam Snead (1937-47-49-51-53-55-59) and J.C. Snead (1971-73-75)

Bob Goalby (1963) and Jay Haas (1983-95)

COUSINS

Jackie Burke Jr. (1951-53-55-57-59) and Dave Marr (1965)

BROTHERS-IN-LAW

Max Faulkner (1947-49-51-53-57) and Brian Barnes (1969-71-73-75-77-79)

Jerry Pate (1981) and Bruce Lietzke (1981)

HIGHEST WINNING MARGINS – 18 HOLE TEAM

7 and 6 (1979) Hale Irwin and Tom Kite beat Ken Brown and Des Smyth

7 and 6 (1991) Paul Azinger and Mark O'Meara beat Nick Faldo and David Gilford

7 and 5 (1981) Lee Trevino and Jerry Pate beat Nick Faldo and Sam Torrance

7 and 5 (1983) Lanny Wadkins and Gil Morgan beat Sam Torrance and JosJ Maria Canizares

7 and 5 (1985) JosJ Maria Canizares and Jose Pinero beat Tom Kite and Calvin Peete

7 and 5 (1993) Bernhard Langer and Ian Woosnam beat Paul Azinger and Payne Stewart

HIGHEST WINNING MARGINS – 36 SINGLES

10 and 8 (1929) George Duncan beat Walter Hagen

9 and 8 (1929) Leo Diegel beat Abe Mitchell

9 and 8 (1933) Abe Mitchell bean Olin Dutra

9 and 7 (1953) Fred Daly beat Ted Kroll

HIGHEST WINNING MARGINS – 18 SINGLES

8 and 7 (1997) Fred Couples beat Ian Woosam

8 and 7 (1989) Tom Kite beat Howard Clark

7 and 6 (1969) Miller Barber beat Maurice Bembridge

7 and 6 (1971) Lee Trevino beat Brian Huggett

7 and 6 (1997) Tom Lehman beat Ignacio Garrido

6 and 5 (1963) Gene Littler beat Tom Haliburton

6 and 5 (1973) Lee Trevino beat Neil Coles

6 and 5 (1999) Davis Love III beat Jean Van de Velde

UNDEFEATED AND UNTIED IN TWO OR MORE MATCHES IN RYDER CUP PLAY

USA

Jimmy Demaret – 6 wins; Billy Maxwell – 4 wins; Ben Hogan, Billy Burke, Johnny Golden – 3 wins; Chick Harbert, Wilfred Cox, Ralph Guldahl, Lew Worsham – 2 wins

EUROPE

Paul Broadhurst, John Jacobs, Bob Rosburg – 2 wins

☆☆☆☆☆☆☆☆☆☆☆☆☆ ODDITIES ☆☆☆☆☆☆☆☆☆☆☆☆☆

CATEGORY	EUROPE	USA
Wins	5	4
Matches won	123	116
Points won	143.5	136.5
Foursome points won	39.5	39.5
Fourball points won	49	32
Single points won	55	65
Winning on the 18th hole	36	19
Rookies record	37 wins, 50 losses, 19 halves	53 wins, 58 losses, 12 halves
Captain's Picks	34 wins, 41 losses, 5 halves	24 wins, 19 losses, 4 halves

PRINCIPAL RESOURCES

Concannon, Dale, *The Ryder Cup: Seven Decades of Golfing Glory, Drama and Controversy,* Aurum Press, London, 2001.

Hobbs, Michael, *The Ryder Cup: The Illustrated History,* Macdonald/Queen Anne Press, London, 1989.

Jarman, Colin M., *The Ryder Cup: The Definitive History of Playing Golf for Pride and Country,* Contemporary Books, Chicago, 1999.

PGA of America, *2003 PGA Media Guide,* PGA of America: Palm Beach Gardens, Fla., 2003.

Williams, Michael, *The Official History of the Ryder Cup: 1927-1989,* Stanley Paul & Co. Ltd., London, 1989.

OTHER BOOKS

Alliss, Peter, *Peter Alliss' Golf Heroes,* Virgin Books, London, 2000.

Alliss, Peter, *The Who's Who of Golf,* Prentice Hall: Englewood Cliffs, N. J., 1983.

Astor, Gerald, *The PGA World Golf Hall of Fame Book,* Prentice Hall, New York, 1991.

Azinger, Paul, Zinger: A Champion's Story of Determination, Courage, and Charging Back, HarperCollins, New York, 1995.

Barkow, Al, *The Golden Era of Golf,* Thomas Dunne Books/St. Martin's Press, New York, 2000.

Barrett, Ted, *The Chronicle of Golf,* Carlton Books, London, 2000.

Brown, Gene, *The Complete Book of Golf: A New York Times Scrapbook History,* Arno Press, New York, 1980.

Burka, Bob, and Tom Clavin, *The Ryder Cup: Golf's Greatest Event,* Crown, New York, 1999.

Crenshaw, Ben, with Melanie Hauser, *A Feel for the Game: To Brookline and Back,* Doubleday, New York, 2001.

Dabell, Norman (also known as "Abnormal Doorbell" and much loved by all European Ryder Cuppers), How We Won the Ryder Cup: The Caddies' Stories, Mainstream, 1997.

Darwin, Bernard, *Golf Between Two Wars* (The Classics of Golf Edition), Ailsa, Inc., New York, 1985.

Darwin, Bernard, et al., *A History of Golf in Britain* (The Classics of Golf Edition), Ailsa, Inc., New York, 1990.

Davies, David and Patricia, *Beyond the Fairways: The Past, Present and Future of World Golf,* CollinsWillow, London, 1999.

Eubanks, Steve, *At the Turn,* Crown; New York, 2001.

Feinstein, John, *A Good Walk Spoiled,* Little, Brown and Company, Boston, 1995.

Graffis, Herb, *The PGA: The Official History of the Professional Golfers' Assocation,* Crowell, New York, 1975.

Hagen, Walter, *The Walter Hagen Story,* Simon & Schuster, New York, 1956.

James, Mark, *Into the Bear Pit,* Virgin Publishing Ltd., London, 2000.

McCord, Robert R., *Golf: An Album of Its History,* Burford Books, Short Hills, N. J., 1998.

McCormack, Mark H., *The Wonderful World of Professional Golf,* Atheneum, New York, 1973.

McDonnell, Michael, *Great Moments in Sport: Golf,* Pagurian Press, Toronto, 1974.

Nelson, Byron, *How I Played the Game,* Taylor, Dallas, Tex., 1993.

Nicklaus, Jack, with Herbert Warren Wind, *The Greatest Game of All,* Simon & Schuster, New York, 1969.

Nicklaus, Jack with Ken Bowden, *My Story,* Simon & Schuster, New York, 1997.

PGA Tour, *PGA Tour 2003 Official PGA Tour Media Guide,* PGA Tour, Ponte Vedra Beach, Fla., 2003.

PGA Tour, *PGA Tour 2003 Official Champions Tour Media Guide,* PGA Tour, Ponte Vedra Beach, Fla., 2003.

Peper, George, and the editors of Golf Magazine, *Golf in America: The First One Hundred Years,* Harry N. Abrams, Inc., New York, 1988.

Sampson, Curt, *Hogan,* Rutledge Hill Press, Nashville, Tenn., 1996.

Sarazen, Gene, *Thirty Years of Championship Golf* (The Classics of Golf Edition), Ailsa, Inc., New York, 1987.

Snead, Sam, with Al Stump, *The Education of a Golfer,* Simon & Schuster: New York, 1962.

Steel, Donald, and Peter Ryde, eds., *The Encyclopedia of Golf,* Rainbird Reference Books/The Viking Press; New York, 1975.

Swales, Andy, ed., *Sporting Statistics Guide to the Ryder Cup: 1927-2002,* Absolute Publishing, Inc., London, 2002.

Various, *20th Century Golf Chronicle,* Publications International, Ltd., Lincolnwood, Ill., 1993.

PERIODICALS

Golf Digest

Golf Magazine

Golf World

☆☆☆☆☆☆☆☆☆☆☆☆☆☆☆☆☆

☆☆☆☆☆☆☆☆☆☆☆☆☆☆☆☆☆

☆ WHAT THE HELL IS GOING ON? ☆

CONFUSED BY THE DIFFERENT FORMATS IN USE DURING THE RYDER CUP?
You aren't alone. Over the years, players have forgotten if they are in foursomes or fourballs (hold on, I'll get to them), and have hit the wrong ball, hit out of turn, or otherwise acted just as dumb as your friend Clarence last Saturday at the club. In the interest of public service (and not, I swear, to fill out a few more pages), here are descriptions of the games pros play.

☆☆☆☆☆☆☆☆☆☆☆☆☆ FOURSOMES: ☆☆☆☆☆☆☆☆☆☆☆☆☆☆

THIS FORMAT has been in use since the first Ryder Cup and actually even before, showing up in the pre-pre-Cup matches of 1921.

In America you call it "alternate shot" because that's what it is: Each side is a two-man team, its players alternating shots. Player A hits the first shot off the tee, Player B hits the next (usually an approach or a putt, or if Player A sucks, something back into play from the trees, deep rough, or sand), then back to A, to B, and so on. The team that uses the fewest shots to complete the hole wins the hole; if the scores are the same, the hole is halved.

Because players must alternate hitting first (that is, one will tee off on all the even holes, the other on the odd), there is strategy in determining who is better on par-threes or long holes and then trying to arrange it so the right player will start on those holes.

☆☆☆☆☆☆☆☆☆☆☆☆☆ FOURBALLS: ☆☆☆☆☆☆☆☆☆☆☆☆☆☆

THIS IS probably what you're used to in your weekly rounds with your mates. It's a team match but everyone plays his own ball from tee to green, with the lower score of the two teammates compared to the lower score of the other two clowns.

Too confusing? Try this. Alan and Arnie are playing Bob and Bill (get it? Team A and B? I'm just too damn cute). On a par-four, Alan scores a five and Arnie blows up to a seven; on the same hole, Bob pulls one out of his ass and gets a rare par while Bill shoots his usual bogey (he hasn't had a par since the Nixon Administration). Team A's better score was a five, Team B's was a four, so Team B wins the hole. If the two best scores are the same, the hole is halved.

☆☆☆☆☆☆☆☆☆☆☆☆☆ SINGLES: ☆☆☆☆☆☆☆☆☆☆☆☆☆☆

I REALLY shouldn't have to explain this one, but there's sort of a legal commitment to see this through, so here goes.